A THEORY OF COMMUNICATION AND JUSTICE

This book outlines a theory of communication and justice for the digital age, updating classic positions in political philosophy and ethics, and engaging thinkers from Aristotle through Immanuel Kant and the American pragmatists to John Rawls, Jürgen Habermas, and Amartya Sen.

In communication seeking to define justice and call out injustice, there is such a thing as the last word. The chapters in this book trace the historical emergence of communication as a human right; specify the technological resources and institutional frameworks necessary for exercising that right; and address some of the challenges following from digitalization that currently confront citizens, national regulators, and international agencies. Among the issues covered are public access to information archives past and present; local and global networks of communication as sources of personal identities and imagined communities; the ongoing reconfiguration of the press as a fourth branch of governance; and privacy as a precondition for individuals and collectives to live their lives according to plans, and to make their own histories.

This book will be of interest to students and researchers in media and communication studies, cultural studies, political philosophy and ethics, and interdisciplinary fields examining the ethical and political implications of new information and communication infrastructures.

Klaus Bruhn Jensen is Professor, Department of Communication, University of Copenhagen, Denmark. His research centers on communication theories and research methodologies regarding digital media. Previous publications include *Media Convergence: The Three Degrees of Network, Mass, and Interpersonal Communication*

(2010), *International Encyclopedia of Communication Theory and Philosophy* (2016, coedited with Robert T. Craig), and *A Handbook of Media and Communication Research: Qualitative and Quantitative Methodologies*, 3rd ed. (2021). He is Life Member for Service of the Association of Internet Researchers and a Fellow of the International Communicology Institute.

"A timely and scholarly work that focuses attention on the imperative to deepen the normative turn in communication studies and the communicative turn in philosophy, with focus on the articulation and practice of the contested concept of justice. Drawing on a diverse range of philosophical traditions and thinkers through a communications lens, Jensen succeeds in bringing together philosophy and communications research to propose a seminal theory of justice that speaks to our contemporary global dilemmas."

Anjali Monteiro, Tata Institute of Social Sciences, Mumbai

"In a world seemingly dominated by polarization and disinformation, Klaus Bruhn Jensen's impressive mastery of both classic philosophy and modern communication science gives his readers a new perspective on how human communication and social justice are fundamentally intertwined."

W. Russell Neuman, New York University

"How can communication research and theory advance the cause of justice in the world? Klaus Bruhn Jensen's theory of communication and justice illuminates many possibilities in the spaces between what is, what ought to be, and what could be."

Robert T. Craig, University of Colorado Boulder

"Grounded in a compelling narrative arc from Charles Sanders Peirce to John Rawls, Klaus Bruhn Jensen provides us with a fresh pragmatist philosophy that recognizes communication and its accompanying goods not only as human rights but as engines of civilizational growth."

John Durham Peters, Yale University

"In an era marked by disturbing shifts towards populism, nativism, identity politics and cancel culture, justice must be done and seen to be done. Communication on and of justice are therefore key. Drawing deeply on philosophical theories and the core foundations of the discipline of communication, Klaus Bruhn Jensen provides us with a reflective and provocative exposition of how justice and communication are deeply intertwined."

Sun Sun Lim, Singapore University of Technology and Design

"Klaus Bruhn Jensen presents a timely deliberation on communication and justice that links philosophy and communication studies to explore theories and practices pertaining to this crucially important matter. Drawing on ethics and pragmatist inquiry, Jensen considers communication as action and suggests a communicative turn that may help us to better understand various forms of justice, including essential environmental concerns. This insightful book should be taken very seriously by academics, policy-makers and the public."

Janet Wasko, University of Oregon

"Jensen offers us a normative theory of communication informed by an historically informed analysis of philosophy and communication theory. His goal is to understand how human communication can better contribute to fairness and justice. Treating communication both as a condition of being and becoming and as deliberative action, its potentials and limitations are critically weighed to assess how communication might make a practical difference. An inspiring and provocative foundation is provided for assessing entitlements to reflection and deliberation in a way that also will spark novel empirical research agendas."

Robin Mansell, London School of Economics and Political Science

"In this timely volume Klaus Bruhn Jensen proposes nothing less than a theory of communication and justice. The volume travels through the history of ideas to explore the meeting points and different avenues of communication research and classic philosophy, as they relate to justice. In a theory-rich, yet practice-oriented manner, Klaus Bruhn Jensen convincingly argues that the study of communication can and should engage with debates about justice."

Rikke Frank Jørgensen, The Danish Institute for Human Rights

A THEORY OF COMMUNICATION AND JUSTICE

Klaus Bruhn Jensen

Routledge
Taylor & Francis Group
LONDON AND NEW YORK

First published 2021
by Routledge
2 Park Square, Milton Park, Abingdon, Oxon OX14 4RN

and by Routledge
52 Vanderbilt Avenue, New York, NY 10017

Routledge is an imprint of the Taylor & Francis Group, an informa business

British Library Cataloguing-in-Publication Data
A catalogue record for this book is available from the British Library

Library of Congress Cataloging-in-Publication Data
Names: Jensen, Klaus Bruhn, author.
Title: A theory of communication and justice/Klaus Bruhn Jensen.
Description: Abingdon, Oxon; New York, NY: Routledge, 2021. |
Includes bibliographical references and index.
Identifiers: LCCN 2020037184 (print) | LCCN 2020037185 (ebook) |
ISBN 9781138807242 (hardback) | ISBN 9781138807266 (paperback) |
ISBN 9781315751207 (ebook)
Subjects: LCSH: Communication–Political aspects. |
Communication–Social aspects. | Justice. | Human rights.
Classification: LCC P95.8 .J46 2021 (print) |
LCC P95.8 (ebook) | DDC 302.23/1–dc23
LC record available at https://lccn.loc.gov/2020037184
LC ebook record available at https://lccn.loc.gov/2020037185

ISBN: 978-1-138-80724-2 (hbk)
ISBN: 978-1-138-80726-6 (pbk)
ISBN: 978-1-315-75120-7 (ebk)

Typeset in Bembo
by Newgen Publishing UK

CONTENTS

ILLUSTRATIONS

Figures

Tables

ANALYSIS BOXES

PREFACE

In a book entitled *The Last Word*, the philosopher Thomas Nagel (1997) confronted relativism and subjectivism, which he associated with

> the already extreme intellectual laziness of contemporary culture and the collapse of serious argument throughout the lower reaches of the humanities and social sciences, together with a refusal to take seriously, as anything other than first-person avowals, the objective arguments of others.
>
> *p. 6*

Elaborating aspects of his more widely known work, *The View from Nowhere* (Nagel, 1986), which had highlighted the human capacity to observe reality from a detached position, with modern science as a prototype, the second volume proposed to answer the question of "where understanding and justification come to an end" (Nagel, 1997: 3), including ethical and other normative issues of what is good and right.

> If there is such a thing as reason, it is a local activity of finite creatures that somehow enables them to make contact with universal truths, often of an infinite range. [...] Reason is an attempt to turn myself into a local representative of the truth, and in action of the right.
>
> *pp. 70, 118*

In the final chapter, Nagel (1997) offered an explanation of why not only philosophers, but large segments of the general public today will resist the idea of a last word about what is the case: Perhaps it is "the fear of religion itself" (p. 130) that inclines people to reject "any cosmic order of which mind is an irreducible and nonaccidental part" (p. 132).

In this book, I return to the question of what might count as the last word, in theory and in practice. Like Nagel, I ask "when understanding and justification come to an end." Unlike Nagel, I neither seek nor find "universal truths," focusing attention instead on the necessary, but contingent conclusion to communication, even when survival and the good life – justice – are at stake, locally and globally. Despite utopian hopes (and dystopian fears) of further conversations and more media, it is the end of communication and its translation into other human actions and social interactions that deliver justice – or not. We can't just talk about it; in practice, there is such a thing as the last word.

The book has been a long time coming, taking shape during time-outs from other obligations and interests in researching and teaching the common practice of communication across time and space, most recently through digital technologies. I have been fortunate to receive continuous inspiration from colleagues and students in the BA and MA programs of Communication and IT at the University of Copenhagen, and in the Peoples' Internet (PIN) project comparing internet use in China, Europe, and the United States, https://comm.ku.dk/research/digital-information-and-communication/peoples-internet/. Much insightful input on related papers and presentations has come from the conferences of the Association of Internet Researchers, the International Communication Association, and NordMedia. And, I have been privileged to serve as Area Editor of Communication Theory and Philosophy for the *International Encyclopedia of Communication*, headed by the late Wolf Donsbach (2008), and as Coeditor, with Bob Craig, of the *International Encyclopedia of Communication Theory and Philosophy* (Jensen & Craig, 2016).

A leave of absence during the fall of 2013 gave me the time and resources to formulate a book project; I am grateful to my then Head of Department, Maja Horst, for supporting the leave. I spent the time as a Visiting Scholar at the New School for Social Research, New York, where Jeff Goldfarb served as my gracious interdisciplinary host, and where Richard J. Bernstein pointed me to the right reference at the right time. During my stay in New York, Michael Schudson kindly facilitated a presentation at Columbia University's School of Journalism as part of a lecture series organized by Todd Gitlin. The period also took me to the University of Illinois at Chicago for a series of lectures, by the generous invitation of Zizi Papacharissi and Steve Jones.

Last but not least, I am deeply thankful to the good people who took the time to read draft chapters. Bob Craig and Russ Neuman offered unfailingly constructive criticisms and detailed suggestions on all the chapters in the book, pushing me to revise and resubmit what are, hopefully, somewhat more coherent and consistent arguments and narratives. I also received many helpful comments and pointers from Rasmus Helles, Nils Holtug, John Durham Peters, Michael Schudson, and Jacob Ørmen.

The text includes edited versions of arguments and examples previously published in Jensen (2010) and Jensen (2012e).

The book in its present form is, of course, my responsibility. For now, this is the last word.

Klaus Bruhn Jensen
Copenhagen, October 2020

NOTE ON THE TEXT

Key concepts and terms are indicated by a marginal note when they are first mentioned in the text.

The symbol < in the text indicates a cross reference to the preceding text which can be found in the relevant marginal note. The symbol > in a marginal note indicates the cross reference linked to its mention on that page.

1

THE END OF COMMUNICATION

Communication is one of the most ordinary of human practices – people talk, type, and text their way through everyday life. Communication is also an extraordinary resource for public deliberation about the ends and means of various kinds of community, increasingly from the local to the global level. Over the last century, communication has emerged as a special source of high hopes and deep disappointments – utopias and dystopias < – when people consider differences and disagreements regarding the conditions of their coexistence. But communication cannot guarantee ideal processes of interaction, let alone ideal outcomes – justice – for the individual or for the collective. In this volume, I reexamine the potentials as well as the limitations of human communication for collective reasoning about the common good; I refocus attention on the end of communication and its translation into other human actions and social interactions. Even when survival or the good life is at stake, our communications must and do end.

> utopias and dystopias of communication – p. 7

Certainly, the capacity to communicate in signs and symbols is a unique feature of the human species. It enables us to transcend ourselves in elaborate make-believe, and to organize ourselves for social revolution. We repeat ourselves, and we resume discussions. Communications end, however, whether by explicit procedure or as contingent outcome. In several of the key institutions where communication today serves to anticipate, motivate, and legitimate collectively binding arrangements – in parliaments, law courts, scientific committees, and other agencies of knowledge and power – the end of communication is to end. Both in principle and in practice, there is such a thing as the last word.

Questions of communication and justice constitute an intersection of classical philosophy and modern communication studies. Surprisingly, this intersection has mostly been neglected in both fields of inquiry. Neither political philosophy nor ethics have traditionally considered the universal human practice of communication as central in either defining or practicing what is good or just. Contemporary communication studies, in their turn, have mostly shied away from normative questions of how to say and do the right thing. Before revisiting, in the middle part of this introductory chapter, some of the roads not (yet) taken by philosophy and communication research, in the following section I briefly map some of the questions they share. Communication theory is heir to what are commonly considered eternal questions of philosophy: How can individuals know about reality through perception, cognition, and communication with others? And how may communities, societies, civilizations, and the human species as such articulate and negotiate different understandings of reality with a view to collaboration and coexistence?

What is, what ought to be, and what could be

A great divide in the history of ideas has separated questions of what *is* from questions of what *ought* to be: facts as opposed to values, and current states of affairs compared to future prospects. Aristotle had introduced a distinction between theoretical sciences that produce true knowledge *of* reality as it is and for its own sake, and practical sciences that offer guidance for human action *in* reality and along with others, further noting a third kind of productive sciences that help people to act *on* reality to make things (Lobkowicz, 1967; Shields, 2014). < At the beginning of modern philosophy, David Hume (2010/1739) reemphasized that humans might never be able to justify deriving any specific ought from any particular is. Ever since, this boundary has troubled the proliferating range of sciences and scholarly fields, leaving them with profound intellectual doubts about the practical relevance and appropriate applications of the growing masses of knowledge they continuously produce. Nevertheless, as institutions and infrastructures, science and scholarship evidently and inevitably serve a wide variety of human purposes and social interests. The study of communication, increasingly through complex and interconnected technologies, is a case in point, having been recruited since the mid-twentieth century as an administrator as

> theoretical, practical, and productive sciences – Chapter 5, p. 130

well as a critic of communicative practices as they currently exist (Lazarsfeld, 1941). The media as we know them would grind to a halt without continuous measurement and monetization of who says what to whom.

A third question – what *could* be – begins to complicate the classic is–ought dichotomy. The question recalls Aristotle's further distinction between potential and actual events in and states of the world. < All research relies on different kinds and degrees of experimentation – thought experiments, *in vitro* experiments in laboratories, and *in vivo* experiments on nature as well as culture – in order to explore and represent what might be in theory, and what could be in practice. In this regard, science and scholarship are special instances of human communication. Since the seventeenth century, the natural sciences have prepared unprecedented means for humans to transform material reality for their own purposes by describing and experimenting with it in increasingly granular detail. From the atomic to the planetary level, concerted and cumulative research programs have enabled ways of life that represent so much more than a side effect of studying what is. Social and human sciences have documented equally complex levels of social organization and cultural expression around the globe. In doing so, they have identified, and advocated, alternatives to social systems and cultural practices in their present form. By offering indications of what could be, the natural, human, as well as social sciences feed into wider public and political deliberations about what ought to be, and what should be done.

> Aristotle on potential and actualization – Chapter 5, p. 137

Communication offers the most generic resource for raising and addressing all these questions – in specialized sciences, public media, and in the interchange between public, private, and professional communications. Communication configures society. Communication also prefigures society, addressing what is not (yet), what could be, and what ought (not) to be done. Communication supports great leaps of the individual imagination and grand collective projects. Communication articulates alternatives and choices. Communication represents the capability of humans to jointly consider whether and how things could be different. Human communication constitutes a window of opportunity between chance and necessity. <

> the window of opportunity between chance and necessity – Chapter 2, p. 23

Consider climate change, which raises the stakes of communication to the global level of the species and the planet. Unless humans conclude their deliberations about this question and translate the answers into timely political and personal actions, we may be done for prematurely. What *is* the present state of planet Earth, and what *could* be its future? The answer to the question of what *ought* to be, might appear self-evident: survival and sustainability for the planet and its peoples and species. But the capacity of scientists, politicians, and citizens to weigh the more specific answers with due diligence depends on the institutions, technologies, practices, and discourses of communication available to them. Communication is a necessary, if far from sufficient, condition for the production and dissemination of knowledge that may help people solve environmental and other practical problems in common. The record shows that, at least in such matters, the answer to the familiar question, 'Can't we just talk about it?' is: No.

ANALYSIS BOX 1.1 CLIMATE AND JUSTICE

Climate change – how to understand it, what to do about it – places communication in long perspectives of natural evolution and human history. Unlike just a couple of generations ago, it is now meaningful to communicate, and to disagree, about the natural environment as a public issue:

> [D]own to about 1960, it was generally assumed that for all practical purposes and decisions climate could be considered constant [...] In any case, many people now know that there have been significant shifts of climate during the twentieth century: at first, a more or less global warming to about 1950, then some cooling. More recently, a notable increase in the incidence of extremes of various kinds in almost all parts of the world has hit agriculture and created difficulties for planning in many fields.
>
> *Lamb, 1995: 2*

the Little Ice Age

The assessment of climate change as a human and social problem that invites collective action depends on geological and meteorological evidence and, to a degree, written sources from historical time. Both kinds of information exist for the so-called Little Ice Age – a period of unusually cold weather around the middle of the last millennium. The dating of the Little Ice Age is subject to some disagreement; its earliest beginning is normally set around 1300, its end around 1850. The disagreements bear witness to conflicting interpretations of both natural evidence and cultural sources as well as to different theoretical conceptions of the relationship between climate change and human civilization – nature and culture. In addition to analyses of ice cores and tree rings, the empirical materials include documentation on the changing prices of grain, following good, bad, and disastrous harvest seasons. A classic contribution by the historian, Emmanuel Le Roy Ladurie (1972/1967), charted "the history of the climate since the year 1000" as a backdrop to the living conditions of ordinary people during the period; his study relied, among other things, on a detailed documentation of the dates of wine harvests. Another study, joining meteorology with art history, showed how, over the centuries, the Little Ice Age affected the color and style of nature paintings (Neuberger, 1970). And the hard times of several centuries gave rise to all manner of both practical and religious reflections, a small portion of which was put into writing by "country clergymen and gentleman scientists with time on their hands." In 1316, one of these sources noted that the mass of rain "seemed as though it was THE FLOOD" (Fagan, 2000: xiii, 38).

Neither environmental determinism nor social determinism is tenable when it comes to recognized problems and potential solutions on the scale of global warming. The natural environment, as found and increasingly modified and made by human societies through tools and technologies, is intertwined with historical developments and social changes:

> Consider, for instance, the food crises that engulfed Europe during the Little Ice Age – the great hunger of 1315 to 1319, which killed tens of thousands; the food dearths of 1741; and 1816, "the year without a summer" – to mention only a few. These crises in themselves did not threaten the continued existence of Western civilization, but they surely played an important role in the formation of modern Europe [...] Some of these crises resulted from climatic shifts, others from human ineptitude or disastrous economic or political policy; many, like the Irish potato famine of the 1840s, from a combination of all three – and a million people perished in that catastrophe. Its political consequences are still with us.
>
> *Fagan, 2000: xv*

Perhaps most famously, a catastrophic wheat harvest in France in 1788, and the resulting shortage of grain and bread, was among the factors contributing to the revolution of 1789.

It is generally accepted that, at least since the nineteenth century, human activity has come to affect the natural environment in fundamental ways and with long-term consequences. In a contemporary perspective, climate change raises fundamental issues concerning justice, not just for "Western civilization" as suggested by the last quotation, but on a global scale:

> Climate change is not simply an environmental issue. Instead, the movement for climate justice asserts that global warming affects, disproportionately, the most vulnerable regions and peoples of the planet and that these peoples and nations often are excluded from participation in the forums addressing this problem.
>
> *Cox, 2013: 263*

The first Climate Justice Summit took place in 2000 in The Hague, the Netherlands, and represented a protest against, and alternative to, the COP-6 United Nations summit on climate change taking place then and there. By 2015, environmental sustainability figured prominently in the United Nations development goals. Climate change also reactualizes classic questions concerning justice across generations (e.g., Bou-Habib, 2019; H. Kim, 2019). The Little Ice Age began approximately 700 years ago, through no known intervention by humans. How might the contemporary human cohort intervene to ensure the livelihood and life quality of generations 700 years and more into the future?

generational justice

The record of lessons learnt about the natural environment, as communicated from the past, provides an invaluable resource for future actions. Over time, formal instruments, complex measurement techniques, and specialized notations have gradually replaced informal observations in natural language in the attempt to predict and plan for shifting weather conditions. Current findings are "acquired by statistical regression analyses from modern instrument records or by proxies from historical records and other sources, [which] are vital to establishing just how warm the late twentieth century has been in comparison with earlier times" (Fagan,

2000: 54). Such evidence was unknown – unavailable – to both scientists and lay observers at the beginning of the Little Ice Age. Today, the evidence is widely available in journal articles and commission reports, online and offline. But it is accessible < primarily to small scientific communities with specialized informational and communicative competences. For all practical purposes, public knowledge of and political debate about climate change becomes possible only when the relevant information is rearticulated in ordinary language, texts, and images – to geographically distributed and culturally differentiated publics – through different media and in multiple steps of communication. And in the end, individuals, communities, and nations must act locally on all this information, also when it comes to global problems such as climate change.

> the availability and accessibility of information – Chapter 6, p. 164

Turns of philosophy

It may come as a surprise that communication was a late arrival in the history of ideas. Of course, the human capacity to communicate in signs and symbols is a distinctive evolutionary feature of the species. But the understanding of communication that currently amounts to common sense – the exchange of information and insight for purposes of coordination as well as contestation – dates from the last half of the nineteenth century. With a memorable quotation from John Durham Peters' (1999: 6) history of the very idea of communication, "mass communication came first." It was only following the rise of electronic communication media, from the telegraph via telephony and broadcasting to the internet, that communication was recognized as a general, inclusive category of human activity – in the flesh, via wires, and over the air. Peters' (1999: 2f.) history, further, tells "the story of how communication became such trouble for us," how communication became "a sink into which most of our hopes and fears seem to be poured." People will blame failures of communication, for example, when intimate relationships split up or international negotiations break down, as if more or better communication could ensure lifelong love and eternal peace. Communication came to stand out, during the twentieth century and into the twenty-first century, as a source of the best as well as the worst of worlds.

the very idea of communication

Also within philosophy and other academic disciplines, communication is a recent addition to their conceptual and analytical repertoires. This is in spite of the founding of Western philosophy on Plato's rendition of Socrates' dialogues and the language-centered traditions of much contemporary philosophy. To appreciate the hesitant engagement of philosophy with communication, it is useful to revisit a few turning points in the history of ideas. This history is normally told with reference to 'turns,' through which the mainstream of philosophy redefined its first premises, key questions, or preferred analytical procedures. While such turns have been motivated, in part, by internal intellectual dynamics, they also bear witness to the changing material and institutional conditions for thinking and communicating in and about the world.

ontology

Much ancient and premodern philosophy held the ambition of accounting for reality in terms of what it is – its ontology – by asking, 'What does the world consist of?' Aristotle and other classical philosophers had referred to four main elements as constituents of the world: fire, air, water, and earth. From the seventeenth and eighteenth centuries onwards, modern philosophers reformulated their question in rather more modest terms as a matter of epistemology: 'What can be known about the world?' Immanuel Kant embodied this position in his so-called Copernican turn. In *On the Revolutions of the Heavenly Spheres* (1543), the astronomer Nicolaus Copernicus had demonstrated that the movements of the planets could be explained without assuming the Earth to be the center of the system, and subsequent scholarship confirmed and consolidated a modern cosmology with the Sun at the center. Kant presented his philosophical system, in the *Critique of Pure Reason* (1998/1787), as a reversal of perspective of similar scope, shifting attention from the objects of knowledge to the so-called transcendental categories by which the human subject might come to know about these objects: time, space, causality, etc. Knowledge came to be understood as a relational phenomenon. What I can know about any object depends on what I am as a subject. And, most recently, during the twentieth century, philosophy came to focus on language as the last line of contact between subject and object, asking 'What is meant by "know" and "world"?'

epistemology

the Copernican turn

In one sense, philosophy had retreated, first from the objects of knowledge and into the human subject as a precondition of knowledge, and next into the formal vehicles that might reunite the two sides of the philosophical equation. In another sense, philosophy increasingly came to recognize linguistic and other means of communication as necessary points of access to the world, vehicles of analysis, and conditions of intersubjective understanding – what is commonly described as a shift from a philosophy of consciousness toward a philosophy of language or communication.

philosophy of consciousness

philosophy of communication

the linguistic turn

The turn of philosophy toward language had two identifiable steps over the course of the twentieth century. The linguistic turn (Rorty, 1967), first of all, refers to the effort, particularly among Anglo-American analytic philosophers, to examine the structures and functions of language in great detail. This strategy could be considered a privileged – perhaps the only – way of approaching either the contents or the forms of reality, while at the same time clarifying the limitations of any knowledge about any reality. In a pivotal volume, *Tractatus Logico-Philosophicus* (1972/1921), the young Ludwig Wittgenstein outlined this approach and the priority it would give to linguistically based and logically formulated propositions about minimal features of reality. Accordingly, laws of nature as well as other types of inference and generalization about what is, must ultimately be reducible to direct observations of elementary phenomena. The purpose of philosophy, in that perspective, was to establish correspondences between the fundamental structures of reality and the linguistic and logical structures that capture and communicate potential human understandings of reality. In this way, Wittgenstein prepared influential arguments that were redeveloped by logical positivism < during the 1920–30s, and which have continued to fuel debates on the methodology and theory of science across natural, humanistic, and social-scientific disciplines.

> logical positivism – Chapter 8, p. 221

The later Wittgenstein himself rejected the approach to the structure of language as a mirror image of the structure of reality. Instead, he came to define language as a complex set of discursive activities – language games – that are inseparable from the broader life forms or practices that they serve to constitute. We constantly play games – in and through language – and we do so for real. A dictum summed up Wittgenstein's (1953: §20) second phase: "meaning is use." Meaning inheres neither in the structure of language, nor in its correspondence with the structure of reality, but in the ordinary as well as extraordinary ends to which language (and other modalities of expression and interaction) are put by individuals and communities, as they communicate in and about reality.

language games

The latest turn of philosophy, thus, has involved a refocusing of attention from language as a medium of representation to language as a resource of interaction, in scientific and other social practices. This turn is not yet associated with any set terminology. In various disciplines and interdisciplinary fields, reference has been made to *the* communicative, narrative, or pragmatic turn (e.g., Bernstein,

language as representation and resource

2010; Herman, Jahn, & Ryan, 2005; Morris, 2001). Still, it is an open question whether recent decades have witnessed a separate turn or one moment of a longer linguistic turn:

> Thinkers frequently speak about the 'linguistic turn' that has characterized twentieth-century philosophy. But the truth is that the so-called linguistic turn really designates many different (and sometimes incompatible) phenomena. Philosophers working in the most disparate traditions turned their attention to the dynamics, role, and significance of language for understanding human beings. From Heidegger to Wittgenstein, from Gadamer to Austin, from Derrida to Searle, language and especially the communicative aspects of language became a dominant concern.
>
> *Bernstein, 2012: x*

In this volume, I proceed from the premise that *a* communicative turn is being taken, even if its progress and outcome are still uncertain. As elaborated in subsequent chapters, the philosophical subdisciplines focusing on justice – political philosophy and ethics – have not yet taken any noticeable turn toward either language or communication, despite noteworthy exceptions.

If philosophy has rarely approached classic questions of right conduct or social justice through a lens of communication, communication research has mostly avoided any sustained examination of normative questions altogether. In this regard, communication research has been a characteristically modern field of inquiry with scientific aspirations. Over the last century, theories of communication have sought to interpret and explain what communication *is*, mostly bracketing questions of what it *ought* to be, but also what it *could* be, as input to present and future practices and institutions of communication.

Theories of communication

> Scientific theory is concerned with what *is*, not with what *ought to be*; the goal of scientific theory is to discover general explanations of phenomena that increase our ability to understand, predict, and control events. Normative theory, in contrast, is centrally concerned with what *ought to be*; it seeks to articulate normative ideals by which to guide the conduct and criticism of practice.
>
> *Craig & Tracy, 1995: 249*

scientific vs. normative theory

In the case of communication, normative theory might "provide a reasoned basis for deliberating about, or critically evaluating, particular communicative acts" (Craig & Tracy, 1995: 248) – what communication ought to be or could be. Faced with these two roads of inquiry, the communication field has traveled the route of scientific theory, at least as its primary and explicit mission, leaving more normative considerations for profitable consultancies and other applied projects. As institutionalized around the world, communication research has widely aspired to become a science (Berger, Roloff, & Roskos-Ewoldsen, 2009) that describes and explains the constituents and processes of human communication. Although this is most manifest in the so-called dominant paradigm of social-scientific communication research (Gitlin, 1978; Webster & Phalen, 1997), also the humanistic and critical traditions feeding into the field (Fink & Gantz, 1996) have tended to produce general and retrospective rather than specific and prospective interpretations and critiques.

In fairness, at least two bodies of research have addressed the normative implications of human communication in detailed fashion. The first literature has examined the mass media as modern institutions supporting public deliberation and debate, with particular reference to the principles and procedures of political democracy (for overview, see C. G. Christians, Glasser, McQuail, Nordenstreng, & White, 2009). Studies have scrutinized the legal, political, and economic frameworks and infrastructures of communication at the national as well as the international levels of social organization. While departing from traditional Enlightenment ideals regarding freedom of expression and equality of participation, research in this vein has also been motivated by particular historical events. An early agenda-setting volume – *Four Theories of the Press* (Siebert, Peterson, & Schramm, 1956) – was published in the shadow of two world wars and at the height of the Cold War, pitting conflicting conceptions of politics and the press in different regions of the world against each other. Later studies have responded to decolonization and North–South divides, to the break-up of the former Eastern bloc and the Soviet Union, and to a process of globalization that is still ongoing (C. G. Christians et al., 2009; MacBride, 1980; Nerone, 1995). One limitation of this literature has been its overriding emphasis on news media and journalism; another characteristic has been its focus on the systemic features of media institutions. As a result, less attention has been given to how a variety of practices and genres of communication – from everyday conversation to serial

institutional conditions of communication

fiction – articulate questions of social privilege or cultural identity. In Chapter 6, I return to the overlaps of such institutional communication studies with the traditional concerns of political philosophy.

contextual practices of communication

A second and more heterogeneous body of work has addressed the specific ethical and political concerns that arise from communicative practices in different social and cultural contexts. The contexts studied have included domains of practice with associated subfields of research such as journalism, health communication, and marketing research (for overview, see Cheney, May, & Munshi, 2011; Plaisance, 2018). How, for example, should reporters, doctors, and marketers address citizens, patients, and consumers? Central contributions have come from the areas of intercultural and intergroup communication studies (Giles, Reid, & Harwood, 2010; Gudykunst & Mody, 2002; Y. Y. Kim, 2018), which were founded after 1945 on the hope that communication might serve as a means to avoid or manage conflict between different national, cultural, and ethnic groups. Work in these areas, however, has tended to invoke abstracted norms such as "the intercultural person as a model for human development" (Gudykunst & Kim, 1992: 253). More generally, the lines of contact between the concrete cultural contexts and the general normative theories of communication have remained tenuous. One main exception has been the work of Jürgen Habermas, which has been massively influential within communication research; I return to Habermas' contributions to normative communication theory in Chapter 3.

intergroup and intercultural communication research

Western communication theory

It should be added that communication theory, as practiced around the world, has largely grown out of Western philosophies and models of science. Whereas a number of publications over the decades have explored the relationship between communication theory and different ontologies, epistemologies, and axiologies (value systems), including world religions (e.g., C. Christians & Nordenstreng, 2014; C. Christians & Traber, 1997; Dissanayake, 1988; Kincaid, 1987; Wang, 2011), it is fair to conclude that no shared, substantive research agenda has emerged to date. This is in spite of continued and concerted interventions by a small community of researchers (e.g., Couldry, Madianou, & Pinchevski, 2013; Ess, 2020; Rao & Wasserman, 2015). In sum, as a field of inquiry communication research has had surprisingly little to say about the evident normative implications of the universal practice of human communication. After half a century of consolidation as a scientific discipline with journals, conferences, major private and public funding, and affiliations with international organizations such as the United Nations, the field still rarely engages the implicit utopias and dystopias being entertained by researchers and other communicators alike.

Up to now, I have identified some of the key questions that classic philosophy and current communication research share, but also the mostly separate ways that the two fields of inquiry have traveled in matters of communication and justice. In the remainder of this chapter, I outline the agenda for the rest of the volume, which is to develop a conceptual and methodological architecture for the study of communication and justice. I note the special status of the concept of justice in public communication; emphasize the constitutive role of communication in anticipating and enacting justice; and outline a practice-based approach to the definition and administration of justice, in and through communication.

Justice – an essentially contested concept

In communication, we agree and disagree about – contest – the ends and means of our existence and coexistence. With climate justice as illustration, < we contest the unequal distribution and the final depletion of the Earth's natural resources. We contest each other's facts and worldviews in these respects. And we contest the social institutions that regulate and condition our natural survival and cultural cohabitation. We do so both in dedicated scientific, artistic, and political institutions-to-think-with < (Jensen, 2010: 104) and in the many informal interactions of our everyday lives. In contesting all of these things, we rely on certain shared and thoroughly familiar concepts that, nevertheless, generate recurring and fundamental disagreements. Justice is one such contested concept, from Aristotle's account of a good life in alignment with the *polis* and the cosmos, via modern conceptions of equality through democracy, to contemporary considerations of justice at the global level of the species and the planet.

> climate and justice – p. 4

> institutions-to-think-with – Chapter 2, p. 27

Justice belongs to a special set of concepts in the history of ideas that have been referred to as essentially contested (Gallie, 1956). Especially concepts that capture what may be considered good or beautiful (or the opposite) have generated seemingly endless disputes, not only in philosophy and scholarship, but in public debate and everyday conversation, as well. Even though most people will agree about the general or abstract meaning of words such as 'art,' 'freedom,' 'democracy,' or 'justice,' each concept carries implications that give rise to discussion, conflict, even violence and war, when the concept is applied to particular artifacts or practices. It is not simply that some people will contest some aspects and uses of these concepts some of the time; nor do people merely misunderstand the *terms* being used to express an understanding of the underlying *concepts*. And because these concepts inform and orient both communications and actions that have decisive practical consequences for the welfare of individuals and the maintenance of community, they simultaneously unite and divide people.

contested and contestable concepts

The status of such concepts has been clarified through an additional distinction: The concepts are not merely *contested* in concrete instances, but are inherently *contestable* (Clarke, 1979). One may contest the definition and use of any concept at any time, but people rarely do so, because it would be impractical and mostly irrelevant. The point concerning these special concepts is that their meanings and implications are unstable or polysemous, and perhaps internally contradictory, in distinctive ways and to such a degree that they have remained at issue. The disagreements typically cannot be resolved through argumentation, because the parties to a controversy can go on presenting additional and often quite valid reasons for the positions they are taking, for example, regarding the definition of art or the practice of justice. Contestation may, further, question the boundaries between what is, what ought to be, and what could be. What some consider a shared reality – liberty or equality – others will see as a distant possibility or an unrealizable utopia. Communication about essentially contestable concepts might never end.

Essential contestability follows from the *phenomena* that these *concepts* denote and to which the *terms* refer. The concepts are contestable because the realities that the concepts capture are subject to fundamental contingencies and conflicts that entail existential uncertainty. Such uncertainty was formulated by Immanuel Kant, in his *Critique of Pure Reason*, in three questions from the individual's perspective: "What can I know?", "What ought I to do?", and "What may I hope?" (Kant, 1998/1787: n.p.). In a contemporary perspective, Kant's questions can be reformulated in collective and communicative terms: What can *we* know? What ought to be the ends and means of our coexistence? And how may we express and negotiate our shared as well as conflicting interests? The reformulation shifts attention from conscience and ethics toward communication and politics, and toward the communal and increasingly distributed processes of addressing what will count as the common good.

from conscience to communication

Essentially contestable concepts have largely remained a niche interest within the discipline of philosophy (but see, e.g., Collier,

Hidalgo, & Maciuceanu, 2006). Yet, they represent an intellectual legacy of issues and agendas that citizens and communities continue to communicate about – agree and disagree on, live and die for – under changing institutional and technological circumstances. The concepts are contested because their interpretation makes a real difference: When all is said and done, a particular understanding of justice will be practiced. Communication anticipates particular actions; communication also serves to enact specific understandings, values, and ends. Communication, conceived as a form of action, provides a common denominator for philosophy and communication theory to begin to address questions of justice.

Communication as action

The most recent and still ongoing turn of philosophy < has suggested how language games – communication – frame human understandings *of* reality as well as actions *in* and *on* reality. Whereas some niches of communication research have detailed the performative aspects of different discourses, practices, and institutions of communication, the mainstream of the field is still premised on the common-sense notion that communication is the transmission or sharing of information – representations of reality that feed intersubjective understanding.

> a communicative turn – p. 9

Communication is that, and more. First, to communicate is to act, in a context and for a purpose. Whenever I say something to someone, I do something, to and with that someone. Second, human actions are communications in and of themselves. Regardless of my intentions or preconscious inclinations, others will associate meaning with the behaviors, however casual and contingent, that I constantly engage in. Golden or not, also silence – the apparent absence of communication – is a form of action. Third, communication anticipates action. Communication is a vehicle of recursive and self-reflective agency, introducing doubt and delay into human affairs. Both senders and receivers will assess and evaluate the actions that communicate and the communications that enact. Communication itself establishes the links between what was said, what could have been said, and what ought to be said in the future.

communication as action

The first understanding – that communication is action – was one of the central insights of twentieth-century philosophy. Whereas the early Wittgenstein (1972/1921) had treated language primarily as a representation *of* reality, his later work (Wittgenstein, 1953) conceived language as a resource *in* reality. Wittgenstein foregrounded the language games that people play with each other, when they interact about ordinary as well as extraordinary aspects of their lives. Language games are inseparable from the life forms, social practices, and cultural traditions that they both maintain and modify. This understanding was elaborated and systematized in speech-act theory (Austin, 1962; Searle, 1969), and it has been profoundly influential across many disciplines and interdisciplinary fields over the past half century.

action as communication

The second perspective – action as communication – is one legacy of sociology and anthropology, even if a communicative perspective on society and culture has remained a minority position in the social sciences. An action may be the intentional expression of something to particular others; it may be an incidental or even instinctual behavior; or it may belong to the significant gray area in between the other two types. At the intentional end of the scale, terrorism, in one sense, is communication: The loss of life and the material destruction accomplish a symbolic purpose, which may be primary for the perpetrators. Toward the incidental end, people continuously communicate with each other through gestures, clothing, and general conduct. Indeed, any action, event, or object in the world may serve as a medium of communication (Peters, 2015). Humans are forever ascribing meaning to both their cultural and their natural environments in order to make sense of their condition. Humans "cannot *not* communicate" (Watzlawick, Beavin, & Jackson, 1967: 49), productively and receptively.

communication anticipates action

Finally, communication anticipates action, exploring what has been referred to, in several areas of inquiry, as possible worlds. Many realities are conceivable, as exemplified by science fiction and by so-called counterfactual historiography exploring what might have happened if key historical events had taken a different turn (Hawthorn, 1991), say, if Nazi Germany had won World War II. Only some of these realities, however, are possible in either a material or a logical sense, as examined by the full range of natural and other empirical sciences, in philosophical logic (Divers, 2002), and in literary theory (Ryan, 1991). And, of course, possible worlds may be far from preferable worlds. Having explored which worlds could be, communities and societies will compare, contrast, evaluate, and enact only some possible worlds. <

> possible worlds – Chapter 3, p. 81

A robust framework for studying such multiple realities was presented by the philosopher and theorist of science, Karl R. Popper, who counted three worlds. World 1 refers to physical objects or states of affairs; World 2 is the world of consciousness, mental states, or behavioral dispositions to act. Linking these 'external' and 'internal' worlds, World 3 covers "the world of the objective contents of thought," whether scientific or poetic (Popper, 1972b: 106) – fact and fiction as represented and communicated in more or less durable media. Popper himself gave priority to World 1 as a bottom line of brute reality, and proposed to extend natural-scientific criteria and approaches to other domains of reality; Popper did not recognize the extent to which World 3 serves as a necessary communicative coin of exchange for collectives to deliberate about any world. In and through World 3, we are in a position to describe and explain World 1; to understand and interpret our individual Worlds 2 to each other; and to criticize and reformulate any perspective on any world, including World 3 as we know it here and now. While far from self-correcting, World 3 represents the individual's point of access to other people and to collective arrangements regarding the natural and social circumstances in which we find ourselves, together. Humans engage nature from within culture, and each other in and through communication. Simultaneously process and product, it is communication that maintains possible worlds in common, across time and space, depending on the historically available media of record and interaction – from cave paintings and cuneiform script to the internet and virtual realities.

Worlds 1, 2, and 3

Theories of communication have remained uneasily poised between questions of what is and what ought to be, between scientific and normative notions of research. Behind this dilemma lurks a final dualism – that of theory and practice. Philosophy, science, and other scholarship have always responded to human and social concerns – perceived problems and proposed solutions, both of which involve facts as well as values. Still missing in many attempts to resolve scientific-normative dilemmas in various domains of inquiry and activity is that third question: What *could* be? Communication studies must ask: What could *communication* be and do? A central, but neglected question for the study of communication today is – ought to be – what communication could be.

Communication research has a role to play and a place to find among the disciplines and fields contributing to research and debate on justice; it is a latecomer to issues that have occupied philosophy, economics, political science, and other disciplines for decades, centuries, millennia. More than three decades ago, John Durham Peters (1986) critiqued the field of communication for considering itself all of China whereas it might, in fact, be the equal of Taiwan. In a similarly self-critical vein, Robert T. Craig (1999: 155) added:

> Might communication studies even claim to be *the* fundamental discipline that explains all other disciplines, since disciplines themselves are social constructs that, like all social constructs, are constituted symbolically through communication? Yes, of course, but only as a joke! [...] The irony that makes the joke funny is that every discipline occupies the precise center of the universe in its own perspective. Communication is no exception, but communication as a metaperspective – a perspective on perspectives – may help us to appreciate the irony of our situation.

I go on to argue that communication is key to also appreciating the seriousness of our situation. As an intellectual commitment and a public service, communication research could reasonably be expected to work out the potentials and limitations of communication as a condition and constituent of justice. How could communication serve justice? What could communication be, before it ends?

The chapters of the volume

To contextualize my argument, in the first half of the volume I devote substantial attention to the different disciplines, fields, and traditions of inquiry that have prepared premises and arguments for a theory of communication and justice. I offer a capsule history of changing ideas of justice since Antiquity, followed by a reassessment of two recent thinkers – Jürgen Habermas and John Rawls. Habermas is the most distinguished exception to the rule that communication scholars have avoided normative questions; Rawls remains the essential point of departure for contemporary inquiry into justice. Before outlining a theoretical and methodological architecture for the study of communication and justice, I also introduce the wider intellectual legacy that the volume draws on – the long substream of pragmatism throughout the history of ideas, from Aristotle via Kant and Marx to Wittgenstein and Rawls.

Chapter 2 provides an overview of the main conceptions of justice, including their understanding – mostly implicit – of the role of communication in defining and practicing justice. The history of justice can be seen to "revolve around three ideas: maximizing welfare, respecting freedom, and promoting virtue [...] ancient theories of justice start with virtue, while modern theories start with freedom" (Sandel, 2009: 6, 9). Bracketing virtue, modern theories of justice have struggled with the question of

welfare, freedom, virtue

how to balance freedom and welfare, or the interests of the individual and the collective. Over the last two centuries, answers to this question have converged on two philosophical positions, emphasizing first principles and final consequences, respectively. The first or deontological position requires people to do the right thing by following rules; the second or teleological position, also referred to as consequentialism, assesses human actions and social interactions according to their outcomes. All along, the virtues of individuals have provided a thematic background to modern treatments of justice; the realization of social justice depends, in part, on the moral agency of individuals.

deontology

consequentialism

Chapter 3 turns to the work of Jürgen Habermas, who has presented the most elaborated and sophisticated normative theory of communication to date; his *oeuvre* has been widely influential in communication research, philosophy, and beyond. From an early historical account of the public sphere (Habermas, 1989/1962), via a general theory of communicative action (Habermas, 1984/1981, 1987b/1981) followed by a volume focusing on law and democracy (Habermas, 1996/1992), to more thematic treatments of international politics and globalization (Habermas, 2001/1998, 2009/2008) and the place of religion in public life (Habermas, 2008/2005), capped by a two-volume history of philosophy (Habermas, 2019a, 2019b), his publications have provided a sustained examination of communication as a human expression and a social practice, from both historical and systematic perspectives. Tracing a long-term shift from historical and implicitly normative analyses toward systematic and explicitly normative typologies of human communication, I highlight one of Habermas' main lines of argument since the early 1970s, namely, the reconstruction < of other thinkers, their terms and concepts, models and findings (Habermas, 1973). I conclude that, over the course of more than 50 years, Habermas has engaged in – by his own terminology – strategic and systematically distorted communication. In a tragic irony, Habermas' communicative practices come back to haunt his theoretical understanding of communication as a realm without end or ends.

historical and systematic analysis

> reconstruction – Chapter 3, p. 63

Chapter 4 presents the thought of John Rawls, who reinvigorated political philosophy, ethics, and related fields (but not communication research) with *A Theory of Justice* (Rawls, 1971). While specifically challenging utilitarianism – the principle of the greatest happiness for the greatest number – his theory of justice as fairness further sought to balance two classic considerations, namely, the absolute rights and duties of individuals versus the contingent intentions and outcomes of their actions

justice as fairness

(deontology and consequentialism, as examined in Chapter 2). In an amended version of his theory, Rawls (2005/1993) clarified that the principles and procedures of justice do not – cannot – constitute any comprehensive, complete, or coherent consensus, given the diversity of worldviews that inform modern societies. Instead, it might be possible to arrive at what Rawls termed an overlapping consensus: By bracketing some aspects of their worldviews, citizens may agree on a set of political institutions and procedures which, in practice, could ensure peaceful coexistence and social stability over time. The amended version gave rise to an important debate between Rawls and Habermas in the 1990s, but without significant *rapprochement* between their positions (Finlayson & Freyenhagen, 2011b). I argue that Rawls' work offers an unduly neglected point of departure for a contemporary normative theory of communication.

pragmatism as tradition and substream

> *erro, ergo sum* – Chapter 5, p. 127

As a last step in preparing the ground for a theory of communication and justice, *Chapter 5* recovers key tenets of philosophical pragmatism. Though mostly associated with an American philosophical tradition that took shape in the decades around 1900, pragmatism constitutes a significant substream in the longer history of ideas since Aristotle (Lobkowicz, 1967), and it has witnessed a recent revival (Dickstein, 1998) following the linguistic and communicative turns of twentieth-century philosophy. Whereas the pragmatist tradition has been invoked by Habermas, and implied by Rawls, I suggest that pragmatism remains an untapped intellectual resource for working out the relationship between human communication and social justice. In comparison to René Descartes' *cogito, ergo sum* – I think, therefore I am – the motto of pragmatism can be expressed as *erro, ergo sum* < (Jensen, 1995: 192) – I err, therefore I am, always in relation to something else: the natural environment, but also the other humans that I depend on, in and through communication. It is via more or less formalized, specialized, and institutionalized communications that individuals and collectives arrive at knowledge and beliefs that they can and will act on.

Shifting the emphasis from historical to systematic analysis, the second half of the volume outlines a theory of communication and justice in the form of a conceptual and methodological architecture. Whereas the normative implications of human communication have typically been presented in communication studies as either first premises or final conclusions, I treat theoretical, empirical, and normative-practical perspectives as complementary for the study of communication and justice.

practical concepts

Chapter 6 first examines different *practical concepts* of communication and justice – historically accumulated ways and means of communal problem-solving. In pragmatist terminology, practical concepts respond to what John Dewey (1903) labeled problematic situations. < When individual doubts or social conflicts frustrate or complicate the ongoing flow of human activities, this situation calls for inquiry, whether as instantaneous reflection or as a prolonged time-out from practice. Characteristic doubts and conflicts bearing on problems of justice have been articulated in social institutions of reflection and deliberation, including the modern media. Chapter 6 reviews the normative principles and practical procedures that gradually emerged regarding general access to information, universal rights of communication, and public participation in the long chains of governance that may deliver an approximation of justice. Such principles and procedures have been variously implemented – and contested – through different institutions, technologies, practices, and discourses of communication, from early newspapers to the internet.

> problematic situations – Chapter 5, p.141

Practical concepts are the accomplishments of social collectives over the *longues durées* of evolution and history, rather than of scientists and scholars undertaking second-order analysis and synthesis – even if practical and theoretical endeavors cross-fertilize. < As such, practical concepts belong to what anthropologists call 'emic' categories (Pike, 1967), which are grounded in the common experiences and ways of life of the natives of a culture, and which are studied in anthropology with reference to abstracted, 'etic' categories. As noted by John Rawls (1999b/1971: 5) in the case of justice, people may agree on a general *concept* of justice even while advocating distinctive *conceptions* of justice. If practical concepts respond to problems and anticipate solutions, theoretical conceptions pose systematic questions concerning the relationship between problems and solutions: What *is* the problem, and what *could* and *ought* the solution be?

> the double hermeneutics of research – Chapter 2, p. 25

theoretical conceptions

Chapter 7 presents a *theoretical conception* of communication as both a condition and a constituent of justice. Introducing the capabilities approach of Amartya Sen and Martha Nussbaum as an amendment to the Rawlsian agenda, I define the availability of *information* resources, the accessibility of *communication* resources, public *participation* in political governance, and personal *privacy* as primary social goods that enable people's actualization of their potentials or capabilities: Communication conditions justice. Communication is also a constituent of justice, an essential source of self-respect and self-realization, of becoming and being an individual within the community. It is in and through communication that a life lived according to a plan and to the full can be imagined, represented, and shared. Communication in-forms and per-forms the future on behalf of individuals as well as collectives.

Theoretical conceptions depend for their relevance – as descriptions, interpretations, explanations, and orientations toward action – on evidence: intersubjective, communicated manifestations of actual problems and possible solutions. Philosophy, notoriously, has been low on empiricism; communication research remains low on normativity. *Chapter 8*, accordingly, turns to *empirical conceptualizations* (Jensen, 2013a: 204), approaching the relationship between communication and justice from a position of critical realism, which is realist in recognizing the material as well as institutional boundaries to the good life, critical in probing such boundaries. As part of an agenda for further research on communication and justice, I note the relevance of diverse forms of inquiry and inference, from quantitative indexes of the freedom of expression to qualitative interpretations of the existential meaning of privacy, all of which feed into public debate and political governance. More than describing what is and what has been, empirical studies of communication and justice anticipate what will be or could be.

empirical conceptualizations

The final chapter, *Chapter 9*, returns to the normative aspects of human communication and its place in the longer history and future of justice. It is time for communication research to join other scholarly and public conversations about justice, locally and globally; it is time for contemporary philosophy to revisit the implications of its communicative turn for the understanding of justice. We can't just talk about it. But by exploring what communication could be, and by embracing its end, the study of communication may make a practical difference for justice in the future. <

> difference – the pragmatic maxim – Chapter 5, p. 135

2

A BRIEF HISTORY OF JUSTICE

Between chance and necessity

In a book entitled *Chance and Necessity*, the Nobel-prize-winning biologist, Jacques Monod (1997/1970), summed up the understanding that life on planet Earth evolved by chance. Mutations, embodied in self-replicating genetic structures and (de)selected over time by environmental necessity, eventually led to the human species. Being a special species – what Aristotle referred to as *zoon politicon*, a political or social being – humans depend on each other for coordination and collaboration, day to day and generation to generation. Over time, our interactions accumulate and solidify as social structures that may appear to us as equally necessary or given – second nature. As noted by Karl Marx, "men make their own history, but they do not make it just as they please; they do not make it under circumstances chosen by themselves, but under circumstances directly encountered, given, and transmitted from the past" (in Feuer, 1969: 360). Questions of justice arise in a narrow and distinctively human window of opportunity between natural and social chance and necessity. In that window, communication about justice explores answers to the question of what ought to be, if it could be. <

humans as social beings

> what is, what ought to be, and what could be – Chapter 1, p. 2

Questions about justice have been posed and answered for millennia; both the framing of the questions and the implications of the answers have remained contested. < The purpose of this chapter is to provide a basic overview of different ideas of justice so as to place the relationship between communication and justice in a long and broad perspective. First of all, I consider theories of

> communication as contestation – Chapter 1, p. 13

justice as products of history; philosophers have always responded to the issues of their times. The interplay between practical problems and philosophical responses is captured by the concept of double hermeneutics. < The point is that, compared to natural and material sciences, human and social sciences interpret realities that have already been interpreted by the people inhabiting them and, further, that people frequently interpret things differently once they have been presented with alternatives. A case in point is the work of Sigmund Freud (1911), whose idea of the subconscious pervades modern life. Also when people debate justice, they will attribute subconscious, less than noble motivations to the practices (as well as the theories) that others present to them.

> double hermeneutics – p. 25

> the prehistory of justice – p. 28

cognitive science

The second section takes up the prehistory of justice < – the evolutionary background to the very idea of justice as a cognitive and communicative category. Whereas histories of justice have traditionally focused on abstract theories with ideal ambitions, the study of (other) great apes by cognitive science (Eysenck & Keane, 2020) is of considerable interest for a better understanding of how humans came to think of and talk about justice in the first place (on evolutionary approaches to communication, see Lull, 2020). The window of opportunity for communication about justice is framed not only by historical institutions and social structures but, simultaneously, by natural circumstances and human capabilities.

ends and means

individuals and collectives

conditions and consequences

In the longest section of the present chapter, I summarize and illustrate the three main traditions within Western political philosophy and ethics and their proposals for civilizing "the animal in man" (Monod, 1997/1970: 178): virtue ethics, deontological ethics, and consequentialism. I characterize the historical trajectory of each position with reference to three dimensions along which they differ, but which are sources of dilemmas that they share: how to relate the ends and means of justice; what roles to assign to individuals and collectives in achieving justice; and how to assess the future consequences of (what appears to be) doing the right thing right now. As the saying goes, the end does not justify the means, but what justifies the end – on the time scale of individuals, families, communities, nations, civilizations, the species, the planet, or some sense of eternity? Next, whereas all individuals depend on other individuals, what is good for the individual may not be right for the collective. Finally, the human window of opportunity is opaque: However much they communicate, neither individuals nor collectives will have perfect insight into the conditions and motivations underlying their actions, nor can they predict or guarantee the long-term consequences of what they do.

Both the practical dilemmas of justice and the double hermeneutics of theory and practice have been reemphasized by contemporary research and debate beyond the nation-state. Changing practical perspectives on justice, in response to decolonization and globalization, have challenged philosophy to revisit past theoretical notions of justice. The fourth section of the chapter, accordingly, takes up international justice, < multiculturalism, and cosmopolitanism. With global means of communication have come new conditions for philosophers to know more about the different faces of injustice, and for anyone to communicate about justice as a global issue.

> international justice – p. 41

In the final section, I consider an intervention by the economist and philosopher, Amartya Sen (2009), who, in *The Idea of Justice*, suggested that the world does not need another – or any – theory of justice in order to counteract injustice in practice. I argue, in this and the following chapters, for the continued importance of theorizing justice, communicating about and reinterpreting past and present injustices with a view to the future.

ANALYSIS BOX 2.1 THE DOUBLE HERMENEUTICS OF JUSTICE

hermeneutics

Hermeneutics – the art and science of interpretation – has traditionally been associated with the reading of written texts, originally the classics, religious scriptures, and law, but increasingly a wider range of artworks and other human artifacts (Ricoeur, 1981). A general insight from a century of social sciences was summed up by the sociologist, Anthony Giddens (1979), under the heading of double hermeneutics: Social scientists study a reality that has already been interpreted by the people being studied. And when a Freud or a Marx reinterprets how reality works, it also changes people's interpretations of themselves and others, sometimes in fundamental ways and with long-term consequences.

The wider implication of double hermeneutics is that theory is conditioned by and, in turn, conditions practice; the mechanism also applies to natural and material sciences. Darwin joined Marx and Freud as one of the most influential modern interpreters of the human condition. In matters of justice, philosophers since Aristotle have addressed perceived problems and proposed solutions, always from within what hermeneutics terms a horizon of expectations (Jauss, 1982).

horizons of expectations

When readers encounter a text, and when researchers witness reality, they inevitably do so with prejudices or preconceptions – premises and preunderstandings that condition their interpretations. Aristotle inherited a closed universe of deep meaning and great beauty; modern philosophers faced an open universe in which humans had to devise the ends as well as the means, at their own risk. When philosophers and other theorists communicate their interpretations of the right and the good, they participate in a double hermeneutics of justice – a process that has unfolded across decades and centuries, in more or less durable media, and in dialogue with practitioners and publics.

Social institutions are key to the dynamics of double hermeneutics. Whereas individual philosophers, scientists, and citizens have employed their expanding freedoms of conscience and expression to represent facts and values to each other, it is the institutions they build and leave behind that serve to maintain principles and procedures of justice across time and space. As noted by John Rawls (1999b/1971: 47), an institution is "a public system of rules" that both precedes and succeeds individuals. Institutions of knowledge and institutions of communication are both necessary, if far from sufficient, conditions for the practice of justice.

institutions of knowledge

Institutions of knowledge, first, have accumulated ideas and instruments for human existence and social coexistence; they also have witnessed radically shifting definitions of what knowledge is (Kjørup, 2001: 20–22). During Greek antiquity, the Delphi oracle's admonition to "Know thyself!" conceived knowledge as *self-awareness* within a closed cosmos; other premodern conceptions approached knowledge as accumulated *learning*, administered by a class of already learned people. It was the modern period that came to approach knowledge as the open-ended outcome of *research*, subject to continuous scrutiny, also of the very first premises of how to interpret evidence and arguments. At the height of the Enlightenment, when the university was still taking shape as a modern research institution (Fallon, 1980; Rudy, 1984), Immanuel Kant (1992/1798) noted an ongoing power struggle among its faculties. To ensure the rule of reason, he found, it must be the humanities (the philosophical faculty), not the theological faculty, that define the foundations for inquiry into natural and cultural realities within the other faculties. Justice could be considered either a divine duty to be deduced through introspection or a democratic principle to be induced from scientific inquiry and public debate.

institutions of communication

Institutions of communication – media – are normally treated as different in kind from institutions of knowledge. However, scholars have always depended on records, archives, and libraries for their studies, and on technologies of writing and, later, print, electronic, and digital media for the dissemination of and discussion about their findings and insights. Both kinds of institutions engage in public-ation: They make information available and accessible to publics, professional or political, large and small, for further communication about its social uses. Much research is disseminated, not in scientific journals or at scholarly conferences, but through collaboration with commercial and public partners (sometimes to make sure that it is *not* publicized to competitors and other stakeholders). Institutions communicate. To appreciate the double hermeneutics of justice, it is essential to revisit the role of communication in the interchange between different social institutions. Both institutions of knowledge and of communication constitute institutions-to-think-with (Jensen, 1991: 21), articulating and exchanging the best hopes and worst fears of humans.

public-ation

institutions-to-think-with

In Chapter 6, I return to the historical formation of institutions of knowledge and communication and their engagement with questions of justice through institutions of governance. Philosophers have participated in this process, though not on the scale envisioned in Plato's (2016) *Republic*, which imagined philosopher-kings as ideal rulers of ideal communities. In dialogue with other disciplines – from classic political economy (which had a moral agenda) to modern economics (which redefined itself as a science) – philosophers have interpreted and reinterpreted principles and procedures of the right and the good. With varying degrees of hermeneutic self-awareness, they have responded to the questions of their times, sometimes as public intellectuals. Like other members of the intelligentsia, philosophers have never been free-floating (Mannheim, 1976/1922: 134–146), but have been suspended in historical webs of significance (Geertz, 1973: 5).

institutions of governance

public intellectuals

One reason for telling the history of justice once again is to appreciate the practical implications of a term and a concept that has been reinterpreted throughout history in a variety of media and communicative practices. Justice had presented itself as a moral-metaphysical issue since premodern times. It was reconceptualized as a political-institutional issue during the Enlightenment. And, at the time of writing, its meaning is widely contested and communicated about in a global perspective.

Justice also has a prehistory; the human condition is both historical and natural.

The prehistory of justice

In *A Natural History of Human Morality*, Michael Tomasello (2016) explored the relationship between evolution and justice, and identified communication as a central condition of how justice came to be understood and practiced by the human species. By way of introduction, the book makes a distinction between two kinds of morality:

morality of sympathy and fairness

> The morality of *sympathy* is the most basic, as concern for the well-being of others is the sine qua non of all things moral. The evolutionary source of sympathetic concern is almost certainly parent care of offspring based in kin selection. [...] In contrast, the morality of *fairness* is neither so basic nor so straightforward – and it may very well be confined to the human species.
>
> *p. 1f., emphasis added*

In the latter case of fairness, "there is typically a complex interaction of the cooperative and competitive motives of multiple individuals. [...] it is not just that I want to be fair to all concerned, but that one *ought* to be fair to all concerned" as a general principle. If others (or oneself) are not fair, the result is "interpersonal judgments of responsibility, obligation, commitment, trust, respect, duty, blame, and guilt" (p. 2).

the interdependence hypothesis

The background to such judgments is expressed in Tomasello's (2016) interdependence hypothesis: From a "great ape starting point, early human individuals became ever more interdependent with one another for cooperative support," an evolution that "took place in two key steps, both of which involved new ecological circumstances that forced early humans into new modes of social interaction and organization: first collaboration and then culture." In the first step, a shared intentionality emerges, a "'we,' as

shared intentionality

in what 'we' must do to capture a prey or how 'we' should defend our group from other groups" (p. 3). In the next step, as "human groups started becoming larger, they split into smaller bands that were still unified [as a] tribal-level group – call it a culture." Now humans "evolved new cognitive skills and motivations of *collective intentionality* – enabling the creation of cultural conventions, norms, and institutions [which] represented the right and wrong ways to do things" (p. 5). Over a span of hundreds of millennia, *Homo sapiens* created cultures that amounted to possible worlds < within which individuals would construct increasingly elaborate representations, including accounts of what they and others could and ought to do, together. All the while, bands, tribes, and cultures would contest each other's representations, to the extent that they shared the same possible worlds through languages and other means of communication.

collective intentionality

> possible worlds – Chapter 3, p. 81

Human communication is a precondition of thus entertaining and acting on the idea of justice. In communication, morality presents itself as a social or collective issue, something to agree and disagree about, beyond individual minds and immediate kin. Communication translated the private into the public and, with time, ethics into politics. Tomasello (2016) referred to the simple, but decisive fact that "when something is explicitly communicated it is 'out in the open' [...] there can be no question of not knowing this information, and so if it has interpersonal consequences one cannot hide from them by claiming ignorance." It is this mechanism that sustains "joint commitments, which create interpersonal feelings of 'ought'" (p. 53). Communication points inward to individual conscience, outward toward social commitments. Revisiting social-contract theories from Hobbes to Rawls, < Tomasello further noted that, today, "contractualist moral philosophers are wont to say that the structure of societies is 'as if' there were an agreement." But the evolutionary evidence suggests that "early humans created new supraindividual social structures by actual explicit agreements"; such agreements could be considered "the first evolutionary step in a natural history of the human social contract" (p. 78). Across prehistorical and historical time, Tomasello and John Rawls pointed to similar communicative and cognitive mechanisms, in almost identical wordings, of how the social contract has been both externalized and internalized: Where Rawls (1999b/1971: 48) indicated that a participant in a social institution < not only knows "what the rules demand of him and of the others," but "also knows that the others know this and that they know that he knows this, and so on," Tomasello (2016: 123) suggested that, as part of their joint

> the social contract – Chapter 4, p. 98

> Rawls on social institutions – Chapter 4, p. 103

intentionality, "everyone knew that everyone knew how to perform in the ideal way."

Extrapolations from evolution must be made carefully, as should philosophical generalizations about principles and procedures of justice across historical time and cultural space. Tomasello (2016: 162f.) noted that, of course,

> it did not have to be this way. It just so happens that, on the whole, those of us who made mostly moral decisions most of the time had more babies [...] morality appears to be somehow good for our species, our cultures, and ourselves – at least so far.

Monod (1997/1970: 163) further suggested that, "Thanks to the progress of scientific knowledge and the social ethic, the mechanism [of the weeding out of the physically and also mentally least fit] now hardly functions at all." He also reminded readers, however, that as part of ethical and political deliberation, it is essential "to confront the animal in man" and to maintain "a clear-sighted appreciation of the urges and passions, the requirements and limitations of the biological being" (p. 178).

the animal in humans

History represents an extended intervening variable between relatively constant evolutionary conditions and the specific ideas of justice that philosophers and other thinkers have proposed. Karl Jaspers (2010/1949) drew attention to the pivotal position of what he termed "the Axial Age" between roughly 800 BCE and 300 BCE, when ideas in several regions of the world – China, India, and the Eastern Mediterranean – underwent a decisive transformation. "In this age were born the fundamental categories within which we still think today, and the beginnings of the world religions" (p. 2): Buddhism, Hinduism, Daoism, Judaism, Christianity, and Islam. A recent summary of Jaspers' point noted how, during this period, the regions in question "saw the emergence of highly similar religious traditions with an unprecedented emphasis on self-discipline and asceticism and with 'otherworldly,' often moralizing, doctrines" (Baumard, Hyafil, Morris, & Boyer, 2015: 10). These authors went beyond Jaspers' argument in suggesting that the three geographically dispersed and culturally distinctive regions had all crossed a boundary condition of economic development or affluence, as measured by energy uptake (20,000 kcal/capita/day). Their conclusion was that "absolute affluence would have impacted human motivation and reward systems, nudging people away from short-term strategies (resource acquisition and coercive interactions) and promoting long-term

the Axial Age

strategies (self-control techniques and cooperative interactions)" (p. 10), as articulated in belief systems emphasizing virtue and, with time, additional conceptions of the good life. The same authors also considered "the emergence of a new class of scholars or priests who had the resource and the time to elaborate more abstract religions" (p. 12), supported by literacy and schooling, which equally bore witness to a significant material and mental surplus among their practitioners.

Political and moral philosophers addressing justice typically have not considered its prehistory (Renfrew & Bahn, 2014), nor have they examined the natural and other empirical preconditions of communication about justice around the world. < Nevertheless, the three main traditions in the history of justice all bear witness to the practical contexts – historical configurations of natural circumstances – that have circumscribed and motivated the theories.

> empirical studies of communication and justice – Chapter 8

Three traditions of justice

Do good – virtue ethics

Virtue ethics is by far the oldest tradition of justice, growing out of ancient Greek philosophy with Aristotle as the key reference, and it remained massively influential in shifting formulations until the Enlightenment and beyond (for overview, see Hursthouse, 2016). As suggested by the term, the emphasis is placed on the moral character of individuals as their source of guidance in interpersonal interactions, with implications for their standing both in the community and in the cosmos. While subject to secular interpretations, virtue ethics has commonly involved adherence to religious or other metaphysical principles.

The Greek term for virtue – *arête* – is normally explained in relation to two sister terms: *phronesis* (practical wisdom) and *eudaimonia* (flourishing or happiness). To practice virtue in concrete instances, people must rely on practical wisdom; in contrast to scientific knowledge that seeks general truths, practical judgments are contextual and contingent on previous experience, including past virtuous acts. Individuals may, of course, hold various virtues to different degrees, but virtues amount to deep dispositions and orientations toward action; they are not specific means to specific ends. As manifestations of a meaningful and coherent cosmos, *arête*, *phronesis*, and *eudaimonia* intersect in individuals, who will actualize these capacities and, hence, their own potential to varying degrees. <

arête, phronesis, and *eudaimonia*

> the Aristotelian Principle – Chapter 4, p. 102

telos

A central aspect of classical virtue ethics is the understanding of life as teleological. Life has a *telos*: certain ends that are predefined by the way the world is, and which human beings can and should pursue by the appropriate means. The good is given, and it precedes the principles and procedures by which humans establish the right. A case in point is the exercise of virtue by the members of a community, state, or *polis*. In his *Politics*, Aristotle suggested that "The end of the state is the good life, and [...] the state is the union of families and villages in a perfect and self-sufficing life, by which we mean a happy and honorable life." Honor is the public side of the coin of virtue, a collective recognition that an individual is virtuous. Aristotle further assumed that "the state is a creation of nature and prior to the individual," so that

the good before the right

honor

> the individual, when isolated, is not self-sufficing; and therefore he is like a part in relation to the whole. But he who is unable to live in society, or who has no need because he is sufficient for himself, must be either a beast or a god: he is no part of a state.
>
> *Aristotle, 2015: n.p.*

As elaborated in the *Nicomachean Ethics*, citizens become part of the *polis* through the joint efforts exercised by representatives of the collective and by themselves as individuals. On the one hand, "legislators make their citizens good by training," by installing the right kinds of habits in people. On the other hand, citizens *become* just or good by *doing* – practicing – what is just or good: "by doing just acts we become just, and by doing acts of temperance and courage we become temperate and courageous" (Aristotle, 1886: 35).

learning the good

What ought to be, then, already is – a potential to be actualized through cultivation. Aristotle recognized that a person's exercise of virtue is, in part, a matter of luck. Virtue depends on contingencies of whether and how that particular individual is in a position both to learn and to do the good. The general conditions and specific limitations of justice are, however, predetermined, because the world is what it is – a closed structure of potentialities. To Aristotle, both slavery and the subordinate role of women in the *polis* were part of the order of the universe; neither group were seen to hold the potential for citizenship. A slave is "by nature a slave," and "master and slave have the same interest" (Aristotle, 2015: n.p.). While such arguments do not in themselves invalidate other aspects of Aristotle's politics and ethics, or virtue ethics as such, they highlight a categorical difference between premodern

what ought to be, already is

luck

slavery

virtue ethics and the modern positions of deontology and consequentialism. The conditions of leading a virtuous and honorable personal and public life were understood as universal and eternal, and they called for contemplation rather than critique. Human actions do have consequences, as indicated through Aristotle's distinction between different kinds of causality – material, formal, efficient, and final. < But the final cause of something, its immanent end, is just that – final. Humans are means to an end, not the origin of deliberation and debate about their own ends.

> Aristotle's four causes – Chapter 5, p. 131

Being a versatile thinker drafting disciplines of ethics, politics, rhetoric, and more, Aristotle also considered the role of communication – speech – in articulating what is good or just: "the power of speech is *intended* to set forth the expedient and inexpedient, and therefore likewise the just and the unjust" (Aristotle, 2015: n.p., emphasis added). Language and its social uses, to him, were part of the design of the universe. In other works on language and metaphysics, Aristotle (2007a, 2007b) explored the interrelations between things in the world, mental impressions of these things, and oral or written expressions about the things as well as the impressions. A common denominator for his explorations was a distinctive kind of realism. Whereas Plato had approached reality as an essential, unified, primary realm of ideas, Aristotle developed the understanding that reality is available and accessible for theory and practice in multiple forms – material, mental, and discursive. As a potential, < reality lends itself to different types of actualization. Discursive expressions and mental impressions are no less real than the material objects they capture, and which the thoughts and the discourses may be designed to change. Reality is diversified and distributed.

communication articulates the good

> potential and actualization – Chapter 5, p. 137

reality – diversified and distributed

Virtue ethics was eclipsed by the Enlightenment even if virtue, in the sense of personal morality, has remained part of the agenda of different conceptions of justice up to and including John Rawls and his critics during the twentieth century. < An article by G. E. M. Anscombe (1958) signaled a revival of sorts, identifying limitations of the deontological and consequentialist traditions, and calling for a renewed examination of the relevance of virtue for a modern understanding of justice. Nevertheless, virtue ethics has remained a minority position, in part because of the difficulty of operationalizing and institutionalizing virtues in principles and procedures of justice. In a contemporary perspective, moreover, the individual's exercise of *arête*, as informed by *phronesis*, occurs against the background of many competing definitions of *eudaimonia* that have been accumulated over time, as documented and widely available in writing and other media. The ends and

> Rawls on personal morality – Chapter 4, p. 107

means of justice are continuously communicated about in a variety of social institutions and practices. Aristotle's definition of humans as social beings still applies, but across the centuries, the species itself has redefined what it means to be social.

One noteworthy recent formulation of virtue ethics was advanced by Alasdair MacIntyre (2007/1981) (who has also been associated with communitarianism, although he himself denies this lineage (p. xiv)). < The title of his most influential work, *After Virtue*, suggested "a context that has since been lost, a context in which moral judgments were understood as governed by impersonal standards justified by a shared conception of the human good" (p. ix). This condition of loss is the modern condition, in which neither religion nor philosophy provide a guide to the good, and where, arguably, a pursuit of pleasure and "a specifically emotivist culture" have become dominant ways of life (p. 22), circumscribed by social systems that are governed by "the theoretically informed managerial expertise of the contemporary technocratic expert" (p. 86). MacIntyre's alternative involved a return to Aristotle and a projection of his virtue ethics forward in history. Narratives are said to play a special role in mediating virtue and situating the individual in the community. Human beings are in their "actions and practice, as well as in [their] fictions, essentially a story-telling animal." Both the plot and the end of the story are uncertain since "the narratives which we live out have both an unpredictable and a partially teleological character." MacIntyre takes for granted, however, that "I can only answer the question 'What am I to do?' if I can answer the prior question 'Of what story or stories do I find myself a part?'" (p. 206). In this vocabulary, individuals are characters in, not authors of their own stories, which are part of grander narratives with ends that the individuals do not – cannot – know, but must, nevertheless, serve.

> communitarianism – Chapter 4, p. 121

After Virtue

narratives mediate virtue

It was the received understanding of individuals as means to ends that had been predefined, perhaps by a current community or de facto authority, perhaps by a historical or eternal logic, which the deontological tradition of justice challenged. The stories that people tell (about) themselves – the conditions in which they find themselves – could and should be subject to revision even if the end of the story – the telling and its consequences – remains unpredictable.

Do the right thing – deontology

If Aristotle has informed more than two millennia of Western thinking about virtue and other aspects of ethics and politics,

Immanuel Kant has provided guiding lights for more than two centuries of modern philosophy. As an Enlightenment thinker, he was standing on the shoulders of a renaissance that had installed humans at the center of the universe, nature as well as culture. Addressing the epistemological question, "What can I know?", Kant (1998/1787: n.p.) recognized that human subjects can only grasp their objects through certain mediating transcendental categories (time, space, causality, etc.). In further considering ethical and existential questions, "What ought I to do?" and "What may I hope?", Kant took reason to be the general mode through which humans might discover the good and the right. His motto for the Enlightenment summed up the view that reason, as a distinctive human capability, comes with duties that have epistemological as well as ethical implications: "The motto of the enlightenment is therefore: *Sapere aude!* Have courage to use your *own* understanding!" (Kant, 1970/1784: 54). Modern humans must seek to know, so that they may know what to do.

reason as duty

The idea of duty is implicit in the term deontology, which joins the Greek *deon* (duty) with *logos* (science or study). Duties, moreover, imply rights: My duty constitutes your right, and vice versa, once it is articulated in discourse, enacted in practice, and enforced by social institutions. Although Kant still observed the world from the individual's viewpoint, his argument extrapolated from ethics to politics as he elaborated on the idea of a social contract. Kant thought of this contract as hypothetical or imaginary, but founded in reason:

duties and rights

> Kant simply calls [the imaginary contract] "an *idea* of reason, which nonetheless has undoubted practical reality; for it can oblige every legislator to frame his laws in such a way that they could have been produced by the united will of a whole nation," and obligate each citizen "as if he had consented."
>
> *Sandel, 2009: n.p.*

For Kant, human actions were to be governed by "a law we give ourselves" (Sandel, 2009: n.p.), anticipating a kingdom of ends in which all humans select, consent to, and act by the same fundamental normative principles. Two hundred years on, the same figure of thought was reiterated by John Rawls in his influential theory of justice as fairness with reference to the so-called original position that would lead to the social contract. < But neither Kant nor Rawls elaborated on the sharing of reason – as reasons – in and through communication.

the kingdom of ends

> Rawls' original position – Chapter 4, p. 99

agents and patients of justice

obligations and permissions

causings and omissions

intentions and actions

free will

The relationship between rights and duties, and their implementation in actions, has been examined in detail by the tradition of deontological ethics, with variable emphases on the agents and patients of justice: Who acts (or doesn't act), and who benefits (or not)? (for overview, see Alexander, 2016). First of all, actions may be conditioned by either obligations or permissions. A person can be obliged to contribute to the welfare of others by paying taxes, and is permitted to do the same by making payments to charities. Second, in both respects, a person may engage in either causings or omissions. Paying taxes is a human action, but it also constitutes a cause with (short-term and) long-term consequences for the rest of society; an omission in this regard can be a criminal offense, whereas *not* making a voluntary contribution cannot. Third, actions and intentions are interrelated. Good intentions may never materialize as good actions (similarly for bad intentions). A distinction also is generally made between intended and unintended actions, whether hurting one's best friend in conversation or killing a stranger with a car. Taken together, these various distinctions recall the issue of free will – one conception of the window of indetermination between chance and necessity. Like the idea of virtue, the idea of duty presupposes a measure of human agency: The presupposition is that choosing *not* to do the good or the right thing is a real option.

positive and negative freedom

> liberalism and/ vs. libertarianism – Chapter 4, p. 120

Whereas it may be intuitively easier to grasp ideas of the good and the right in a perspective of personal morality than of public policy, it was the political perspective that moved to front and center in modern philosophy. Humans employ reason in order to make individual choices, but also to collectively plan ahead, in part to avoid certain choices. Free will in the classical sense translates into modern questions of freedom: Which social institutions should be in place to enable and constrain what individuals can do? Debates have revolved around two conceptions of freedom, one positive, the other negative (Berlin, 1969/1958). Probably the most widespread current understanding of freedom or liberty is negative, as associated with liberalism and libertarianism. < Here, freedom is the absence of constraints on individuals' exercise of their ideas and ambitions, specifically a freedom from interference by government authorities. *Less* government equals *more* freedom, would be the motto. Positive freedom, in comparison, implies that individuals will be in a better position to pursue their ends in life if certain collective arrangements are in place: *More* government of the right kind enables *more* freedom for all. The duality of positive and negative freedom pervades modern politics from the local to the global level. The issue has become what duties the collective has for realizing the rights of the individual.

> deductions about justice – Chapter 8, p. 240

Like the other traditions of justice, deontology has faced its share of conceptual and practical dilemmas. Since the model underlying deontology is one of deduction, < of deriving duties from rules, questions arise of how, concretely, to interpret rules before or as they are implemented. In the example of taxation, the chains of deduction from a constitution through legislation to concrete policies and administrative decisions leave wide margins of interpretation, regarding legitimate levels of taxation under the social contract and concerning the relative contribution of taxes on property, income, or consumption. Different rules may take precedence in different contexts, for instance, in view of a current economic crisis. Moreover, some duties will be considered more central than others; Alexander (2016: n.p.), for instance, contrasted "the wrongness of stepping on a snail" with "the wrong of stepping on a baby." The application of rules to such cases has invited sophistry: What if the snail is on top of the baby? One proposed solution to such construed dilemmas has been threshold deontology. As part of a division of ethical labor, rules could be considered absolute up to a certain threshold (don't step on babies), beyond which actions may be justified with reference to context-dependent consequences (don't step on a snail that is on top of a baby) or presumed virtues (don't take a life – any form of life).

threshold deontology

the categorical imperative

Kant's categorical imperative constituted a rule of rules, with two aspects: "Universalize your maxim" and "Treat persons as ends" (Sandel, 2009: n.p.). All human beings are ends in themselves, and they are entitled to pursue their different ends as long as they observe maxims or rules that apply equally to all. If one asks what, then, is the source of this overarching rule, the modern answer is simple: human reason. Compared to virtue ethics, which tends to assume some form of cosmic order – with or without personalized deities, with or without popes and emperors as their authoritative representatives on Earth – deontological ethics delegated the decisions concerning duties to the individual human being. To Kant, human reason still did not place the existence of God in doubt: "God and a future life are two hypotheses which, according to the principles of pure reason, are inseparable from the obligation which this reason imposes upon us" (Kant, 1998/1787: n.p.). Other modern thinkers went on to question any cosmological order, as a secular understanding of nature and culture gradually gained ground in scientific theory and social practice.

> philosophy of consciousness – Chapter 1, p. 9

To Kant, the individual remained the site of reason; Kant was the quintessential philosopher of consciousness. < *Sapere aude* was an imperative in the singular, addressed to individuals of the eighteenth-century Enlightenment. Over the course of the nineteenth century, philosophers, along with emerging publics, increasingly dared to communicate about justice. But it would take another century before a philosophy of communication became conceivable, including public communication as a condition and constituent of justice.

Do the math – consequentialism

> the view from nowhere – Chapter 4, p. 110

While growing out of the same Enlightenment, consequentialism reverses the perspective of deontological ethics, judging acts by their consequences rather than by the duties or intentions motivating them, and observing the course of events from the outside rather than from inside the agents' consciousness (for overview, see Sinnott-Armstrong, 2015). Consequentialism could be seen to aspire to the scientist's objective view from nowhere (Nagel, 1986), < whereas deontology had retained the philosopher's ambition of merging (all) subjective viewpoints. What the two traditions shared, nevertheless, was the premise that human reason can identify the principles and procedures by which human beings may coexist peacefully. Both consequentialist and deontological ethics, further, lent themselves to extension and extrapolation from individual morality to political institutions. The institutional level of analysis became central to different conceptions of and debates about justice during the modern period.

utilitarianism

Utilitarianism is the prototypical example of consequentialism. The founder of utilitarianism, Jeremy Bentham, held that, ultimately, the utility or desired consequence of human actions is the achievement of pleasure and the absence of pain. According to this logic, the diverse hopes and desires of individuals can be translated into one formula. It might be considered cynical, or a reductive conception of what it means to be human, but to Bentham, it was the realistic and rational option: "When a man attempts to combat the principle of utility, it is with reasons drawn, without his being aware of it, from that very principle itself" (Bentham, 1823: 4f.). However much people may protest that they are preoccupied with rights or duties, the animal within < still rules their pursuit of pleasure.

> the animal within humans – p. 30

Like deontology, utilitarianism has confronted dilemmas, particularly of how to define and operationalize pleasure or happiness. Whereas deontological ethics might appear too weak or general to distinguish between just and unjust actions in concrete instances, utilitarianism invites strong and sometimes abhorrent conclusions based on the measure of pleasure. Philosophers have designed various moral dilemmas in order to pinpoint theoretical principles with reference to empirical instances; one classic dilemma is Transplant (see, e.g., Sandel, 2009; Sinnott-Armstrong, 2015). The point in different versions of the story is that the lives of several individuals suffering from organ malfunction could be saved if the organs of a healthy individual were transplanted to them. Though this last person would die, two or more persons would live, which would constitute a greater sum of pleasure than if they had died and the (unwilling) donor had lived. In a pure or literal version, utilitarianism would seem to justify such a scenario. While extreme, the Transplant dilemma helps to explain why philosophers of different stripes have aimed to devise procedures balancing human pleasure with other values.

Transplant

Also advocates of utilitarianism recognized that a quantitative conception of utility along a single scale of pleasure would be untenable. Representing a second generation of utilitarianism, John Stuart Mill (the son of another first-generation utilitarian, James Mill) advanced a qualitative understanding of the consequences or ends that people pursue. Invoking the role of human reason, he specified that, "I regard utility as the ultimate appeal on all ethical questions; but it must be utility in the largest sense, grounded on the permanent interests of man as a progressive being" (Mill, 2011/1859: n.p.). At the very least, the good life must be assessed in the long run, not in terms of instant gratification. Furthermore, Mill (2004/1861: n.p.) distinguished between higher and lower pleasures: "It is quite compatible with the principle of utility to recognise the fact, that some *kinds* of pleasure are more desirable and more valuable than others." In making utilitarianism more palatable to contemporary audiences, Mill was, in effect, reintroducing elements of both virtue ("more valuable" pleasures) and deontology ("the permanent interests of man as a progressive being") into the ethical equation. *On Liberty* (Mill, 2011/1859) summed up the liberal position that "people should be free to do whatever they want, provided they do no harm to others" (Sandel, 2009: n.p.). This general formulation was also compatible with Kant's deontological position, summed up in the categorical imperative.

happiness in the long run

high and low pleasures

If deontology operates through deduction, consequentialism is premised on induction. < Mill's (2009/1843) *A System of Logic* had elaborated an inductivist theory of science, and his utilitarianism assumed that utility could be anticipated and, to a degree,

> inductions about justice – Chapter 8, p. 241

predicted. After all, future outcomes are supposed to guide present actions. At the same time, both Bentham and Mill realized that predictions are uncertain and may be cumbersome in practice. Bentham (1823: 31) noted that, "It is not to be expected that this process [of calculating pleasure] should be strictly pursued previously to every moral judgment, or to every legislative or judicial operation. It may, however, be always kept in view." Mill (2004/1861: n.p.) added that it is not possible to aim for what is generally or universally good, so that "it is a misapprehension of the utilitarian mode of thought, to conceive it as implying that people should fix their minds upon so wide a generality as the world, or society at large." Instead, utility or happiness should be measured at the individual level: "The great majority of good actions are intended, not for the benefit of the world, but for that of individuals, of which the good of the world is made up." The question, however, remained how individuals would be in a position to predict and plan for pleasure or happiness. As later argued by Rawls (1999b/1971: 24), "Utilitarianism does not take seriously the distinction between persons," the fact that people have different principles of happiness, or different ends in life, also when it comes to long-term and higher-order variants.

A common feature of the different traditions of justice has been their admixture of conceptual abstractions and anecdotal dilemmas. Non-philosophers may be struck by the number of subpositions *within* each tradition, spawned by reflections and dilemmas over time. The Transplant dilemma and the sophistry of stepping on snails and babies both suggest a mode of reasoning detached from empirical contexts of practice, as examined in other human and social sciences. Additional textbook dilemmas, shared by consequentialists and deontologists, include Trolley and

Trolley

Fat Man (Alexander, 2016; Sandel, 2009). The Trolley dilemma refers to a situation in which a run-away trolley is headed towards five workers who are trapped at the end of one track; at the end of another track, one worker is trapped, and it is possible for someone to change the course of the trolley so that it likely will kill one rather than five people. A variant of the story introduces

Fat Man

the Fat Man, a bystander, who might be pushed onto the tracks so as to stop the trolley, thus saving all the workers at the end of the tracks. At issue are several questions concerning an absolute right to life, a contingent decision on which lives to save, and whether taking the life of the fat man is morally more wrong than taking that of (one of) the workers. Textbooks rarely include the insight of Bentham and Mill, namely, that no detailed moral reflection is likely to take place before any such action (or inaction); it also is not common for textbooks to shift the agenda toward practical questions of trolley maintenance (or lack thereof) as overseen by social institutions. It is cognition and communication long before and after such choices of the moment that are most likely to make a practical difference for justice. <

> how to make a practical difference – Chapter 5, p. 155

The three traditions of justice have all contributed to an understanding of the window of opportunity between chance and necessity; additional interventions from political philosophy and adjoining disciplines have informed different models of modern political democracy; < and the various traditions and models have been synthesized and restated by contemporary thinkers, notably John Rawls and Jürgen Habermas, who are examined in detail in the following chapters. In recent decades, moreover, both philosophy and interdisciplinary research have drawn particular attention to questions of international justice, specifically how local and global conceptions of justice intersect and crisscross. In this process, communication has taken on added importance: Global communications have disseminated new agendas for theorizing justice and new resources for debating and practicing justice.

> models of political democracy – Chapter 6, p. 182

The global futures of justice

Migration as communication

When individuals migrate, their baggage includes memories of the past and projections of the future. When collectives migrate, their memories and projections amount to cultures that are reinterpreted in response to, and perhaps in opposition to, new social circumstances. Both individuals and collectives depend on communication in order to interpret their changing selves and changing others. In seminal essays collected in a volume entitled *Communication as Culture*, James W. Carey (1989b) made the point that communication is not only, or even primarily, a transmission of concrete items of information, but a continuous ritual in which humans come together to deliberate on the circumstances they share. Carey defined communication as "a symbolic process whereby reality is produced, maintained, repaired, and transformed" (p. 23). When different cultures make contact, new realities are produced, maintained, repaired, and transformed.

communication as transmission and ritual

The prehistory of humans is, in part, a story of migration among more or less hospitable habitats (Sachs, 2020), while bands, tribes, and cultures developed moralities and social contracts through face-to-face communication. < In historical time, writing came

> the prehistory of human morality – p. 28

to facilitate the conquest of and control over territories, when migration turned into settlement and empire (Innis, 1972/1950). And in the modern period, territories became increasingly interconnected through communication as well as transportation. Carey (1989) illustrated the close relationship between communication and migration with reference to the telegraph, which "marked the decisive separation of 'transportation' and 'communication'" (p. 213). Until the invention of the telegraph, all communication had required the physical movement or migration of humans and the written or printed materials they came to carry. Now, humans could have virtual contact across space in real time, and they could act at a distance. The telegraph "allowed communication to control physical processes actively" (p. 203), with railroad signals as one early example. In hindsight, the telegraph has been dubbed "the Victorian internet" (Standage, 1998).

Centuries of migration and communication, enhanced by technologies of transportation and information, have resulted in a networked world (Castells, 1996), as also summarized under a heading of globalization (Robertson, 1992). Global economic, political, and cultural networks condition whatever justice and injustice people experience where they currently find themselves. Some forms of migration, crucially, have amounted to forced displacement and the subjugation of indigenous peoples and national minorities. Multiculturalism denotes a contemporary reality in which collectives with distinctive and conflicted histories coexist within modern nation-states (for overview, see Song, 2016). In Europe, this is the legacy of liberal democracies that are former colonial powers, and where multiculturalism has provided a backdrop to academic and public debate about justice in recent decades. Also beyond Europe, the issues have been debated under a heading of identity politics (Heyes, 2016), including the relative importance of cultural identities for social justice and the interrelation of identities with material and institutional conditions.

globalization

multiculturalism

identity politics

Perhaps the most contentious issue of multiculturalism has been group-based rights. Do particular groups of individuals hold specific rights because of a shared cultural identity or historical trajectory? Are some people, further, entitled – as groups – to specific goods or preferential treatment, such as affirmative action, as compensation for past grievances with present consequences? Whereas the reference points in such debates typically have been ethnic or religious communities, arguments concerning multiculturalism have also been applied more broadly to disadvantaged groups as associated with gender, sexuality, and physical or mental ability. In some instances, the groups in question may be subject

group-based rights

to multiple or intersectional discrimination (Crenshaw, 1989), or they may themselves be at odds, for example, when a religious group discriminates against women, making them a minority within a minority (Eisenberg & Spinner-Halev, 2005).

intersectionality

minorities within minorities

The terminology of multiple *cultures* might suggest that the contentious issues relate primarily to what Marxists have referred to as the superstructure of society – ideas and identities. In fact, research in the area has recognized that also the material and economic bases of society are at stake: The institutions, practices, and discourses of culture constitute points of access to other social goods and to the procedures regulating their distribution. In other fields, interdisciplinary literatures have explored, for example, intercultural communication (Kim, 2018) and the interrelations between different kinds of subcultures (Gelder, 2005). Key strands of this work have pursued a critical agenda with a family resemblance to multiculturalist philosophy, referring to media as agents of cultural imperialism (e.g., Tunstall, 1977) and to postcolonial cultures pervading contemporary nation-states (Ashcroft, Griffiths, & Tiffin, 2006). Whereas these other fields have commonly shared a definition of cultures as whole ways of life (Williams, 1975/1958: 18) that are maintained in and through communication, multiculturalist philosophy has mostly been silent on the common practice through which cultures share aspects of their different ways of life, potentially anticipating whole new ways of life.

cultural imperialism

postcolonial cultures

Multiculturalism has itself been subject to multiple interpretations. On the one hand, one influential formulation, by Will Kymlicka (1996), started out from the liberalism of John Rawls, and suggested that culture constitutes both a background to the exercise of individual autonomy when people make various choices in life, and a source of their basic self-respect. Considering both aspects of culture, he contributed a distinction between "'multination' states (where cultural diversity arises from the incorporation of previously selfgoverning, territorially concentrated cultures into a larger state) and 'polyethnic' states (where cultural diversity arises from individual and familial immigration)" (p. 7). Kymlicka, further, introduced a parallel to what Rawls had referred to as natural and social lotteries: Just as any person happens to be born with certain natural capacities, and into certain social circumstances, so persons grow up to become part of a certain culture, which may be a minority culture, perhaps despised by the majority. This gives rise to what is known, in multiculturalism, as a politics of difference, which, in turn, motivates a politics of recognition. Cultural differences, accordingly, should be recognized through institutional procedures, so

multination states

polyethnic states

politics of difference

politics of recognition

that resources may be allocated for different cultures to flourish. As part of a contemporary theory of justice, "we should treat access to one's culture as something that people can be expected to want, whatever their more particular conception of the good" (p. 87). The requirement is not just the absence of discrimination (negative freedom), but the cultivation and even celebration of difference (positive freedom). <

> positive and negative freedom – p. 36

On the other hand, critics of liberal multiculturalism have argued that the reality has, instead, been a politics of indifference and misrecognition. In a case study of indigenous peoples in Canada, Glen S. Coulthard (2014) suggested that the politics of recognition reproduces the power relations of the colonial past through a combination of "forced *exclusion* and *assimilation*" (p. 4): the exclusion of minorities from social goods and positions of power, and their assimilation to the majority culture. Recognition does not yield reciprocity because, in practice, some groups remain more equal than others. This is in spite of initiatives such as "state apologies, commissions of inquiry, truth and reconciliation commissions, individual reparations, and so forth" (p. 22). With reference to "settler-colonialism as a structure of domination predicated on the dispossession of Indigenous peoples' lands and political authority" (p. 151), Coulthard concluded that colonialism is not a thing of the past, but persists throughout contemporary institutions, practices, and discourses of culture.

Both multination states and polyethnic states are crisscrossed by long memories of deep divisions, carried by media and addressed in communication. In and through media and communication, individuals and collectives migrate across past, present, and future. With modern means of communication, the agenda for discussions about justice, increasingly, has come to include the whole world.

Communication as migration

If physical migration entails embodied communication, communication also involves virtual migration. At issue are not just science fictions of humans traveling in deep space or time, but deliberations that concrete individuals and communities engage in, about the future, and with reference to present institutional arrangements bearing on justice. Long before virtual-reality technologies (Levy, 1993) and the "declaration of the independence of cyberspace" from the "Governments of the Industrial World, you weary giants of flesh and steel" (Barlow, 1996: n.p.), humans have imagined and exchanged different possible worlds < in signs

> possible worlds – Chapter 3, p. 81

and symbols. Virtual worlds are real – they make a practical difference for how people orient themselves, make plans, and act. As illustrated by Carey (1989), the telegraph enabled communication with absent others and action at a distance, affording far-flung physical infrastructures such as the railroad. The notion of an interconnected world inhabited by world citizens, as articulated through shifting technologies and institutions of communication, has been a long time coming.

virtual worlds

Complementing and overlapping with multiculturalism, research and debate on cosmopolitanism have considered the possibility and desirability of global institutions and procedures of coexistence and collaboration – in moral, political, economic, as well as cultural matters (for overview, see Kleingeld & Brown, 2013). While recorded since Antiquity, the idea of cosmopolitanism was reemphasized during the Enlightenment:

cosmopolitanism

> The historical context of the philosophical resurgence of cosmopolitanism during the Enlightenment is made up of many factors: The increasing rise of capitalism and worldwide trade and its theoretical reflections; the reality of ever expanding empires whose reach extended across the globe; the voyages around the world and the anthropological so-called 'discoveries' facilitated through these; the renewed interest in Hellenistic philosophy; and the emergence of a notion of human rights and a philosophical focus on human reason.
>
> *Kleingeld & Brown, 2013: n.p.*

In philosophy and other scholarship, these factors, again, took effect through double hermeneutics. < Modern scholarship was responding to a world that presented itself as a new and different sort of environment, and which invited reinterpretation of the place of humans in it. The world was there to be discovered, but also to be reconstructed for human ends, whatever they might be.

> the double hermeneutics of justice – p. 25

Moral cosmopolitanism, first of all, refers to a wide variety of reflections on the good and the right that have featured in virtue ethics, deontological ethics, as well as consequentialism, in addition to world religions. The idea has been that all human beings constitute one community. Because of its general formulation, and because it is typically embedded in traditions with more specific commitments, moral cosmopolitanism is perhaps best characterized as a utopian vision shared across civilizations. Even as it was emerging in its modern form, cosmopolitanism faced "a pluralism of comprehensive religious, philosophical, and

moral cosmopolitanism

moral doctrines" (Rawls, 2005/1993: xvi) that seemed incompatible. A second variant – *economic* cosmopolitanism – has been described, in the philosophical literature, as a source of problems rather than of their solution. A common argument has been that a global free market, when coupled with minimal political regulation, as advocated most emphatically by libertarianism, < contributes to economic inequality and general misery around the world. Economic cosmopolitanism might even be thought of as the antithesis of moral cosmopolitanism, as immoral.

economic cosmopolitanism

> libertarianism – Chapter 4, p. 120

political cosmopolitanism

Political cosmopolitanism, third, has been the central focus of research and debate in the area. The shared assumption is that international institutions are needed to regulate the more or less blind forces of the market as well as the more or less moral inclinations of individuals and communities, so as to counteract, at least, the worst excesses and contingencies of the global human condition. Since Kant's 1795 *Perpetual Peace* (2016/1795), thinkers have explored alternatives to a world government, which, arguably, would result in "either [...] a global despotism or [...] a fragile empire torn by frequent civil strife" (Rawls, 1999a: 36). Despite interventions such as Habermas' constitution for a world society (Chapter 3) and Rawls' Law of Peoples (Chapter 4), it is fair to conclude that international justice has remained theoretically underspecified. It was, instead, the practice of injustice during two world wars, and the de facto powers emerging by the mid-twentieth century, that shaped contemporary international institutions of justice – which are themselves being reconfigured in response to globalization and digitalization.

cultural cosmopolitanism

Cultural cosmopolitanism, finally, returns to issues of multiculturalism: how to recognize distinctive cultural practices as ingredients of a good life, while avoiding a world of cultural camps, defined and divided by their differences. Culture is more than a source of self-identity; it is also a point of access to the identities of others. Cultures are produced, maintained, repaired, and transformed in shifting configurations. Culture and cultures are accumulated in and through communication, from the local to the global level.

Globalization, today, refers to an interplay of economic, political, and cultural forces. It is not a recent phenomenon, and the forces are not in sync. Economic globalization has been ongoing at least since the sixteenth century (Wallerstein, 1974). Political globalization, as noted, remains limited in institutional terms, despite international treaty systems and a regional entity like the European Union. Cultural globalization has depended on shifting communication infrastructures – writing, print, cinema, broadcasting, the internet – and has been intensifying in recent decades. A unique feature of cultural globalization is that it enables, in principle, anyone anywhere to represent and reflect on the rest of the world. The world is, of course, a concrete, material context of human endeavors: business investments, political negotiations, tourism, and more. For most people most of the time, however, the world is a virtual frame of reference for their communications and actions (Tomlinson, 1999: 11) – an imagined entity, sometimes an imagined community (Anderson, 1991). This is the technologically mediated condition of modernity, as accentuated by globalization, which is also the condition for communicating about justice in a future perspective.

the world as a context of action

the world as a frame of reference

Does the world still need a theory of justice?

The difficulty of arriving at a consensus on principles and procedures of justice – across decades and centuries, and around the globe – has prompted proposals for alternative strategies of counteracting manifest injustice ad hoc and in practice. Theories of justice might even be seen as distractions from the urgent business of avoiding or alleviating human suffering. Such a position was presented by Amartya Sen, a Nobel Prize-winning economist, who has devoted specific attention to issues of justice, with famines as a case in point. The title of the volume in question – *The Idea of Justice* (Sen, 2009) – signaled an attempt to reframe the very idea of justice and to develop

> a theory of justice in a very broad sense. Its aim is to clarify how we can proceed to address questions of enhancing justice and removing injustice, rather than to offer resolutions of questions about the nature of perfect justice.
>
> *p. ix*

Toward this end, Sen joined two perspectives on global justice: Western science and Eastern philosophy. On the one hand, he advocated a comparative, empirical approach: How do problems of justice and potential solutions actually manifest themselves in particular historical and cultural circumstances? On the other hand, he took inspiration from concepts deriving from Indian philosophy and jurisprudence: *niti* and *nyaya*. Whereas *niti* emphasizes "organizational propriety as well as behavioral correctness," *nyaya* directs attention to "what emerges and how, and in particular the lives that people are actually able to lead" (p. xv).

Sen (2009) contrasted his own position with "the pre-eminent theories of justice in contemporary moral and political philosophy" (p. ix) and in particular with John Rawls' work (which I address in Chapter 4). Sen's critique of the established traditions of justice was summed up in a notion of "transcendental institutionalism" (p. 5). His argument was, first, that philosophers have focused so much on "getting the institutions rights" that they have tended to lose sight of "the actual societies that would ultimately emerge." Second, the focus on institutions was said to have a transcendental quality: "It tries only to identify social characteristics that *cannot be transcended* in terms of justice" (p. 6, emphasis added). It takes a careful reading and a charitable interpretation to realize that Sen uses transcendence as a synonym of perfection, not as a reference to Kantian, necessary conditions of grasping or exercising justice in the first place.

transcendental institutionalism

To Sen (2009), institutionalism and transcendentalism (perfectionism) had come together in the model of the social contract, < as developed from Hobbes through Rawls. He contrasted it with another much more recent model – social choice theory – to which Sen himself has made central contributions. Addressing how groups of people could and should arrive at collective decisions in economic and other matters, social choice theory proceeds by practical, comparative assessment, and allows for multiple principles, iterative procedures, and partial resolutions. Sen further contrasted this model with another widely influential school of economics, namely, rational choice theory: the "remarkably alienating belief" and "peculiar understanding that rational choice consists only in clever promotion of self-interest." His outlook was different: "A person may have well-thought-out reasons other than the promotion of personal gain for acting in a socially decent way" (p. 32). And he supported his position with reference to a heterogeneous legacy of "realization-focused comparison" (p. 7), emerging from the Enlightenment and incorporating ideas from thinkers as diverse as Adam Smith and Karl Marx. In particular, Sen aligned himself with Adam Smith's idea of an impartial spectator. Smith's moral and political philosophy was premised on "the need to invoke a wide variety of viewpoints and outlooks based on diverse experiences from far and near [...] scrutinizing not only the influence of vested interest, but also the impact of entrenched tradition and custom" (p. 45). Concrete solutions to real problems of justice, then, would be based on empirical evidence, but assessed from the perspective of a supposedly impartial spectator.

> the social contract – Chapter 4, p. 98

social choice theory

realization-focused comparison

the impartial spectator

Like other contemporary philosophers, including Rawls and Habermas, Sen (2009) pointed to public reasoning as a general process through which "realization-focused comparison" can be undertaken (p. 7), also beyond the election seasons of institutional politics. Moreover, he highlighted "the global origins of democracy," and rejected the view of democracy as "a quintessentially 'European' or 'Western' idea" (p. 327). At the same time, he noted the crucial role of the press and other media as vehicles of public reasoning. "And here the traditions established in Europe and America over the last three hundred years have indeed made a gigantic difference [and] have been transformational for the world as a whole." But Sen's cursory treatment of communication, toward the end of the volume, did not actually clarify – compare – how, concretely, "unrestrained and healthy media" could and should operate in different national and cultural contexts (p. 335). Like most theorists of justice, Sen stopped short of addressing how imagined entities such as impartial spectators would communicate and translate their assessments into realizable and sustainable arrangements – institutions, in some sense of the word.

global origins of democracy

The main contribution of Sen's (2009) volume was to reemphasize the importance of empirical reasoning, along with non-ideal theory, < regarding global justice; I return in Chapter 7 to Sen's capabilities approach < and its application to contemporary communication infrastructures. His critique of "transcendental institutionalism" (p. 5), however, conflated perfectionism and institutionalism. He targeted the "transcendentalist institutionalists in search of perfectly just institutions," even while adding that the same thinkers "have sometimes also presented deeply illuminating analyses of moral or political imperatives regarding socially appropriate behaviour" (singling out "Immanuel Kant and John Rawls" for special praise, p. 6f.). But any comparison of any "imperatives" or "behaviors" requires standards, whose definition and enforcement depend on institutions, however preliminary and imperfect. To combat injustice in practice, both individuals and collectives need at least a working theory of justice in order to communicate about what it ought to be, and what could and should be done to achieve it. The most influential theory of communication and justice to date has been developed by Jürgen Habermas, whose work is the topic of the following chapter.

> non-ideal theory – Chapter 4, p. 107

> the capabilities approach – Chapter 7, p. 193

3

THE STRUCTURAL TRANSFORMATION OF JÜRGEN HABERMAS

From the coffeehouse to the internet

In a keynote address to the annual conference of the International Communication Association, Jürgen Habermas (2006) took stock of the conditions of public communication at the beginning of the twenty-first century. Having reaffirmed the "truth-tracking potential" (p. 413) of human communication, Habermas contrasted "the confused din of voices rising from both everyday talk and mediated communication" with a need for checks and balances, "a cleansing mechanism that filters out the 'muddy' elements" (p. 416f.). In the absence of such mechanisms, he found, public communication has deteriorated through "the colonization of the public sphere" into "the covert displacement of one category of communication by another: Issues of political discourse become assimilated into and absorbed by the modes and contents of entertainment" (p. 422). The keynote, thus, reiterated a 50-year critique of media that was first expressed in Habermas' (1989/1962) historical account of the structural transformation of the public sphere < across two and half centuries – from the extension of face-to-face coffee-house debates into early newspapers of the eighteenth century, to the cooptation of political communication by full-fledged commercial media systems by the mid-twentieth century.

> the public sphere – p. 52

The most remarkable moment of the keynote was an assessment of the internet that only appeared in a footnote of the published version, asking the reader to "allow me in passing a remark on the Internet" (Habermas, 2006: 423). For Habermas, there could be no talk of the internet redressing some of the democratic deficits of press and broadcasting, except in one special case: "computer-mediated communication in the web can claim unequivocal *democratic* merits only for a special context: It can undermine the censorship of authoritarian regimes that try to control and repress public opinion." Beyond that instance, the internet was said to represent another step backward: "In the context of liberal regimes, the rise of millions of fragmented chat rooms across the world tend instead to lead to the fragmentation of large but politically focused mass audiences into a huge number of isolated issue publics." The only hope, according to Habermas, would be yet another cleansing of internet din through the intervention of classic quality mass media: "Within established national public spheres, the online debates of web users only promote political communication, when news groups crystallize around the focal points of the quality press, for example, national newspapers and political magazines" (Habermas, 2006: 423).

It was puzzling to find the chief chronicler of the public sphere from the early eighteenth to the late twentieth centuries discounting the potentials of the internet even as it was emerging and taking shape as a public medium in the early twenty-first century. In other writings, Habermas (2009: 53, 131) has reaffirmed both the specific point about the internet and the general priority given to the traditional press. This chapter presents a solution to the puzzle through an analysis of his *oeuvre* as communication. I identify a long-term structural transformation of premises, evidence, and conclusions as Habermas has been struggling to come to terms with two modes of thought and discourse, one historical-empirical, the other systematic-normative. Compared to the structural transformation of the public sphere, which Habermas, speaking as a social theorist, attributed to economic and other historical forces, his own transformation has followed from the philosopher's quest for transhistorical standards to evaluate and reform present forms of life. While there is every reason to appreciate Habermas' continued commitment as an academic scholar and a public intellectual, I document equally compelling reasons to engage in a hermeneutics of suspicion (Ricoeur, 1981: 46), not of Habermas' ideal intentions, but of his actual communications. Despite many protestations that his philosophy of communication represents a turn toward detranscendentalized and *Postmetaphysical Thinking* (Habermas, 1992d), his writings can be seen to pursue practical ends by transcendental terminologies and metaphysical conceptions of the human condition over the course of half a century and through distinctive stages.

historical and systematic analysis

> the theory of communicative action – p. 65

By way of introduction, I revisit the first, historical *magnum opus* on the development of public sphere (Habermas, 1989/1962). Following a 1960s–70s interlude during which Habermas explored diverse macrosocial implications of microdiscursive practices, the theory of communicative action < (Habermas, 1984/1981, 1987b/1981) summarized and elaborated his second, systematic position, which became the pivot for numerous subsequent publications that engaged a host of classic epistemological questions and contemporary political and cultural issues. A third *magnum opus*, on law and democracy (Habermas, 1996/1992), sought to integrate elements of the first two works by working out the institutional consequences of the ideal requirements of communicative action. During recent decades, a shift of emphasis has been in evidence in Habermas' publications toward a range of public issues, notably global communication and religious communication; his newest *magnum opus*, a two-volume history of philosophy (Habermas, 2019a), charts reconfigurations of faith and knowledge in the longer and wider history of ideas. As part of a comparative analysis of the different stages and themes of these *magna opera*, I present evidence and arguments regarding fundamental contradictions crisscrossing the *oeuvre*. I conclude that Habermas has practiced – if one were to accept his vocabulary – both strategic and systematically distorted communication, canceling the theory of communicative action on its own terms. Amplified in an era still resonating with utopias of communication (Peters, 1999), and recommended by the relative poverty of other normative communication theory, as outlined in Chapter 1, Jürgen Habermas' philosophy of communication has come to stand out as so singularly attractive that it tends to block the way of inquiry < into communication and justice.

> the way of inquiry – Chapter 5, p. 141

The rise and fall of the bourgeois public sphere

Historical norms

the public sphere

The volume on *The Structural Transformation of the Public Sphere* (Habermas, 1989/1962) provided, at once, a history of the rise of modern political democracy in Europe and a critique of how public communication came to be practiced as part of this new system of governance. Habermas' analysis made clear that the public sphere took shape, and was repeatedly reshaped, in and through social conflict. Whereas the public sphere could be defined, most basically, as "the sphere of private people come together as a public" to deliberate and communicate on their common affairs, it was a particular group of private people – the rising bourgeoisie – who "soon claimed the public sphere" in their own interest and turned it "against public authorities themselves" (p. 27), namely, the ruling feudal order. From the outset, then, it was a "*bourgeois* public sphere" (p. 27, emphasis added). Structurally speaking, it served as the means to a particular end of transforming society, in opposition to nobility and monarchy, and in the interest of what would become a new dominant economic and political class.

the feudal order

In later stages of its development, the public sphere acquired a less proactive, more reactive function. It became a discursive arena in which conflicts between classes, and between the state and different sectors and interests in society, could be represented, negotiated, and, to a degree, resolved. Throughout its transformation, however, the public sphere "was based on the fictitious identity of the two roles assumed by the privatized individuals who came together to form a public: the role of property owners and the role of human beings pure and simple" (p. 56). The notion that historically situated individuals could engage in disinterested communication about the common good of all must be considered, in Habermas' 1962 words, "fictitious," because, as property owners, they would go on pursuing their own economic interests. Also in the public sphere, some were more equal than others. Such a fundamental ambiguity was destined to generate institutional antagonisms and discursive ambivalences within a public that would remain divided along economic, political, and cultural fault lines. And it was an ambiguity that would continue to trouble Habermas' own conceptions, not just of the public sphere, but of the universal human practice of communication throughout the different stages of his work.

proactive and reactive public spheres

citizens and property owners

Table 3.1 lays out what Habermas (1989/1962: 27–30) referred to as "the basic blueprint" of the public sphere in an amended and elaborated version of his original diagram (see further Jensen, 2012b: 17; Mortensen, 1977). The figure identifies, to the right, the various state agencies that maintain the material, legal, and other infrastructural conditions and frameworks of social interaction, ultimately with recourse to a monopoly on the use of physical force. To the left, private economic enterprise unfolds in the social sphere, while the intimate sphere represents a different category of 'private' or personal family life. (Habermas (1989/1962: 55) used the term "private" exclusively to refer to the economic sphere of production; here, I prefer the alternative terminology to highlight the overarching distinction between the state and a private realm of existence, centered in the individual and his [historically, not her] enterprise and family.)

the state

the social sphere

the intimate sphere

TABLE 3.1 The public-sphere model

	Society		*State*
	Private sphere	*Public sphere*	
	Intimate sphere	*Cultural public sphere*	The (agencies of the) state ensure(s) the material infrastructure, overall economic stability, law enforcement, and regulation of conflicts by economic, coercive, legal, and ideological means
Object	Religion, sexuality, emotion, friendship, etc.	Preaching, art, literature, music, etc.	
Institution	Family	Organizations, clubs	
	Social sphere	*Political public sphere*	
Object	Private economic activity, production and sale/ purchase of commodities, including labor	'Politics' and 'the economy', including social issues	
Institution	Private enterprises and stores	Parliamentary organs, representing political parties, and the press	

the political public sphere

the cultural public sphere

The mediating element of the model is the public sphere, comprising the main political and cultural institutions of modern society: parties, parliaments, and presses, but also cultural organizations and aesthetic movements. Importantly, Habermas distinguished two functionally differentiated public spheres, one political, the other cultural (a distinction that has been neglected in much of the secondary literature in English on Habermas). In historical perspective, Habermas further noted how the cultural public sphere of literary journals and *salons* had been a crucial "training ground" and "precursor" (p. 29) for political deliberation and debate in a contemporary sense. Fictions help individuals and communities understand and put into perspective what they will count as facts. Also today, communicative competences will carry over from the cultural to the political realm, and vice versa, even if the existential questions of personal life and the political questions of public coexistence mostly will be addressed in separate genres of communication and with reference to distinctive agendas.

real and imagined models

The public-sphere model represents both a real and an imagined conception of society. Markets, parliaments, families, state agencies, and media are all real: The model *locates* media and communication on a map of modern society alongside other major social institutions. However, far from providing a neutral organizational chart, the model entailed a particular understanding of how these institutions *relate* to each other, specifically how they could and ought to interact. To be operational and effective, a particular configuration of the model had to become ingrained in the hearts and minds of self-defined citizens as a plan of action that would enable them to construct a different social order; the public sphere itself had to be conceived as a source of political alternatives and collective agency. A key question, in the longer historical perspective and for Habermas' retrospective analysis and assessment, was whether and how a sphere of public communication could have such transformative capacity at the level of the institutional and material structures of society.

From the opening of his first volume, Habermas (1989/1962) underscored the reflective, deliberative, and, ultimately, transformative potential of communication. The public sphere could be understood as unique, "without historical precedent: people's public use of their reason (*öffentliches Räsonnement*)" (p. 27). The vision of public debate was one in which "the public competition of private arguments" would result in "the consensus about what was practically necessary in the interest of all" (p. 83). Habermas readily acknowledged that what took shape was far from any free marketplace of idea, noting in particular the fundamental problem of unequal access to participate: "The public sphere of civil society stood or fell with the principle of universal access" (p. 85). Gender, age, property ownership, and education still determined whether a person would be in a position to speak (and to be heard) in public. And yet, the self-conception of those who gained access to speaking and participating in the public sphere could be considered "more than mere ideology." This was because "the dominant class nevertheless developed political institutions which credibly embodied [...] the idea of their own abolition [...] the idea of the dissolution of domination into [...] the compelling insight of a public opinion." In sum, the imagined public sphere was real enough that it could "lay a claim to truth inasmuch as it transcends the status quo in utopian fashion, even if only for purposes of justification" (p. 88). A utopia for the many had been articulated even if, from the outset, it only served the few, and even if the utopian window, according to Habermas' (1989/1962) analysis, would soon close.

more than mere ideology

It was this closure that the book title summed up as a "structural transformation," and which went far beyond the particular contents and forms of reflection and deliberation in the public sphere. Habermas (1989/1962) specified the closure as a process of "refeudalization" (p. 142): an intertwining, once again, of private interests and governmental authority without the transparency afforded by public disclosure and scrutiny. The resulting

refeudalization

reconfiguration of the basic constituents of Table 3.1 suggests the nature of the forces at work. In a first step, the public sphere had driven a wedge into the feudal order of the medieval era, supposedly natural as well as divine, which had subordinated and bonded social subjects to their sovereign. In a second step, the two sides of the split-open structure, now in the shape of private capital and emerging modern state apparatuses, pushed back the domain of the public sphere as they entered into new and mutually beneficial alliances. For one thing, various forms of legislation and regulation, including monetary and fiscal intervention, were designed to save private enterprise from the worst crises of its own making, both within national borders and as part of an international system in which "gradually all the capitalistically advanced countries abandoned the sacred principles of free trade [...] in favor of a new protectionism" (p. 143). For another thing, responding to grievances and protests from the economically and politically disenfranchised, state agencies acted to serve the long-term interests of capital by ensuring some "protection, compensation, and subsidies to the economically weaker social groups, to workers and to employees, tenants, consumers, etc." (p. 147) as part of a rudimentary system of social welfare.

national and international economic regulation

social welfare

The overriding historical logic was one of "translating economic antagonisms into political conflicts" (Habermas, 1989/1962: 146). While avoiding open class warfare, the resulting "blurred blueprint" also amounted to a "disintegration" of the public sphere as originally envisioned (p. 175). Most important, it entailed the gradual transformation of an arena of dialogue and deliberation about "the interest of all" (p. 83) into one of negotiation and bargaining: "Competition between organized private interests invaded the public sphere" (p. 179). In the *political* public sphere, citizens became audiences rather than agents:

economic antagonisms and political conflicts

from deliberation to bargaining

> The process of the politically relevant exercise and equilibration of power now takes place directly between the private bureaucracies, special-interest associations, parties, and public administration. The public as such is included only sporadically in this circuit of power, and even then it is brought in only to contribute its acclamation.
>
> *p. 176*

In the *cultural* public sphere, the setback registered in a shift from "rational-critical debate" toward mere "consumption" in "a pseudo-public sphere" and "a culture that no longer trusts the power of the printed word" (pp. 161–163). The decline of both public spheres was attributed, first and foremost, to the full-scale introduction of commercial, advertising-supported mass media, so that "the laws of the market governing the sphere of commodity exchange and of social labor also pervaded the sphere reserved for private people as a public" (p. 161). Because businesses and governments increasingly communicated to consumers and citizens in an interconnected marketplace of attention, also "the state [had] to 'address' its citizens like consumers" (p. 195). In effect, Habermas suggested, citizens had been pacified as they enjoyed their entitlements alongside other goods: "Citizens entitled to services relate to the state not primarily through political participation but by adopting a general attitude of demand – expecting to be provided for without actually wanting to fight for the necessary decisions" (p. 211).

commercial media

citizens as consumers

Retrospective systematics

Not surprisingly, Habermas' dystopian diagnosis of the mid-twentieth century, as contrasted with the communicative utopia of the eighteenth-century bourgeois public sphere, attracted widespread scholarly (and some public) attention. The lines of argument, among critics as well as in his responses, came together at a high-profile international conference and in a subsequent anthology (Calhoun, Florence, & Mirchandani, 1992), following the belated translation of *Structural Transformation* (ST) into English. The anthology included formal papers as well as transcripts of plenary discussions at the conference; Habermas' own interventions in both genres begin to suggest some of his strategies of communication – strategies that he had disowned, in principle, in the theory of communicative action that had appeared in between ST and the retrospective conference.

At one level, Habermas' (1992b) formal paper recognized that the narrative about the political and cultural decline of the public sphere had been "too simplistic" (p. 438): It had "the ring of a contrast between an idealistically glorified past and a present distorted by the mirror of cultural criticism" (p. 430). At the same time, he reconfirmed that "I continue to stay with the intention that guided the study as a whole" (p. 441). Even if the discursive means had been less than ideal, perhaps the intention or consciousness behind the communication had expressed the right end. However, Habermas' oral contributions left listeners and later readers in further doubt as to what, in fact, his intention had been in the 1960s, or had become by the 1990s. On the one hand, he pleaded guilty to conflating ideal type and ideal:

ideal and ideal type

> I can rightly be accused of having idealized what were presented as features of an existing liberal public sphere; I was at least not careful enough in distinguishing between an ideal type and the very context from which it was constructed.
>
> *Calhoun, 1992: 463*

On the other hand, he quickly modified such self-criticism by claiming that the "collapsing of norm and description" amounted to only a "slight idealization" (p. 463). Even if one were to grant this forgiving self-interpretation 30 years on, the question remained how a revised position would take into account the empirical reality of the many conflicts involving all those social groups and practices that had been "excluded from the public sphere *and from my analysis of it too*: gender, ethnicity, class, popular culture" (p. 466, emphasis added).

At this point of his oral intervention, Habermas adopted the familiar argumentative strategy of defending one's own conclusion by challenging anyone to disagree with its first premise. Rather than elaborating or exemplifying, for example, the place of gender perspectives on, or of popular culture in, the original vision of an inclusive and comprehensive public sphere, he reasserted the core premise of the bourgeois public sphere:

> Once you invent these universalistic Enlightenment concepts, forms of communication [...] that are meant to settle practical conflicts in terms of mutual understanding and intended agreement manifestly rely on the force of more or less good reasons as the only alternative to overt or covert violence. So, the question is, How could you critically assess the inconspicuous repression of ethnic, cultural, national, gender, and [identity] differences if not in the light of this one basic standard, however interpreted, of procedures that all parties presume will provide the most rational solution at hand, at a given time, in a given context?
>
> *p. 467*

one basic standard

The devil is in the discursive detail: By immediately adding the qualification, "however interpreted," to his reaffirmation of "one basic standard," Habermas left conveniently ambiguous how, in fact, that standard might come to include and recognize different genders, ethnicities, classes, and cultural layers, not least in a future perspective. It is this 'standard' that has been reasserted in shifting historical and systematic guises through the different stages of Habermas' thinking – it is the point beyond which he will entertain no doubt and engage in no further communication. Admittedly, the specific ambiguity might be attributed to the ad hoc, oral format of the argument in this particular conference session; most thinkers will occasionally defend past positions with questionable arguments. But Habermas has gone on, before and after the 1992 anthology, to claim the continuity of his own position and its compatibility with other sources of modern philosophy and additional fields in ways that are at odds not only with standard academic practice, but with the standards that his own theories have held up for all communication.

Habermas (1992b) summed up his practical-political project, initially outlined in the volume on the public sphere, as one of working out the conditions under which "the mass democracies constituted as social-welfare states [...] can claim to continue the principles of the liberal constitutional state" (p. 441). After all, large numbers of citizens, pacified or not, were spared great suffering by their entitlements under the social-welfare schemes that, arguably, compromised the bourgeois public sphere, or at least its self-conceived promise. How might the historical *ideal type* of the public sphere help to articulate and advance a universal *ideal* that would serve citizens' rights and their welfare in present and future communities and societies? Such questions were not addressed in any detail in the first book. In retrospect, Habermas (1992b) found that "further advances [had been] necessary to produce a theoretical framework within which I can now reformulate the questions and provide at least the outline of an answer" (p. 441). That framework or systematics – the theory of communicative action – was in the making for two decades after the historical study of the public sphere. But the continuity of the 1962 problem with the 1981 solution was not quite what it seemed in Habermas' retrospective 1992 reply. In between, his intellectual trajectory had taken a decisive, if seldom debated turn in defense of the "one basic standard" (Calhoun, 1992: 467).

the theory of communicative action

Reconstructed interests

Interested knowledge

The interlude between 1962 and 1981 witnessed a gradual configuration and consolidation of two enduring elements of Habermas' thinking. At the macro level of modern institutions and ideas, the study of the public sphere was followed by inquiries into the very idea of knowledge, including the status of science

> formal pragmatics – p. 67

human knowledge and social action

> Kant on knowledge – Chapter 1, p. 14

and scholarship as undertaken by disciplinary specialists and of rationality as practiced, potentially, by anyone. At the micro level of language and communication, Habermas began to probe some of the formal structures and preconditions of science as well as democracy, which were elaborated as a comprehensive formal pragmatics < of human communication. The two levels of analysis came together in a communicative conception of knowledge that was presented in a preliminary form in *Knowledge and Human Interests* (Habermas, 1971/1968). Within a few years, however, a postscript to the same volume proposed a fundamentally revised agenda for thinking about the relationship between human knowledge and social action. Immanuel Kant had asked: "What can I know?", "What ought I to do?", and "What may I hope?" (Kant, 1998/1787: n.p.). < In search of updated answers, Habermas transitioned from an understanding of the production of knowledge as necessarily interested and historically grounded, to an understanding of communication as a primordial category in and through which humans might transcend their own history and interests.

scientism

Knowledge and Human Interests bore witness to intense and still unfinished debates about the relationship between hard science and soft scholarship that were unfolding in post-1945 social science, including a 1960s *Positivismusstreit* or positivism dispute in Germany (Adorno, 1976). Habermas, among others, sought to reclaim forms of knowledge beyond a scientism deriving from modern natural and experimental sciences, and to recuperate "the forgotten experience of reflection." His book-length intervention was guided by "the systematic intention of analyzing the connections between knowledge and human interests," which "is possible only as social theory" (Habermas, 1971/1968: vii). Reality does not speak up to explain itself; it only responds to questions raised by humans against the background of their perceived interests in particular historical and social contexts.

knowledge interests: technical, practical, and emancipatory

While the volume included detailed discussion of key thinkers from Kant, through Hegel and Marx, to Nietzsche and Freud, its main legacy was the formulation of three basic knowledge interests. First, a "*technical*" knowledge interest is associated with "the empirical-analytic sciences" that concern themselves with the production of "possible predictive knowledge" (Habermas, 1971/1968: 308). Although the primary example of this "cognitive interest in technical control over objectified processes" (p. 309) is various natural sciences, it may spill over into the study of humans, cultures, and societies in a scientistic or positivist perspective, which was perhaps Habermas' main motivation for insisting on multiple knowledge interests. Second, the "historical-hermeneutic sciences" engage in "the interpretation of texts" and "the understanding of meaning, not observation" (p. 309). As such, these sciences can be said to have a "*practical* cognitive interest, in contrast to the technical." This is because "the understanding of meaning is directed [...] toward the attainment of possible consensus among actors in the framework of a self-understanding derived from tradition" (p. 310). Again, if one approaches meaning – the understanding of self, others, and tradition – in an "objectivist" perspective, Habermas suggested, this "locks up history in a museum" (p. 316).

The third, "*emancipatory*" knowledge interest was the hopeful element of Habermas' (1971/1968: 308) typology. In this respect, he was careful to distinguish "the systematic *sciences of social action*, that is economics, sociology, and political science" from "a critical social science" that targets "ideologically frozen relations of dependence that can in principle be transformed." At the time, his candidates for accomplishing this were "*the critique of ideology*" and "*psychoanalysis*," whose insights would be disseminated more widely to set off "a process of reflection [...] so that the level of unreflected consciousness [...] can be transformed" (p. 310) in a process of double hermeneutics. < Such self-reflection would be privileged in an absolute sense: Unlike "all other cognitive processes [...] the standards of self-reflection" do not "require critical evaluation. They possess theoretical certainty. The human interest in autonomy and responsibility is not mere fancy, for it can be apprehended a priori." Humans can simply know their interests: "*in the power of self-reflection, knowledge and interest are one*" (p. 314).

> double hermeneutics – Chapter 2, p. 25

Toward the end of his argument, Habermas (1971/1968) inched closer to a communicative conception of knowledge. Perhaps reflection on knowledge and interests is anchored not in our consciousness, but in our communication with others: "What raises us out of nature is the only thing whose nature we can know: *language*. Through its structure, autonomy and responsibility are posited for us. Our first sentence expresses unequivocally the intention of universal and unconstrained consensus" (p. 314). In the wider history of ideas, such a shift of emphasis from individual reflection toward public communication represented a turn from a philosophy of consciousness toward a philosophy of communication. < What particularly occupied Habermas in this wider shift was the capacity of philosophy and other scholarship to exercise a critical knowledge interest so as to promote collective reflection in "unconstrained communication":

from individual reflection toward collective deliberation

> philosophies of consciousness and communication – Chapter 1, p. 9

unconstrained communication

> Only when philosophy discovers in the dialectical course of history the traces of violence that deform repeated attempts at dialogue and recurrently close off the path to unconstrained communication does it further the process whose suspension it otherwise legitimates: mankind's evolution toward autonomy and responsibility.
>
> *p. 314f.*

The bourgeois public sphere had risen, but fallen again as a forum of political and cultural reflection and debate. In the longer perspective of human evolution and history, the question for Habermas had become how to ascertain the full reflective, liberating, and empowering potential of communication across all spheres of social activity. As prelude to an answer, he soon abandoned his position in *Knowledge and Human Interests* (KHI) and reconstructed the common practice of communication as the original and universal medium for defining and defending what is true and good.

Disinterested communication

The 1973 postscript to KHI represented a paradigm shift in Habermas' writings, as suggested by its inclusion as an erratum of sorts in subsequent editions of the original work. Whereas the book had been committed to reclaiming multiple knowledge interests with different historical legacies, against the presumption of a unified scientism, the postscript (Habermas, 1973) reversed the perspective, assuming one and only one grounding of any and all forms of knowledge: "In all sciences, argumentation is subject to the *same* conditions of governing the discursive redemption of truth claims, [which are] conditions of a rationality free of scientistic constraints" (p. 172). That grounding was understood in explicitly communicative terms as *discourses*, but in a very specific sense of this widely used term. Referring back to the 1968 volume, Habermas found that "at that time, the crucial distinction that must be made between communications (which belong to experience and action) and discourses (which make corroborated, i.e. theoretical, knowledge possible) had not yet occurred to me" (p. 174). He now sought to identify certain necessary conditions of intersubjective knowledge, at first in the domain of science and scholarship, but with implications for any human enterprise. As such, Habermas' reworked argument had a Kantian scope, even as he shifted the emphasis from cognitive categories < toward discursive practices of arriving at both descriptive and normative

discourse as grounding of all knowledge

> Kant's transcendental categories – Chapter 1, p. 8

agreement. For now, he summed up his position as "*transcendental pragmatism*" (p. 179); I return in Chapter 5 to Habermas' relationship with the pragmatist tradition. <

> Habermas and pragmatism – Chapter 5, p. 150

The postscript described a particular analytical procedure for establishing the transcendental conditions of authentic discourse: rational reconstruction, or simply reconstruction, which Habermas (1973) contrasted with the "self-reflexion" that he had advocated in the parent volume (p. 182). There, as noted, "the standards of self-reflection [did not] require critical evaluation" (Habermas, 1971/1968: 314). But according to the postscript, those standards now had to be reconstructed with inspiration from disciplines such as psychology and linguistics that seek to account for basic human competences of thinking and speaking: "Wittgenstein's analysis of the notion of 'following a rule' and, in the Humboldtian tradition, Chomsky's concepts of 'generative rules' and 'linguistic competence'" (Habermas, 1973: 182). It was no longer self-reflective subjects, but their communicative interactions that could be said to hold transcendental qualities: It had become "unnecessary to add a transcendental subject to the system of conditions, categories or rules established by linguistic theory" (p. 182). And Habermas' ambition went far beyond linguistic competences and included the attempt to also establish moral capacities on transcendental grounds: "Even moral philosophy will achieve the status of a reconstructive science to the degree that it can derive the universal rules of a communicative ethic from the basic norms of rational speech" (p. 183). Under the right conditions, communication would serve as both legislator and final court of appeal regarding any fact, value, or practice, including the ideal execution of communication itself.

rational reconstruction

communication as transcendental category

reconstructed morality

A rare in-depth examination of the merits of Habermas' reconstructive approach started by noting how "surprising" it is "that the methodology from which Habermas has developed his theoretical ideas has not been subject to more attention" (Pedersen, 2008: 458). This is in spite of the fact that the centerpiece of his philosophy, namely, the theory of communicative action "is the most fundamental result of Habermas's rational reconstruction" (p. 468). While I return to the theory of communicative action in the next section, Pedersen's (2008) detailed analysis identified several problems for Habermas' reconstructive approach to scholarship. In summary, Habermas could be seen not to follow "the methodological program that [he has] drawn up," returning instead to "more classical philosophical ways of working with a material: reflection on his own intuitions, conceptual analysis in addition to a critical appropriation of the relevant literature"

> Austin's speech-act theory – p. 70

(p. 481). By inclination, "Habermas frequently starts from existing theories, picks them apart, and then puts them back together again in a novel fashion." As I elaborate below with special reference to Habermas' appropriation of Austin's speech-act theory, < there are "positions that have their own logic and that cannot be picked apart without significant loss," and there are additional "positions that should not be united" (p. 480). Ultimately at issue is whether, or to what degree, Habermas himself has been guided by the discursive ethics that he has stipulated as the universal standard for all scholarship, and all human communication.

empirical tests of reconstructed theories

One concrete, methodological question is how different kinds of (reconstructed and empirical) theories may be said to either confirm or disconfirm each other. Habermas holds that reconstructions have a hypothetical character and are "dependent on indirect verification through other empirical theories" (Pedersen, 2008: 466). In Habermas' own words, the point is "to put rational reconstructions of supposedly basic competences on trial and to test them indirectly by employing them as input in empirical theories" (cited in Pedersen, 2008: 466). In the postscript to *Knowledge and Human Interests*, he illustrated this line of thinking by suggesting that "Piaget's cognitivistic developmental psychology has confirmed Kant's analyses: the basic notions of substance, space, time and causality are the minimum conditions for determining a system of reference for objects of possible experience" (Habermas, 1973: 173). But this is quite different from the standard and received understanding of transcendental categories as *conditions* of knowing, rather than phenomena that can be known or "confirmed" empirically. In the Kantian example, the unaddressed question is whether and how empirical evidence might conceivably *disconfirm* one or more of Kant's transcendental categories. More important, in the case of Habermas' reconstruction of communication, "what kind of empirical falsification can be accepted against the claim that communication oriented toward agreement is the primary form of communication?" (Pedersen, 2008: 480). Surprisingly, Habermas has never addressed this decisive question in any sustained fashion.

The transition that Habermas had signaled in the postscript was reconfirmed and elaborated in the theory of communicative action a decade later. His mature theory involved a general reorientation from historical categories – a public sphere being shaped and reshaped in and through social struggle, and a complex of knowledge interests deriving from different intellectual traditions and institutional frameworks of research – toward systematic and ontologizing conceptions of both research and democracy, anchored in one communicative ideal. The multiple knowledge interests of the book title were giving way in the postscript to a singular, disinterested form of human communication. Immanuel Kant (2004a/1790) had spoken of disinterested pleasure in the domain of aesthetic experience. Two hundred years on, Habermas was returning to a notion of disinterested knowledge, not just of what is, but also of what ought to be done – in scientific, political, and other public matters. What had started out as a universalistic, but historically articulated ideal of public communication – practiced by the few, but of interest and value to the many – was being reconstructed as an anthropological given, at once fact and norm. (The relationship between facts and norms became an explicit focus of attention in the third phase of Habermas' (1996/1992) work.) < The motivation behind the reorientation has remained part of the puzzle up to and including Habermas' (2006) stock-taking of press and internet: What has been Habermas' interest in disinterested communication? Part of an answer was suggested by the two-volume *The Theory of Communicative Action* (TCA) (Habermas, 1984/1981, 1987b/1981).

historical and systematic inquiry

> between facts and norms – p. 74

From the categorical imperative to communicative action

"A third, somewhat less demanding way"

On the last page of TCA, Habermas (1987b/1981: 403) characterized this work as offering a "theory of modernity." Over 900 pages, he had contrasted the civilizing potential of modernity with the forces endangering that process: "the type of social pathologies that are today becoming increasingly visible, by way of the assumption that communicatively structured domains of life are being subordinated to the imperatives of autonomous, formally organized systems of action" (Habermas, 1984/1981: xl). His summary term for the sources of the crisis was "systematically distorted communication" (p. 332), also referred to as the "unconscious deception" (p. 333) that follows from the conditions under which both media and individual citizens must communicate. Habermas' premise was that the contemporary predicament calls for a concerted intellectual defense of certain universal principles on the order of Immanuel Kant's (2004b/1785: n.p.) categorical imperative of ethical conduct: <"Act always on such a maxim as thou canst at the same time will to be a universal law." As part of the wider shift from an individualist philosophy of

modernity

systematically distorted communication

> the categorical imperative – Chapter 2, p. 37

consciousness toward a communalist philosophy of communication, Habermas set out to amend Kant by replacing the categorical imperative with the principles of communicative action: "What was intended by the categorical imperative can be made good by projecting a will-formation under the idealized conditions of universal discourse" (Habermas, 1987b/1981: 95). Human communication would itself deliver the models of disinterested dialogue and the ultimate standards with which to assess the truth, sincerity, and moral rightness of concrete historical instances of communication.

> reconstruction – p. 63

rationality vs. rationalization

Frankfurt School critical theory

functionalist social science

The two volumes of TCA broadened and deepened Habermas' strategy of reconstruction. < While departing from Max Weber's sociology, Habermas distanced himself from *rationalization* as commonly understood since Weber: the organization of social life according to a logic of ends and means, which came to guide modern markets, state bureaucracies, and, to a degree, personal life. To reconstruct his alternative of communicative *rationality*, Habermas recombined diverse critical and functionalist traditions in modern social theory. To one side, he endorsed the general project of first-generation Frankfurt School critical theorists such as Theodor Adorno and Max Horkheimer (Habermas is normally associated with a second generation of the Frankfurt School (Jay, 1996)), but rejected both their radical critique of instrumental reason and Georg Lukacs' notion of a resulting reification of consciousness and culture. To Habermas (1984/1981), early critical theorists had remained trapped in a philosophy of consciousness in which "the subject relates to objects either to represent them as they are or to produce them as they should be" (p. 387). The first-generation critical vision of social change trusted not in communicative rationality, but in a collective subject that might change the course of history, as exemplified by Lukacs' "enthronement of proletarian class consciousness as the subject-object of history as a whole" (p. 364). To the other side, Habermas drew on mainstream sociology – Émile Durkheim, Talcott Parsons, and George Herbert Mead, in particular – to formulate an understanding of society as, at once, a functional system and an inherently meaningful experience of self in the context of others. If critical theory had stated Habermas' long-term ends – his knowledge interest under a different name – functionalist social science was recruited to deliver the necessary conceptual means for present purposes.

Habermas' (1984/1981, 1987b/1981) detailed readings of earlier social theorists in TCA were summed up in a sequence of "intermediate reflections" leading into final conclusions about the prospects for communicative action as theory as well as practice.

The intellectual profile of the two volumes was suggested by the choice of one of the "basically three ways" in which one might undertake what represented, by Habermas' own admission, a rather grand proposal to "expound the universality of the concept of communicative rationality." First, formal pragmatics could offer the means of "rationally reconstructing universal rules and necessary presuppositions of speech actions oriented to reaching understanding." Such universalistic claims might be "rendered plausible" by formal-pragmatic means, but again, "hypothetical reconstructions [...] must [...] be capable of being checked against speakers' intuitions." Second, then, one would have to demonstrate "the empirical usefulness" of formal pragmatics – but Habermas immediately bracketed this route, which would "require a great effort [...] even if only through secondary evaluation of the empirical research in [the relevant areas]." Instead, he pursued "a *third*, somewhat less demanding way [...] to work up the sociological approaches to a theory of societal rationalization." He did so, "not with the intention of carrying out historical investigations; rather, I shall take up conceptual strategies, assumptions, and lines of argument from Weber to Parsons" (Habermas, 1984/1981: 138f.) in order to specify and validate a theory of communicative action.

formal pragmatics

In order to assess the status of TCA and its place in Habermas' *oeuvre*, it is important to recognize two of its distinctive features. First, TCA never elaborates on the empirical applications of the theory in further research, as might have been expected in view of Habermas' (1973) characterization of his reconstructive approach; I return in the following sections to the relationship between TCA and specific empirical domains. Second, TCA proceeds by reconstruction, "work[ing] up the sociological approaches" of other thinkers, but not in the sense of Habermas' (1973) original brief. In the postscript to KHI, reconstruction entailed uncovering and recovering fundamental human competences as identified by central disciplines and key thinkers; in TCA (and later works by Habermas), reconstruction has involved an ad hoc recycling and recombination of a much broader range of ideas and positions. As also noted by Pedersen (2008: 482), "The concept of reconstruction is used by Habermas in (at least) two distinct ways, without it always being equally clear what is meant."

no empirical research agenda

How to do things with other people's words

Two of the key building blocks in the conceptual architecture of TCA – world and action – were derived (and then reconstructed)

> World 1, World 2, World 3 – Chapter 1, p. 16

phenomenology

the lifeworld

> German Idealism – p. 78

> philosophy of consciousness – Chapter 1, p. 9

from two twentieth-century philosophers, Karl R. Popper and John L. Austin. Early in the first volume of TCA, Habermas (1984/1981) introduced the concept of 'worlds' as developed by Popper (1972b). Popper distinguished between World 1, World 2, and World 3: < the world of physical objects or states, the world of states of consciousness, "or perhaps of behavioral dispositions to act; and thirdly, the world of *objective contents of thought*, especially of scientific and poetic thoughts and of works of art" (cited in Habermas, 1984/1981: 76). Whereas this third world might have been thought to provide a communicative coin of exchange between individually subjective and socially objective domains of reality, Habermas was at pains to distance himself from "the ontological concept of 'world'" and to overlay Popper's typology with "the phenomenological tradition," from Edmund Husserl to Alfred Schütz. Accordingly, he preferred to "adopt the pair of concepts 'world' and 'lifeworld.'" As part of this duality, Habermas posited the lifeworld as primary – an "unthematically given horizon within which participants in communication move in common when they refer thematically to something in the *world*" (p. 82). The lifeworld, thus, represents a realm that is both subjective and shared, but without being communicated in any thematic or focused fashion; it constitutes what I, you, and we know in common without ever having to say so. The idea of an immediate awareness of self and others, which was fed from German Idealism < into the phenomenological tradition, was a legacy of the philosophy of consciousness < that reemerged at the center of Habermas' variant of a philosophy of communication.

Aside from the fact that Habermas (1984/1981) ended up doubling rather than discarding "the ontological concept of 'world'" (p. 82), his reconstruction of Popper's typology raised basic questions of motivation and justification: What is the explanatory value of the concept of a lifeworld for a theory of communication, and to what extent will Popper's original framework accommodate this additional type of world? Habermas' explicit motivation was to move beyond "*the cognitivistically abridged interpretation of the third world*" (p. 78) and to foreground the place of "cultural knowledge" (p. 83) in framing and making validity claims about different kinds of worlds. "The lifeworld [...] stores the interpretive work of preceding generations" (p. 70) – even if Habermas nowhere specifies what either the process of storing or the site of storage consist in. As he proceeds to relate different worlds to different kinds of social action, it becomes clear that, for Habermas, the lifeworld constitutes an ontological bottom line – an original mode of human existence and a historical residual, subject to the violence of social systems. On the one hand, taking on board Popper's three-world typology, Habermas recognizes that "speakers and hearers operate with a *system* of several equally primordial worlds [that] lie in one and the same evolutionary plane" (p. 84) (as previously suggested in his own early critique of scientism). On the other hand, the lifeworld qualifies as more primordial than any other world. Much more than a negative ground or horizon against which objects and events become understandable and actionable, in the theory of communicative action the lifeworld maintains a manifest existence as something inalienably, if precariously human.

Habermas' reconstruction of Popper might have been considered a justified means of protecting and promoting an uncompromising ideal of "unconstrained communication" (Habermas, 1968/1971: 315) – but not according to the principles and procedures of communicative action. Habermas goes on to identify different types of social action with a relative orientation toward either shared understanding or self-centered success. Deriving "four sociological concepts of action" from earlier thinkers, Habermas (1984/1981: 75) distinguishes strategic and other teleological action as means to an end; normatively regulated action establishing interpersonal relations; dramaturgical action presenting oneself to others; and communicative action oriented to mutual understanding. In his further discussion of worlds, the point is that whereas the first three action types each concerns one world, communicative action takes all these worlds and "all the functions of language equally into consideration" (p. 95). Beyond its specific forms and contents, any instance of communicative action is said to make three validity claims (p. 99), later summed up in terms of truth, truthfulness or sincerity, and normative rightness (p. 329). The intervening argumentation had further singled out communicative action as part of a different, if related three-fold action typology: *instrumental* action, which seeks technical control over nature and other resources; *strategic* action, which pursues social outcomes by influencing the rational choices of others; and *communicative* action, which aims at social coordination through reaching an understanding with others (p. 285). Grounded in the lifeworld, communicative action is held up as "the original mode of language use," upon which other uses of language are even deemed "parasitic" (p. 288). The upshot of the extended argument is a dichotomization of social actions into the communicative and the strategic (p. 333).

strategic and other teleological action

normatively regulated action

dramaturgical action

communicative action

truth, truthfulness, and rightness

Habermas is very clear that communicative and strategic actions are not just "two analytic aspects under which the same action could be described" (p. 286), but categorically different, essential kinds of action with radically different social implications. Strategic actions involve a second-level dichotomy of open and concealed strategy; concealed strategic actions hold a third-level dichotomy of conscious deception or manipulation and unconscious deception, also referred to as systematically distorted communication. This last notion of social systems distorting original forms of human expression and social interaction runs through Habermas' *oeuvre* as an Ariadne's thread, from ST on the refeudalization of the public sphere through TCA to recent publications on global communication (Habermas, 2001, 2006).

systematically distorted communication

The problem is that, in TCA, Habermas himself does not seek any disinterested or intersubjective understanding, for example, about the idea of worlds; Popper is not an equal, but an other in Habermas' communication. Instead, he strategically reconstructs Popper's three-world typology for the manifest purpose of installing a predefined fourth realm, namely, the lifeworld, at the center of an alternative ontology. Whereas Habermas appears convinced that he is doing the normatively right thing, by his own standards he is not sincerely or truthfully weighing his own ontology against Popper's, so the outcome of his reflections cannot be true in the required sense of a rationally achieved consensus. I return in the conclusion of this chapter to the implications for the theory of communicative action of what, on its own terms, amounts to a systematically distorted communicative practice.

speech-act theory

> Wittgenstein on language games – Chapter 1, p. 9

locutions, illocutions, and perlocutions

If TCA went against the spirit of Popper's writings, Habermas' reconstruction of Austin (1962) went further in disregarding the letter of speech-act theory. The strategy was to recruit this theory as the linchpin of the wider theory of communicative action. Drawing on Wittgenstein's (1953) understanding of language use not as representations of reality, but as language games constituting social reality, < Austin developed an understanding of language use as actions. Each action is said to consist in three component acts: locutions, illocutions, and perlocutions – which is "to say *something*, to act *in* saying something, to bring about something *through* acting in saying something" (Habermas, 1984/1981: 289). In saying something about the national economy, politicians make predictions and promises and, as a result, increase or decrease their credibility and following. Habermas, however, divorced illocution from perlocution on the assumption that it is not only practically possible, but normatively essential to perform the first act (representing something to someone) without simultaneously performing the second act (achieving something): "I count as communicative action those linguistically mediated interactions in which all participants pursue illocutionary aims, and *only* illocutionary aims, with their mediating acts of communication" (p. 295).

Austin (1962) had prefaced his elaboration of the three component acts with the comment that, "It is the distinction between illocutions and perlocutions which seems likeliest to give trouble" (p. 110); he went on to detail and exemplify the several senses in which illocutions have consequences that are, at once, linguistic and social. Austin was acutely aware that illocutionary intentions, whether oriented toward understanding or not, may have unintended perlocutionary consequences:

> The perlocutionary act may be either the achievement of a perlocutionary object (convince, persuade) or the production of a perlocutionary sequel. Thus the act of warning may achieve its perlocutionary object of warning and also have the perlocutionary sequel of alarming, and an argument against a view may fail to achieve its object but have the perlocutionary sequel of convincing our opponent of its truth ('I only succeeded in convincing him'). What is the perlocutionary object of one illocution may be the sequel of another.
>
> *Austin, 1962: 118*

Recognizing the many cognitive and social contingencies of human communication, a key premise of Austin's model was the interdependence of locution, illocution, and perlocution. In Habermas' terminology, Austin's three acts would constitute equally primordial aspects of communication.

Heedless of Austin's cautions, Habermas staked his claim to disinterested communicative action on a selective use of Austin's concepts, noting that his own argument will hold:

> only if it can be shown that the use of language with an orientation to reaching understanding is the *original mode* of language use, upon which indirect understanding, giving something to understand or letting something be understood, and the instrumental use of language in general, are parasitic. In my view, Austin's distinction between illocutions and perlocutions accomplishes just that.
>
> *Habermas, 1984/1981: 288*

the original mode of language use

But "Austin's distinction" is not represented in TCA in any truthful fashion. If the reconstruction of Popper at least preserved his three worlds (subordinated to the lifeworld), Austin's conceptions were used in piecemeal fashion to claim the place of TCA in a lineage from Wittgenstein < through Austin. Habermas even summarily corrected Austin, who was said to be "fixated on the model of institutionally bound speech acts":

> Habermas on Wittgenstein – p. 90

> Austin did not keep these two cases [communication with illocutionary and perlocutionary aims, respectively] separate as different types of interaction, because he was inclined to identify acts of communication, that is, acts of reaching understanding, with the interactions coordinated by speech acts. He didn't see that acts of communication or speech acts function as a coordinating mechanism for *other* actions.
>
> *Habermas, 1984/1981: 295*

Fixated or not on his own reconstruction, Habermas did not respect Austin's position as both argued and arguable. Instead, he jumped to the conclusion that Austin did not understand – "see" – the implications of his own theory. The immediate question is not who may be right; the point is that Habermas' own communicative practice – about the conceptual distinction by which TCA, in his own words, stands or falls – is inadmissible according to the most fundamental standard stipulated by TCA.

Like the volume on the public sphere (Habermas, 1989/1962), TCA gave rise to a voluminous literature, including another anthology with a lengthy reply by Habermas to his critics (Honneth & Joas, 1991). As in the first anthology (Calhoun, 1992), while offering clarifications and elaborations, Habermas basically reiterated his position: "I am of the opinion that social pathologies can be understood as forms of manifestation of systematically distorted communication" (Habermas, 1991: 226). <

> systematically distorted communication – p. 70

In the special case of speech-act theory, he recognized that "my usage of Austin's expressions 'perlocutionary' and 'illocutionary,' diverging as it does from conventional philosophical usage, leads to misunderstandings. This prompts me to provide some *terminological clarification*" (p. 239). The reference here is to other scholars' "misunderstandings" of Habermas, not his own potential misunderstandings of Austin or other scholars, and the solution offered is terminological, not conceptual. The next few pages of the reply suggest, among other things, a further distinction between "*immediate*" and "*more far-reaching*" illocutionary aims, but only to more precisely distinguish illocution from perlocution. Habermas was replying, in part, to Alexander (1991), who had noted that the inseparability of the two "was, indeed, exactly Austin's point" (p. 68). But Habermas declined more communication about this point: "In the light of these philosophical observations a number of the misgivings that Alexander [...] and others have with respect to my basic action-theoretic assumptions evaporate" (Habermas, 1991: 242).

conceptual dichotomies

The divorcing of perlocution from illocution is one example of the conceptual dichotomies, noted by critical and sympathetic commentators alike (Bernstein, 1998), which permeate Habermas' thinking. With further reference to the overarching lifeworld/system dichotomy, < Alexander (1991) added that "the oppressive and dangerous parts of modern society are almost always portrayed as emerging from rationalized, material systems, whereas the 'good parts' are associated with the personal intimacy of moral life" (p. 62), which, to him, recalled "the continuing influence on [Habermas'] work of German Idealism" (p. 61). <

> lifeworld and system – p. 68

> German Idealism – p. 78

juridification

therapeutocracy

Dichotomies such as lifeworld/system have posed perhaps the main difficulty for any concrete assessment of the explanatory value of TCA regarding communication in particular historical and social contexts. This came out, for instance, in a rare section late in TCA where Habermas ventured into relatively more detailed empirical argumentation. In his "Concluding Reflections" (Habermas, 1987b/1981: 301ff.), he recognized "the danger of overgeneralization" when making conclusions about the "internal colonization of the lifeworld," and admitted that his theory "must be able to specify at least *the type* of empirical research that is appropriate to it." But when he elaborated on a specially selected test case in order to empirically document the subjugation of the lifeworld to formal law – "the juridification of communicatively structured areas of action" (p. 356) – the reference was not to concrete processes of communication, but to general legal principles as instantiated by "German examples from the spheres of family and school law" (p. 357). On the basis of such legal sources, Habermas concluded that "the net of welfare guarantees" has colonized citizens, so that "it is now the very means of guaranteeing freedom that endangers the freedom of the beneficiaries," thus echoing the earlier argument regarding the public sphere that ordinary citizens have been pacified by their entitlements. The form as well as the contents of modern welfare are said to be at fault: The problem is both the "*bureaucratic implementation*" of "*monetary compensation*" and "*social services* [that] have been set up to lend *therapeutic assistance*," which diverts citizens from participation in an active communicative democracy and leaves them as the victims of a passive "therapeutocracy" (p. 362f.).

TCA reaffirmed and consolidated the reorientation toward systematic and ontologizing perspectives on human communication

> rational reconstruction – p. 63

that had been begun by Habermas' turn to the reconstruction < of other thinkers and ideas. As he entered a third phase focusing on deliberative democracy in *Between Facts and Norms* (BFN) (Habermas, 1996/1992), both the conceptual coherence and the empirical support of his mature position remained in question. In one sense, BFN turned to a specific empirical domain, namely, the institutions and practices of political democracy, without, however, introducing substantial evidence of its own or from established disciplines such as political science. Instead, the volume extended the founding premise of TCA – the understanding of disinterested communication about the common good as an anthropological reality as well as a universal ideal – to law and democracy. In the process, Habermas performed not just reconstructions, but additional

self-reconstruction

self-reconstructions – reworking his own previous conceptions – without explicating motivations and implications in any detail. These self-reconstructions presumed some form of reconciliation of the historical-empirical approaches of his first phase with the systematic-normative positions of the second phase. The difficulty of such reconciliation became apparent in Habermas' renewed treatment of the notion of an ideal speech situation, < which, for decades, had represented a capsule summary of his position.

> the ideal speech situation – p. 77

Laws of communication

The power of communication

The title of *Between Facts and Norms* (BFN) (Habermas, 1996/1992) signaled a return to political democracy and the public sphere < as historical facts, refracted through the transhistorical norms expressed in TCA. How could communication serve to legitimate de facto laws according to the principles and procedures of modern political democracy? To answer this question, Habermas returned to the interrelation of knowledge and action: "Law is two things at once: a system of knowledge and a system of action" (p. 79). In order for rules that have practical and sometimes existential consequences to be not just legal, but legitimate, they must be based in reasoning and reasons that are established and maintained through the exercise of rationality in public. Because the law, in part, treats citizens as objects, regulating and disciplining them, it is essential that the same citizens see themselves as subjects or authors of the law in the first place. The consent of the governed presupposes communication by the governed, and some measure of consensus, about both the ends and the means of their community.

> the public sphere – p. 52

law as knowledge and action

citizens as subjects and objects of law

The translation of knowledge into actions, including the use of physical or symbolic force, brings up the concept of power, which Habermas (1996/1992) went on to reconstruct in BFN. As in TCA, he distanced himself from a functionalist rationalization of society and from Max "Weber, who sees the fundamental phenomenon of power as the probability that in a social relationship one can assert one's own will against opposition" (p. 147). Instead, Habermas took his cue from Hannah Arendt, who had previously inspired his account of the public sphere (Habermas, 1989/1962: 19). "Arendt views power as the potential of a *common will* formed in noncoercive communication. She opposes 'power' (*Macht*) to 'violence' (*Gewalt*)" (Habermas, 1996/1992: 147f.). In Arendt's own words: "Power is actualized only where word and deed have not parted company, where words are not empty and deeds not brutal" (cited in Habermas, 1996/1992: 150). The question was how Arendt's poetic expressions – empty words and brutal deeds – might be rearticulated as precise concepts for analytical purposes.

In social theory as in common parlance, power has often had negative connotations, even if some social scientists have proposed a neutral understanding of power as transformative capacity (Giddens, 1984): the capacity of humans to change their social and material circumstances. In contrast to both negative and neutral notions, Habermas reasserted a positive perspective on power by introducing yet another dualism of communicative and administrative power. His definition suggested that "law [is] the medium through which communicative power is translated into administrative power." The implication, again, was that the exercise of power by social systems, including the legislative, executive, and judicial branches of government, must always be grounded in the lifeworld as expressed in communicative action. But in his further explanation of how such translation works, more puzzling ambiguities surfaced:

power as transformative capacity

communicative and administrative power

> We can then interpret the idea of the constitutional state in general as the requirement that the administrative power, which is steered through the power code, be tied to the lawmaking communicative power and kept free of illegitimate interventions of social power (i.e., of the factual strength of privileged interests to assert themselves).
>
> *Habermas, 1996/1992: 150*

Here, there are two devils in the discursive details. For one thing, the dualism immediately breaks down; a third form of "social power" is introduced. Being dubbed "illegitimate," it is evidently contrasted with "communicative power," but it is not clear whether "social power" is identical with the "administrative power" of the state, or perhaps part of a refeudalized formation of state and capital. < For another thing, administrative power is said to be "steered through *the power code*" (emphasis added), but without a specification of what type of power is exercised through which kind of code. Presumably, the reference is to the negatively valorized, systemic aspects of power, "the oppressive and dangerous parts of modern society [...] emerging from rationalized, material systems" (Alexander, 1991: 62). But Habermas himself appears overpowered by the rhetorical force of his own dualisms as he slides back into a commonsensical equation of the power code with the exercise of force. (The German original holds the same ambiguity: "*das über* den Machtkode *gesteuerte administrative System*" (Habermas, 1992a: 187, emphasis added). Following Arendt, a reference to *Gewalt* (force) rather than *Macht* (power) would have been the appropriate terminology.) Taken together, these conceptual slippages bear witness to a figure of thought and discourse that had become familiar in Habermas' writings: Communicative power was introduced in BFN as one more term for an original, but precarious manifestation of a lifeworld that is subject to contingent, but systemic powers threatening "the autonomy and responsibility" (Habermas, 1971/1968: 314) of human beings.

> refeudalization – p. 55

Later sections of BFN fail, in the end, to reconcile historical-empirical and systematic-normative perspectives on the translation of communicative action into law. Habermas' (1996/1992) premise remains that "we should carefully distinguish between forms of communication – or types of communication processes – and the legal procedures in which they can be institutionalized" (p. 177). The essentializing understanding of human communication is witnessed in the description of "an argumentation process whose *internal* structure eludes legal institutionalization." And yet, Habermas goes on to recognize and endorse legal principles and procedures as necessary constraints on communication "in specific places at specific times": "Although the *embeddedness of different types of argumentation in legal procedures* leaves the inner logic of such discourses intact, legal institutionalization subjects them to specific temporal, social, and substantive constraints" (p. 178). The claims are incommensurable: The "internal structure" of argumentation eludes legal formalization – but the legal procedures that leave "the inner logic" of argumentative discourses intact, nevertheless, take effect through formalized constraints. Early in

communication processes and legal procedures

BFN, Habermas had indicated that the "background knowledge" of the lifeworld accomplishes a "unique *leveling out of the tension between facticity and validity*" (p. 23): The norms of the lifeworld are facts. The untenable implication by the end of BFN had become that, at least in the case of law, there is no conflict between "the original mode of language use" and what had been considered, since TCA, "parasitic" communication as administered through social systems – such as law (Habermas, 1984/1981: 288).

The claim to be squaring the communicative circle in the case of law and on the scale of another *magnum opus* was especially remarkable because, in TCA, juridification < had been one of the central descriptions and diagnoses of how social systems colonize communicative action and the lifeworld as such. In BFN, Habermas did not acknowledge or reflect on this fundamental conceptual shift and its implications for the wider theory of communicative action. Instead, he presented BFN as the extension of an already established, general theory of communication into a domain-specific theory of law and democracy. In doing so, he was returning both to his historical interest in political democracy and to the ideal speech situation, which has served as a moving signifier absorbing shifting premises of the same practical-political project. The changing accounts of the ideal speech situation provide indicators of Habermas' long-term structural transformation. In the obligatory international anthology with critical interventions about BFN and a reply from Habermas, he referred back to "the expression 'the ideal speech situation,' which I introduced decades ago as a shorthand for the ensemble of universal presuppositions of argumentation" (Habermas, 1998: 418); it is the status of this "shorthand" that has been changing with the times and with his shifting knowledge interests.

> juridification – p. 73

the ideal speech situation

Speaking of ideals

In BFN, Habermas had suggested that, "As the reflexive form of communicative action, argumentation distinguishes itself socio-ontologically, one might say, by a complete reversibility of participant perspectives that *unleashes* the higher-level intersubjectivity of the deliberating collectivity" (Habermas, 1996/1992: 228). But what is the nature of this "intersubjectivity" that is said to be "unleashed" through argumentation as an instance of communicative action? Readers familiar with Habermas' (1992c) claim to be engaging in postmetaphysical thinking may be surprised to encounter, in the very next sentence, the following characterization of the "socio-ontological" nature of argumentation: "In

German Idealism

Hegel

this way, Hegel's concrete universal is sublimated into a communicative *structure* purified of all substantive elements" (Habermas, 1996/1992: 228). As described most fully in TCA, such a purified structure carries more than a family resemblance with German Idealism and Georg Wilhelm Friedrich Hegel's understanding of the Spirit suffusing the material and immaterial universe and communicating itself in and through multiple minds (Redding, 2015). In Habermas' preferred terminology, it is the lifeworld that underlies and overlays all other known and knowable worlds. In the present formulations, to the extent that it is not colonized or otherwise incapacitated by social systems, the lifeworld is articulated in the communicative action by "the deliberating collectivity" and sublimated into its "higher-level intersubjectivity." It is understandable that Alexander (1991: 61), for one, might get the impression of a "continuing influence on [Habermas'] work of German Idealism."

liberal, republican, and deliberative models of politics

> rational reconstruction – p. 63

Habermas was concerned, in BFN, to relate communicative action generally to political democracy as a process and to law as both a precondition and a product of democracy. To develop a deliberative model of politics, as contrasted with liberalism and republicanism, he turned again to reconstruction. This time around, the reconstruction was performed not on basic human competences, or on key thinkers, but on "the *self-understanding* of [...] modern legal orders" (Habermas, 1996/1992: 82). < While this self-understanding was traced in BFN through historical sources, the reconstructive ambition remained transhistorical: "I take as my starting point the rights citizens must accord one another if they want to legitimately regulate their common life by means of positive law" (p. 82). Again, the hope was to recover surviving residuals of the lifeworld and potentials for the exercise of rationality. "A reconstructive sociology of democracy" must seek to "identify particles and fragments of an 'existing reason' already incorporated in political practices, however distorted these may be" (p. 287).

The analysis of political communication presented a relatively more complex task than the examination of prototypical examples of speech acts and communicative genres in TCA. In BFN, Habermas (1996/1992) related the ideal of communicative action, on the one hand, to "the institutionalization of the corresponding procedures and conditions of communication" and, on the other hand, to "the interplay of institutionalized deliberative processes with informally developed public opinions" (p. 298). Political communication takes place, in other words, both in parliamentary proceedings and in public debate. This familiar fact was expressed by Habermas in a "two-track" model of deliberative politics (p. 304), in which "decision-oriented deliberations, which are regulated by democratic procedures," are informed by "informal processes of opinion-formation in the public sphere." To suggest the implications of this division of communicative labor, Habermas introduced a comparison between political and scientific communication, referring to the classic distinction in the theory of science between "context of discovery" and "context of justification" (p. 307) (Reichenbach, 1938). In the case of political communication, the public sphere represents an unpredictable context of discovery whereas parliaments constitute a regularized context of justification, in which conclusions are drawn, decisions enacted, and their implementation anticipated.

two-track model of politics

context of discovery, context of justification

The decisive issue for the legitimacy of both law and political democracy is how the two tracks or levels of deliberation are to be related. On this point, Habermas came face to face with a dilemma of his own making, already noted: How to reconcile a purportedly original mode of communicative action with systemically organized political and legal procedures? How to communicate when we can't just talk about it? His first step was to recognize that "no complex society could ever correspond to the model of purely communicative social relations." In several further steps, Habermas described communicative action variously as an actual fact and as a counterfactual potential. In one formulation, "this model is merely a methodological fiction" (Habermas, 1996/1992: 326), a perfect ground on which imperfect figures of actual communication and law can be observed and, if need be, criticized. (This fiction recalls the "fictitious identity" of property owners and human beings as such in the public sphere (Habermas, 1989/1962: 56).) < In a later formulation in BFN, he addressed the more concrete or factual question of whether contemporary publics make up their minds about current issues through "a process of becoming informed" or as part of "a more or less concealed game of power" (Habermas, 1996/1992: 375). With only passing mention of and no references cited to a "wealth of empirical investigations," Habermas' response was that:

> citizens as property owners and human beings – p. 53

> we still do not have a well-established answer to this cardinal question. But one can at least pose the question more precisely by *assuming* that public processes of communication can take place with less distortion the more they are left to the internal dynamic of a civil society that emerges from the lifeworld.
>
> *p. 375, emphasis added*

Within 50 pages, the *fiction* of ideal communication had become an *assumption*, which, next, was said to feed into a more precise empirical *question* – which has not been addressed as such in BFN or elsewhere.

> counterfactuality – p. 81

thesis, antithesis, synthesis

Instead, the fiction has been treated, in Habermas' communicative practices, as a fact. What had emerged, in ST, as a historically discovered norm, was reconstructed or transformed, in TCA, into an ontological systematics, comprising both an anthropological reality and a universal ideal. In logical terms, Habermas' argument has continued to beg the question with reference to an unconventional understanding of counterfactuality, < presupposing what was to be examined, conceptually and empirically. By the time of BFN, the dilemma had become acute, as he proposed to synthesize historical and systematic modes of argument with reference to a deliberative and "procedural concept of democracy" (Habermas, 1996/1992: 326). The surprising claim of BFN was that the dilemma had been resolved or, perhaps, dissolved: The abstract or pure "democratic idea of self-organization" was said to translate into "a self-organizing *legal* community." Through the medium of law, human communication becomes communicative action, at least in the domain of political democracy. In sum, "the discursive mode of sociation is to be implemented through the medium of law alone. And the law as such already incorporates those features from which the model of 'pure' sociation abstracts" (p. 326). Somehow, a historical thesis (the public sphere) had been negated by a transhistorical antithesis (communicative action), and had finally been sublated into a synthesis (law).

> formal pragmatics – p. 67

a superdiscourse

Habermas' (1998) reference to the ideal speech situation in his reply regarding BFN occurred in response to one critic who highlighted this idea. Although it was Habermas himself who had reintroduced this "shorthand" in BFN (Habermas, 1996/1992: 322f.), he found it "disturbing" to be reminded that "the expression 'ideal speech situation' [...] suggests an end state that must be strived for in the sense of a regulative ideal" (Habermas, 1998: 418). He went on to insist that "I am not simply *stipulating* a normatively loaded concept of discourse," reiterating that a formal-pragmatic, "presuppositional analysis" can and will always show that "anyone who earnestly takes part in argumentation *unavoidably* accepts certain communicative presuppositions with a counterfactual content" (p. 418f.). < In response to another critic in the anthologized reply, Habermas (1998) protested that his discourse theory is not cast in the role of a "superdiscourse" (p. 431). In the present chapter, I have argued and presented evidence that this, in fact, has been the unacknowledged knowledge interest driving three *magna opera*.

The conceptual contradictions of Habermas' reconstructions have been so fundamental and pervasive that also his translators and close conversational partners have differed quite substantially in their understanding of the ideal speech situation. Already in the English version of TCA, its translator, Thomas McCarthy, had suggested that "the 'ideal speech situation' is *not* the image of a concrete form of life," but instead is a counterfactual category that enables research "to identify *empirically* the actually existing possibilities for embodying rationality structures in concrete forms of life" (in Habermas, 1984/1981: 405–406, emphasis added). In contrast, James Bohman and William Rehg (2014: n.p.) found that, at least into the decade of BFN, the 1990s, Habermas still referred to "an ideal condition that real discourses must measure up to, or at least approximately satisfy."

In their characterization of what might be Habermas' current position, following TCA and BFN, Bohman and Rehg (2014) credited (the German version of) Habermas (2008) with attenuated formulations referring to the "idealizing performative presuppositions of communicative action" (p. 28), which might suggest that communicative action is something that could be, not something that already is or has to be, even if it ought to be. < Despite these disagreements among Habermas scholars about its timing, the idea of counterfactuality must be considered central to his argumentation at least from BFN onwards. Habermas' version of this idea, however, differs significantly from established conceptions of possible worlds in philosophical logic (Divers, 2002), literary theory (Ryan, 1991), and historiography (Hawthorn, 1991). Standard counterfactual arguments address what might be, or might have been the case under specified alternative circumstances: If Y rather than X had happened, then Q rather than Z might have been the outcome. If Nazi Germany had won World War II, then Habermas would not have published (been in a position to publish) his critique of Martin Heidegger. < In contrast, Habermas has reconstructed the notion of counterfactuality to claim that human communication as such would be inconceivable without presupposing that acts of communication simultaneously stake a claim to truth, truthfulness, and rightness < – unless, that is, these acts have already been canceled or distorted by systemic forces.

> what is, what ought to be, what could be – Chapter 1, p. 2

counterfactuality

possible worlds

> Habermas on Heidegger – p. 83

> claims to truth, truthfulness, and rightness – p. 69

In a postmetaphysical world (Habermas, 1992d), such absolute claims produce a heavy burden of proof, which Habermas has never attempted to lift in empirical terms. One black swan disproves the presupposition, premise, or hypothesis that all swans are white (Flyvbjerg, 2006: 224). Empirically, swarms of black swans populate communicative practices of varying quality and with variable outcomes; they are both conceivable and quite possible in practice without assuming transhistorical laws of communication, even if people perhaps could or ought to communicate differently. In BFN, the premise of a purified and higher-level structure of intersubjectivity (Habermas, 1996/1992: 228) strongly implied a metaphysics of communication. By the time of the essays collected in the 2008 volume, the terminology that, once, referred to a "transcendental" position (Habermas, 1973: 179) had been replaced by references to a "detranscendentalized" use of reason (Habermas, 2008: 24), but with reference to identical lines of argument. The ideal speech situation, by any name, has remained a shorthand for transcendental premises and metaphysical pretensions on behalf of the common human practice of communication.

black swans

metaphysics of communication

BFN summed up Habermas' mature position in two principles. The discourse principle (D), first, emphasizes equal access to argumentation, and states that, "Just those action norms are valid to which all possibly affected persons could agree as participants in rational discourses" (Habermas, 1996/1992: 107). The universalization principle (U), further, focuses on the norms themselves and their consequences for all concerned:

> For a norm to be valid, the consequences and side effects that its general observance can be expected to have for the satisfaction of the particular interests of each person affected must be such that all affected can accept them freely.
>
> *p. 566*

It is the absence of these ideal conditions that has fueled Habermas' communications in a variety of media and genres beyond journals and monographs. If media institutions were not a particular center of attention in either TCA or BFN, they remained an important concern from the 1962 volume through the 2006 article and beyond. Also in BFN, he repeated his critique of media as they currently exist: "The sociology of mass communication," in Habermas' interpretation, "depicts the public sphere as infiltrated by administrative and social power and dominated by the mass media" (p. 379). Despite these circumstances, or because of them, Habermas has been an active participant in debates not only *on*, but also *in* the public sphere.

Communicative action in the public sphere

Religious communication

Beginning with an indictment of Martin Heidegger, "not as a philosopher, but as a political personality" with National-Socialist sympathies, when Habermas (Habermas, 1977/1953: 155) was still a graduate student in his twenties, he has confronted the great issues of his times. By his own account, philosophers, in the role of public intellectuals, have a special role to play in "an autocritique of reason," partly because, unlike "experts," they are able "to think in terms of the whole," partly because "philosophy has an inherent capacity to address basic normative issues of the 'just' or well-ordered society" (Habermas, 2003: 290). At the same time, he has worried that "the recalibration of communication from print and the press to television and the Internet" has entailed a specific weakening of intellectuals, who "seem to be choking on this life-sustaining element like an overdose. The blessing seems to be turning into a curse" (Habermas, 2009: 53). Following BFN, the engagement with public issues has even taken center stage in his publications (Corchia, 2020), with special emphases being placed on religious practices and global politics. In one sense, these issues have come to represent practical-political focal points, still not as objects of empirical study, but as social domains in which the discourse principle, the universalization principle, and other theoretically derived axioms might be brought to bear on future practices of communication. Also in public debate, Habermas has encountered the dilemma that came to a head in BFN: how to make history and reinvent the future with reference to transhistorical norms.

critique of Martin Heidegger

experts and intellectuals

On the question of religion, Habermas has joined efforts to develop alternatives to the perspective of a clash of civilizations (Huntington, 1993) in a post-Cold War and globalizing world. Could the theory and practice of communicative action help to avert one more world-historical confrontation between different religious worldviews with political ambitions? Habermas' response has been cautiously optimistic. In TCA, drawing on Max Weber, he had reviewed world religions with a view to their potential for being reconstructed as sources of rationality. In recent decades, he has dedicated specific attention to religion, both as a form of knowledge in its own right and as a condition of crosscultural communication in a postsecular world where comprehensive or thorough secularization may not be an option (key publications collected in Habermas, 2008).

clash of civilizations

religion as a form of knowledge

a postsecular condition

As part of the historical background to the continued relevance of religion for philosophy as well as other disciplines, he referred to "the cross-fertilization of Christianity and Greek metaphysics" that generated important normative philosophical concepts such as "responsibility, autonomy and justification, history and remembrance, rebirth, innovation and return, emancipation and fulfillment, renunciation, internalization and incarnation, individuality and community." To Habermas, "Although philosophy transformed the original religious meanings of these terms, it did not deflate them or exhaust their meaning" (Habermas, 2008: 110). In a later section examining Immanuel Kant's attempt to assimilate religion and philosophy, Habermas recognized that, "Reason cannot have its religious cake and eat it. Nevertheless," he suggested, "we want to know what we can learn from the articulatory power of the major world religions for the practical use of reason under conditions of postmetaphysical thinking" (p. 227).

A conspicuous absence in Habermas' (2008) systematic accounts of religion has been its relation to, and difference from, communicative action, the ideal speech situation, and other aspects of "the original mode of language use" (Habermas, 1984/1981: 288). Given the historical and anthropological record, religious cognition and communication can be considered originally and universally human, predating and exceeding organized religion as social systems. The question might even be posed whether religious expression qualifies as communicative action. In some of his arguments, Habermas has held up communicative action as the model for civilizing religious practices – a cleansing mechanism for religious din. Importantly, religion is at stake not just between individuals with different religious worldviews, but between communities and societies defining themselves, to varying degrees, by religious principles and procedures. In social formations that, worldwide and increasingly, are characterized by "religious pluralism," in part through mass and networked communication, "the constitutional freedom of conscience and religion" can only be a first step (Habermas, 2008: 120). In order to move beyond what he has labeled "condescending" forms of tolerance that merely protect minorities, "Fair arrangements can be found only if the parties involved also learn to adopt the perspectives of the others. The deliberative mode of democratic will-formation is the most appropriate for this purpose" (p. 102f.).

religious tolerance

As it turns out, however, deliberation on other religious perspectives may be beyond the communicative competences of ordinary citizens against the background of their lifeworld. Instead,

interreligious communication

Habermas has proposed entrusting interreligious understanding to the systemic, institutionalized level of deliberative politics. Because "the liberal state" allows religious beliefs that cannot be separated from the rest of the believer's existence, this state:

> cannot at the same time expect *all* citizens in addition to justify their political positions independent of their religious convictions or worldviews. This strict demand can only be made of politicians operating within state institutions who have a duty to remain neutral among competing worldviews.
>
> *Habermas, 2008: 128*

Not only does this line of argument pose a real danger that "even fundamental political questions would be settled on the basis of reasons that are inaccessible to many citizens" (Boettcher, 2009: 227). It squarely contradicts the first and essential premise of communicative action: that the original and ordinary communication of citizens is the only legitimate grounding of any system of social regulation: "the lifeworld remains the subsystem that defines the pattern of the social system as a whole. Thus, systemic mechanisms need to be anchored in the lifeworld" (Habermas, 1987b/1981: 154). As in the case of BFN regarding law and communication, the dilemma is intractable: Even in the laudable attempt to promote interreligious communication and coexistence, Habermas cannot have his lifeworld cake and eat it.

Habermas' (2019a) most recent *magnum opus* directed renewed attention to religion, as a contemporary intellectual and political issue, but more importantly as a background to modern, secular forms of knowledge and communication. While the details of this two-volume, 1,700-page history of philosophy and ideas fall outside the scope of the present book, the work retraces the two modes of inquiry – one historical-empirical, the other systematic-normative – running throughout Habermas' *oeuvre* in its several stages and transformations. From a historical-empirical perspective, the text traces the articulation and application of ideas and worldviews as guides to human existence and social coexistence across the millennia; the Axial Age < and the modern turn toward science and reason < stand out as pivotal periods in a reconfiguration of faith and knowledge as mental categories and social institutions. From a systematic-normative perspective, Habermas offers an appreciation of the history of ideas as a collective learning process < in which secular knowledge has remained indebted to religious vocabularies. In this last perspective, "religious legacies"

> the Axial Age – Chapter 2, p. 30

> political, economic, and cultural modernization – Chapter 6, p. 168

> learning processes – p. 88

are said to represent "a normative core" of concepts and values which lend themselves to appropriation and adaptation for human emancipation and social progress, also in a future perspective (Habermas, 2019b: 589, author's translation). As candidates for such a normative core, the concepts and values that constitute his own theory of human communication on lifeworld terms suggest themselves, and they come across, by the last chapter of the second volume on "the embodiment of reason in practices of research and politics" (p. 749), as lessons learnt. In sum, Habermas' latest *magnum opus* presents, at once, a history of progress through dialogue between the otherwise separate worlds of faith and knowledge, and a Whig history (Butterfield, 1931) of their synthesis in his theory of communicative action, still subject to reconstruction and, perhaps, revelation.

Global communication

national languages, national public spheres

Overlapping with religious communication, global communication has presented a renewed challenge for scholars and intellectuals in recent decades, including issues of how to couple local, mundane practices with global, overarching institutions of communication. 'National' languages have always differed around the world; public spheres have remained national. Whereas economic globalization has been ongoing for centuries (Wallerstein, 1974), and while cultural globalization has been on the rise during and following a century of broadcast media, political globalization has remained limited, despite the United Nations, international treaty systems, and the European Union as a regional pilot project of sorts. < The world wars and other international confrontations of the "'short' twentieth century (1914–1989)" raised concerns of whether and how "cosmopolitan solidarity" < would be practicable, even conceivable (Habermas, 2001: 43, 57).

> economic, political, and cultural globalization – Chapter 2, p. 42

> cosmopolitanism – Chapter 2, p. 45

In a range of essays, Habermas (2001, 2009) has returned to a central theme of his public-sphere volume (Habermas, 1989/1962), namely, "the public use of reason (Kant)" alongside "the pursuit of self-interest and the realization of political freedom" (Habermas, 2001: 110) in a global perspective. As necessary components of "a discourse-theoretical understanding of democracy" at the global level, he has noted a "functioning public sphere, the quality of discussion, accessibility, and the discursive structure of opinion- and will-formation" (p. 110f.). Even though he recognizes that "all of these could never entirely replace conventional procedures for decision-making and political representation," Habermas, again, has expressed a cautious optimism:

> [T]hey do tip the balance, from the concrete embodiments of sovereign will in persons, votes, and collectives to the procedural demands of communicative and decision-making processes. And this loosens the conceptual ties between democratic legitimacy and the familiar forms of state organization.
>
> *Habermas, 2001: 111*

In perhaps his most detailed treatment of the topic so far, Habermas (2009: 109–130) outlined three elements and three levels of "a constitution for world society" (p. 109). His "decisive conceptual move" was to open up the contingent "historical form of the constitutional state" and to distinguish its three elements: "statehood, democratic constitution, and civic solidarity" (p. 112). Transposing these elements to the global scale, the question becomes how infrastructures, constitutions, and forms of solidarity may be reconfigured and interrelated in international institutions and practices of communication. Habermas' proposal included three levels of governance so that, first, "the lowest, but supporting, '*national*' level of the political system of the world society would be occupied by the states which currently comprise the United Nations" (p. 115, emphasis added). *Above* the national level, "the classical function of the state as the guarantor of security, law, and freedom would be transferred to a *supranational* world organization specialized in securing peace and implementing human rights worldwide" (p. 112). *Across* these levels, "*transnational* negotiations systems" would be tasked with:

a constitution for world society

national, supranational, and transnational institutions

> a global domestic policy designed to overcome the extreme disparities of wealth within the stratified world society, reverse ecological imbalances, and avert collective threats, on the one hand, while endeavoring to promote an intercultural discourse on, and recognition of, the equal rights of the major world civilizations, on the other.
>
> *Habermas, 2009: 112f*

Compared to various hierarchical structures, "interactions at the transnational level would be heterarchical" (p. 113) – which anticipates the question of how citizens' public use of reason might, in practice, legitimate and sustain the world society that they share.

In an intermediate reflection, Habermas (2009) noted the importance of including both "individuals and states as subjects of a world constitution" (p. 118). Ever since Thomas Hobbes' (2009/

individual and collective subjects

1651) account of the idea of a social contract, social theorists have undertaken "the thought experiment of 'leaving the state of nature'" (Habermas, 2009: 118) and transferring state power to a legitimate sovereign. In a globalized society, it becomes essential to reconsider "the thought experiment of a 'second state of nature'" in which states make up "collective subjects" (p. 119 – an idea that parallels John Rawls' proposal for a Law of Peoples). < At the same time, Habermas distinguishes between "cosmopolitan" and "national" individuals or citizens. Cosmopolitan citizens "take their orientation from universalistic standards"; national citizens emphasize "the effective pursuit of *national or regional* interests" (p. 116). Part of Habermas' solution within such a three-level system of governance is to design a "General Assembly composed of representatives of the cosmopolitan citizens on the one side, and of delegates from the democratically elected parliaments of the member states on the other," in either one or two chambers. In its more permanent form, this assembly would become "a World Parliament" whose function would be to interpret and elaborate the charter or constitution of the world society (p. 120).

> the law of peoples – Chapter 4, p. 115

cosmopolitan and national citizens

It may be too much to expect a specification of the communicative practices of that multi-level institutional design in an essay format; the wider set of essays might point toward yet another *magnum opus* on communicative action and deliberative democracy at the global level. It seems clear, however, that, since the time of BFN, Habermas has come to devote ever greater attention to the system side of the lifeworld-system dualism – generally to the institutional frameworks circumscribing the communicative practices of deliberative politics, and specifically to certain "learning processes" (Habermas, 2009: 123) by which communication might be funneled through institutional frameworks to arrive at public policies and address practical problems. In the case of global communication, beyond the need for "a *functional global public sphere*" (Habermas, 2009: 124) that would serve to monitor the General Assembly and other branches of global government, he has pointed to "two pillars" supporting the "democratic legitimacy" (p. 126) of the full institutional structure. The first, unsurprising reference is to the national level, where "the legitimacy of the negotiating partners" participating in transnational negotiations must be secured through the institutions, principles, and procedures of each national democracy. A second, more innovative suggestion is for an arrangement in which "the national public spheres would have to become responsive to one another to such a degree that transparency would be created for transnational politics within regional regimes and major powers"

learning processes

a global public sphere

(p. 126). The details of such a process – from literal translation to cultural mediation – remain to be specified, of course, especially in a historical situation where the public sphere(s) are said to be colonized, intensively and increasingly, by commercial systems (Habermas, 2006).

Although Habermas (2019a) elaborated his understanding of "learning processes" with particular reference to faith and knowledge in his recent history of philosophy and ideas, the references to such processes in the context of political communication return debate on his *oeuvre* to the basic question of what is the nature or status – the ontology – of the ideal speech situation, communicative action, and deliberative politics. For global communication to work, Habermas (2009) now submits, learning processes are necessary conditions, in parallel with the "legitimation requirements" (p. 123) of the two pillars, which together place individuals and collectives in a position to reflect, deliberate, and govern themselves. Habermas assumes that, in a global perspective, "both governments and populations would have to adopt new orientations and, in this sense, 'learn'" (p. 127) how to communicate and act politically. A further premise is (or has become) that the ideal conditions of communicative action "set standards for a self-correcting learning process" (Habermas, 2008: 84). What, then, *is* the status of the original mode of human communication oriented toward mutual understanding: an anthropological fact; a counterfactual norm; a reconstruction of a latent, but transhistorical reality; or a historical lesson to be learnt by individuals, generations, and civilizations, over and over again, as part and parcel of their struggles for survival, coexistence, and good lives? Habermas cannot have all of these cakes and eat them.

ANALYSIS BOX 3.1 SIGNS IN ACTION

Umberto Eco (1976) once proposed a surprising definition of signs in terms of their use, not for telling the truth, but for lying: "Thus *semiotics is in principle the discipline studying everything which can be used in order to lie*" (p. 7). While presented, in part, as a poststructuralist provocation, the definition pinpointed the insight of twentieth-century philosophy that signs and symbols – words, numbers, images – serve not only or even primarily as representations of the world, but as resources for acting in and on the world. < It was summed up in Wittgenstein's (1953: §20e) dictum that "meaning is

> signs as representations and resources – Chapter 1, p. 9

> meaning is use – Chapter 1, p. 9

use." < In linguistic terminology, the meaning and status of words is decided not by their grammar or semantics, but by pragmatics: how signs are used in social contexts. Fictions rely on vocabularies and sentence structures similar to news in order to tell stories about imagined or impossible worlds. The exact same sentence may tell either the truth or a lie.

In his formal pragmatics (originally referred to as "universal" pragmatics), Habermas (1979/1976: 1–68) has vacillated between the two primary conceptions of language and communication – as either formal representations or practical resources. Whereas his mature theory of communicative action aligned itself with Austin's (1962) speech-act theory, Habermas has returned throughout his writings to a formal understanding of the concrete vehicles of communication and of their relationship with cognition. In the third *magnum opus* (BFN), one reads: "Thoughts are propositionally structured. One can get a clear sense of what this means by considering the grammatical form of simple assertoric sentences. I do not need to go into this here" (Habermas, 1996/1992: 11). Notwithstanding the last formulation (which Habermas uses regularly to indicate what he takes for granted, or finds that he has already established elsewhere), there are good reasons to unpack precisely this reasoning. Compared to the late Wittgenstein (1953), who inspired speech-act theory, and who is regularly invoked by Habermas, the last quotation rather recalls the early Wittgenstein (1972/1921), who gave priority to the logical structure of propositions as points of access to the

> the early and late Wittgenstein – Chapter 1, p. 9

structure of reality. < For Habermas, a special attraction of propositional structures and simple verbal assertions likely is that they (appear to) model rational thinking with an orientation to reaching a common understanding about what is the case.

The same point is suggested by Habermas' reconstruction of the Wittgenstein (1953) that he takes as his ally. A passage in TCA refers to "Wittgenstein's central insight and the starting point for his use theory of meaning," which Habermas (1984/1981: 115) takes to be that a communicator or interpreter "can understand the meaning of communicative acts only because they are embedded in contexts of *action* oriented to reaching understanding." Habermas put action in italics; I would italicize *oriented to reaching understanding*. Even though the late Wittgenstein is notoriously difficult to interpret, it is hardly the case that his language games are characterized in any primary sense by communicative action as defined by Habermas. The examples in one important section on language games in *Philosophical Investigations* (Wittgenstein, 1953: §23) include reporting on an event, but also speculating about an event, play-acting, and making a joke. Where Wittgenstein (1953) opened up philosophy to the analysis of human cognition and communication as contingent, informal, messy phenomena, Habermas has sought to regularize and sanitize Wittgenstein's concept of language games for his own ends, significantly limiting the bandwidth of signs, genres, and styles of communication that are considered fit for analysis.

Habermas' preference for formalized communications – as forms of interaction and as objects of study – is evident across his *oeuvre*. In ST, he had referred to "a culture that no longer trusts the power of the printed word" (Habermas, 1989/1962: 163), but was instead turning its attention to movies, radio, and television. Like other cultural critics then and now, Habermas has worried about the lures of images and improvised speech. In TCA, the systematics of communicative action specifically excluded bodily expressions as instances of communication in themselves: "*A bodily movement is an element of an action, but not an action*" (Habermas, 1984/1981: 97); empirically, this view is disconfirmed by an entire subfield of interpersonal communication research (Knapp & Daly, 2011) which was consolidated during the same decades that Habermas established his position. In a special irony, Habermas' view of nonverbal communication cries out against the insight that is commonly cited to account for Wittgenstein's transition from logic to pragmatics. In a famous episode, the Italian economist, Piero Sraffa, challenged Wittgenstein to describe the logical form of a Neapolitan gesture of contempt (Malcolm, 1958: 69), which, of course, Wittgenstein could not. In BFN, Habermas still took the foundational figure of human cognition and communication to be propositional-logical.

words and images as communications

nonverbal communication

At the level of concrete communicative interactions and cultural practices, Habermas has been remarkably reluctant to recognize the relevance and potential value of popular forms of culture. "In mass culture, value contents have been deflated into stereotypical and, at the same time, manipulable elements" (Habermas, 1987b/1981: 108).

popular culture

At the other end of the high–low cultural spectrum, in "the hermetic works of modern art," value contents have been "subjectivized." More hopefully, a primordial middle ground is available in the form of a lifeworld where "cultural values [...] stand at the disposition of processes of mutual understanding which are not prejudged" (p. 108). The paradoxical implication is that the values of the lifeworld only come to fruition through rationally cultivated and formalized modes of understanding – which are products of the system world. And, at the level of media systems, the argument, reiterated by Habermas (2006), has been that everyday din must be subjected to cleansing by quality media.

> Habermas on Peirce – Chapter 5, p. 150

As part of an early criticism of Charles Sanders Peirce, < who started out from logic to develop his versions of semiotics and pragmatism, Habermas (1971/1968: 137) had commented that "it is possible to think in syllogisms, but not to conduct a dialogue in them." Habermas' synthesis of formalism and idealism recalls syllogisms rather than dialogues.

Remember Habermas!

Under the title *Forget Foucault* (2007/1977), Jean Baudrillard launched an all-out attack on the critical discourse analysis of Michel Foucault (who was on the editorial board of the French journal *Critique* to which the manuscript was originally submitted). The wider aim of Baudrillard's postmodernist philosophy was to *deconstruct* the sort of stable discursive positions from which critiques of society and culture could be launched. (Echoing Baudrillard in 2006, a German cultural magazine, *Cicero*, circulated accusations that Habermas had held Nazi sympathies during his youth with a front page reading, "Forget Habermas!" (Müller-Doohm, 2016: n.p.).) In comparison to Baudrillard, Habermas' strategy has been to *reconstruct* one discursive position as not just stable, but primordial. While I go on, in Chapter 5, to elaborate on *construction* as a third mode of inquiry, I conclude the present chapter by recognizing the important contributions that Habermas has made to scholarship and to the history of ideas, most of which fall outside the scope of a book chapter with a specific focus and an openly strategic purpose. His account of the development of the bourgeois public sphere, < for one, stands as a pivotal contribution to the understanding of communication and society; his volume on *The Philosophical Discourse of*

construction, deconstruction, reconstruction

> the bourgeois public sphere – p. 52

Modernity (Habermas, 1987a/1985), for another, provided what remains one of the most insightful analyses of the premises and arguments feeding into the communicative turn of modern philosophy. It is in the transition from analysis to synthesis that his own premises and arguments crisscross and contradict themselves. The structure that Habermas built and, over time, reconstructed to house a philosophy of communication will not provide a sustainable framework for reinvigorating or consolidating normative communication theory. This is the other good reason to read and remember his works: Falsification – being wrong in either conceptual or empirical terms, or both – is a finding in itself and part of the human condition. <

> falsification and fallibilism – Chapter 5, p. 127

Reviewing the distinctive stages of Habermas' published works and their implications for practical-political issues, I have identified three main lacunae. First, since his reconstructive turn, Habermas has been reasserting, time after time, the complementarity of his systematics of communication with empirical inquiry. His publications do not, however, include substantial empirical findings, nor has he reviewed relevant disciplinary and interdisciplinary literatures that might either confirm or disconfirm conclusions regarding particular aspects of communication and social life. My analysis has concentrated here on Habermas' own formulations; many researchers in communication research and other fields have taken inspiration from his works (see, e.g., Corchia, 2020; Hansen & Gregersen, 2020). In a comment on an anthologized reprint of Habermas (2006), the translator found that, there, "Habermas offers one of his most detailed analyses to date of the empirical data that tend to support [his] conclusions" (Habermas, 2009: xv) about the deliberative potential of a technologically mediated public sphere. What Habermas (2006) presents and cites is, in fact, a handful of strategically selected studies. Habermas' theories and hypotheses call for more empirical inquiry, but also more critical deliberation by his many readers on the presumed relationship between historical evidence and transhistorical claims.

Second, considering best academic practice, Habermas' reconstructions of earlier thinkers and received concepts have involved clear and consequential misrepresentations. His accounts of at least three supposed allies – Austin, Peirce, and Wittgenstein – have been so selectively self-serving on decisive points that it undermines the coherence and validity of his wider position. At the same time, he has been unwilling – or unable – to engage criticism from other scholars concerning key premises and central lines of his own argument. Third, then, Habermas' communicative practice contradicts and cancels his communication theory. His *oeuvre* represents a clear instance of sustained strategic communication, and his non-negotiable presuppositions regarding a primordial lifeworld hosting ideal communicative action – his

> metaphysics of communication – p. 82

unacknowledged metaphysics of communication < – foreclose further communication, strategic or otherwise, about the merits of his theories.

A final question is why Habermas has pursued this particular strategy, and why so many readers have been attracted to his project. In a courageous and moving essay on the biographical background to his focus on communication, Habermas (2008: 11–23) referred to his cleft palate, which "undoubtedly sharpened my awareness of the deep dependence of one person on others" (p. 14), and to "the caesura of 1945" (p. 17), which prompted his commitment to inquiry at the intersection of philosophy and social theory (on Habermas' biography, see Müller-Doohm, 2016). In response to a question in conversation of why, despite his invocation of the philosophy of practice – pragmatism – he has aligned himself with transcendentalism and universalism, "his answer was straightforward: the Holocaust" (Aboulafia, Bookman, & Kemp, 2002: 4).

But neither historical nor biographical circumstances will justify transhistorical premises and arguments, even if the circumstances help to explain their recurrence. To account for the prevalence of "systematically distorted communication" (Habermas, 1984/1981: 332), he has indicted the many social systems that are said to violate and incapacitate communicative action. Habermas and Habermasians might respond that their best conceptual and analytical efforts are being colonized by social systems. In this chapter, I have suggested that it is, instead, the utopian attractions of the lifeworld – the idea and ideal of a lifeworld as a primordial human condition – that has been a source of systematically distorted, in the specific sense of historically and practically disorienting, communication by Habermas. If the present text were a critique of ideology of the sort advocated by the younger Habermas (1971/1968: 310), it might have referred to a case of false consciousness. Instead, I follow Max Weber and Clifford Geertz (1973: 5) in concluding that Habermas has remained suspended in historical webs of significance which he has repeatedly reconstructed, but cannot transcend.

what ought to be, already is – or was

What ought to be, already is – or was. In shifting historical and systematic guises, Habermas has presupposed a utopian lifeworld as both fact and norm, a bottom line from which to reconstruct human history. The guiding figure of thought and discourse has been one of loss and lack of the sort of enlightened collective agency that is informed and empowered by unrestrained communication. The solution to the opening puzzle of this chapter, about the future of the internet (Habermas, 2006), is that any new medium will be subject to the same transhistorical logic of loss by system. The structural transformation of Jürgen Habermas has involved, not any transition to a different position, but a series of twists and turns within the same foundational figure of thought and discourse. As summarized by John Rawls in his mid-1990s debate with Habermas: <

> the Rawls–Habermas debate – Chapter 4, p. 96

> Habermas's own doctrine, I believe, is one of logic in the broad Hegelian sense: a philosophical analysis of the presuppositions of rational discourse (of theoretical and practical reason) which includes within itself all the allegedly substantial elements of religious and metaphysical doctrines. His logic is metaphysical in the following sense: it presents an account of what there is. And what there is are human beings engaged in communicative action in their lifeworld.
>
> *Rawls, 2011/1995: 50–51*

4

JOHN RAWLS BEHIND THE VEIL OF COMMUNICATION

Habermas vs. Rawls

In the mid-1990s, Jürgen Habermas and John Rawls came head to head in a debate about their respective conceptions of law and politics. Habermas opened his critical discussion of Rawls' (2005/1993) *Political Liberalism* in the following way:

> Because I admire this project, share its intentions, and regard its essential results as correct, the dissent I express here will remain within the bounds of a familial dispute. My doubts are limited to whether Rawls always brings to bear against his critics his important normative intuitions in their most compelling form.
>
> *Habermas, 2011b/1995: 25–26*

The first sentence of Rawls' response read: "First, I want to thank Jürgen Habermas for his generous discussion and acute comments on my work, and for his setting the stage for me to reply to the instructive criticisms he raises" (Rawls, 2011/1995: 46). Following a long and detailed counterargument, Rawls found, nevertheless, that he now understood his own views better: "For that I shall always be in Habermas's debt" (p. 91). A volume revisiting the debate two decades later noted "the received opinion that neither thinker had properly understood the other" (Finlayson & Freyenhagen, 2011a: 1) in a failure to communicate. I go on to suggest that the two thinkers did communicate, and did understand each other quite well – they just did not agree, neither at the outset nor in the end. As such, their interchange offered an illustrative example of the limitations not only of heated public debate, but also of polished academic communication about what justice is, ought to be, and could be. <

> what is, what ought to be, and what could be – Chapter 1, p. 2

Observing the juncture of communication and justice from within communication studies, the first giant in sight is Habermas; observing the same juncture from within philosophy, the first contemporary giant is Rawls. In this chapter, I give an outline of Rawls' *oeuvre* and refer to some of the debates that it both addressed and stimulated. Like Habermas' works, Rawls' writings can be divided into three main stages. The first section characterizes the volume that set a new agenda for political philosophy and ethics, *A Theory of Justice* (Rawls, 1971); I present the idea of justice as fairness, < focusing on the key concepts of the original position, < the veil of ignorance, < and reflective equilibrium. < I further discuss the implications of these concepts for an understanding of communication as a component of and a vehicle for justice. Whereas Rawls, like Habermas, expressed faith in the public use of reason, communication did not figure centrally in *A Theory of Justice*. I argue that, contrary to Rawls' implication, his famous veil of ignorance – behind which, in an imagined state of nature, people must decide on the principles that will govern their future lives together – can never be lifted entirely in and through communication.

> justice as fairness – p. 98

> the original position – p. 99

> the veil of ignorance – p. 99

> reflective equilibrium – p. 105

Like Habermas, Rawls changed his position significantly from the first to the second stage of his thinking. Unlike Habermas, Rawls explicitly recognized the discontinuity of the two positions. Rawls also traveled in the opposite direction of Habermas en route from a universalizing or comprehensive doctrine of justice < toward a historically inflected framework allowing for multiple doctrines of the good life. The revised position was laid out fully in *Political Liberalism* (Rawls, 2005/1993) (which was the occasion for the Rawls–Habermas debate). Here, Rawls reemphasized the practical purpose of political philosophy with reference to the idea of an overlapping consensus. < More than just a *modus vivendi*, this refers to the possibility of people endorsing and practicing similar principles of the right, but for different reasons. In the second section of the present chapter, I explore the relevance of the general idea of an overlapping consensus for the institutional structures and practices of communication in matters of justice. At the end of communication, < an overlapping consensus may enable individuals and collectives to go on, together, even when they cannot agree on some, even most, of the premises and arguments motivating their conclusions and actions.

> comprehensive doctrines – p. 108

> the overlapping consensus – p. 113

> the end of communication – Chapter 1, p. 1

The third stage of Rawls' *oeuvre* began to address questions of international justice. In *The Law of Peoples*, Rawls (1999a) transferred the concepts of the original position and the veil of ignorance from the national to the transnational level. His suggestion was that, like individuals, peoples (which Rawls distinguished from states) < depart from an original position behind a veil of ignorance to arrive at agreements and arrangements concerning sustainable institutions of global justice. Although the transfer of the basic model from individual citizens to peoples might be considered a category mistake (Ryle, 1949), Rawls' text served to specify key issues of international relations and global governance that have only become more urgent in academic research and public debate since the 1990s. Transnational institutions and practices of communication hold at least the promise that problems of justice may be addressed in a global perspective, and that the proposed solutions might articulate an overlapping consensus beyond local, national, or regional interests.

> peoples vs. states – p. 116

In twentieth-century philosophy, Rawls' *oeuvre* stood out by setting an agenda for subsequent political philosophy and ethics. Whereas most of the voluminous literature that it has stimulated falls outside the scope of this chapter (for overviews, see Kukathas, 2003; Mandle & Reidy, 2014; Richardson & Weithman, 1999), I consider selected responses to Rawls' interventions and some of their implications for communication and justice. In line with Rawls' practical and procedural approach, I take his framework as offering not a comprehensive systematics, but a point of departure for reinvigorating normative inquiry into the common practice of communication. So far, a surprisingly limited number of studies have explored the relevance of a Rawlsian framework for the study of human communication, mostly with reference to (new) information technologies (e.g., Bay, 2017; Duff, 2012; Hoffmann, 2014; Schejter & Tirosh, 2016).

Justice as fairness

Principles and consequences

the social contract

Rawls (1999b/1971) summed up his position in a terminology of justice as fairness, "a theory of justice that generalizes and carries to a higher level of abstraction the traditional conception of the social contract" (p. 3). *A Theory of Justice* (TJ) emphasized that "we are not to think of the original contract as one to enter a particular society or to set up a particular form of government" in advance and in detail. In matters of justice, the market principle of *caveat emptor* will not suffice: Citizens do not have perfect knowledge to guide them as they enter into contracts with long-term consequences for their life and welfare. And, like individual citizens, societies need institutional mechanisms to compensate for the unforeseen and the unpredictable, and for the unavoidable errors of fact and judgment by citizens as well as their representatives. < Still, to initiate any deliberation or decision, an agreement on certain fundamental "principles of justice for the basic structure of society" is necessary; to Rawls, these are "the principles that free and rational persons concerned to further their own interests would accept in an initial position of equality as defining the fundamental terms of their association" (p. 10). Concretely, "a group of persons must decide once and for all what is to count among them as just and unjust" (p. 11). It is this crucial decision that is made in the so-called original position behind a veil of ignorance.

> fallibilism – Chapter 5, p. 127

the original position

The original position "corresponds to the state of nature in the traditional theory of the social contract" (Rawls, 1999b/1971: 11). It is "not, of course, thought of as an actual historical state of affairs [but] as a purely hypothetical situation" (p. 11) in which a specific conception of justice "would be agreed to" (p. 14) behind a veil of ignorance:

the veil of ignorance

> Among the essential features of this situation is that no one knows his place in society, his class position or social status, nor does any one know his fortune in the distribution of natural assets and abilities, his intelligence, strength, and the like. I shall even assume that the parties do now know their conceptions of the good or their special psychological propensities. [...] This ensures that no one is advantaged or disadvantaged in the choice of principles by the outcome of natural chance or the contingency of social circumstances.
>
> *p. 11*

The resulting principles of justice (described below) are presented in TJ not as "necessary truths or derivable from such truths" (p. 19), nor does Rawls, by the end of the volume, consider them "self-evident." Instead, he assumes the general persuasiveness of the basic model, "the naturalness of these conditions" (p. 507), at least in the ideal version of the theory. < While hypothetical, the original position is offered as a concrete point of reference for the assessment of justice in different historical contexts. "At any time we can enter the original position" (p. 17) to assess the state of justice in past, present, and future societies. This is in spite of the fact that, like most philosophers, Rawls did not pursue

> ideal and non-ideal theory – p. 107

an empirical line of inquiry and argument. He also seemed to accept that the idea of justice as fairness itself is historical and fallible: "The most we can do is to study the conceptions of justice known to us through the tradition of moral philosophy and any further ones that occur to us, and then to consider these" (p. 43).

rationality and mutual disinterest

moderate scarcity and conflict of interests

> the ideal speech situation – Chapter 3, p. 77

In the original position, the parties share two features as they seek "the most effective means to given ends": they are "rational and mutually disinterested" (Rawls, 1999b/1971: 12). TJ did not mean to suggest that people are "egoists, that is, individuals with only certain kinds of interests, say in wealth, prestige, and domination." Rather, the theory proposes to avoid any ideal presupposition that people can and will take "an interest in one another's interests" (p. 12). Rawls' point was "to assume as little as possible" about how humans could and should shape their societies (p. 112). As part of the original position, TJ further referred to conditions of "moderate scarcity" and "conflict of interests." Even though the theory of justice as fairness centers on historical societies with adequate resources to satisfy the basic needs of all, "conflicting claims to the division of social advantages" (p. 110) were seen as unavoidable. Embracing conflict as a fact of life, Rawls followed in the social-contract tradition from Hobbes through Locke and Rousseau to Kant (p. 10), rather than assuming the potential dissolution of conflict through deliberation and communication; I compare Rawls' original position and Habermas' ideal speech situation < at the end of this chapter.

The central claim of TJ was that, behind the veil of ignorance in the original position, the parties would agree on two principles to guide all future interactions:

> [T]he first requires equality in the assignment of basic rights and duties, while the second holds that social and economic inequalities, for example inequalities of wealth and authority, are just only if they result in compensating benefits for everyone, and in particular for the least advantaged members of society.
>
> *Rawls, 1999b/1971: 13*

the difference principle

This important last point is referred to as the difference principle. The opening formulation was elaborated throughout the volume and summarized in "a full statement" (p. 266f.). Rawls first specified the priority of the first principle to the second: "infringements of the basic equal liberties [...] cannot be justified, or compensated for, by greater social and economic advantages" (p. 53f.). At the same time, he included both liberties and entitlements or compensations among the so-called primary social goods: "rights, liberties, and opportunities, and income and wealth" (p. 79). They are primary because these are things that all humans will want, "whatever else they want" (p. 230) in life:

primary social goods

> All social values – liberty and opportunity, income and wealth, and the social bases of self-respect – are to be distributed equally unless an unequal distribution of any, or all, of these values is to everyone's advantage. [...] Injustice, then, is simply inequalities that are not to the benefit of all.
>
> *p. 54*

Rawls even considered the natural and social endowments of concrete historical individuals as collective assets: "No one deserves his greater natural capacity nor merits a more favorable starting place in society. [...] These are simply natural facts. What is just or unjust is the way that institutions deal with these facts" (p. 87).

natural and social lotteries

In contextualizing his redevelopment of the social contract, Rawls recalled another traditional distinction, that between the good and the right, or the ends and means of justice, submitting that "the concept of the right is prior to that of the good" (Rawls, 1999b/1971: 28). The right derives from the original position, and is expressed in the two principles of justice that "specify the boundaries that men's systems of ends must respect" (p. 27f.). In comparison,

the good and the right

> there is no need to set up the account of the good so as to force unanimity [...] it is, in general, a good thing that individuals' conceptions of their good should differ in significant ways, whereas this is not so for conceptions of right.
>
> *p. 393*

In this way, arguably, the individual liberty to define the good is served by collectively agreed boundaries to the right, which have been predefined and accepted by all in the original position.

Rawls was well aware that a theory of the good is a necessary component of any theory of justice regarding its "Ends" (the heading of Part Three in TJ). It is typically the ends or principles of justice, more than its means or procedures, that motivate and divide people, and which tend to generate contestation < and conflict. To accommodate a notion of the good within TJ, Rawls made a distinction between a "thin theory," which yields "the bare essentials" as premises of the two basic principles of justice, and a "full theory of the good" (Rawls, 1999b/1971: 348).

> essentially contested concepts – Chapter 1, p. 13

self-respect

> Rawls and pragmatism – Chapter 5, p. 160

self-realization

> the prehistory of justice – Chapter 2, p. 28

The thin theory of *the good* covers "the rational preference for primary *goods*" (emphasis added) as general resources for living (p. 349). In a stepwise argument thickening his theory of the good, Rawls made special reference to self-respect as "perhaps the most important primary good" (p 386). Self-respect is cultivated through "a human life lived according to a plan" (p. 358 – an idea that he credited to Josiah Royce and other pragmatists), < and not just any plan, but a plan that is recognized as rational by oneself and others. In a further step, Rawls linked self-respect to self-realization with reference to the so-called Aristotelian Principle: "human beings enjoy the exercise of their realized capacities (their innate or trained abilities), and this enjoyment increases the more the capacity is realized, or the greater its complexity" (p. 374). Rawls also found support for his argument in the prehistory of justice: < "Natural selection must have favored creatures of whom this principle is true" (p. 378). A good human life, then, is a life lived to the full.

> the kingdom of ends – Chapter 2, p. 35

In the final chapter of TJ, Rawls discussed the relationship between justice and goodness as part of "a social union": "it is only in active cooperation with others that one's powers reach fruition. Only in a social union is the individual complete" (p. 460). Recalling Immanuel Kant's kingdom of ends, < in which human beings define their own ends, and are never treated as means, Rawls envisioned a "community of mankind" in which the members "enjoy one another's excellences and individuality" (p. 459).

> deontology – Chapter 2, p. 34

utilitarianism

> consequentialism – Chapter 2, p. 38

In summary, Rawls (1999b/1971) characterized TJ as "a deontological theory" (p. 26), departing from rules or principles regarding a person's rights and duties. < A central motivation behind TJ was to challenge and move beyond utilitarianism as the paradigmatic instance of teleological or consequentialist theories, which assess human actions and social interactions according to intentions and outcomes, and which had become entrenched as a mainstream of academic philosophy. < In utilitarianism, "the right is defined as that which maximizes the good" (p. 22). According to Rawls, however, a definition and justification of the good is simply missing in utilitarianism. The problem and the "striking feature of the utilitarian view of justice is that it does not matter, except indirectly, how this sum of satisfactions is distributed among individuals" (p. 23). Utilitarianism appears to require an "impartial spectator," who not only is "perfectly rational," but who is "endowed with ideal powers of sympathy and imagination," and who, therefore, "identifies with and experiences the desires of others as if these desires were his own." By "conflating all persons into one," utilitarianism does not recognize different and potentially conflicting conceptions of the good: "Utilitarianism does not take seriously the distinction between persons" (p. 24).

In developing his agenda in TJ, however, Rawls appeared to overstate its distance from consequentialism, while at the same time understating its reconfiguration of the traditional philosophical mainstreams. On the one hand, he presented a circular or, at least, negative definition of his deontological theory as a "non-teleological" one. On the other hand, he argued that, "All ethical theories worth our attention take consequences into account in judging rightness. One which did not would simply be irrational, crazy" (Rawls, 1999b/1971: 26). TJ took on board the common experience that equal starting points do not guarantee fair (let alone equal) end results. The theory of justice as fairness, accordingly, sought to address the balance between certain absolute rights and various compensations for the contingencies of a human life in a social and historical context. TJ also considered justice in relation to human virtues, < which represent the third mainstream of theories of justice and ethics. The enactment of principles of justice through agreed procedures will depend on the capacity of both individuals and collectives to appreciate what is right and what may be good. Rawls' reconfiguration, rather than rejection, of classic insights from the history of ideas helps to explain why he set a new and abiding agenda for thinking and communicating about justice. <

> virtue ethics – Chapter 2, p. 31

> a Rawlsian agenda – p. 120

Procedures and communications

The first page of TJ indicated that, "Justice is the first virtue of social institutions, as truth is of systems of thought" (Rawls, 1999b/1971: 3). Institutions (the heading of Part Two in TJ) constitute the pivot of justice as fairness; the major institutions of politics, economy, family, etc., together make up what Rawls termed the basic structure of society. An institution is "a public system of rules" (p. 47). Systems of law and politics are maintained in and through the actions or practices that citizens continuously engage in according to rules or procedures that are public and, therefore, subject to both individual reflection and communal deliberation: "A person taking part in an institution knows what the rules demand of him and of the others. He also knows that the others know this and that they know that he knows this, and so on" (p. 48).

the basic structure of society

Already in the original position, publicity is presented as one of the central conditions of agreeing to what is right, even if

publicity

> Kant's categorical imperative – Chapter 2, p. 37

TJ did not associate publicity in any detail with institutions or practices of communication. To Rawls, the condition of publicity was already "clearly implicit in Kant's doctrine of the categorical imperative" < (p. 115). Indeed, the entire original position could be understood as "a procedural interpretation" of Kant "within the framework of an empirical theory" (p. 226).

the four-stage sequence

constitutional convention

legislature

To specify how the principles of justice as fairness are to be translated into empirical or practical procedures, Rawls (1999b/1971) referred to a "four-stage sequence" (p. 171). Throughout these stages, the veil of ignorance is gradually lifted. The first stage covers the initial choice of the two basic principles, considering also social stability over time and including a principle of "just savings" (p. 252) for later generations. (Behind the veil of ignorance, people do not know which historical period they live in, and would therefore choose arrangements that are fair across generations.) The second stage witnesses a constitutional convention that takes place with reference to more information on the economic level of development of the society in question and its political traditions. In the third stage, with further knowledge about actual social structures and available theories of society, a legislature writes the general principles, as framed by the constitution, into concrete and actionable laws. In the fourth and final stage, laws and legal procedures are applied "to particular cases by judges and administrators," coupled with "the following of rules by citizens generally." "At this stage," in Rawls' words, "everyone has access to all the facts" (p. 175).

> information, communication, and action – Chapter 6, p. 163

TJ referred only briefly and mostly indirectly to communication as concrete vehicles of the reflective and deliberative procedures that put justice into practice. The importance of the basic rights of "freedom of speech and assembly, and liberty of thought and conscience" (Rawls, 1999b/1971: 197) was explained with reference to how information and communication help to anticipate (rational) action: <

No one [even of the representative legislators] knows everything the others know, or can make all the same inferences that they can draw in concert. Discussion is a way of combining information and enlarging the range of arguments. At least in the course of time, the effects of common deliberation seem bound to improve matters.

p. 315

"Discussion" and "deliberation," thus, serve to identify and justify rational courses of action, first when the basic choices are made in the original position, later at the different levels of political democracy. When people choose a constitution and adopt "some form of majority rule," they "accept the risks of suffering the defects of one another's knowledge and sense of justice in order to gain the advantages of an effective legislative procedure." Not only does Rawls see "no other way to manage a democratic regime," but the individual's submission to a collective "democratic authority [...] is simply recognizing and being willing to work within the limits imposed by the circumstances of human life" (p. 312). Communication about the ends and means of coexistence is a constitutive element of the human condition, a precondition for any form of civilized community.

reflective equilibrium

In TJ, the emphasis was placed on personal reflection, as summed up in the idea of a reflective equilibrium, not on communal deliberation. The individual's attempt to arrive at reflective equilibrium responds to doubts and errors, when even "our considered judgments" may fail (Rawls, 1999b/1971: 42). < In a first step, doubts can be resolved at the level of "a person's sense of justice more or less as it is although allowing for the smoothing out of certain irregularities," as that person seeks to arrive at a coherent or consonant position. In a next step, such resolution is challenged by "all possible descriptions" of different judgments regarding justice "together with all relevant philosophical arguments for them" (p. 43), as people (ideally) confront the length and breadth of the history of ideas in the present. In later work, Rawls (2005/1993: 8) introduced a terminology of narrow and wide reflective equilibrium to capture this distinction; at least the wide equilibrium presupposes some form of communicative interaction – conversation or reading – about the available repertoire of judgments and arguments. In TJ, however, the focus remained on the more or less extensive process of reflection through which one person arrives at particular conceptions of and judgments about justice: The site of rationality in TJ is individual consciousness.

> fallibilism – Chapter 5, p. 127

narrow and wide reflective equilibrium

procedural justice

Communication was implicit in another central concept in TJ: procedural justice. Compared to distributive justice, which addresses the social distribution of rights and resources, and retributive justice, which attends to sanctions and punishments, procedural justice covers those institutions and interactions that are designed to determine what is right with reference to explicit and operational principles. As such, procedural justice is a distinctively modern notion. Like modern science and scholarship, procedural justice gives priority to methodologies for arriving at conclusions through the presentation of evidence and arguments, rather than to ontological or epistemological axioms, thus counteracting the random exercise of power by religious or secular authorities.

Both science and justice, of course, face questions of how to justify both *their* first principles *and* the methodologies for assessing the relevance and application of these principles. Rawls' (1999b/1971) approach in TJ was to start from "pure procedural justice" where "there is no independent criterion for the right result: instead there is a correct or fair procedure such that the outcome is likewise correct or fair, whatever it is, provided that the procedure has been properly followed" (p. 75). Invoking the veil of ignorance, he argued that "justice as fairness is able to use the idea of pure procedural justice from the beginning" (p. 104). Rawls compared this pure type with perfect procedural justice (exemplified by one person dividing a cake and getting the last piece) and with imperfect procedural justice (e.g., criminal trials where one may expect "the right results, not always but at least most of the time" (p. 75)). He further recognized that, already at the stage of devising a constitution, the "best attainable scheme is one of imperfect procedural justice" (p. 173), and he noted that, in practice, one must "fall back upon a notion of quasi-pure procedural justice" in which laws and policies stay within an "allowed range" (p. 176). Still, given their grounding in the original position, Rawls suggested, the resulting constitutions, laws, policies, and administrative applications and decisions could be expected to produce the best (or least worst) approximation of the right.

pure, perfect, and imperfect justice

The most explicit engagement with communication occurred in the last part of TJ, which examined the good that the right is supposed to serve. Rawls (1999b/1971) indicated that not only is the good relative to people's different ends in life; the good is defined and, simultaneously, enacted through speech and other communication. < The good is not a quality inherent in either objects or events, nor does it follow from metaphysical or transcendental principles: "There is no necessity to assign 'good' a special kind of meaning which is not already explained by its constant descriptive sense and the general theory of speech acts" (p. 356). Observing the principles of what is right, and staying within the bounds of rationality, people are free to pursue and perform *their* good, so that "once we establish that an object has the properties that it is rational for someone with a rational plan in life to want, then we have shown that it is good for him" (p. 351).

> speech-act theory – Chapter 3, p. 70

It was striking that TJ did not consider the same logic of performative speech acts as part of a definition of the right. Echoing Rawls, there would seem to be no reason to assign 'right' a special kind of meaning that is not already explained by its constant descriptive sense and the general theory of speech acts. Justice is neither pure nor perfect; the right is not predefined or primordial. Laws passed in parliaments and sentences pronounced in courtrooms are textbook examples of speech acts with institutional consequences (Austin, 1962). The implication in TJ seemed to be that the procedures establishing the right do not require the same (kind or degree of) performative affirmation as the good. I return, in the next section on *Political Liberalism*, to Rawls' (2005/1993) attempt at resolving this ambiguity by reformulating key constituents of justice as fairness.

Both TJ and Rawls' later works made a distinction between ideal and non-ideal theories of justice. The main concern of TJ was the development of an ideal theory about the basic structure of society that would address the principles of justice characterizing "a perfectly just society, given favorable conditions," and which "will be strictly complied with and followed by everyone." Non-ideal theory considers various "unjust arrangements" and "includes, among other things, the theory of punishment and compensatory justice, just war and conscientious objection, civil disobedience and militant resistance" (Rawls, 1999b/1971: 309). His premise was that ideal theory provides the necessary background and "the only basis for the systematic grasp" of problems of injustice (p. 8). In the case even of fundamental disagreements, shared ideals would still provide the yardstick. For example, in a detailed examination of civil disobedience, Rawls emphasized that one cannot justify such behavior with an "appeal to principles of personal morality or to religious doctrines," but must invoke "the common shared conception of justice that underlies the political order. [...] By engaging in civil disobedience a minority forces the majority" to reconsider its practices in the light of shared principles and through public deliberation (p. 321).

ideal and non-ideal theory

civil disobedience

TJ took note of the dynamic interrelation between ideal and non-ideal perspectives on justice, between theory and practice, which obtains simultaneously at the individual and the institutional levels. Although he grounded justice as fairness in deontological principles rather than in human virtues, Rawls (1999b/1971) found that, "To some degree [...] moral sentiments are necessary to insure that the basic structure is stable with respect to justice" (p. 401), and that "the conception of justice [...] is to be learned" (p. 404) through socialization in families and educational institutions. TJ further assumed that individuals and collectives can and will make substantial revisions to their conceptions of the good across biographical and historical time: "free persons conceive of themselves as beings who can revise and alter their final

moral sentiments

learning justice

ends" (p. 131). It is this liberty to both define and redefine the good within the limits of the right that the institutions of justice must be designed to serve. In TJ, justice as fairness was advanced as a comprehensive doctrine that would be accepted for a given society by all citizens regardless of their different worldviews. In the second stage of his thinking, it was the viability of *any* such comprehensive doctrine that Rawls came to question.

comprehensive doctrines

An overlapping consensus

The rational and the reasonable

Political Liberalism (PL) summed up Rawls' (2005/1993) revised understanding of "justice as fairness as a form of political liberalism" (p. xxix). Liberalism here denoted the acceptance of "a plurality of reasonable yet incompatible comprehensive doctrines," while politics referred to "the free institutions of a constitutional democratic regime" that make such incompatible doctrines not just possible, but "the normal result" (p. xvi). By way of introduction, Rawls outlined the historical background to political liberalism with reference to a shift from ancient civic religions, which had been based on relative tolerance and ecumenical participation, to competing religions of salvation. In the aftermath of the Reformation, "people's conceptions of their good" came to incorporate "a transcendent element not admitting of compromise." This seemed to present just two alternatives, "either mortal conflict moderated only by circumstance and exhaustion, or equal liberty of conscience and freedom of thought" (p. xxvi). The task for modern political governance became one of accommodating "a pluralism of comprehensive religious, philosophical, and moral doctrines" (p. xvi) within the basic structure of society as identified by TJ. In effect, PL reopened the central question of TJ: How may citizens practice a consensual approach to the right despite their sometimes fundamentally different conceptions of the good?

political liberalism

civic religions

religions of salvation

Rawls' (2005/1993) short answer to this complex question was "*reasonable* pluralism" (p. xvii, emphasis added): "No society can include within itself all forms of life" (p. 197); "the principles of justice set limits to permissible ways of life" because of "the priority of the right" over the good (p. 209). The most obvious challenge followed from the existence of different religious doctrines. The motivation for separating church and state is that this "protects religion from the state and the state from religion; it protects citizens from their churches and citizens from one another" (p. 476). Rawls underscored that he did not endorse varieties of "Enlightenment Liberalism" that would attack religion as such (p. 486): Political liberalism leaves scope for the possible worlds of religion. < Instead, PL started out from a "criterion of reciprocity" (p. xliv) that called for translatability between worldviews. People are permitted to introduce aspects of their comprehensive doctrines in a public, political forum, provided that "in due course public reasons [...] are presented sufficient to support whatever the comprehensive doctrines are introduced to support" (p. xlixf.). Rawls added that, in a world of incompatible doctrines, conflict is unavoidable and, indeed, a welcome first step in interactions – communications – toward an argued consensus: "Citizens learn and profit from conflict and argument, and when their arguments follow public reason, they instruct and deepen society's public culture" (p. lv).

> possible worlds – Chapter 3, p. 81

criterion of reciprocity

translatability

In TJ, Rawls (1999b/1971: 190–194) had taken up the so-called paradox of tolerance: whether and how to be tolerant toward the intolerant. There, he indicated that societies are justified in defending their security and basic institutions against individuals and groups who prove intolerant of these. PL introduced additional steps on the road from a situation pitting mutually intolerant doctrines against each other, toward a culture that would promote reciprocal tolerance and feed overall social stability. The volume opened with the remarkable claim that "political liberalism applies the principle of toleration to philosophy itself" (Rawls, 2005/1993: 10). Rawls' point was that, in contrast to its traditional self-conception, philosophy could no longer be expected to deliver first premises and final ends – the truth about the good life. Instead, "The aim of justice as fairness, then, is practical" (p. 9), working out the principles and procedures that may enable people to lead good, if different lives together. PL clarified that Rawls' revised conception of justice was not a comprehensive doctrine, but "a freestanding view," a "political" framework that did not embrace any "specific metaphysical or epistemological doctrine." The freestanding view, further, delimited the political domain, bracketing "other values that apply, say, to the personal, the familial, and the associational" (p. 10). Rawls, again, explained this delimitation in practical terms with reference to "the need for [a] division of labor between different kinds of principles" (p. 469). At the same time, PL noted the interdependence of political and other kinds of values and institutions. On the one hand, the family has relative autonomy in its central role of arranging "in a reasonable and effective way the raising of and caring for children, ensuring their moral development and education into

the paradox of tolerance

a freestanding view of justice

justice as politics

the family

the wider culture" (p. 467). On the other hand, "The family as part of the basic structure cannot violate [...] the basic rights of equal citizens who are members of families" (p. 469).

a practical turn

common sense

The practical turn of PL entailed a categorical distinction not only between the freestanding, political view of justice and metaphysics or epistemology, but also between political philosophy and science in the modern sense: "we need not explain [the] role and content [of political philosophy] scientifically, in terms of natural selection, for instance" (Rawls, 2005/1993: 88). (In TJ, he had pointed to natural selection to support the claim that the Aristotelian Principle of living life to the full is true (Rawls, 1999b/1971: 378).) Science still counted in PL for its practical relevance, but on a par with common sense. Rawls argued that "the basic structure and its public policies are to be justifiable to all citizens," and "in making these justifications we are to appeal only to presently accepted general beliefs and forms of reasoning found in common sense, and the methods and conclusions of science when these are not controversial" (Rawls, 2005/1993: 224). Because justice is extraordinarily important, it must be conceivable and communicable in ordinary terms.

objectivity

> political constructivism – p. 112

> fallibilism – Chapter 5, p. 127

PL went on to conceive even objectivity as a practical rather than an epistemological issue, defining objectivity as an outcome of those procedures that serve to construct the principles of political justice. < In opposition to Thomas Nagel's (1986) influential formulation of a neutral or impersonal "view from nowhere," Rawls (2005/1993) maintained that "the objective point of view must always be from somewhere [...] the point of view of persons, individual or corporate" (p. 116). He associated objectivity with "a public framework of thought" (p. 110) that seeks to "specify an order of reasons" as to why "our thinking something is just or reasonable" (p. 111), and which is able to account for both agreements and disagreements. And in contrast to the common understanding of objectivity as the elimination of error, PL, like TJ, embraced error, holding that being wrong is part of being reasonable. With "the liberty of conscience" comes "the liberty to fall into error and to make mistakes" (p. 313), a condition that applies equally to philosophers and other humans. < In the end, (political) philosophers can only invoke "the overall success over time of the shared practice of practical reasoning by those who are reasonable and rational" (p. 119).

In an important footnote, Rawls clarified his understanding of the process through which one may practice objectivity: An objective procedure "does not imply that we have knowledge of this procedure; but rather we can use the principles that issue from it" (p. 112). This argument shifted attention from knowing-that to knowing-how (Ryle, 1949), conceiving reason and knowledge not as representations of reality, but as resources for interacting with reality. To Rawls (2005/1993), "reason is the final court of appeal," and its "concepts of judgment and inference, and the rest, are irreducible. With these concepts explanations come to an end; one of philosophy's tasks is to quiet our distress at this thought" (p. 120f.). Philosophy is both a practical and a therapeutic enterprise.

knowing-that and knowing-how

Rawls still faced the decisive practical question of how societies may devise procedures to ensure the peaceful coexistence of people with incompatible doctrines. On this point, PL revisited the concept of rationality. In TJ, rationality had figured as the medium through which all citizens would come to affirm shared principles and procedures of the right, beginning from the original position. But, as already noted, the status of such affirmation had remained ambiguous: Does the medium of rationality *perform* the right, or does it *represent* a right that already exists and, perhaps, always has existed? In PL, Rawls' (2005/1993) solution was to distinguish between the rational and the reasonable. The rational is typically associated with calculations of ends and means by "a single, unified agent (whether an individual or corporate person)" (p. 50). "What rational agents lack is the particular form of moral sensibility that underlies the desire to engage in fair cooperation" (p. 51). In comparison, "reasonable people take into account the consequences of their actions on others' well-being," and they "can reason in common" (p. 49). In this way, "the reasonable is public in a way the rational is not" (p. 53).

rationality and/vs. reason

Conceptually, if not terminologically, Rawls (2005/1993) was approaching a conception of rationality as collective and of reasoning as communicative: public processes through which people subscribing to different doctrines of the good may come to agree on and affirm the right. As in TJ, PL held that citizens can "enter [the original position] at any time" (p. 27) as part of their participation in political democracy. Compared to TJ, however, PL described several different procedures through which societies may imagine and reflect on institutions of justice, distinguishing between "as-if historical" and "as-if non-historical" processes. Whereas the latter is exemplified by the original position, as-if historical processes take into account various "fundamental social laws [and] natural facts" (p. 264) as people consider reasonable courses of action. Communication about justice can be understood as a practical enterprise anticipating the future with reference both to historical experience, past and present, and to additional possible or counterfactual worlds. <

as-if historical and as-if non-historical processes

> counterfactual worlds Chapter 3, p. 81

The revised position of PL clarified the practical and historical status of several constituents of justice as fairness. The original position is described in PL as "simply a device of representation" (Rawls, 2005/1993: 25) for initiating processes or procedures of reflection and deliberation about the principles of justice. "The procedure itself is simply laid out using as starting points the basic conceptions of society and person, the principles of practical reason, and the public role of a political conception of justice." Having accepted this device, people go on to construct "the substantive principles specifying content of political right and justice" (p. 104). Rawls further recognized that the original position offers one possible starting point or criterion for the exercise of reason in arriving at principles of justice. "Many will prefer another criterion" (p. 227). PL, nevertheless, reasserted that "in order to find an appropriate conception of justice to regulate [the basic structure of society], something like the notion of the original position seems inevitable" (p. 275).

The public uses of reason

political constructivism

Rawls (2005/1993) summed up his revised approach to justice under a heading of political constructivism. At one level, PL reiterated the reliance on procedures as the necessary means of arriving at the principles that will govern the basic structure of society: "the principles of political justice (content) may be represented as the outcome of a procedure of construction (structure)" (p. 93). But Rawls' political constructivism held radical implications for received ideas of rationality and truth. Just as he no longer approached rationality as a singular perspective on the right, PL proposed an understanding of justice that "does without the concept of truth" (p. 94). At least in matters of justice, several truths and rationalities may be admissible. Throughout the history of ideas,

truths and rationalities

> One of the deepest distinctions between conceptions of justice is between those that allow for a plurality of reasonable though opposing comprehensive doctrines each with its own conception of the good, and those that hold that there is but one such conception to be recognized by all citizens who are fully reasonable and rational.
>
> *p. 134*

Rawls distanced himself from the idea of one true good that had been "the dominant tradition" since "Plato and Aristotle, and the Christian tradition as represented by Augustine and Aquinas," into modernity, and through to "classical utilitarianism" (p. 134f.). With reference to past practical experience, he found that, "History tells of a plurality of not unreasonable comprehensive doctrines" (p. 140), among which he counted "all the main historical religions" (p. 170). The peaceful coexistence of people holding incompatible worldviews, in addition to being practicable in history, might also be conceivable in philosophy.

the overlapping consensus

The overlapping consensus was Rawls' term for the understanding that there can be several routes to the right. He underscored that "an overlapping consensus is not a mere modus vivendi" (p. 147), which would involve a series of compromises that are more or less acceptable to the parties in question. Regarding the "depth" of such a consensus, it "goes down to" such fundamental ideas as "society as a fair system of cooperation and of citizens as reasonable and rational, and free and equal." Regarding its "breadth," the overlapping consensus "applies to the basic structure as a whole" (p. 149), i.e., the major institutions of politics, economy, family, and so forth. The acceptance by all of a unifying political conception, such as justice as fairness, is premised on the translatability of "the totality of reasons specified within the comprehensive doctrine affirmed by each citizen" (p. 171) into public reasons. < The translation back and forth between separate doctrine and shared consensus may, simultaneously, promote self-respect and social stability. Citizens can agree to disagree on the premises that, in the end, motivate their shared conclusions about how they should act, as individual members of the same collective.

> translatability – p. 109

public reason

Compared to TJ, PL contained ingredients for a more explicitly communicative conception of justice, including the overlapping consensus and another key concept: public reason. Whereas TJ had referred to the exchange of information and the interaction between citizens as aspects of how individuals arrive at a reflective equilibrium, < PL elaborated on their exercise of reason in a variety of public practices and institutions. However, Rawls (2005/1993) offered an unusual definition of what is 'public,' as indicated through a distinction between "the public political forum" and "the background culture." The public political forum, on the one hand, has three components:

> reflective equilibrium – p. 105

the public political forum

> the discourse of judges in their decisions, and especially of the judges of a supreme court; the discourse of government officials, especially chief executives and legislators; and finally, the discourse of candidates for public office and their

> campaign managers, especially in their public oratory, party platforms, and public statements.
>
> *p. 443*

the background culture

The terminology of "discourses" at least suggested a communicative understanding of each of the three institutional branches of modern politics: legislative, executive, and judicial. The background culture, on the other hand, "is the culture of civil society. In a democracy, this culture is not, of course, guided by any one central idea or principle, whether political or religious." This is the "culture of churches and associations of all kinds, and institutions of learning at all levels" (p. 443). Civil society institutions and associations operate in and through communication, feeding their interests and viewpoints into the formal institutions of politics.

Surprisingly, Rawls (2005/1993) did not associate the background culture with any form of public reason: "The idea of public reason does not apply to the background culture with its many forms of nonpublic reason nor to media of any kind" (p. 443f.). According to his definition, public reason "is public in three ways":

> as the reason of free and equal citizens, it is the reason of the public; its subject is the public good concerning questions of fundamental political justice, which questions are of two kinds, constitutional essentials and matters of basic justice; and its nature and content are public, being expressed in public reasoning by a family of reasonable conceptions of political justice reasonably thought to satisfy the criterion of reciprocity. <
>
> *p. 442*

> the criterion of reciprocity – p. 109

The definition, thus, focused on a core of political institutions, rather than on the basic structure of society, which would have included those institutions of communication and culture, broadly speaking, that mediate different kinds of reasoning across space, time, and collectives. What remained unaccounted for was the ongoing translation between the background culture and the public political culture – between 'private' reasoning by citizens and their associations and 'public' reasoning by their representatives, but also among the incompatible comprehensive doctrines that inform the background culture. Only in a brief footnote to the main text did Rawls note the existence of a "*nonpublic* political culture" (emphasis added) that "mediates between the public political culture and the background culture. This comprises media – properly

a nonpublic political culture of media

so named – of all kinds: newspapers, reviews and magazines, television and radio, and much else" (p. 443f.).

The modern media of communication, and the multi-step communications < that traverse Rawls' (2005/1993) public political culture and background culture in both directions, simply fell outside his purview. While reiterating TJ's general commitment to "the freedom of political speech and press" (p. 340), PL approached political communication in basic terms of citizen-to-citizen exchanges and any practical obstacles to such encounters:

> multi-step communications – Chapter 6, p. 178

> [W]hile we might want to include in our freedom of (political) speech rights to the unimpeded access to public places and to the free use of social resources to express our political views, these extensions of our liberty, when granted to all, are so unworkable and socially divisive that they would actually greatly reduce the effective scope of freedom of speech. [...] Thus, the delegates [to the constitutional convention] accept reasonable regulations relating to time and place, and the access to public facilities, always on a footing of equality.
>
> *p. 341*

The individual's reflective equilibrium still overshadowed the overlapping consensus that collectives may arrive at, increasingly through technologically mediated communication. The basic structure, as defined and later revised by Rawls, did not consider institutions of communication (public or commercial) as central constituents of the political reality being constructed. The idea of public reason had essentialist connotations, reminiscent of the unified, universal rationality from which PL was otherwise distancing itself. If, as Rawls suggested, *public reason* is "the reason of free and equal citizens [...] the reason of the public" (p. 442), then surely the *public uses* of reason extend far beyond the agency of candidates running for election, government officials, and judges within the formal institutions of politics. <

> social agency and social structure – Chapter 6, p. 188

The laws of the lands

Throughout his writings, Rawls updated and amended his ideas, as suggested by the "revised" and "expanded" editions of TJ and PL that I cite here. *The Law of Peoples* (Rawls, 1999a) (LP), which extended the argument to international relations, also included the central article, "The Idea of Public Reason Revisited," that had been integrated into the expanded edition of PL, as well.

the law of peoples

LP was much shorter and less detailed in its argumentation than either TJ or PL; several strokes impaired Rawls' ability to work from the mid-1990s until his passing in 2002 (on Rawls' biography, see Pogge, 2007). Nevertheless, LP presented both a specific treatment of international justice and supplementary analyses of the place of individuals and institutions, reason and publicity, in the accomplishment of justice, locally and globally. LP also held implications for general questions of communication: How might people – and peoples – engage in deliberation and debate about the right and the good across national, linguistic, and cultural boundaries to work out the laws applying to their different lands?

a realistic utopia

> what is, what ought to be, and what could be – Chapter 1, p. 2

> the criterion of reciprocity – p. 109

Rawls (1999a) framed the Law of Peoples as a "realistic utopia" in that it "extends what are ordinarily thought to be the limits of practicable political possibility" (p. 11). LP continued a hopeful line of argument, developed from TJ through PL, for a basic institutional structure of international justice with fairness as the end and reason as the means. Citing Jean-Jacques Rousseau's (1920/1762) *The Social Contract*, LP observed the difference between what is and what could be, < and started from a premise of "men being taken as they are and laws as they might be" (p. 98). Again, priority was given to the right and to laws, as least as they might be, rather than to the good as variously defined by "men." According to agreed principles and procedures of the right, the purpose must be to approximate basic equality for all human beings in pursuing *their* good. Rawls (1999a) was acutely aware that his argument could be construed as "ethnocentric or merely western," but responded that the Law of Peoples could be considered "objective" in the practical and procedural sense already noted: a reasonable structure of cooperation that "satisfies the criterion of reciprocity" (p. 121). <

the second original position

peoples vs. states

LP relied, once again, on the model or criterion of the original position: "The content of a reasonable Law of Peoples is ascertained by using the idea of the original position a second time with the parties now understood to be the representatives of peoples" (Rawls, 1999a: 17). Two aspects of this proposal, in particular, called for clarification. First, "why peoples and not states?" (p. 23). Rawls' intention was "to highlight their moral character and the reasonably just, or decent, nature of their regimes" (p. 27). Here, LP picked up on a central theme, namely, the distinction between the rational and the reasonable, which had motivated the practical-political turn of PL, away from the comprehensive doctrine of TJ. Following a principle of rationality, "world politics is still marked by the struggles of states for power, prestige, and wealth in a condition of global anarchy." In the world that Rawls observed, public reason was, in fact, not being practiced. "If *rationality* excludes the *reasonable* [then] a state [...] ignores the criterion of reciprocity in dealing with other societies" (p. 28, emphasis in original).

Second, why does the second original position not feature individual citizens reasoning about the principles and procedures of a basic structure for world society? Rawls (1999a) offered two kinds of responses. On the one hand, he assumed that such an arrangement would be impracticable, even considering the reflective and deliberative role of "peoples" through their various "associations and federations":

> Here I follow Kant's lead in *Perpetual Peace* (1795) in thinking that a world government – by which I mean a unified political regime with the legal powers normally exercised by central governments – would either be a global despotism or else would rule over a fragile empire torn by frequent civil strife.
>
> *p. 36*

On the other hand, to Rawls, the general status of the model of the original position is not affected in any way by the practical and political difference between citizens and delegates: "the use of the original position at the second level [is] a model of representation in exactly the same way it is at the first" (p. 33). This is because "it models what we would regard – you and I, here and now – as fair conditions under which the parties, this time the rational representatives of liberal peoples, are to specify the Law of Peoples, guided by appropriate reasons" (p. 32). Given the difference between people and peoples as cognitive and communicative entities and agents, at least this aspect of Rawls' utopia seemed less than realistic or practicable.

The outcome of the second original position is the Principles of the Law of Peoples, covering the freedom, independence, and equality of peoples; their observance of treaties and of a duty of non-intervention, coupled with a right of self-defense as moderated by restrictions on the conduct of war; and the honoring of shared human rights. In addition, "Peoples have a duty to assist other peoples living under unfavorable conditions that prevent their having a just or decent political and social regime." Rawls (1999a) characterized these as "familiar and traditional principles of justice among free and democratic peoples" (p. 37), and he implied that they might be self-evident: "the representatives of well-ordered peoples simply reflect on the advantages of these principles of

the Principles of the Law of Peoples

equality among peoples and see no reason to depart from them or to propose alternatives." Compared to both TJ and PL, then, in LP the "parties are not given a menu of alternative principles and ideals from which to select." Rawls took the Principles of the Law of Peoples to be "superior to any others" (p. 41). In this way, LP eliminated procedural or deliberative elements from the second original position, which left open the question of where, then, the principles of international justice come from: Are they absolutely rational or contingently reasonable?

liberal peoples

In the second original position, it is liberal peoples that arrive at the Principles of the Law of Peoples – liberal in the sense anticipated by PL for one people: having "a reasonably just constitutional democratic government" and "a moral nature," and being united by "common sympathies" (Rawls, 1999a: 23), but holding no overarching comprehensive doctrine of the good. The next question is "how far liberal peoples are to tolerate nonliberal peoples" (p. 59). Rawls first identified what he called peoples with a "decent consultation hierarchy," so that

decent peoples

> the basic structure of the society must include a family of representative bodies whose role in the hierarchy is to take part in an established procedure of consultation and to look after […] the important interests of all members of the people.
>
> *p. 71*

well-ordered peoples

outlaw states

benevolent absolutisms

burdened societies

the duty to assist

Together, liberal and decent peoples make up a category of "well-ordered peoples" (p. 63). In contrast, a third type of outlaw states "think a sufficient reason to engage in war is that war advances, or might advance, the regime's rational (not reasonable) interests" (p. 90). (The terminology seemed to suggest that only states and their regimes, not peoples, can be outlaw.) Fourth, "we have benevolent absolutisms: they honor most human rights, but because they deny their members a meaningful role in making political decisions, they are not well-ordered" (p. 63). The fifth and final type is societies burdened by unfavorable conditions, that is, societies that "lack the political and cultural traditions, the human capital and know-how, and, often, the material and technological resources needed to be well-ordered" – which implies why "well-ordered peoples have a *duty* to assist burdened societies" (p. 106).

Rawls (1999a) emphasized that, as in the case of the overlapping consensus at the national level, a *modus vivendi* will not do at the international level, either. The peaceful coexistence of peoples must represent "stability for the right reasons," not merely "stability as a balance of forces" (p. 44f.). The long-term perspective is what Rawls referred to as democratic peace, which depends on a number of factors both internal and external to states and peoples. Internally, "the idea of a democratic peace" is promoted if "constitutional democratic societies" have "a certain fair equality of opportunity, especially in education and training [...] a decent distribution of income and wealth," basic social security and health care for all citizens, and "public financing of elections and ways of assuring the availability of public information on matters of policy" (p. 49f.). Externally, human rights represent "a special class of urgent rights" that obtain across borders: "First, war is no longer an admissible means of government policy and is justified only in self-defense, or in grave cases of intervention to protect human rights. And second, a government's autonomy is now limited" (p. 79). People have rights, in short, as subjects of states, but also as citizens of the world. On a rare empirical note, Rawls voiced a cautious optimism concerning the prospects for democratic peace as part of his realistic utopia, in light of international relations since 1945: "The absence of war between major established democracies is as close as anything we know to a simple empirical regularity in relations among societies" (p. 52f.).

democratic peace

human rights

LP returned to the question of who exercises what kind of reason, as part of which kind of public, introducing a distinction between public reason as idea and ideal. As an *idea*, PL had reserved public reason for the institutions and functions of formal politics, as contrasted with the background culture and Rawls' "nonpublic" culture of media. As an *ideal*, however, public reason was now credited to ordinary citizens, who "are to think of themselves *as if* they were executives and legislators" and, in the case of international relations, "ask themselves what foreign policy supported by what considerations they would think it most reasonable to advance" (Rawls, 1999a: 56f.). At least in this last respect, reason could be considered a general human capability, which may be put to a wide variety of public (and, presumably, private) uses by different social agents, from the local to the global level.

public reason as idea and ideal

Media and communication were almost entirely absent from LP. The press did not figure as a fourth estate, < an institution facilitating public reason as ideal and idea, whether locally or globally, nor did Rawls (1999a) consider how the peoples of the world come to know about, or reason with, each other, through literal and intercultural translation. LP did reaffirm the understanding emerging from TJ and PL that language is a resource *in* rather than a representation *of* the world, still without citing speech-act theory. < Having noted with regard to decent peoples that, "just

> the fourth estate – Chapter 6, p. 186

> speech-act theory – Chapter 3, p. 70

as with the idea of the reasonable in political liberalism, there is no definition of decency from which [particular] criteria can be deduced," Rawls (1999a: 67) found that, "We give it meaning by how we use it," echoing Wittgenstein (1953). With reference to the less-than-ideal conditions that decent peoples must live under, he confronted the obvious question suggesting itself, namely, "why religious or philosophical doctrines that deny full and equal liberty of conscience are not unreasonable." His response was that reason is a matter of degree: "I do not say that [decent societies] are reasonable, but rather that they are not fully unreasonable; one should allow, I think, a space between the fully unreasonable and the fully reasonable" (1999a: p. 74). Like justice as fairness, *The Law of Peoples* approached international justice as a practical question.

In the conclusion to LP, Rawls (1999a) also reaffirmed the limits of philosophy in defining and designing the institutions of justice. The premise of PL had been that political philosophy must apply "the principle of toleration to philosophy itself" (Rawls, 2005/1993: 10): Philosophy cannot deliver first premises or final ends of human existence and social coexistence. LP recalled that "it is often thought that the task of philosophy is to uncover a form of argument that will always prove convincing against all other arguments. There is, however, no such argument" (Rawls, 1999a: 123). In theory as in practice, justice comes without guarantees, locally and globally.

ANALYSIS BOX 4.1 A RAWLSIAN AGENDA

If European philosophy amounts to "a series of footnotes to Plato" (Whitehead, 1978/1929: 39), political philosophy during recent decades can be read as a set of commentaries on Rawls. Disciples and critics alike have recognized his works as agenda-setting for political philosophy and ethics; several central publications constituted direct responses to Rawls' interventions. To one side, his early version of egalitarian liberalism was challenged a few years after the publication of TJ by libertarianism in the form of Robert Nozick's *Anarchy, State, and Utopia* (1974). From that perspective, social regulation beyond a minimal state taking care of "protection against force, theft, fraud, enforcement of contracts, and so on" could not be justified (Nozick, 2013/1974: n.p.). Treating the rights of the individual as absolute

libertarianism

and the welfare of the collective as contingent, the libertarian position aligned with neoliberal approaches to politics and economy during the same period (e.g., Friedman, 1962). To the other side, the response to TJ was a revitalized interest in the role of social collectives as part of what came to be known as communitarianism. Although the contributing thinkers, including Michael Sandel (1998/1982), Charles Taylor (1985), Michael Walzer (1983), and Alasdair MacIntyre (2007/1981), resisted such a generalizing categorization, they shared an understanding of collectives as communities emerging from history with particular horizons of understanding, and of individuals as constituted in and through communities. What communitarianism rejected was the view, attributed to Rawls, that, "We are distinct individuals first, and then we form relationships and engage in co-operative arrangements with others; hence the priority of plurality over unity" (Sandel, 1998: 133). Like Nozick's libertarianism, communitarianism represented an engagement with issues beyond the academy, including a perceived decline of community in the United States that was being examined in both public debate and social sciences (e.g., Bellah, Madsen, Sullivan, Swidler, & Tipton, 1985). Taken together, the responses to Rawls came from both the right and the left of the modern political and intellectual spectrum.

neoliberalism

communitarianism

The agenda that Rawls developed, revolved around institutions as the central category for defining, realizing, and evaluating justice. Some of the main limitations and blindspots of his agenda can be identified with reference to the original position. And several of the untapped potentials of the same agenda, notably for communication and justice, follow from the idea of the overlapping consensus. Compared to the more well-known original position, the overlapping consensus, arguably, has been Rawls' most important contribution to the history of ideas and the systematics of philosophy. Whereas the overlapping consensus was not addressed specifically in LP, it holds particular implications for international relations and communications – which have received renewed attention, since the 1990s, in work on multiculturalism < and cosmopolitanism. <

A common denominator for commentaries on *the original position* has been that it offers an intuitively appealing, but ambiguous idea: < It provides a hypothetical model that is meant to orient concrete actions and arrangements in and

> multiculturalism – Chapter 2, p. 42

> cosmopolitanism – Chapter 2, p. 45

> the original position – p. 99

on history. Concerning the very idea of the original position, Nagel (2003/1973: 35) noted that it "serves to model rather than to justify" the conclusions in TJ regarding Rawls' preferred egalitarian liberalism, a point that PL recognized by referring to the original position as one possible criterion or device for arriving at the principles of justice (Rawls, 2005/1993: 227). Concerning the question of how to apply a hypothetical model to concrete historical settings, Schwarzenbach (1999/1991: 272) remarked that Rawls' conception of the

the idea of a person

person – having rights and responsibilities in designing principles and procedures of justice for the future – is a distinctively modern idea. In even longer perspectives, the key ideas of justice as fairness and political liberalism were formulated against the background of a Renaissance that had placed humans at the center of the universe (even as the Earth was being relegated to its periphery), and of an Enlightenment that had expressed renewed confidence in the capacity of human reason to keep the species at the center of everything. When TJ indicated further that, behind the veil of ignorance, the parties will "know the general facts about human society," will "understand political affairs and the principles of economic theory," and will "know the basis of social organization and the laws of human psychology" (Rawls, 1999b/1971: 119), all this background knowledge would, necessarily, be historical and articulated in culturally specific forms.

Social class and gender are among the historically contested "facts," "principles," and "laws" that can be expected to affect the choice of principles and procedures

social class

in the original position. In the case of class, as noted by Miller (2003/1974: 70), if "the general facts about human society" include "Marxist social theory," then "the general facts contained in this theory would be known in the original position," which might lead the parties to question

> the difference principle – p. 100

the difference principle. < People would accept the compensations that follow from the difference principle *only* for a society where "class conflict is moderate; there is no ruling class; [and] the basic desires characteristic of one class are not drastically different from those characteristic of another" (p. 84). Rawls tended to treat politics as a prime mover, a master of the economy, even while indicating that justice as fairness could be served by systems

property-owning democracy

of either capitalist, property-owning democracy or liberal

socialism (Rawls, 1999b/1971: xivf.). In the case of gender, Okin (1999/1989: 279) commented that, although Rawls included the family in the basic structure of society, in TJ it is "heads of families" that convene in the original position, which means that "they are not in a position to settle questions of justice *within* families." Considering PL, Baehr (1999/1996: 304) concluded that "Rawls has written into the idea of reasonableness a distinction between the political and the private" – a distinction which has been debated since the emergence of modern democracies (Habermas, 1989/1962), and which was contested by the feminist proposition that the private is political. More generally, Rawls' relative emphasis on ideal rather than non-ideal theory < entailed a focus on justice for individuals within a normal range of health and other capacities, and a corresponding neglect, for example, of what would constitute fair equality of opportunity for people with disabilities (White, 2014). Regarding the implementation of Rawls' practical theory in non-ideal circumstances, in his *oeuvre* as in Rawlsian scholarship there have been comparatively few attempts to work out the "ways in which fidelity to Rawls's liberal principles of justice requires significant, and in some cases, radical reforms to liberal democratic institutions" as they currently exist (Macleod, 2014: 165).

liberal socialism

gender

> ideal and non-ideal theory – p. 107

disability

The overlapping consensus < could be understood as an approach to historicizing and operationalizing the original position for practical, contemporary purposes. In PL, Rawls (2005/1993) had differentiated between "as-if historical" and "as-if non-historical" processes < of reflecting and deliberating about justice, but neither PL nor LP treated justice as the moving target it is – slowly, but continuously changing objects and subjects of inquiry. As objects of justice, both social structures and natural environments evolve through human interventions; as subjects of justice, individuals and collectives were different kinds of agents, for instance, in 1789 and 1989, with different degrees of hindsight and foresight. Already in TJ, Rawls (1999b/1971: 476) had departed from "a well-ordered society under favorable circumstances" in which basic "needs and material wants" can be fulfilled. As the limits of what is objectively and subjectively, materially and socially conceivable shift, so may conceptions both of the primary goods that all humans will want and of "whatever else" different individuals and groups may want

> the overlapping consensus – p. 113

> as-if historical and non-historical processes – p. 111

the objects of justice

the subjects of justice

(Rawls, 1999b/1971: 230). The basic structure of society is just that – social and subject to historical change.

When Rawls placed *institutions* at the center of justice as fairness, he outlined a social architecture that would be, if not self-correcting, then at least subject to continuous review and revision. As a representative of a second-order institution of science and scholarship that reflects and deliberates on other institutions, he practiced what he preached, revising the comprehensive doctrine of TJ through reference to the overlapping consensus in PL, and extending the model of the original position to the global level in LP. A conspicuously underdeveloped element of Rawls' conceptual architecture has been the institutions and practices of knowledge and culture, specifically the modern media, which, as noted, received a footnote and the heading of "nonpublic" culture. The basic structure of society is articulated, as idea and ideal, by both professional and lay communications traversing the public political forum and the background culture; the overlapping consensus emerges from interactions among all the institutions of the basic structure. The idea of the overlapping consensus was missing from LP (except in reference to the first, national original position and in the appended article on "The idea of public reason revisited" (Rawls, 1999b: 16, 32, 143, 151)). Nationally as well as internationally, however, consensus through public reasoning presupposes communication.

priestly and prophetic readings

Like other recognized classics, Rawls' *oeuvre* lends itself to both priestly and prophetic readings (Liszka, 1998). A priestly reading stays close to the letter and spirit of the original work, and to an established interpretive community of scholars; a prophetic reading allows for inferences and applications to unforeseen contexts of either theory or practice. One challenge for a theory of communication and justice is how to balance the two kinds of readings with a view to theory development and empirical inquiry. In the present chapter, I have identified what could be considered an overlapping consensus regarding the basic structure of Rawls' ideas; some points of priestly contestation; and certain prophetic potentials for a research agenda at the juncture of justice and communication. In subsequent chapters, I rely on the works of Rawls and other thinkers as resources for a theory of communication and justice, seeking to specify what they said, to clarify what this could have meant in context, and to explore how both the sayings and the meanings may inform what we – their readers – may go on to think, say, and do. It is practical to make the most of what people said in the past, for present and future ends. Recent work has begun to draw on archival papers, including unpublished manuscripts by Rawls and his personal notes, to reassess the implications of his *oeuvre* (Bevir, 2017). The cash-value of ideas < – William James' (2013/1907) motto for pragmatism – had been part of Rawls' early motivation, in a 1946 student paper citing the civil rights of African-Americans as an illustration, for redeveloping ethics as a form of science rather than an aspect of theology or metaphysics (Reidy, 2014). Rawls' ideas have uncashed value for a theory of communication and justice.

> the cash value of ideas – Chapter 5, p. 143

The veil of communication

The Rawls–Habermas debate revolved around different conceptions of what Rawls had termed principles and procedures, including how procedural justice might ensure substantive justice – the right outcome. < Following up on Rawls' (2011/1995) response to his opening criticism (Habermas, 2011b), in his second intervention Habermas (2011a/1996: 108) found that Rawls' "remarks do not capture the sense in which I use the expressions 'procedure' and 'procedural rationality.'" Habermas claimed to be procedural, and only procedural: The ideal speech situation is supposed to furnish the ultimate guarantee and justification for both the right and the good. Rawls' corresponding point of departure was the practical device of the original position, which he cast as the best available model from the history of ideas for developing a freestanding theory of justice in contemporary circumstances. In the end, no overlapping consensus could accommodate both Habermas' comprehensive theory of the human condition and Rawls' practical theory of justice.

> justice – procedural and substantive – p. 105

The debate between the giants stimulated an additional stream of scholarship (e.g., Finlayson & Freyenhagen, 2011b; Hedrick, 2010; Pedersen, 2012). (For a detailed analysis of the debate itself, see Finlayson, 2019.) While some contributions have found their positions to be compatible (e.g., Baynes, 2014; Lafont, 2009; McMahon, 2002), or Habermas' stance to be more persuasive (e.g., Ward, 2019), a recurring theme has been a tendency for Habermas' works, notably on global and religious communication, to slide into a Rawlsian position without explicit acknowledgment (e.g., Boettcher, 2009; Corlett, Norzagary, & Sharpless, 2010; Moon, 2003; Rasmussen, 2012). In the longer history of ideas, Rawls and Habermas represent two different philosophical temperaments with a common denominator: the virtual absence of empirical argumentation. Habermas has continued to insist that empirical evidence of *his* principles and procedures *could* be presented, while basically engaging empirical reality only as a public intellectual. Rawls took the more traditional role of a political philosopher leaving further deliberation about the practical merits of his theories up to an unspecified readership and public: "Thus justice as fairness is addressed not so much to constitutional jurists as to citizens in a constitutional regime" (Rawls, 2005/1993: 369). Though shaped by his times, for example, through participation in World War II, when he lost his Christian faith, and speaking out during the 1960s against the US involvement in the Vietnam War (on Rawls' life and work, see Galisanka, 2019; Pogge, 2007), Rawls was not a public intellectual, but a private person and an academic, his communications conditioned by a stutter and what one obituary described as "a bat-like horror of the limelight" (Rogers, 2002: n.p.).

John Rawls did not join the linguistic or communicative turns of twentieth-century philosophy, but he performed a practical turn that has been underestimated, concretely by his adaptation of insights from speech-act theory to political philosophy and ethics, and generally through his idea of the overlapping consensus and a position that "does without the concept of truth" (Rawls, 2005/1993: 94). The metaphor of the veil of ignorance began to suggest how the availability of information and the opportunity for communication are essential conditions of human cognition and social cooperation, facilitating a reflective equilibrium and an overlapping consensus. But even when the veil has been lifted, and "everyone has access to all the facts" (Rawls, 1999b/1971: 175), neither mutual understanding nor self-understanding is assured. What modern communication studies, roughly since Rawls' (1958) earliest formulation of the idea of justice as fairness, have found, is that communication itself constitutes a veil. Even face-to-face, human communication is no point-to-point transmission, no meeting of minds through authentic "contact between interiorities" (Peters, 1999: 21). On this point, Rawls' work recalled longer and wider debates about the relationship between human knowledge, social action, and communication as a mediating resource. Pragmatism – a philosophy of practice and communication that has remained a substream in the history of ideas – is the topic of the following chapter.

5

THE LONG LEGACY OF PRAGMATISM

Erro, ergo sum

In a history of ideas with the surprising title, *Being Wrong*, Kathryn Schulz (2010) told the story not of humans' quest for the truth, but of error as a constant condition of their inquiries. "No matter the domain of life, one generation's verities so often become the next generation's falsehoods [in] politics, economics, technology, law, religion, medicine, child-rearing, education" (p. 9), and, one might add, justice. A trade book written by a journalist, not a philosophical treatise, Schulz' volume was a rare exception to the many publications that, over the centuries, again and again, have claimed to be right. This chapter recovers a substream in the history of ideas that has recognized not only the persistence of error, but the primacy of practice over theory. Practice is both the beginning and the end of theory. The legacy of pragmatism is captured in the proposition, *erro, ergo sum* (Jensen, 1995: 192) – I err, therefore I am. My presence in the world is manifested in constant feedback from the natural environment and through my communicative interactions over time with other humans about the conditions we share and must act on.

In a summary formulation, the philosopher Hilary Putnam (1994: 152) identified four theses of pragmatism:

> (1) *antiskepticism*: pragmatists hold that *doubt* requires justification just as much as belief (recall Peirce's famous distinction between "real" and "philosophical" doubt); (2) *fallibilism*: pragmatists hold that there is never a metaphysical

antiskepticism

fallibilism

> guarantee to be had that such-and-such a belief will never need revision (that one can be both fallibilistic *and* antiskeptical is perhaps *the* unique insight of American pragmatism); (3) the thesis that there is no *fundamental* dichotomy between "facts" and "values"; and (4) the thesis that, in a certain sense, practice is primary in philosophy.

Whereas Putnam was characterizing the American tradition of philosophical pragmatism mostly associated with the names of Charles Sanders Peirce, William James, and John Dewey, the theses captured common themes in a substream of pragmatism throughout the history of ideas. Part epistemology, part methodology, pragmatism represents an intellectual stance at the intersection of theory and practice – or science and society, as currently understood. Compared to other classic questions of philosophy – *what* is reality, and *how* may humans know about reality – pragmatism has foregrounded the *why* of inquiry: Why do individuals and collectives want to know and communicate about particular aspects of reality so as to inform their plans in life? Why is reality, as far as humans are concerned?

why is reality?

In this chapter, I trace the development of pragmatism from ancient through modern to contemporary conceptions of the relationship between theory and practice, reemphasizing the place of communication in translating back and forth between the two endeavors in the pursuit of justice and other important social ends. While the tradition lends itself to normative applications, pragmatists only rarely have broached questions of justice (Dieleman, Rondel, & Voparil, 2017).

> the linguistic and communicative turns – Chapter 1, p. 9

The pragmatist legacy extends from Aristotle, via early modern thinkers, to the linguistic and communicative turns of the twentieth century. < The first section recovers the classical understanding of philosophy and scholarship as reflective and analytical means to human ends – the pursuit of good lives by individuals and collectives. Aristotle's system of sciences counted theoretical, practical, and productive sciences, each of which had different ends and implications. His productive sciences, notably, included rhetoric, which was designed, in part, to enable communities to consider alternative realities with a view to the future.

The second section addresses the turn of modern philosophy toward one prototypical scientific method – a shift from a contemplation of the cosmos toward the control of nature. In the process, the productive sciences were reconceived as instrumental approaches to transforming the material (and increasingly human-made) environment. It was this narrowing of the way of inquiry < that the American pragmatists challenged as they sought to reclaim a place for philosophy within a modern system of sciences. > the way of inquiry – p. 141

The third section characterizes the nineteenth-century American tradition of pragmatism as a distinctive philosophy of communication that, in its various incarnations, gave priority not to individual thinkers, but to communities of inquiry < – philosophical, professional, and public – as the sites and sources of reflection and deliberation about what could be, and what should be done; the remainder of the chapter lays out the legacy of pragmatism for contemporary research on communication and justice. In the early twentieth century, Ludwig Wittgenstein served an important transitional role as an ambivalent heir to the American tradition, before the wider substream of pragmatism fed into current debates about the practical relevance of philosophy for social progress. During the second half of the twentieth century, pragmatism was recruited, most prominently, by Richard Rorty for the cause of postmodernism and by Jürgen Habermas for his practical-political project. > communities of inquiry – p. 141

I conclude the present chapter by restating the untapped potential of pragmatism for further research and debate on communication and justice. In one of his student papers, John Rawls (1946) had motivated his personal turn from theology and metaphysics toward philosophy and ethics with reference to William James' (2013/1907) motto for pragmatism: Ideas about what is good and right can and should have practical or cash value. < > the cash-value of ideas – p. 143

Theoretical, practical, and productive sciences

Aristotle's account of different sciences offered a systematic framework for considering the relationship between theory and practice, and it came to inform centuries of philosophy and scholarship. While originally part of a comprehensive metaphysics, as a heuristic framework his system of sciences helps to identify the main stages in a historically shifting understanding of theory and practice. To Aristotle, the *what* and *how* of any inquiry – the subject matter and the method – were decided by the ends, the *why*. The first book of the *Nicomachean Ethics* (Aristotle, 1886: 1), for example, is entitled simply, "The end." Aristotle explains here that, "every art and every kind of inquiry, and likewise every act and purpose, seems to aim at some good." Depending on what individuals and collectives take to be the aim or purpose of their lives, they will strive to know particular kinds of things, and different ends are served by different sciences that rely on different means: conceptual frameworks, analytical methods, verbal and numerical notations, and means of dissemination.

the Aristotelian system of sciences

Table 5.1 lays out the Aristotelian system (Levine, 1995: 111). The theoretical sciences (*theōria*), first of all, were said to offer certain knowledge about eternal matters; examples include mathematics and physics. Compared to the modern natural sciences, however, in Aristotle's perspective both the eternal matters and the human knowledge about them were imbued with metaphysical meaning. Theoretical truths were not just proven, but contemplated as part of the order and beauty of the universe. Practical sciences (*praxis*), next, provide probable and reasonable knowledge about the conditions and consequences of human actions and social interactions. Ethics and politics are practical sciences that address individual and collective aspects of right conduct. They are practical in the sense that they examine and evaluate the extent to which humans actualize the potential of their lives. In contrast to the eternal universe, which invites appreciation in a passive mode, in practical matters humans can and must make active choices. Productive sciences (*poiēsis*), finally, develop useful and more or less artful things – artifacts. Both the artifacts themselves and the processes of production were understood by Aristotle in a broad sense, including the building of ships (engineering), the healing of diseases (medicine), and the delivery of persuasive speeches (rhetoric). The products of science and scholarship, thus, include physical objects, changes of state in an organism, as well as anticipated or merely imagined realities.

rhetoric as a productive science

In Table 5.1, the interrelations between the three prototypes of science are suggested by another Aristotelian typology, namely,

TABLE 5.1 Aristotle's organization of the sciences

	Theoretical sciences	*Practical sciences*	*Productive sciences*
SUBJECT MATTER (*Material Cause*)	Natural substances (*ta physei*)	Actions (*ta prakta*)	Artifacts (*ta poieta*)
METHODS (*Formal Cause*)	Induction of invariable causes and properties; deduction	Deliberation about variables and opinions	Techniques of construction
COGNITIVE FACULTY (*Efficient Cause*)	Intuitive reason (*nous*) and scientific knowledge (*episteme*)	Practical wisdom (*phronesis*)	Art (*techne*)
AIM (*Final Cause*)	To know	To act well	To make things

Source: Levine, 1995: 111.

material, formal, efficient, and final causes. The four causes together indicate the necessary and sufficient conditions for something to exist or happen in the world. In the second book of his *Physics* (1886), Aristotle used the example of a bronze statue. Its material cause is the bronze; the formal cause is the structure in which the bronze becomes recognizable as a sculpture of a familiar cultural type. The efficient cause is the acting force or agent that brought the sculpture into existence, most likely a trained artist. And the final cause is the *telos* or end of bringing form and matter together in a particular sculpture: The representation might serve to honor either a human being or a god.

material, formal, efficient, and final causes

Behind the seemingly simple example, additional causalities are at work. Bronze is a particular quality of matter, extracted from other matter and refined in a process requiring considerable material and mental resources. The form, similarly, bears witness to sophisticated skills and inherited conventions of how to give matter a meaningful shape. The process, further, requires artistic competences that are embodied in the artist as the immediate efficient cause, but which have been discovered and cultivated through generations. And the final cause amounts to a social institution of sharing – communicating – certain signs and symbols for either secular or religious ends. Ends become causes when they are enacted by humans, on matter through form, typically in several steps requiring collaboration and communication.

The background to the Aristotelian system was existential considerations concerning the human condition: "the Greeks tried to tackle a question highly characteristic of their culture, namely, which is the best and most desirable of lives" (Lobkowicz, 1967: 3). Aristotle identified three different ways or "walks of life" that "a man free of the immediate necessities of life may choose (the life of enjoyment, political life, and the life of contemplation)" (p. 3). He went on to prefer, in the first instance, the philosopher's life of contemplation and, as a second choice, the statesman or citizen's deliberation and participation in the community. In comparison, it is only "the vulgar mob which identifies the Good with pleasure" (p. 4) (even though a life of pleasure must be considered infinitely preferable to the dependent lives of women, laborers, and slaves). In this worldview, the theoretical sciences would support a life of contemplation, whereas the practical sciences were to serve the life of people in the *polis*, leaving the productive sciences to perform ancillary functions. Aristotle recognized, however, that, like the different sciences, the different walks of life intersect. Theory and practice are "dimensions of human existence rather than realizable types of existing," so that

the walks of life

"a good politician could not avoid being a philosopher, and vice versa" (p. 26).

The modern inversion of theory and practice

Aristotle's theoretical sciences were supposed to establish what *is*, always has been, always will be. The practical sciences addressed what *ought* to be through human intervention. And the productive sciences explored what *could* be in either a material or an imagined sense, including the production and sharing of new insights through language and other signs and symbols. In his seminal history of the ideas of theory and practice from Aristotle to Karl Marx, Nicholas Lobkowicz (1967) retraced how the broad mainstream of Western philosophy reconfigured the three ancient sciences, subordinating theory to practice while redefining practice as production: the mastery of nature, including the human body, and of matter in the shape of built environments. This shift entailed a long-term secularization of scholarship, but also residual questions about the order of the universe, the nature of community, and the meaning of a human life. Such questions have continued to challenge the increasingly specialized modern system of sciences regarding the appropriate ends and means of different kinds of inquiry.

secularization

A voice of medieval Christianity, Augustine of Hippo, still referred back to Aristotle's different walks of life and found that, "so long as a man's faith is preserved, he may choose any of them without detriment to his eternal interests" (Augustine, 2009: n.p.). And, to Augustine, the preservation of the faith required both theory and practice, contemplation as well as action: "It no longer counts whether one is a philosopher, a politician, or a combination of both; what counts, regardless of one's walk of life, is the right balance between one's contemplative striving for God and one's actions of charity" (Lobkowicz, 1967: 64). Augustine, further, prefigured modern debates on whether and how humans are in a position to know anything, making specific reference to error: "I am not at all afraid of the arguments of the Academicians, who say, What if you are deceived? For if I am deceived, I am" (Augustine, 2009: n.p.). In an adaptation of Augustine to the Cartesian formula, his dictum has been restated as "*fallor, ergo sum*" (Schulz, 2010: 6) – I fail, therefore I am. Augustine felt reassured, however, that failure and imperfection are characteristic of human practices, not of the theoretical, divine order of the universe. Even if humans can "recognize in ourselves the image of God," they are "very far removed from Him" (Augustine, 2009: n.p.). Like the

fallor, ergo sum

ancients, Augustine would contemplate the universe as an already perfect theory.

The moderns took it upon themselves to prove the existence and nature of reality in practice and painstaking detail. While some aspects of reality could be seen to manifest themselves in the present, others would have to be extracted or made – produced – for the future. Lobkowicz (1967) ascribed the most succinct statement of this practical-productive turn to Francis Bacon:

the practical-productive turn

> what neither the ancients nor the scholastics would have agreed with is Bacon's claim that *theoretical* knowledge has to prove itself by 'fruits and works'; moreover, they probably would not even have understood Bacon's assertion that theoretical knowledge ought to be striven for *because* it has some fruits.
>
> *Lobkowicz, 1967: 90*

In his *Novum Organum* (1620), Bacon clarified that it is not only that "the fruits and [works] are the sureties and vouchers, as it were, for the truth of philosophy." The fruits of true knowledge also serve practice in the sense of production: the human exercise of power over nature and, in turn, over other humans. "Knowledge and human power are synonymous, since the ignorance of the cause frustrates the effect; for nature is only subdued by submission, and that which in contemplative philosophy corresponds with the cause in practical science becomes the rule" (Bacon, 2014: n.p.). Whoever knows the causes that control nature, gains the power to rule the world. Knowledge is power, with the practical potential to advance or impede justice.

knowledge as power

Being an early modern thinker, Bacon "systematized and raised to a method the mentality characteristic of Renaissance artisans and artisan-scientists," but he remained "basically antitheoretical and pragmatic" (Lobkowicz, 1967: 92, 115). Bacon offered "a last articulation of the skepticism which had pervaded philosophy and science after the thirteenth century" (p. 115), as philosophers and scientists were struggling to reconcile "the medieval otherworldly conception" (p. 109) with empirical studies of the cosmos. It was René Descartes who, as the vanguard of a "rationalist reaction" to skepticism (p. 109), advanced a full-fledged modern theory of inquiry. In a first step, Descartes famously confronted the option of absolute skepticism, but concluded that, *cogito, ergo sum* – I think, therefore I am; and therefore I can know and do things in and on reality. In a second step, he identified mathematics as the generic interface between subjects and their objects: "all reality accessible

cogito, ergo sum

to man ought to be deduced from and in a sense even reduced to mathematics" (p. 116).

Descartes' position signaled a break with the classical modes of inquiry that had allowed for "various species and subspecies of knowledge: theoretical and practical, physics, mathematics, metaphysics, knowledge about doing and about making, etc." Now, mathematics was to be conceived as the theory and method of everything. "In a word, there is *a single and identical method* to be applied to each and every field of knowledge – a method discovered hitherto only in mathematics but ultimately reflecting the very nature of human reason itself" (Lobkowicz, 1967: 117). Whereas the many practical fruits and works of the modern experimental sciences helped to legitimate such a single, central perspective on reality, debates on whether there is one and only one scientific method – one privileged repertoire of signs and symbols for capturing and communicating about reality – have continued into the twenty-first century.

a theory and method of everything

Without either an Aristotelian final cause or a divine prime mover to guide them, modern thinkers found themselves alone at the center of the universe. Representing the eighteenth-century Enlightenment, Immanuel Kant was "faced with the problem as to how to preserve the unlimited rights of modern science, its mathematical method, and the ensuing Cartesian spirit without surrendering genuine ethics" (Lobkowicz, 1967: 123). Kant's response was the "radical modern claim" to self-determination through reason: < "it is man's very nature to define for himself his position in the universe, so that in the end all except strictly physical laws are imposed upon man *by himself*" (p. 135). Humans make themselves by giving themselves laws. But human laws intersect with natural laws. Karl Marx added the insight that humans make themselves, not least, by re-making their material environment, with long-term consequences for the structure of human societies and the lives of their individual citizens. Appreciating the fruits and works of modern sciences, "philosophers began to realize that the [notion of self-determination] could be extended beyond the realm of 'doing' to the realm of 'making,' from the realm of ethics and politics to that of economics and technology." The human condition could be seen as subject to change by humans themselves. "Kant's philosophy, later that of German idealism, and, last but not least, the ideas of the young Marx are the last outcome of [a] peculiar self-confidence [...] an expression of the basic intent of postmedieval man" (Lobkowicz, 1967: 139). From the agricultural revolution through the industrial revolution into an unknown Anthropocene future (Lewis & Maslin, 2015), the

> self-determination through reason – Chapter 2, p. 35

human laws and natural laws

the Anthropocene

human species has re-made what once was, with a view to what could be, raising ever more questions of what ought to be.

Across religious and secular orientations, philosophers continued to ponder the nature of human agency – the window of opportunity between chance and necessity. < Descartes, for one, subscribed to the ontological proof of God's existence, which holds that since God is the most perfect being conceivable, existence is necessarily one of His attributes. Descartes' window of opportunity was framed by eternal necessity. Also Kant reaffirmed that the faculty of reason obliges humans to believe in God. < Even Marx, who termed religion the opiate of the people, was ambiguous regarding human agency and the predetermination of human history, whether "man *should* rise and overthrow existing conditions," or whether humans' "'material practice' necessarily *does* overthrow" these conditions in the long run (Lobkowicz, 1967: 418).

> the window between chance and necessity – Chapter 2, p. 23

> Kant on reason and religion – Chapter 2, p. 37

the opiate of the people

From the late nineteenth century, classic debates on materialism and idealism, science and religion, theory and practice, were given a distinctive articulation by a group of American philosophers. American pragmatism, on the one hand, recovered classic conceptions of theory and practice (for overview, see Misak, 2013), recognizing theories as conceptual means to practical ends. On the other hand, the tradition prefigured the linguistic and communicative turns of twentieth-century philosophy. In the following section, I sum up the contribution of the American tradition to the longer substream of pragmatism and its implications for current debates about communication and justice: its operational definition of theories in terms of the practical difference they make; < its communicative conception of humans' interactions with reality and with each other; and its performative understanding of belief as that which individuals and collectives will be willing to act on when everything – or enough – has been said and done.

> how to make a difference – p. 155

The American revival of pragmatism

The pragmatic maxim

"The college philosopher tended to be also the college minister or moral tutor and appointments in philosophy were reserved for the religiously orthodox. This was about to change" (Misak, 2013: ix). Like scholars elsewhere, American philosophers in the late nineteenth century found themselves in an intellectual crossfire of naturalism and empiricism. To one side, Charles Darwin

naturalism

(2013/1859) had introduced evidence of natural evolution, substantiating Friedrich Nietzsche's (2001/1882) subsequent dictum that God was dead. To the other side, empirical sciences of both nature and culture had long been delimiting ever more aspects of reality as fields of increasingly specialized empirical inquiry. The inversion of theory and practice in the longer history of science and society was casting philosophy as a residual field serving other disciplines, in addition to contemplating supposedly eternal questions. The American pragmatists took up the challenge of reinvigorating philosophy and reconnecting it to a modern system of sciences.

empiricism

Several key figures of American pragmatism started out as members of a reading group in Cambridge, Massachusetts, which – under the ironic title, The Metaphysical Club (Menand, 2001) – explored issues ranging from classical and religious metaphysics to the modern idea of one and only one scientific method. The pragmatic maxim, outlining a third position, was presented by Charles Sanders Peirce, first to The Metaphysical Club, then in an 1878 series of publications, and it was disseminated to a wider audience by William James several decades later:

The Metaphysical Club

> There can *be* no difference any-where that doesn't *make* a difference elsewhere – no difference in abstract truth that doesn't express itself in a difference in concrete fact and in conduct consequent upon that fact, imposed on somebody, somehow, somewhere and somewhen.
>
> *James, 2013/1907: n.p.*

The pragmatists were challenging the abstract conceptual analyses of their contemporary colleagues, advancing what Peirce termed critical commonsensism. Reality constantly manifests itself in human experience; real doubts arise in concrete instances, not in blanket skepticism as a philosophical position. Peirce even compared the process of learning from experience to practical jokes: "I don't remember that any one has advocated a system of teaching by practical jokes, mostly cruel. That, however, describes the method of our great teacher, Experience" (Peirce, 1931–58: 5.51). The pragmatists' fallibilism went beyond the contemporary scientific gold standard of falsificationism (Popper, 1972a/1934) that poses and tests null hypotheses. It is not only specific hypotheses, but their underlying premises, and entire paradigms, that regularly fail.

critical commonsensism

Far from rejecting the value and relevance of theory, American pragmatism underscored the productive role of inquiry in anticipating – representing and communicating about – the various elements and processes of reality, including what has not yet been thought about by any individual or affirmed by any community. Thought experiments are as important as laboratory experiments for considering what could make a practical difference. Table 5.1 had suggested the relative focus of different sciences on either material or immaterial objects of inquiry. Aristotle's theoretical sciences focused on natural substances, and the productive sciences were designed to generate (more or less) concrete outcomes. In Aristotle's terminology (Ross, 1923; Wieland, 1962), productive sciences actualize the potentials of reality in material, conceptual, or discursive forms, sometimes all of these: Ships and houses are thought of by individuals and represented to others before they are built through collaboration. In comparison, Aristotle's practical sciences addressed more elusive objects of study – appropriate human actions and social interactions, but also failures to act in the right way or at the right time, all of which may register for no more than an instant in the minds of those involved.

material and immaterial objects of inquiry

potential and actualization

As human projects and social enterprises, however, all sciences depend on means of representation and interaction, from mathematical models and experimental protocols to ethical dilemmas and models of democratic governance. In this regard, the discursively and intellectually productive moments of inquiry are constitutive of all sciences. In his semiotics, Peirce elaborated how language, logic, and other genres and modalities of communication enable inquiry and mediate theory and practice. Like scientific communities, wider social communities and political publics depend on communication to decide what makes – or ought to make – a practical difference for designing principles and procedures to inform their coexistence, for justice.

Communication as representation and resource

Like classical rhetoric, < modern semiotics – the study of signs – is a productive science with important ethical and political implications. Compared to more text-centered variants of semiotics that have drawn on linguistics and literary studies (Barthes, 1973/1957; Saussure, 1959/1916) to perform critical cultural studies, Peirce departed from logic and epistemology, and returned to the foundational issues of modern philosophy: 'What can be known about the world – through which signs and symbols?' While standing on the shoulders of Kant, Peirce proposed to move beyond the residual dualism of Kant's transcendental idealism, < namely, the notion that humans grasp for reality in brief moments

> rhetoric as a productive science – p. 130

semiotics

> Kant's transcendental idealism – Chapter 1, p. 8

and delimited forms of elementary contact between subject and object, through a narrow conduit of transcendental categories. Peirce, instead, approached signs as constitutive of all encounters between subjects and their objects of inquiry as well as between the subjects as they engage objects of common interest. Signs are not secondary *representations* of a primary, brute reality of facts; reality *presents* itself to experience in and through a variety of signs (Bergman, 2004: 299–309). To Peirce, signs were neither troublesome boundaries nor tenuous lifelines between *das Ding an sich* and *das Ding für uns*, but interfaces maintaining our relationship with reality and with each other.

reality as presented and represented

In Peirce's model of the sign, cognition of and communication about reality involve not two, but three components:

> A sign, or *representamen*, is something which stands to somebody for something in some respect or capacity. It addresses somebody, that is, creates in the mind of that person an equivalent sign, or perhaps a more developed sign. That sign which it creates I call the *interpretant* of the first sign. The sign stands for something, its *object*.
>
> *Peirce, 1931–58: 2.228*

Peirce's premise was that perception, reflection, and deliberation are all mediated by signs. Signs, accordingly, come in many shapes and forms, from sense impressions and basic statements, to formal and informal arguments, audiovisual narratives, and computer algorithms. The objects to which signs refer, equally, include many levels or aspects of reality. They are grammatical objects – objects of interest and analysis. Material entities, subconscious desires, and collective beliefs can all be considered real, because they "make a difference" for "consequent conduct" (James, 2013/1907: n.p.).

interpretants

Interpretants hold a special place in Peirce's model of signs and in his formulation of pragmatism. The term refers *not* to human interpreters, but to second-order signs, mental constructs by which humans orient themselves in and interact with reality. Each interpretant amounts to a step in a longer process of cognition and communication across time and space, what Peirce referred to as semiosis. Figure 5.1 lays out the dual status of interpretants: they are, at once, orientations toward particular objects and points of departure for further interpretations (interpretants). The dotted line suggests that all interpretations – all awareness of and interaction with reality – is mediated in and through signs. Signs are not secondary representations, but primary resources for the

semiosis

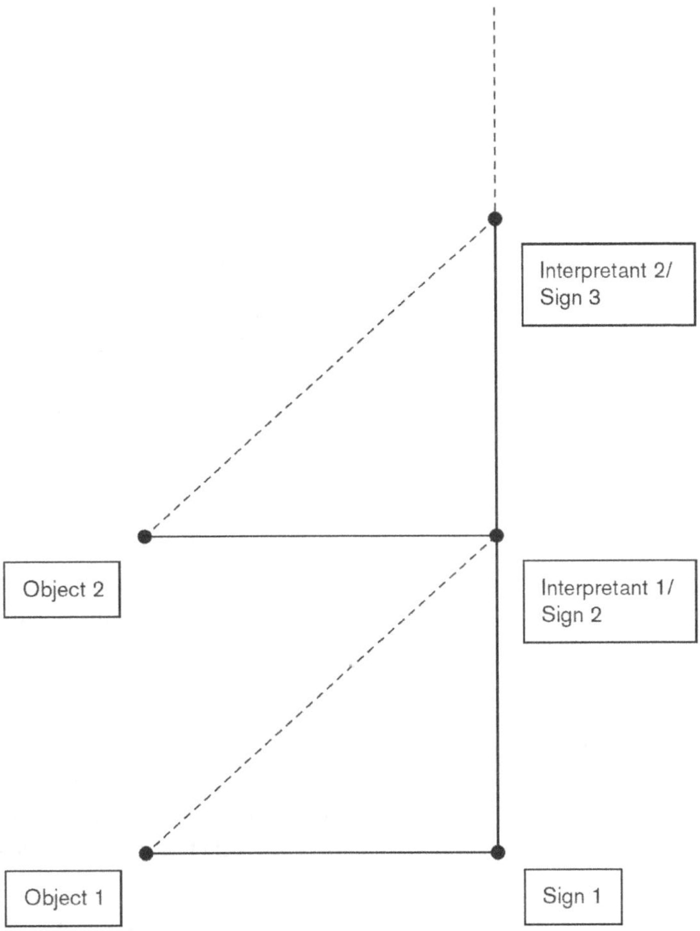

FIGURE 5.1 Peirce's model of signs

(practical and theoretical) engagement of reality. Like interpretants, objects present themselves in sequences of "equivalent" or "more developed" objects of interest and inquiry. The wider implication of Peirce's semiotics was an Aristotelian realism, < which takes reality to consist in a highly differentiated and widely distributed set of phenomena, each with multiple states and interrelations, rather than any primary realm of either matter or spirit. Material, mental, and discursive manifestations of what there is, are all real – different, but equal objects of inquiry.

> Aristotelian realism – Chapter 2, p. 33

different, but equal signs and objects

Different aspects of reality lend themselves to different kinds of research, for different ends, through different kinds of signs. Signs are necessary conditions for justifying that we do know certain things that make a practical difference, and which we will be willing to act on, as individuals and as collectives. American pragmatism advanced an understanding of inquiry as a communal and communicative practice that responds to practical problems. Scientific communities act on behalf of and, at best, in the common interest of greater communities or publics, always with a view to the future.

Individual beliefs and collective actions

> *cogito, ergo sum* – p. 133

Descartes had contrasted absolute doubt with an absolute certainty: *Cogito, ergo sum.* < As suggested by the singular verbs, Descartes' approached the problem of human knowledge from the individual's perspective. The American pragmatists questioned both Descartes' problem and his solution. Peirce commented acidly that "this initial skepticism will be a mere self-deception [...] Let us not pretend to doubt in philosophy what we do not doubt in our hearts" (Peirce, 1958: 40). Doubts only have merit and relevance insofar as they make a practical difference, and as far as a community of inquirers is concerned. Doubts, equally, must be resolved by the community:

truth as public

> Unless truth be recognized as *public* – as that of which *any* person would come to be convinced if he carried his inquiry, his sincere search for immovable belief, far enough – then there will be nothing to prevent each one of us from adopting an utterly futile belief of his own which all the rest will disbelieve.
>
> *Peirce, 1958: 398*

belief as orientation toward action

The antiskepticism of the American pragmatists was expressed in the understanding that beliefs already constitute orientations toward action – which may either succeed or fail in practice. Rather than being a clearly bounded and carefully weighed opinion or attitude – a representation of something in the world – a belief constitutes a readiness to act in relation to that something, one interpretant within an extended process of semiosis and social interaction. Whereas this processual understanding of human consciousness was widespread in philosophy and science when American pragmatism was taking shape, as advocated by John Stuart Mill in his influential *A System of Logic* (Mill, 2009/1843), it was the work of a less famous philosopher, Alexander Bain, that fed into American pragmatism. In line with the emphasis on the practical difference that ideas make, and with the understanding of inquiry as a communal practice, Bain and the pragmatist tradition insisted on the inseparability of human thought and social behavior:

> Belief has no meaning except in reference to our actions. But Aristotle's distinction between potentiality and actuality applies. In respect of matters upon which we have no present occasion to act, our belief is "an attitude or disposition of preparedness to act" when occasion offers. Under civilization and education we acquire numerous beliefs of a scientific and historical kind, upon which it is not likely we shall ever have occasion to act. But the readiness is there if the unexpected occasion should arise, and the readiness constitutes the belief.
>
> *Fisch, 1954: 419f.*

communities of inquiry

problematic situations

In his seminal writings, Peirce tended to treat communities of inquiry in rather abstract terms and with particular reference to philosophy and science. Other pragmatists, notably John Dewey, the youngest of the three classic figures, extended the role of communities to problematic situations (Dewey, 1903) in a broader range of social domains. When individual doubts or social conflicts frustrate or complicate an ongoing flow of activities, this situation calls for inquiry, whether as instantaneous reflection by individuals or as a prolonged time-out from practice in dedicated social institutions, from schools to parliaments. Dewey went on to advocate and practice educational reform, in part as an avenue toward social reform, which would be promoted by the broader and deeper participation of private citizens in public life. Dewey's approach to inquiry as a society-wide and stepwise process helps to explain why, among the founding figures of American pragmatism, it was Dewey who most directly engaged contemporary issues of communication and justice. <

> Dewey and communication theory – p. 143

the long run of inquiry

do not block the way of inquiry

The American pragmatists still struggled with the question of truth. Peirce (1958: 398), as noted, understood truth as public, as that which studies "would" produce if they were to be carried "far enough" by open-ended communities of inquiry. The subjunctive formulation suggested Peirce's reliance on a counterfactual premise or regulative assumption about the long run of inquiry, which also helps to explain Peirce's (1931–58: 1.135) motto for pragmatism: "Do not block the way of inquiry." Reality is what humans *would* come to know if they had unlimited time and resources available for their inquiries and communications – which, of course, they don't. But continued inquiry, in the face of error throughout life and across generations, manifests a constitutive inclination of humans, grounded in evolution and with evident existential ramifications, as we seek to be right in the present with a view to the future.

the will to believe

Recognizing the inevitable end of inquiry in the short run and in practice, William James introduced the idea of a will to believe. His suggestion was that, in matters that are sufficiently "momentous," one cannot wait for all the evidence to be in, or to be finally agreed upon: "*Moral questions* immediately present themselves as questions whose solution cannot wait for sensible proof. A moral question is a question not of what sensibly exists, but of what is good, or would be good if it did exist" (James, 1919/1897: 22). Part of James' motivation was to still reserve a special place among "momentous" beliefs for religion. But the need to conclude inquiries and communications is part of the human condition. Whether critical to life or existence or not, individual reflections and collective deliberations must and do come to an end. < Human rationality is bounded by practical circumstances – time limits, fallible human cognitions and judgments, and the historically available media of deliberation and interaction. <

> the end of communication – Chapter 1, p. 1

> bounded rationality – Chapter 7, p. 199

American pragmatism had reasserted the productively imaginative and practically relevant contribution of philosophy to other sciences and to society, and the tradition fed into the history of ideas in at least two respects. First, the understanding of inquiry as a social activity, conducted by communities and enabled by their communications, prefigured the linguistic and communicative turns of twentieth-century philosophy. < As the following section explains, the later phase of Ludwig Wittgenstein's seminal contributions to contemporary philosophy stood on the shoulders of American pragmatism. Second, the American pragmatists' restatement of the idea that practice is both the beginning and the end of theory, that "belief has no meaning except in reference to our actions" (Fisch, 1954: 419), inspired other disciplines and interdisciplinary fields to draw on pragmatism as an intellectual framework for engaging problematic situations in politics, culture, and society at large.

> linguistic and communicative turns – Chapter 1, p. 9

It may be appropriate that, as a philosophy of practice, American pragmatism has invited multiple and mutually competing prophetic readings regarding its implications and applications (Liszka, 1998). < In the aftermath of its American moment, several theorists of justice, including Habermas and Rawls, became heirs to the longer substream of pragmatism.

> priestly and prophetic readings – Chapter 4, p. 124

Priests, prophets, and heirs of pragmatism

Cambridge pragmatisms

The pragmatism that originated in Cambridge, Massachusetts, was contested from the outset, and the tradition faced several challenges in communicating its message. Peirce never synthesized his seminal ideas in a final form in major publications; his scattered writings are still in the process of being published in an authoritative edition (Peirce, 1982: vol. 1ff.) (for key works, see Peirce, 1992–98). In comparison, his fellow member of the original Cambridge Metaphysical Club, < William James, was a prolific writer and a brilliant communicator, but became the target of scathing criticism from fellow philosophers. Whereas Peirce had emphasized the long run of communal inquiries, key formulations in James' works gave priority to practical difference as it is perceived by individuals here and now: "The whole function of philosophy ought to be to find out what definite difference it will make to you and me, at definite instants of our life" (James, 2013/1907: n.p.). With reference to the true and the right, he further held that, "'The true,' to put it very briefly, is only the expedient in the way of our thinking, just as 'the right' is only the expedient in the way of our behaving," although he quickly added, "expedient in the long run and on the whole of course." Another widely cited summary statement of pragmatism by James was the "cash-value" of ideas, even if, again, he proposed the motto "less as a solution [...] than as a program for more work, and more particularly as an indication of the ways in which existing realities may be CHANGED" (James, 2013/1907: n.p.). It was through James' formulations that contemporary thinkers first encountered the pragmatist tradition, which helps to explain why it was perceived by many philosophers and intellectuals as an expression of "vulgar practicalism or narrow utilitarianism" (West, 1989: 67). Following the wider dissemination of pragmatism, Peirce himself commented that the term had come to be "abused in the merciless way that words have to expect when they fall into literary clutches," and he renamed his philosophy "pragmaticism," which, he hoped, would be "ugly enough to be safe from kidnappers" (Peirce, 1955: 255).

> The Metaphysical Club – p. 136

the expedient

the cash-value of ideas

pragmaticism

The third figure of classic American pragmatism – John Dewey – insisted on ethics and politics as legitimate topics of philosophy, even as the mainstream of the discipline was turning toward linguistic and logical formalisms. Relying on an inclusive conception of experience as the human interface mediating biology and history, he also advanced an understanding of inquiry

experience

as an inclusive, public activity, not the prerogative of philosophers and other specialists (e.g., Dewey, 1927). In this manner, Dewey could be seen to develop "an epistemic justification of a democratic method of inquiry" (Misak, 2013: 136). If communities are to arrive at the right solutions to the problematic situations they share, inquiry must involve everybody – anybody as somebody (Scannell, 2000). (Rawls (1999b/1971: 315) was to develop an identical argument for political democracy: "No one knows everything the others know, or can make all the same inferences that they can draw in concert.") <

anybody as somebody

> Rawls on democratic inquiry – Chapter 4, p. 104

Dewey remained the standard-bearer of pragmatism into the post-1945 period, a nationally and internationally famous public intellectual and educational activist until his death in 1952. As a philosopher, however, Dewey was still inclined toward the conceptual analyses characteristic of a philosophy of consciousness, < as he contemplated ideal theories of the good life and a just society. "In contrast to Wittgenstein who, although he was the paradigmatic twentieth-century *philosopher* was in many ways a nineteenth-century *man*, John Dewey was a twentieth-century man although he was in certain ways a nineteenth-century philosopher" (Murphy, 1990: 79). The philosophy of language and communication that had been anticipated in Peirce's semiotics, and which became the philosophical mainstream during Dewey's lifetime, remained an unfulfilled potential in his own interventions.

> philosophy of consciousness – Chapter 1, p. 9

A missing link in the history of pragmatism as a philosophy of communication was recently identified and named by Cheryl Misak (2016): Ludwig Wittgenstein. While the early Wittgenstein (1972/1921) aligned with the linguistic formalism and logical atomism advanced by his teacher, Bertrand Russell, the later Wittgenstein (1953) foregrounded the practical uses of language in inquiry and other language games. < Nevertheless, histories of philosophy and of ideas have not associated Wittgenstein with the pragmatist tradition. The received history was summed up by Georg Henrik von Wright (cited in Misak, 2016: 1): "The later Wittgenstein, in my view, has no ancestors in the history of thought. His work signals a radical departure from previously existing paths of philosophy." In response, Misak (2016) presented a compelling argument and book-length evidence that Wittgenstein's turn from formal logic toward ordinary language in Cambridge, England, was informed by the pragmatism of Cambridge, Massachusetts.

logical atomism

> language games – Chapter 1, p. 9

The contingencies of Wittgenstein's reorientation involved a long and tortuous sequence of communications: Peirce's correspondence with the independent scholar Lady Victoria Welby

Lady Victoria Welby

in England; her dissemination of the correspondence to, among others, the intellectual entrepreneur and publicist C. K. Ogden, who passed Peirce's writings on to his mentee at Cambridge University, Frank Ramsey; Ogden and Ramsey's participation in the publication of *Tractatus Logico-Philosophicus* (Wittgenstein, 1972/1921); and Ramsey's sustained argumentation for Peirce's ideas in writing and conversation with Wittgenstein during the 1920s, before Ramsey's premature death at 26 in 1930. "Ramsey's pragmatist objections to Wittgenstein's early position were largely responsible for Wittgenstein's turn away from the *Tractatus* and toward ordinary language" (Misak, 2016: 2).

C. K. Ogden

Frank Ramsey

In notes from January 20, 1930, the day after Ramsey had died, Wittgenstein disclaimed his own early ambition of devising a primary language that would provide representations of the minimal constituents of reality:

> The point of talking of sense-data and immediate experience is that we are looking for a non-hypothetical representation. But now it seems that the *representation* loses all its value if the hypothetical element is dropped, because then the proposition does not point to the future any more, but it is, as it were, self-satisfied and hence without any value.
>
> *cited in Misak, 2016: 240*

A representation has value only insofar as one is willing to act on it in the future, and

> it makes no sense to speak of sentences, if they have no instrumental value. The sense of a sentence is its purpose. When I tell someone 'There's a chair over there,' I want to produce in him certain expectations and ways of acting.
>
> *p. 240*

Wittgenstein's example was a textbook illustration of what would develop as speech-act theory. < Also from the perspective of the person acting, representations and the beliefs associated with them amount to orientations toward action in the future. In his final work, *On Certainty*, published posthumously, Wittgenstein added: "the *questions* that we raise and our *doubts* depend on the fact that some propositions are exempt from doubt [...] it belongs to the logic of our scientific investigations that certain things are *in deed* not doubted" (cited in Misak, 2016: 273).

> speech-act theory – Chapter 3, p. 70

While thus adopting the twin theses of antiskepticism and fallibilism, Wittgenstein still reserved judgment on the other two theses of pragmatism: the primacy of practice for philosophy and the normative nature of the whole enterprise. < His ambivalence was suggested by his key concept of language games. Even while shifting his attention from the forms of language to its uses, Wittgenstein still conceived the task of philosophy as one of *describing* how language enters into and constitutes different sorts of encounters with reality, not of *explaining* why questions arise in such encounters and how doubts could or ought to be resolved through language games: "All *explanation* must disappear, and description alone must take its place" (Wittgenstein, 1953: §109). In the end, "all we can say is that we are immersed in a language game or form of life. We cannot say anything normative, anything by way of a meta-philosophy, about those language games or forms of life" (Misak, 2016: 252). In Wittgenstein's pragmatism, language makes a practical difference, but only within delimited, self-satisfied games.

> four theses of pragmatism – p. 127

description, not explanation

Wittgenstein's concept of language games was to become widely influential in social-scientific and humanistic research on society and culture as discursive practices. On philosophy's behalf, however, Wittgenstein had ended up prioritizing "a therapeutic approach" (Misak, 2016: 251), even a desire to become "capable of stopping doing philosophy" (Wittgenstein, 1953: §133) as an intellectual, social, or existential commitment. Wittgenstein, who was a religious person, sought to bracket normative and other practical questions from philosophy proper. The American pragmatists, in comparison, had struggled, in various ways, to accommodate a normative residual within philosophy. James, as mentioned, insisted on the will and the right to believe; Peirce, ever the logician, outlined "A neglected argument for the reality of God" (Peirce, 1998/1908); while Dewey replaced "the religion of his youth with a faith in democracy and non-parochial education" (Misak, 2013: 112).

a therapeutic approach to philosophy

Later heirs of pragmatism have traveled a secular way of inquiry, treating religion not as an element of theory, but as an aspect of the problematic, practical, normative situations that communities must regularly communicate about. In the very last sentence of the *Tractatus*, Wittgenstein (1972/1921) had excommunicated much of reality from philosophy: "What we cannot speak about we must pass over in silence" (p. 151). Following his pragmatist turn, Wittgenstein still aimed "to build a protective fence" between philosophy and "religion, ethics, and what is meaningful in life" (Misak, 2016: 264). There are, however, many questions and doubts regarding social justice or the meaning of a human life that communities, from the local to the global level, cannot pass

what we cannot speak about we must pass over in silence

over in silence even if they are unable to arrive at firm answers and uncontested solutions, or to fully grasp the rules of the language games that they are playing in articulating questions and arriving at answers. It was the role of communication in philosophical inquiry and, by extension, in public debate that took center stage in two recent redevelopments of pragmatism, one minimalist and postmodernist, the other maximalist and transcendentalist. Richard Rorty and Jürgen Habermas, in different ways, cast human communication as the beginning and end of both theory and practice regarding justice.

Postmodernist pragmatism

"Pragmatism survived as a philosophical position from the time of John Dewey to the late 1970s, but it did not flourish" (Prado, 1987: 1). From the 1970s, Richard Rorty became the central figure in another revival of pragmatism (Dickstein, 1998). Drawing on the American classics, Rorty presented a distinctive argument that, while echoing the late Wittgenstein, proposed to end philosophy by replacing it with politics. Having edited a summary volume on *The Linguistic Turn* (Rorty, 1967), < in a later monograph, *Philosophy and the Mirror of Nature*, Rorty (1979) launched a frontal attack on a dominant conception of philosophy as the discipline still providing the foundation for all other sciences. Rorty's publications assigned an increasingly modest role to philosophy, emphasizing "the priority of democracy to philosophy" (Rorty, 1991b: 175). The brief of philosophy, instead, would be to promote the general conversation of mankind. The discipline, accordingly, would shift

> the linguistic turn – Chapter 1, p. 9

the priority of democracy to philosophy

> from a methodologico-ontological key into an ethico-political key. For now one is debating what purposes are worth bothering to fulfill, which are more worthwhile than others, rather than which purposes the nature of humanity or of reality obliges us to have.
>
> *p. 110*

The way to explore and evaluate various human and social ends, to Rorty, was to tell ever more stories.

philosophy as story-telling

Rorty (1979) started out from a relatively traditional understanding of story-telling as a source of individual and collective edification. For doing philosophy in an "ethico-political key," he attributed special significance to other genres than those of science and scholarship, pointing to literature, poetry, and journalism as more important sources of moral progress. Over time, his writings radicalized the position to suggest that story-telling is not just a necessary, but a sufficient condition of interpersonal understanding and social coordination (Rorty, 1982, 1989, 1991a, 1991b, 1998, 2007). While adopting the postmodernist notion that a free flow of narratives and other signifiers might liberate and empower people, Rorty ascribed a limited role even to poststructuralist analyses, denouncing their underlying "tone of urgency": "there is not an urgent task called 'deconstructing metaphysics' which needs to be performed before we can get to work on the rest of culture" (Rorty, 1991a: 104–105). Stories are already being told, and are all that humans need to get along and go on.

pragmatism as an alternative to philosophy

Among the classic American pragmatists, Rorty cast John Dewey as his hero, attributing a special understanding of communities to him. In Rorty's reading, Dewey had approached pragmatism not as an alternative philosophy, but as an alternative *to* philosophy: "pragmatism not as grounding, but as clearing the ground for, democratic politics" (Rorty, 1991b: 13):

> Is the sort of community which is exemplified by groups of scientific inquirers and by democratic political institutions a means to an end, or is the formation of such communities the only goal we need? Dewey thought that it was the only goal we needed, and I think he was right.
>
> *p. 43*

Well aware of the many different vocabularies and values that different political and cultural formations subscribe to in their characterizations of the good life, Rorty (1991b: 218) simply assumed that their differences "can get resolved by hashing things out" through story-telling. Regarding the resolution of inevitable conflicts over the definition of both the ends and the means of coexistence, his recommendations were less specific: "if we take care of political freedom, truth and goodness will take care of themselves" (Rorty, 1989: 84).

humiliation as pain

Rorty did recognize a particularly challenging aspect of story-telling as communications flow within, but also between communities. The only feature that humans initially "share with all other humans is the same thing we share with all other animals – the ability to feel pain." But pain comes in several different forms:

> human beings who have been socialized – socialized in any language, any culture – do share a capacity which

> other animals lack. They can all be given a special kind of pain: They can all be humiliated by the forcible tearing down of the particular structures of language and belief in which they were socialized (or which they pride themselves on having formed for themselves).
>
> *Rorty, 1989: 177*

At this point of his argument, however, Rorty would slide from a position of narrative relativism into one of political absolutism, which he summed up as "postmodernist bourgeois liberalism" (Rorty, 1991b: 197). In a related formulation – anti-anti-ethnocentrism – he distanced himself from anti-ethnocentrism as unwanted political relativism. Certain ideals "may be local and culture-bound, and nevertheless be the best hope of the species" (p. 208).

postmodernist bourgeois liberalism

anti-anti-ethnocentrism

Speaking on behalf of "we heirs of the Enlightenment," Rorty (1991b: 187–188, emphasis in original) concluded that opponents of liberal democracy "are crazy because the limits of sanity are set by what *we* can take seriously." Whereas several of the ideals in question, including representative democracy, privacy rights, and procedural justice, might serve as consensual points of departure for many different stories and arguments, Rorty's conception of liberalism was blind especially to market forces – the practical difference that (de)regulation of the entire domain of economic activity makes for the freedom to tell stories, and for many other endeavors that people have reason to value. Rorty's vision was of "a large private and a small public sector, sectors which have no particular relation to one another" (Rorty, 1989: 100). In sum, his position neglected the concrete institutions, practices, and discourses that would keep story-telling, by all and for all, going – or not.

private and public sectors

Rorty performed prophetic readings of the works of Dewey and other thinkers, with few priestly checks and balances; one of his interventions painted Rawls as an ally of Rorty's (2003/1988) postmodernist pragmatism, and met with fierce criticism from another prominent pragmatist, Richard J. Bernstein (1987). When Rorty proposed to enlist one more fellow philosopher, Donald Davidson, as his ally, and when Davidson declined, that did not phase Rorty: "Davidson cannot be held responsible for the interpretation I am putting on his views, nor for the further views I extrapolate from his" (Rorty, 1989: 10). Compared to Habermas, Rorty engaged in self-consciously strategic communication for political ends and by postmodernist means. < In response, yet another philosopher, Daniel Dennett (1982),

> Habermas' strategic communicative practices – Chapter 3, p. 93

the Rorty Factor

tongue-in-cheek, proposed introducing a "Rorty Factor," specified as 0.742, to indicate the extent to which Rorty misrepresented the position of others. Adopting a Rortyan storyline, "we heirs" of pragmatism might even choose to consider Rorty "crazy." On a more practical note, one may conclude that Rorty left unaddressed many questions concerning the concrete difference that unspecified numbers and kinds of stories might make for "truth and goodness" (Rorty, 1989: 84).

Transcendental pragmatism

> the metaphysics of communication – Chapter 3, p. 82

retranscendentalization

Conferring Jürgen Habermas' pragmatism with his own, Rorty (1989: 68) found that both thinkers have advocated "as much domination-free communication as possible," but added that, "the trouble with Habermas is [...] that he is not content to let the narratives that hold our culture together do their stuff" (Rorty, 1991b: 167). In Chapter 3, I argued and presented evidence that, notwithstanding Habermas' protestations, his *oeuvre* has reconstructed and recommended a metaphysics of communication as "the best hope of the species" (Rorty, 1991b: 208). < In this section, I briefly trace Habermas' retranscendentalization of American pragmatism, which occurred in several stages and with reference to shifting terminologies including "transcendental pragmatism" (Habermas, 1973: 179), "Kantian pragmatism" (Habermas, 2003: 30), and "semiotic idealism" (Habermas, 2019b: 705). The secondary literature on Habermas has noted pragmatism as one important influence, but also his ambivalence regarding central tenets of the tradition (e.g., Aboulafia et al., 2002; Bernstein, 2010). Habermas' strategic appropriation of pragmatism has been most apparent in his treatments of Charles Sanders Peirce.

In a retrospective self-assessment, Habermas found that, among the American pragmatists, Peirce had been the most important to his intellectual development. "In epistemology – and the theory of truth – Peirce had the strongest influence, from my Frankfurt inaugural lecture on *Knowledge and Human Interest* (1965) onwards up to *Wahrheit und Rechtfertigung* [Truth and Justification (Habermas, 2003)]" (Aboulafia et al., 2002: 227). This was in addition to "Mead's theory of social interaction" (p. 227), which became key to the theory of communicative action, and the more general "anti-elitist, democratic, and thoroughly egalitarian *attitude* that shapes and penetrates the work of all the pragmatists" (p. 228). The influence was channeled, in part, through the early interest of Habermas' friend and fellow philosopher, Karl-Otto Apel (1981), in Peirce's philosophy.

One of Habermas' (1971/1968) most elaborate treatments of Peirce's ideas is still to be found in the early volume on *Knowledge and Human Interests* (KHI). Before his reconstructive turn, and in an Aristotelian lineage, Habermas had recognized the different ends or knowledge interests of different sciences, < assigning special importance to the practical, emancipatory potential of critical social science. Through the exercise of double hermeneutics, < scientific communities would be in a position to empower citizens by enhancing their self-understanding as a prelude to wider political communities reshaping their own history. At the time of KHI, however, Habermas found Peirce's conception of the communities of inquiry seriously deficient. For Habermas, the right kind of community was:

> knowledge interests – Chapter 3, p. 60

> double hermeneutics – Chapter 2, p. 25

> a community that constitutes the world from transcendental perspectives. This would be the subject of the process of learning and inquiry that is itself involved in a self-formative process until the point in time at which a definitive and complete knowledge of reality is attained. But it is this very subject that Peirce cannot conceive.
>
> *Habermas, 1971/1968: 135*

Without a transcendental subject, Habermas suggested, Peirce's notion of the long run of inquiry was regressing to scientism and resulting in a general "logic of scientific progress" (p. 94) – which was precisely what the idea of multiple knowledge interests was meant to counteract. Habermas' 1968 verdict was that "a hidden but unyielding positivism finally prevails" in Peirce (p. 135).

the transcendental subject

In KHI, the charge of positivism was coupled with a second charge, that Peirce was simultaneously veering toward (German) idealism. In a first step, Habermas found that, without transcendental grounding, language cannot deliver the sort of reflective inquiry that keeps humans at the center as the subjects of history; instead, Peirce could be seen to be reinstating "nature as an absolute subject" (Habermas, 1971/1968: 111). Peirce, arguably, was replacing "the logic of language" with "a doctrine of categories that tacitly abandons the transcendental approach and restores ontology in an only barely concealed manner." In a second step, Peirce's ontology was said to presuppose "the identity of concept and object (*Sache*)" in a way that could "only be justified in terms of an idealism that is not unlike Hegel's" (p. 111). Habermas' alternative to this perceived, surprising marriage of positivism and Hegelianism in Peirce's thinking was a "transcendental pragmatism" that he reconfirmed in the postscript to KHI (Habermas, 1973: 179).

nature as an absolute subject

Over the decades, Habermas has returned to Peirce multiple times, in passing and in at least three substantial interventions. In an essay entitled, "Peirce and Communication," and included in the collection on *Postmetaphysical Thinking* (Habermas, 1992d), he modified his original criticism of Peirce, praising "the great achievement of Peircean semiotics in its consistent expansion of the world of symbolic forms beyond the borders of linguistic forms of expression" (Habermas, 1992c: 107). In KHI, one of his assertions had been that Peirce based his epistemology on "his linguistic concept of reality," so that "reality is defined by the totality of possible true statements," and that "these statements are symbolic representations" (Habermas, 1971/1968: 102) – a reading which is clearly untenable. Even so, Habermas did not clean up his communicative act. The 1992 essay was silent on the glaring differences between the 1968 and 1992 versions of "the strongest influence" of pragmatism on Habermas. Instead, he once again asserted the primacy of "the structure of the simple predicative sentence, which is the semiotic form of perceptual judgments," according to Habermas (1992c: 98) – but not according to Peirce.

linguistics and/or semiotics

predication and perception

What appeared unacceptable, or incomprehensible, to Habermas was Peirce's starting point: Signs come in different, but equal forms, and they constitute orientations toward action, not predications or representations in any primary sense. As part of his 1992 criticisms, Habermas still insisted that Peirce had been preoccupied with scientistic representation rather than authentic deliberation and humane reflection. For Peirce, "communication is not for the sake of reaching mutual understanding between ego and alter about something in the world; rather, interpretation only exists for the sake of the representation and the ever more comprehensive representation of reality" (Habermas, 1992c: 109). For Habermas, the two conceptions of communication amounted to a clear-cut dichotomy, which he projected onto Peirce. The most distinctive feature of Peirce's epistemology and semiotics was precisely the triad of subject, sign, and object, not any subject–object or subject–subject dyads. The dichotomy was in the eye of the beholder, the mind of the transcendentalist: Habermas.

communication for representation or understanding

A second elaborated treatment of Peirce appeared in Habermas' (2003) introduction to *Truth and Justification*. Several formulations were in line with a general consensus of Peirce scholarship regarding his key concepts; these formulations, however, were again offered without commentary on the slippages between 1968 and 2003. On the one hand, Habermas reiterated his own position, namely, that "nonlinguistic practices, too, are characterized by the propositional structure of language" (p. 13). On the other hand, Habermas outlined an ontology of "weak naturalism" that was premised on a continuum of natural evolution and human learning, and which had clear affinities to both American pragmatism and the longer pragmatist legacy:

weak naturalism

> From a pragmatist perspective, reality is not something to be copied; we take note of it performatively – as the totality of resistances that are processed and are to be anticipated – and it makes itself known to us solely in the constraints to which our problem-solving activities and learning processes are subject.
>
> *p. 27*

The same introduction, moreover, endorsed the antiskepticist premise < that language users and social actors necessarily "presuppose a shared objective world as the totality of objects to be dealt with and judged" (p. 16). Habermas also relaxed his previous dichotomizations of communication and representation, which he now considered "equiprimordial," so that "the representational and communicative functions of language mutually presuppose one another" (p. 5).

> antiskepticism – p. 127

communication and representation as equiprimordial

Toward the end of the text, however, Habermas (2003) went so far as to inscribe Peirce's concepts into his own terminology, ascribing a "discursive concept of truth" to Peirce. The reference was to the view that

> a statement is true if and only if, under the rigorous pragmatic presuppositions of rational discourse, it is able to withstand *all* efforts to invalidate it, that is, if and only if it can be justified in an ideal epistemic situation.

Habermas commented that, like Karl-Otto Apel and Hilary Putnam, he had been "inspired by C. S. Peirce's famous suggestion" to defend "some version of such a discursive concept of truth" (p. 36). But Peirce had spoken of the long run of inquiry < in contingent practical circumstances, not of any "ideal epistemic situation." Habermas, having added his own specifications and "idealizing presuppositions" concerning the nature of rational argumentation, in the next paragraph repeated the reference to "*the* discursive concept of truth" (p. 37, emphasis added), now with a definite article, as if his own special concept of discourse < were identical with Peirce's conception of communication and inquiry.

> the long run of inquiry – p. 141

> Habermas' concept of discourse – Chapter 3, p. 62

Not only has Habermas performed several quite different reconstructions of Peirce, but the seminal influence that was said, in 1968, to harbor an unhealthy hybrid of positivism and German Idealism thus came out, by 2003, as Habermas' ally *avant la lettre*. In a third substantial treatment – the recent history of philosophy and ideas (Habermas, 2019a) – Peirce, once again, occupied a pivotal position in Habermas' narrative, but with another surprising twist to the plot. Centering on Peirce's > pragmaticism – p. 143 late works and the 'pragmaticism' < he invoked late in life to distinguish himself from the pragmatism of William James and others, Habermas described Peirce, this time approvingly, as a thinker who "continues the tradition of transcendentalism in the spirit of Kant and Hegel" (p. 560, author's translation of this and the following quotations). Now, Peirce could even be thought of as one of the "Young Hegelians" along with Ludwig Feuerbach and Karl Marx (who are traditionally included in this line) as well as Søren Kierkegaard (p. 703). And, Peirce's (late) semiotics was said to amount to "a theory of the objective Spirit" (p. 725), which had been a key concept in Hegel's account of the development over time of (human understanding of) the world. Peirce's "decisive contribution" (p. 749), for Habermas, was that his ideas enabled the transition from the idealisms of Kant and Hegel – philosophies of consciousness – to a position with more than a family resemblance to Habermas' own philosophy of communication:

> In this perspective, the semiotic idealism of [Peirce's] late works must be understood as a metaphysical attempt to, once again, make familiar a nature that had been alienated by nominalism and objectified by natural sciences, in terms of communicatively socialized subjects themselves constructing their *lifeworld* from the symbolic material of their language.
>
> *p. 705, emphasis in original*

Peirce, as noted, never arrived at a final synthesis of his seminal ideas; his late semiotics does lend itself to interpretation along these lines. But Habermas' shifting interpretations of Peirce for shifting purposes since 1968 must be understood, in Habermas' vocabulary, as strategic and systematically distorted communication. <

> systematically distorted communication – Chapter 3, p. 93

ANALYSIS BOX 5.1 THE DIFFERENCES THAT MAKE A DIFFERENCE

The American pragmatists' idea that conceptions of reality and their expression in signs and symbols make a practical difference had intellectual ancestors in both ancient logic (Bobzien, 2015) and modern humanities (Bod, 2013), and it came to inform much twentieth-century social science and interdisciplinary research, if only with occasional reference to pragmatism. Gregory Bateson (1972: 351) offered an influential definition of communication in terms of the difference it makes: "'information' may be succinctly defined as *any difference which makes a difference in some later event*." Bateson duly noted that reality holds an infinite number of differences. Returning to Immanuel Kant's point that, in a piece of chalk, as a *Ding an sich*, "there are an infinite number of potential facts," he underscored the very small number of facts that will ever acquire relevance as information:

> There are differences between the piece of chalk and the rest of the universe, between the chalk and the sun or the moon. And within the piece of chalk, there is for every molecule an infinite number of differences between its location and the locations in which it *might* have been. Of this infinitude, we select a very limited number, which become information.
>
> *p. 428*

Of all the potential states of the world – from the subatomic to the planetary level – only some are ever actualized, and an even smaller set of differences will ever be realized in human cognition and social interaction. Some differences make a greater difference than others, as far as humans are concerned; some differences enable people to say and do things that change their lives for the better in either the short or the long term.

The American pragmatists had foregrounded the process in which scientific and social communities arrive at beliefs that they are willing to act on; Peirce had elaborated the semiotic and interpretive constituents of this process (Johansen, 1985: 250f.). His typologies of the interpretant

> the interpretant – p. 138

< – the discursive and mental constructs by which people orient themselves toward particular actions, with variable levels of self-awareness – corresponded to the basic communication model whose elements, over the past century, have become part of common sense: < senders, messages, receivers, channels, codes, and contexts (Jakobson, 1960; Lasswell, 1948). To explore the practical difference that communication could make in matters of justice, all of these elements lend themselves to further conceptualization, operationalization, empirical study, and normative debate.

> the very idea of communication – Chapter 1, p. 7

- *Discursive difference.* While most people will think of information, in positive terms, as the stuff contained in messages and delivered by either a human being or a communication technology, it is helpful to think of information, in negative terms, as configurations of differences – minimal items that could have been selected differently and combined differently. What is *not* communicated, and what *could* have been communicated instead? Advertisements draw attention to particular products or services by verbal and visual appeals; newscasts prioritize certain events over others and cover them according to debatable journalistic standards and conventions. The category of discursive difference directs attention to important public issues concerning the availability and accessibility of information: < What is known – and who knows? Who is in a position to know what, compared to others? Even if both advertisements and newscasts give rise to different interpretations and actions, the presence or absence of certain discourses in specific media and communities represents a bottom line of communication, what Peirce had spoken of as the *Immediate Interpretant* – "the total unanalyzed effect that the Sign is calculated to produce, or naturally might be expected to produce" (Peirce, 1958: 413).

> rights of information – Chapter 7, p. 201

- *Interpretive difference.* If discursive difference is a property of messages, interpretive difference is an accomplishment of their recipients or users. Peirce had referred to a *Dynamic Interpretant* that is the "direct effect actually produced by a Sign upon an Interpreter of it" (Peirce, 1958: 413). Communication occurs in the dynamic encounter between the discursive differences on offer and the interpretive difference that socially and culturally situated audiences make, as they participate in the production, maintenance, repair, and transformation of reality (Carey, 1989a: 23). In contrast to a widespread understanding of communication as the mechanistic transfer of items of information, media studies have long documented the productive role of audiences in communication (Jensen, 2012c, 2012d). Advertisements may be construed as casual entertainment or capitalist propaganda; news may be considered biased by either political or commercial interests, or both. Individual literacy and the institutions of communicative participation raise additional political issues. Depending on their receptive and productive capabilities, < citizens may or may not be in a position to exercise their rights of communication as persons and publics. <

> capabilities of communication – Chapter 7, p. 193

> rights of communication – Chapter 7, p. 204

- *Performative difference*. The third type of difference, which most obviously makes a practical difference, takes effect at the end of communication, as information is translated into beliefs and, in additional steps, other human actions and social interactions. When Peirce referred to a *Final Interpretant*, he was mostly considering truth in the long run and in counterfactual terms as "the effect the Sign *would* produce upon any mind upon which circumstances should permit it to work out its full effects" (Peirce, 1958: 413). But his writings also addressed more concrete aspects of interpretations performed by embodied individuals embedded in social settings: Emotional, Energetic, and Logical Interpretants, including an "ultimate logical interpretant" that was said to constitute a habit-change or a "modification of a person's disposition or tendency, when actuated by certain desires, to respond to perceptual conditions by conduct of a certain kind" (cited in Johansen, 1993: 165). Also in the short run, interpretations feed into beliefs and a readiness or predisposition to act (or not): buying or boycotting advertised goods, engaging or neglecting the news of the day. All of these actions depend on, and are conditioned by, rights of participation in politics, economy, and culture. <

> rights of participation – Chapter 7, p. 207

A competing conception of difference, which has been widely disseminated in recent decades, is advocated by poststructuralists. As reflected in Rorty's call for story-telling without end, poststructuralism describes a human condition

différance

in which no stable or dependable knowledge of reality, other minds, or oneself is possible. The key formulation – *différance* – was due to the philosopher, Jacques Derrida (1973/1967), who twisted the French verb *différer*, which means both to differ and to defer. The suggestion is that all insight and intersubjectivity is forever delayed in a play of differences. And that, to poststructuralists, is a good thing, because the fixation of meaning is a way of exercising power, even a form of discursive violence. Poststructuralist studies, accordingly, have commonly presented themselves as contributions to a socially progressive enterprise of deconstructing and decentering established discourses, occasionally as having revolutionary potential (Kristeva, 1984/1974).

Derrida depicted Peirce as a prophet of poststructuralism:

> Peirce goes very far in the direction that I have called the de-construction of the transcendental signified, which, at one time or another, would place a reassuring end to the reference from sign to sign. [...] The self-identity of the signified conceals itself unceasingly and is always on the move.
>
> *Derrida, 1976/1967: 49*

Peirce scholarship has generally dismissed such interpretations, but as he himself realized, signs are never "safe from kidnappers" (Peirce, 1955: 255). Rorty's deconstruction of pragmatism swung the pendulum to one extreme of narrative chance; Habermas' reconstruction took pragmatism to another extreme of transcendental necessity.

Pragmatism, communication, and justice

In communication research as in philosophy, pragmatism has been a minority interest and a marginal position. This is in spite of the many family resemblances of both the American tradition and the longer legacy of pragmatism with disciplinary questions of what media do to people, and what people do with media (Katz, 1959) – the discursive, interpretive, and performative differences that communication makes. The most direct influence registered in James W. Carey's presentation of a ritual model of communication as an alternative to the still dominant transmission model. < A key

> communication as transmission or ritual – Chapter 2, p. 41

reference was to John Dewey's point that, "Society exists not only by transmission, by communication, but it may fairly be said to exist in transmission, in communication" (in Carey, 1989a: 13f.). Communication is not external, but internal to, and constitutive of, society. Communication makes a difference not only through specific effects on the attitudes and behaviors of media audiences, but throughout the interactions involving individuals as well as institutions "whereby reality is produced, maintained, repaired, and transformed" (p. 23). Carey further emphasized the role of media as technological infrastructures < that enable and delimit historical windows of opportunity for communication.

society exists in and by communication

> medium theory – Chapter 6, p. 162

An elaboration of the implications of pragmatism for communication theory and practice has been offered by Robert T. Craig, with references ranging from Aristotle via John Dewey to Richard J. Bernstein (1983). On the one hand, Craig's influential typology and metamodel of seven traditions of communication theory was a way of spelling out what difference each of them might make for the understanding and conduct of communication (Craig, 1999; Craig & Muller, 2007). In response to a critical discussion of his original article (Russill, 2005), Craig (2007: 141) amended the metamodel, describing his own vision of theory in terms of tools for addressing practical problems of communication and as an eighth tradition, "a largely pragmatist project." On the other hand, Craig (1989, 2018) has aimed to redevelop communication research as a "practical discipline," specifically through grounded practical theory (GPT) (Craig & Tracy, 1995), which proposes to tackle problematic situations of communication with simultaneous reference to a technical level of solutions or means and a normative level of ends concerning the "elaborated normative ideals and overarching principles" that the communicative practices in question can be seen to express (p. 253). So far, however, GPT studies (Craig, 2014; Craig & Tracy, 2021) have devoted more attention to domain-specific problems and local solutions than to the wider normative principles that are at stake in and across social contexts. In a self-critical vein, Charmaz (2006: 135) noted that, as an empirical methodology that claims to derive concepts and categories from the domain of study itself, the wider tradition of grounded theory has, in fact, generated little theory. Craig and Tracy (2014) themselves recognized that at least "some GPT studies can be criticized for being excessively descriptive, thus lacking normative potential" (even while adding that other GPT studies "can be criticized for excessive idealism that departs too far from the realities of practice" (p. 237)).

Craig's metamodel of communication theory

grounded practical theory

humanistic semiotics

Deweyan social and political theory

The American tradition of pragmatism has been referenced in communication research (Perry, 2001) as in other social sciences and humanities. In the humanities, Peirce's semiotics has received growing attention in recent decades (e.g., Bergman, 2008; Jensen, 2012e). In sociology and political science, it is, above all, Dewey's works that have fed into pragmatist studies of political institutions (e.g., Bray, 2011; Knight & Johnson, 2011), even if a few scholars have explored the relevance of Peirce's ideas for theories of democracy (Misak, 2000; Talisse, 2011) (for critical discussion, see MacGilvray, 2014). Deliberative models of democracy and the public sphere, departing from Habermas' position, have incorporated components of pragmatism (e.g., Elstub, 2010; O'Mahoney, 2013); Misak (2019) briefly relates Peirce and Habermas in the history of pragmatism. Even Wittgenstein's understanding of practice, of being able to go on in one's language games, has informed theory development regarding society and communication (e.g., Bloor, 1983; Shotter, 1996).

> why is reality? – p. 128

> Rawls' practical turn – Chapter 4, p. 110

> Rawls on the cash-value of ideas – Chapter 4, p. 129

The legacy of pragmatism has continued to challenge the range of scientific disciplines and interdisciplinary fields regarding the ends and means of their inquiries: Why do scholarly communities, and the wider social communities they serve, want to know about particular aspects of reality? < In matters of justice, John Rawls performed a practical turn and took up a position that "does without the concept of truth" (Rawls, 2005/1993: 94). < Following his student commentary on the cash-value of ideas, < Rawls rarely referred to the American pragmatists in his publications. Recent work, however, drawing on unpublished papers and annotations in Rawls' personal library, has suggested a substantial influence not least from Peirce's understanding of inquiry and an implicit engagement with pragmatist positions and scholarly debates of the 1980s–90s (Botti, 2019). (On pragmatist elements of Rawls' thinking, see also, e.g., Alexander, 2003; D'Agostino, 2004; Hay, 2012; Weber, 2010.) Rawls' (2005/1993) understanding of the overlapping consensus < as a practical accomplishment by fallible communities of inquiry can be seen to update and extend pragmatist themes in the longer history of ideas.

> the overlapping consensus – Chapter 4, p. 113

Amartya Sen's (2009: 5) critique of Rawls for advocating a "transcendental institutionalism" stimulated another round of debate on theories of justice. Endorsing Sen's characterization of Rawls, for example, Hannan (2015: 317) suggested reading Sen's project as a "fallibilistic approach to justice [that] bears a strong affinity to classical and contemporary pragmatism." In the following chapters, I take Rawls' practical conception of justice as my point of departure, to be complemented by Sen's attention to empirical contingencies and human capabilities and, most important in the present context, to be balanced by both empirical and theoretical research on the technologies and institutions that historically have enabled communication about and for justice. Communication is both a constituent and a condition of justice < – a human right and a resource for articulating the principles and procedures that may approximate justice in practice.

> communication as constituent and condition of justice – Chapter 7, p. 214

6

MEDIA OF JUSTICE

Medium theory

Communication is a means of justice, as humans engage the problematic situations of their coexistence (Dewey, 1903). Communication is also an end of justice: a social good in itself and a resource for further reflection and deliberation about what justice *could be*. Communication about justice has been enabled over time by the historically available technologies and institutions. Relying on Aristotle's distinction between potentiality and actuality < as sensitizing concepts (Blumer, 1954), in this chapter I review the development of media as social infrastructures – what media are and have been, as actualizations of material, institutional, and discursive potentials. In the two following chapters, I return to normative questions of how media ought to serve justice, and to empirical questions of how they could serve justice in practice.

> Aristotle on potential and actualization – Chapter 5, p. 137

Compared to the understanding of communication as either transmission or social sharing, < medium theory (Meyrowitz, 1994), and the wider tradition of media ecology (Strate, 2016), has focused attention on the ways in which, and the degree to which, media circumscribe what can be thought, said, and done in any given community or civilization – its worldviews, sciences, arts, and forms of governance. Media constitute environments enveloping individuals and collectives, conditioning how they relate to natural circumstances and received cultural conventions. Far from endorsing technological determinism, medium theory makes the simple, but crucial point that societies with access to writing systems, printing presses, telegraphy and telephony,

> communication as transmission and ritual – Chapter 2, p. 41

media as environments

broadcasting, and digital networks – none, some, or all of these – have been different in kind. The implication was suggested by Stuart Hall (1983) in a reassessment of the terminology characteristic of critical social science which suggests that, in the *final* instance, the material base of society determines its ideological superstructure: When all is said and done, money still talks. Hall proposed an alternative perspective of determination in the *first* instance: Like comparable infrastructures, media redraw the lines between what it is possible and impossible to say, know, and do. But media technologies do not in themselves predict which institutions, practices, and discourses of communication will prevail over time. Media have had, and still have, unforeseen and unforeseeable consequences.

determination in the first instance

As social institutions, media have been shaped and reshaped in a process of double hermeneutics, < as philosophers, scientists, politicians, entrepreneurs, and other practitioners have participated in thought experiments and real-life experiments on the private and public ends that media might serve. The integration of various media into the basic structure of society < has made them essential conditions of justice, giving rise to contestations of how they ought to operate in practice. As noted by John Rawls (1999b/1971: 5) regarding justice, people will agree on the relevance and importance of the general or practical *concept* even while advancing alternative theoretical *conceptions* of the good life. For more than a century, communication has been considered key to human collaboration and coexistence. < Whereas Chapters 7 and 8 develop systematic conceptions of the relationship between communication and justice, the present chapter tracks the historical development of different media and the practical concepts of communication associated with them. Media history represents a natural experiment exploring *what communication could be.*

> double hermeneutics – Chapter 2, p. 25

> the basic structure of society – Chapter 4, p. 103

> the idea of communication – Chapter 1, p. 7

The chapter is structured around three practical or lay concepts (Furnham, 1988) which have become part of common parlance and common sense: information, communication, and action. Which kinds of information have been available – depending on technological infrastructures and shifting understandings of what humans could and ought (not) to know about in the first place? Next, who, and how many, have been in a position to access and communicate about the available information, depending on formal rights and functional literacies? Last, how have different interests in society – religious, secular, economic, political, private, and public agents – fed their information and communications into the institutions of governance that regulate coexistence?

practical concepts

data, information, knowledge, wisdom

the availability of information

rights of information

In the first section, I consider what has been counted as information, data, knowledge, or wisdom (Bellinger, Castro, & Mills, 2004) in matters of justice. I rely on a contemporary understanding of information as data that are processed by humans and technologies, resulting in knowledge or beliefs that are acted on, and which may later be recognized as wisdom – or fatal error. Chapter 2 recounted how virtue-ethical, deontological, and consequentialist traditions of justice have disagreed fundamentally on what constitutes valid, reliable, and relevant information about justice. In the present chapter, the central question is which qualities and quantities of information have been available for anyone at all to reflect on, frequently only a fraction of the community in question. Writing, printing, and computing each changed the ground rules for representing, communicating about, and engaging reality and other people. In each case, information has been redefined and fought over as an emergent human right.

rights of communication

access to communication

rights of privacy

The second section traces how rights of communication – freedoms of conscience, expression, assembly, and more – have been reformulated in view of what a sequence of 'new' media have afforded individuals and collectives: What could, in fact, be said and done by humans, in the flesh, via wires, and over the air? Here, the central issue is access. Who has had access – potentially and actually – to what kinds of information, through which media? I lay out the options in a typology of communicative practices – one-to-one, one-to-many, and many-to-many – noting their relative prominence and interrelations in different historical contexts, and reemphasizing that 'old' media rarely die, but are redefined as part of an ongoing division of communicative labor. I highlight a fourth type of many-to-one communication, which has recently come to the fore: the registration of users' activities in digital systems through the bit trails they leave behind. People "cannot *not* communicate" (Watzlawick et al., 1967: 49) in digital media, with implications for justice that are only beginning to be appreciated. Rights of privacy or data protection belong up there with the classic rights of conscience and expression.

> institutions of governance – p. 182

from government to governance

The third and final section of the chapter turns to institutions of governance and collective agency, < which traditionally have been given priority in philosophical and social-scientific treatments of justice. Whereas Rawls (2005/1993: 443) reserved "public reason" for political officials and only admitted citizens and media into the "background culture," I include additional cultural and other social institutions within the purview of governance. Several disciplines and fields have recognized their importance in a terminological shift from 'government' to 'governance.' < Habermas

(1989/1962: 29) noted how the cultural components of the early public sphere < had served as a "training ground" and "precursor" for political and public debate in a modern sense. Fictional genres are part and parcel of socialization and education for democratic participation; they facilitate the identification and enactment of facts. At stake are rights of participation, not just in expressing particular opinions on policy issues and electing representatives at regular intervals, but in co-constructing discursive and material realities, being productive in Aristotle's sense and performative in Austin's (1962) sense.

> the cultural public sphere – Chapter 3, p. 54

rights of participation

Marshall McLuhan (1964: 23), the most widely known medium theorist, had suggested that "the medium is the message": Each new medium has carried a distinctive outlook on reality. In more scholarly statements, McLuhan's main source of inspiration, the political economist and historian Harold A. Innis (1951, 1972/1950), transferred the principles of economic monopolies to information monopolies to suggest how power can be both exercised and subverted through media. Entire empires and cultures could be seen to hold a 'bias' toward either time or space because their dominant media favored either stability over time or extended territories. Stone tablets last a long time, but do not travel well; papyrus and paper support the administration of distant regions, but are vulnerable to decay and destruction, and to being appropriated for purposes of opposition and social change. A related literature on the affordances of both natural objects and cultural artifacts has suggested that such biases are not absolute (Gibson, 1979; Hsieh, 2012; Hutchby, 2001). Objects and structures in the world afford different relational uses by different organisms. Unlike humans, insects can walk on water. Unlike other living organisms, humans rework the natural resources they find, and they reprogram the forms and contents of the media they inherit. Media have been materially and "culturally invented" (Carroll, 1988: 143) in incremental and iterative fashion – clay into tablets, metal into types, electromagnetism into broadcasting, silicon into computers.

biases of time and space

affordances

The in-formation of justice

Saying, writing, and printing it

For most of the existence of the species, humans themselves were the only media around. Itinerant poets, bards, or singers of tales (Lord, 2000) constituted institutions of communication: embodied archives of past experience and received tradition

oral cultures

offering lessons on how to hunt, gather, cultivate the land, raise the young, build houses and ships, and resolve disputes, always in the form of good, memorable stories. Scholarship on prehistoric and non-literate societies has pointed to the context-bound and present-oriented nature of their communications (Goody & Watt, 1963; Ong, 1982; Scribner & Cole, 1981). It is not only that, today, our knowledge of past oral cultures is limited; then and there, our ancestors had no stable external representation of

writing systems

the past, to agree or disagree about in the present, and to work on with a view to the future. Writing allowed humans to capture and compare different possible worlds.

> possible worlds – Chapter 3, p. 81

< And the historical sources suggest that writing originated not as a representation of or contemplation on reality, but as a resource for mundane, essential tasks such as "temple bureaucrats recording economic transactions" (Lerner, 2009: 1). Before anything else, media are practical accomplishments affording humans a communicative resource for acting in the present and planning for the future. Writing was the first medium to in-form – re-present and reproduce – both the past and potential futures.

When Plato, in the *Republic*, attacked the poets, he was announcing the passing of a primary oral culture and the coming of literate society (Havelock, 1963). Poets, to Plato, could no longer be trusted in practical matters of what was, in fact, the case and what ought, therefore, to be done – science and politics – although poetry could still be appreciated as personal opinion or myth: stories rather than history. Poetic justice, after all, was and is different from social justice. With writing also came more

genres of communication

differentiated conventions and genres of communication for diverse purposes, expert as well as lay. As part of a growing division of communicative labor, writing became the medium of record for vast and complex economic, political, and scientific systems around the globe (for overview, see Powell, 2009). Scribal communication, however, still depended on oral mediation. Because copies were precious and few, they were distributed selectively to a few trusted individuals – priests, generals, literate servants – who would pass on even more selective and contextually adapted information with oral commentary within established institutional hierarchies (Camargo, 1996). Not only was public access to information for survival and a good life (and to the necessary literacy), thus, policed by religious as well as secular authorities. Even a utopian state that were to materially support the literacy and learning of all its citizens, promoting their copying by hand of as many manuscripts as possible for as inclusive a group of readers as possible, would require human labor on a scale that makes anything approaching equal access to the culturally available information and to public participation in communication about the common good inconceivable – impracticable. Mass communication is not an affordance of the medium of writing.

the printing press

The printing press spawned a range of media for both recording and disseminating information, fact as well as fiction: books, journals, pamphlets, newspapers (for overview, see Briggs, Burke, & Ytreberg, 2020). Their common features were, first, precise one-to-one reproduction and storage of a particular content or message. Compared to the laborious copying by hand of manuscripts with many accidental (and a good number of intentional) mistakes, print media introduced a different category of 'information.' Print afforded the systematic identification of errors of fact and judgment over time, < facilitating reflective beliefs and recursive actions. Second, print media radically extended the dissemination of and access to the available information, including the philosophical and scientific insights recovered by the Renaissance and the source texts of world religions (Eisenstein, 1979). Whereas the printing press did not determine the Reformation, it decisively changed who was in a position to define the meaning of life and eternity: "the medieval Church's monopoly over religious information, and thereby over salvation, was broken by the printing press" (Meyrowitz, 1994: 51). Still, it was the scribal culture of religious and political elites that was transformed by print media. Mass literacy lay far ahead, in the nineteenth and twentieth centuries.

> *erro, ergo sum* – Chapter 5, p. 127

The implications of the printing press for public communication recall the insight that, among great apes, "when something is explicitly communicated it is 'out in the open' [...] there can be no question of not knowing this information" (Tomasello, 2016: 53). < It was not only new information, but a radically new medium of communication that now was out in the open, a generic resource with a wide range of uses. With the embedding of print media into the basic structure of society, communication became a central constituent of ongoing intellectual struggles and equally endless wars, as a modern scientific and social order was taking shape. At the juncture of science and religion, when Galileo Galilei had been forced by the Inquisition, in 1633, to recant the view that the Earth moves around the Sun, tradition has it that he spoke the words, *Eppur si muove* [And yet it moves] (Drake, 1978: 357), and scientific communities would confirm this to one another in print in the years ahead. At the juncture of politics and religion, post-Reformation elites certainly knew about the several competing, uncompromising religions of salvation, < and

> communication in prehistory – Chapter 2, p. 28

> religions of salvation – Chapter 4, p. 108

yet, all sides would force their illiterate subjects, by the spoken word and any other means, into "mortal conflict moderated only by circumstance and exhaustion" (Rawls, 2005/1993: xxvi). The Westphalian peace accords of 1648 ended both a Thirty Years' War and an Eighty Years' War, and the accords marked the onset of nation-states – sovereign states with delimited territories, if crisscrossed by religious denominations – as the modern principle of inter-national relations. And it was print media – the daily and periodical press, but also novels and maps – and additional institutions-to-think-with < such as museums and the census that would maintain each nation as an imagined community (Anderson, 1991). Modern nations are imagined (but not imaginary) communities because each citizen will never have face-to-face or direct contact with the vast majority of other community members, but will nevertheless think of them as an 'us,' even while the community may be divided on the ends and means of their coexistence.

nation-states

> institutions-to-think-with – Chapter 2, p. 27

imagined communities

Mediated modernity

Philosophical debates about justice were given a modern form by print technologies. Print media made historically unprecedented quantities and qualities of information available, if initially only to a small minority of populations. But information was recommunicated, acted upon, and fed into collective projects and abiding institutions. As social systems, nation-states and their constituent communities reconsidered basic questions of 'what is' in either a religious or secular sense, 'what ought to be' in a political and ethical perspective, and 'what could be' produced in both economic-material and cultural-discursive terms. The long and still ongoing process of modernization can be summarized with reference to its economic, political, and cultural strands, all of which relied on, and were related to each other through, infrastructures of information and communication (for overview, see Thompson, 1995).

modernization

First, the modern *economy* became characterized by capitalization and industrialization. A growing division, mechanization, and rationalization of labor, increasingly also at the international level, and with variable phases of market competition, concentration, imperialism, and conglomeration, all set the stage for renewed physical and discursive conflicts over the distribution of natural resources and primary social goods. < New productive capacities were being cultivated as natural and material sciences redefined themselves as practical undertakings, and their findings

capitalization and industrialization of the economy

> primary social goods – Chapter 4, p. 101

were disseminated far beyond learned journals and academies. < The French *Encyclopédie* (1751–72), along with other large-scale reference works, symbolized a distinctively modern ambition of making all the world's knowledge universally available and practically applicable.

> the modern inversion of theory and practice – Chapter 5, p. 132

Second, modern *politics* witnessed a decisive, if gradual process democratizing public participation in the institutions of representation and governance. The massive transformation of the natural environment through human intervention with manifestly unequal, unjust outcomes – experienced by individuals within the span of their own lifetime (Ord, 2020: 15) – motivated the idea that also society and history would have to be re-made by humans. Print media documented and debated problems and proposed solutions; they also enabled the organization of mass parties as popular action movements and electoral systems as institutional bureaucracies. Communication about injustice had become an open-ended process with concrete political ramifications.

democratization and bureaucratization of politics

Third, *culture* acquired new meanings and implications, beyond tradition and learning as received from the past. The moderns faced the possibility of daring to know about several comprehensive doctrines < at the same time, or of rejecting any such doctrine. Modern culture can be characterized in terms of a stepwise, double secularization, as "the principle of toleration [has been applied] to philosophy [and culture] itself" (Rawls, 2005/1993: 10): Both organized religion and elite arts have been called into question. Cultural tradition, including philosophy and religion, was no longer able to deliver first premises or final ends regarding what is and what ought to be. The world had no evident or experienced *telos* orienting and guiding virtuous action. Accordingly, modern thinkers found themselves in a predicament where they not only could, but had to make the future – by self-legislation through reason (deontology) or by measuring the likely consequences of their more or less rational actions (consequentialism).

> comprehensive doctrines – Chapter 4, p. 108

the double secularization of modern culture

Cut loose from tradition and ritual, culture lent itself to different formulations. On the one hand, the modern arts conceived themselves as the site and source of extraordinary insights without practical purpose or, in Immanuel Kant's (2004a/1790: n.p.) terms, "disinterested delight." These insights would be separate from economic and political preoccupations, and superior to other cultural forms. On the other hand, the modern arts proposed to replace an *eternal* metaphysical order with a canon that could, nevertheless, be considered *universal*. Such a canon was soon confronted by *historical* and contingent standards of meaning

disinterested delight

folk culture

popular culture

and beauty. 'Folk' culture, for one, was becoming key to the legitimation of different (more or less nationalistic) nation-states, their culture and politics. 'Popular' culture, for another, embraced both high and low formats and contents, as carried by print media and, with time, audiovisual entertainments for the masses and across national borders. For better or worse, the commercialization of culture promoted a democratization of the very idea of culture.

modernity

> institutions of knowledge and communication – Chapter 2, p. 26

The distinctive experience of modernity was that of an open future, full of potential, but also holding fundamental uncertainties and ambivalences regarding what to do next (Berman, 1982; Giddens, 1991; Huyssen, 1986). What futures were possible; which might be preferable or just according to human, collective reasoning; and how could such a future be enacted? Reflection and deliberation on these questions were carried on in modern institutions of knowledge and communication, < which have relied on several overlapping media.

Media of discovery, justification, application, and dissemination

> contexts of discovery and justification – Chapter 3, p. 79

media of registration

Over the last century, scientific disciplines and fields have sought to stand out from other human endeavors with reference to a distinction between contexts of discovery and justification < (Popper, 1972a/1934; Reichenbach, 1938). The aim has been to separate the more or less brilliant discoveries by individual scholars (which are said to simply happen) from the long-term, regularized, communal activity of justifying specific conclusions and inferences. In a first step, discoveries are enabled by media of registration or documentation – microscopes and telescopes, the census and fine-grained typologies of the natural world. In a next step, linguistic, mathematical, and other systems of notation support critical reflection and intersubjective deliberation on findings and implications, as recorded and exchanged for the longest time through print media, enhanced by advances in the visual display of information (Tufte, 1983, 1990), with time in photography and moving images. In this understanding, scientific communication can be seen as a world unto itself.

contexts of application

the industrial revolution

Both before scientific discovery and after scientific justification, however, practice enters into the equation. As reviewed in Chapter 5, modern scientific discovery subordinated theory to practice and redefined practice as production in an attempt to master nature, including the human body, and to rebuild the natural environment for human ends in diverse contexts of application. Summed up as an industrial revolution, the scale and scope of material production grew massively and on a global scale during the nineteenth century and into the twentieth. Whereas the modern sciences had depended, from the outset, on increasingly specialized media of registration, the resulting deliveries presented additional challenges of how, in practice, to master the rebuilt environment. The solution became yet another reconception of 'information' and what it might afford social planning. Matter was getting out of control, and had to be in-formed in new ways. In an innovative analysis of the crisis of control that resulted, James R. Beniger (1986) showed how, from the late nineteenth century, a control revolution anticipated what would later be dubbed the information society (Bell, 1973; Porat, 1977). The guiding principles were bureaucratization and rationalization; the concrete instruments were newly available means of information and communication such as telegraphy, telephony, and punch-card processing, to be followed by digital technologies, which may equal, or surpass, print and electronic technologies in their global practical consequences (Baldwin, 2016).

the control revolution

the information society

The implications for justice, as modernity unleashed new productive capacities and new political and cultural energies, were twofold. First, and most evidently, primary social goods – what people will want "whatever else they want" (Rawls, 1999b/1971: 230) – were becoming more plentiful, and their distribution gave rise to renewed social struggles: Who would benefit, how much, compared to whom, from a greatly increased material (and immaterial) production to lead good or, at least, better lives? Second, the uses of media for defining and enacting – producing and practicing – justice were becoming key to working out the intersection between human laws and natural laws. Who would have the necessary and sufficient information to address and resolve conflicts and crises of control? Who would know what, to do what, compared to others? Rights of information, < accordingly, entered diverse political agendas, regarding the role of the public sphere, but also concerning the scientific systems producing ever more knowledge and the schools and other civil society institutions disseminating knowledge and deliberating on its implications for the general public.

> rights of information – Chapter 7, p. 201

The oral mediation of written materials in scribal cultures had suggested how media feed into social contexts of dissemination through several steps of communication. The insight was rediscovered (without reference to the scribal past) as twentieth-century communication studies (Park & Pooley, 2008) began to address widespread worries that the mass media would have massive effects on audiences' attitudes and behaviors. An early

contexts of dissemination

> two-step flow of communication – p. 179

finding was summed up in the two-step flow model of communication, < which suggested that people take their guidance in politics, consumption, and other matters of choice, less from 'the media' than from small-group interactions *about* media content and from opinion leaders *within* such groups. It is essential to look beyond individual media, new and old, and to follow the flows of communication, not just between individuals, but among institutions, beyond small scientific and other specialist communities and into wider public communities. As opined by Fowler (1911: 730) more than a century ago, scholars seem to be "getting to know more and more about less and less." And, as noted by Rawls (1999b/1971: 315), "No one [...] knows everything the others know, or can make all the same inferences that they can draw in concert."

Communication flows

One-to-one, one-to-many, and many-to-many communications

Human communication can be categorized into basic types, covering face-to-face as well as technologically mediated interaction (Jensen & Helles, 2011). Table 6.1 outlines how such basic practices have related to different historical technologies of communication. Along its vertical dimension, the table divides communicative practices according to the number of participants: How many are in a position to say something to how many others? Along the horizontal dimension, the reference is to three broad variants of information and communication technology; for purposes of this overview and a contemporary theory of justice, I treat oral and scribal communication as part of one category (see further Jensen, 2010).

> the affordances of media – p. 165

Each practice is associated with a prototype of distinctive material affordances < and institutional arrangements. First of all, embodied human beings are necessary and sufficient conditions of communication, here and now; face-to-face exchanges remain key to all social life; but one-to-one interactions are limited in the scale and scope of what they may achieve. Telephony and other messaging technologies offered, literally, "extensions of man" (McLuhan, 1964) across space and time. Second, analog technologies, from printing to broadcasting, made one-to-many or mass communication conceivable – practicable. Despite their one-way bias, print and broadcast media significantly enhanced access to the available information. Third, digital technologies

media as extensions of humans

analog technologies

digital technologies

TABLE 6.1 Communicative practices across media types

Communicative practices	*Media types*		
	Embodied technologies	*Analog technologies*	*Digital technologies*
One-to-one	PROTOTYPE Face-to-face conversation, hand-written letters and records	Telegraph, telephone, fax	Email, text message, instant messaging, IP telephony
One-to-many	Manuscript, theater, painting, sculpture, architecture, musical composition	PROTOTYPE Book, newspaper, magazine, broadcasting, audio and video recording	Web 1.0 / webpage, download, streaming (mass) media
Many-to-many	Cave painting, gaming, graffiti, notice board, agora, marketplace, stadium	Community media, public-access radio and television, telephone chat services	PROTOTYPE Web 2.0 / wiki, file-sharing site, online chat, massively multiplayer online gaming, social network site, blog, auction site

have extended access to also sending information in many-to-many configurations, with implications that are only beginning to be felt and understood.

One-to-one communication is the evolutionary and historical archetype that models of communication will invoke so as to characterize other forms of communication. Basic to all socialization and acculturation, one-to-one communication, further, represents the minimal manifestation of an individual vis-à-vis others, an articulation of one's existence and identity in private as well as public settings. Walter J. Ong (1982) described orality as a primary mode of consciousness and communication, which was given a secondary, scripted form in radio and television (and which, in a tertiary form, reappears in the many informal features of digital genres (Jensen, 2010: 67)). Transferred to writing, one-to-one communication in the form of both personal letters and official communications served as essential practical means of contact and organization for centuries (Walker, 2007), given increasing literacy, but absent telephony.

one-to-one communication

secondary and tertiary orality

Compared to the one-to-one (and few-to-few) communications of the itinerant poets of oral culture who were institutions in

> the communicative structuration of society – p. 188

> communication and transportation – Chapter 2, p. 42

their own right, one-to-one communication in analog and digital technologies also contribute to the informal and ongoing communicative structuration of society. < Communication prefigures and configures society: the constituent institutions of the basic structure of society, from families and friendships to markets and parliaments. Telegraphy and telephony extended one-to-one communication across space and time in ways that reshaped both public infrastructures and private businesses. The telegraph helped to coordinate railroad schedules as part of an emerging separation of communication and transportation; < the telephone facilitated urban and suburban sprawls of work and leisure (de Sola Pool, 1977). Gradually, the landline telephone became both a household item with personal uses and a generic resource for cultural participation and political activism (Fischer, 1992; Winston, 1998). And the communicative structuration of society has become increasingly manifest and obvious with digital media, such as email and messaging services, through which one-to-one communication becomes ubiquitous, crisscrossing work, leisure, private and public relations. With digital technologies, imagined communities (Anderson, 1991) beyond mass-communicated nation-states, as well, have become conceivable and practicable, if not always pursued and actualized.

transnational imagined communities

one-to-many communication

manuscripts

presentations and performances

Print media introduced one-to-many communication as an institutionalizing force of society and history. In retrospect, mass communication was prefigured not just by manuscripts, as disseminated by authorities and their emissaries, but by secular and religious presentations and performances in local settings. From theater and musical composition to sculpture and painting, cultural events and artifacts articulated visions both of eternity and of the more immediate future, in different genres and styles for different strata of society. Music, in the modern period, came to be understood as mass communication to passive and silent listeners. The convention of how to appropriately attend to music became one of focusing attention on the performance on stage, and on one's individual, interior experience; this represented a marked contrast to music as a communal practice giving priority to participation and interaction with others in the venue about the experience on offer (Johnson, 1995). Closer to power as conventionally understood, the bourgeois public sphere had been preceded by a 'representative' public sphere in which sovereigns would present themselves to their underlings in public as the embodied representatives of power (Habermas, 1989/1962).

the representative public sphere

> the bourgeois public sphere – Chapter 3, p. 52

As summarized in Chapter 3, the bourgeois public sphere < was premised on the notion that societies might govern themselves through communication, flowing between and among coffee-houses, clubs, *salons*, journals, and newspapers. The idea took hold that news presses, above all, would serve as a political fourth estate or branch of government. < It should be reemphasized, however, that both fine arts and popular entertainments enabled the moderns' imagining of alternative realities. Novels presented full-fledged universes for exploration and emulation by a rising middle class (Watt, 1957). Visual arts moved beyond eternal themes and divine tableaux to portray contemporary social sceneries (Davies et al., 2015), and from the late nineteenth century came to include abstract depictions of a reality in flux, not captured by life-like photography and cinema (Hughes, 1991). For popular audiences, as well, print fictions helped to place the lived social realities of the majority in perspective (Denning, 1987). Print was joined by sound recordings and portable gramophones for mobile music consumption (Millard, 1995; Nott, 2002) and, in turn, by audiovisual and electronic media – cinema, radio, television, the internet – that made representations of nature, culture, and other regions of the world (and more injustices) more accessible in additional modalities of communication.

> the fourth branch of governance – p. 186

All the while, verbal language remained a privileged modality – in evolutionary, psychological, and social terms. Language relays categorical information that can be recategorized – restated, rejected, responded to – in ways that no other modality can. The linguist, Émile Benveniste (1985/1969: 236), noted that "the signs of society can be interpreted integrally by those of language, but the reverse is not so." Verbal language interprets images, but rarely vice versa, except in the occasional aesthetic experiment. The human capability of language, as extended in other media of expression and interaction, has been key to the formulation of general rights, concrete alternatives, and responses to questions of justice. <

language as a privileged modality

> the capability of communication – Chapter 7, p. 193

The third communicative practice – many-to-many – has received special attention in recent years, in research and public debate. In the words of a book title by Clay Shirky (2008), "Here comes everybody," as senders, receivers, and co-creators of information and communication. In Table 6.1, I note many-to-many communication as the prototype of communication in the case of digital technologies; in the cells immediately above, I also indicate that a very large proportion of all digital communication is still of the one-to-many (and one-to-one) varieties. Searching for practical information from websites, and streaming films and television series, do involve choices, but are more akin to being a mass media audience than to being a cultural entrepreneur or political

many-to-many communication

the 90/9/1 ratio

activist. The point has been summed up in a 90/9/1 ratio or 1-percent rule (Nielsen, 2006). The implication is that, in online communities, 1 percent of participants will deliver most of the contributions by far; 9 percent may contribute from time to time; and the 90-percent majority lurk or, in a positive formulation, appreciate what others have to say. While I return to digital media and communication in the next two sections, both public and scholarly debates about the potentials of the internet for human emancipation and social progress can be seen to replay the utopias and dystopias that have been associated with each generation of 'new' media. <

> utopias and dystopias of communication – Chapter 1, p. 7

Like one-to-one interactions, many-to-many communicative practices have entered into the communicative structuration of society. Social network sites, blogs, file-sharing sites, and more have become integral to private business, public governance, civil society, and the personal lives of a majority of the world's population (Internetlivestats, 2020). The convergence of previously separate media *and* their integration into the everyday practices of so many users are explained by the distinctive affordances of the digital computer as a meta-medium. The digital computer reproduces and recombines all previous media of representation and interaction (and introduces new ones) on a single material platform of hardware and software. At the beginning of the era of personal computers, Alan Kay and Adele Goldberg (1999/1977) described computers as meta-media. As means of representation, digital media join text, image, and sound in some new and many old genres, as inherited from mass media as well as from face-to-face interaction: narratives, debates, gaming, etc. As modes of interaction, moreover, digital media integrate and interrelate one-to-one, one-to-many, and many-to-many forms of communication. The ongoing digitalization of social institutions and practices, and of infrastructures and utilities, < entails that the very idea of communication is in for another round of theory development.

the computer as meta-medium

> the Internet of Things – Chapter 7, p. 211

Many-to-many communication is not unprecedented or unheard of, as suggested in Table 6.1, but its scale and scope has been limited by technological, professional, and other practical circumstances. Community media, including public-access channels in radio and television systems, gave voice to citizen groups and other non-professionals regarding shared, public concerns of the twentieth century (Rennie, 2006). In more private settings, telephone chat services enabled romantic and other forms of personal contact. In the cultural domain, coauthored publications relating to the media themselves have taken the shape of fanzines and fan fiction (Jenkins, 1992; Lewis, 1991). In

public access

fan media

retrospect, many-to-many communication may be said to have unfolded, in embodied forms, in marketplaces, stadia, agoras, and other community settings; even cave paintings and graffiti might be thought of as many-to-many communication.

community fora

Throughout the twentieth century, public intellectuals – from Bertolt Brecht (1993/1932) to Hans-Magnus Enzensberger (1972/1970) to Larry Lessig (1999) – have considered how more participatory forms of communication might compensate for the limitations of mass media. However, the relative predominance of one-to-many and, recently, many-to-many communication is only half the story of how communication relates to justice. Communication flows not just one-to-one, one-to-many, and many-to-many, but in multiple, interlinked steps. As already mentioned, contemporary communication research, which took shape at the apex of mass communication, developed the idea of two-step flows, highlighting the interdependence of one-to-many and one-to-one (or few-to-few) communications. With digital technologies have come a third step of many-to-many communications (Jensen, 2009, 2010). New media reconfigure old flows of communication; they also suggest new ways of understanding how communication flows, new practical concepts of communication.

Information flows, user flows, and context flows

In the current digital media environment, people still pass along news, tall tales, and jokes in face-to-face interactions; they still attend to legacy media as (more or less) preferred sources of fact and fiction; and people rely on social media as both points of departure and final destinations for their other communications – people do all of these things in long sequences and complicated networks. To identify both the potential and actual flows of these communications, I next address two questions: *What* flows in communication? And, what is the *number and type of steps* that enter into different communicative practices? (Analysis Box 6.1.)

The concept of flow has been associated, in communication studies, with Raymond Williams' (1974) characterization of broadcasting as technology and cultural form. Especially in commercial television and radio, viewers and listeners have been encouraged to go with the flow – to keep watching and listening throughout commercial breaks and transitions between programs. In a more fine-grained analysis, broadcasting is constituted through different types of flow: The *channel flow* of one station enters into the *super flow* of all the contents on offer in a given market, and

radio and television flow

channel flow, super flow, audience flow

the actual *audience flows* are the product of people's selections and combinations from the various channel flows (Jensen, 1994). Also other communicative practices can be thought of in terms of such sequences and transitions between several available flows of contents, from turn-taking in a face-to-face conversation to selections from an online news or shopping service. On the internet, the corresponding super flow is, of course, more complex than any classic television market (or traditional conversational setting); the channel flow of any site or service is multi-layered and integrated with other sites and services; and the user flows involve both navigation between sites and interactivity with each site. Most important, digital networks, increasingly in conjunction with mobile terminals, enable more widely distributed contexts of communication: interactions with other users anywhere, and coordinated actions in dispersed physical locales.

Three types of flows can be identified across different kinds of communication:

- *Information flows.* Like broadcast channels, human beings and internet sites can be understood as potential or available flows of information, sources of fact as well as fiction.
- *User flows.* Users will flow across the available and accessible media types; other humans constitute embodied media of consultation and interaction.
- *Context flows.* With mobile media has come a distinctive kind of contextual mobility (Kakihara & Sørensen, 2002). What's mobile in mobile communication is not so much the information, the user, or the technology, but the contexts in which they come together in communication (Jensen, 2013b). In and through communication, entire formations of social relations – present and absent – move about.

It is these elements that enter into diverse configurations, as part of contemporary social practices and institutions involving multiple steps of communication.

ANALYSIS BOX 6.1 ONE-STEP, TWO-STEP, AND THREE-STEP FLOWS OF COMMUNICATION

one-step flows

One-step flows of communication refer to interpersonal or one-to-one communication as well as to the individual's (mass) media use. In this sense, both individuals and collectives make themselves available for exposure to information and communication or interaction. The understanding that there might be more to human communication followed from early findings in the emerging field of communication research: Media did not, and do not, have massive direct effects on their audiences, despite recurring suggestions to the contrary. Instead, studies found, media work in a two-step flow involving interpersonal communication and with embodied opinion leaders in a pivotal role (Katz & Lazarsfeld, 1955; Lazarsfeld, Berelson, & Gaudet, 1944). The two-step model, thus, contributed to a more nuanced understanding of what (mass) communication is and does. Later studies have found that although media may not tell people *what* to think, they do tell us what to think *about* (agenda-setting – McCombs & Shaw, 1972) and *how* to think about various issues (framing – Gamson, 1992; Scheufele, 1999). The accumulated evidence consistently indicates that communication in society is a multi-step as well as a multi-level process (for overview, see Jensen, 2012c). A further implication of the two-step flow model was that mass and interpersonal communication (and, today, online and offline communication) are interdependent (Rogers, 1999). Recently, many-to-many communication in internet communities, social network sites, mobile messaging, and other formats yet to be imagined and invented, have been added to the classic two-step model that coupled one-to-one and one-to-many communication. Three-step flows are constitutive of the contemporary media environment (Jensen, 2009, 2010).

the two-step flow model

agenda-setting

framing

three-step flows

It should be underlined that these various steps and flows are different in kind; the point is not the number of steps or their quantity, but their quality, their respective contributions to different kinds of communication throughout society. Not all communicative steps or flows are created equal. In the 1940s, news announcers and political columnists addressing their audiences was one type of communicative event; listeners and readers, whether opinion leaders or not, conversing locally with one or a few other people about their preferred political candidate, was rather a different type of social interaction. Today, as well, there is a categorical difference between, on the one hand, A listening to a podcast and, next, engaging in online interactions with B and C

not all communication is created equal

about it and, on the other hand, A telling something to B in the street, who later relates it to C at home or at work.

Following two world wars, the two-step flow model of the 1940s–50s appeared to offer new hope for democracy as it modeled an inclusive public conversation involving both centers and peripheries. In the early years of the twenty-first century, much research and public debate held up the promise and potential of many-to-many communication as a source of reinvigorated public participation, a resource for achieving justice across social domains. While the jury is still out, there is little to suggest that many-to-many communicative practices may reverse the traditional flows of communication from the few to the many (except in the case addressed in Analysis Box 7.1). Empirical studies have indicated, for example, that legacy media still predominate as information providers and agenda-setters (e.g., Himelboim, 2010; Meraz, 2009). Other research has suggested that the comparatively participatory genre of blogs may not promote dialogue among citizens (Kenix, 2009). Communication still "may simply be two people taking turns broadcasting at each other" (Peters, 1999: 264). Rights of communication < must be defined with reference to several steps and flows.

> rights of communication – Chapter 7, p. 204

To begin to assess the implications of different flows of communication for justice, it is important to introduce a final specification of the two-step flow model (Katz & Lazarsfeld, 1955; Lazarsfeld et al., 1944): Communication flows among the various institutions of society, not just between individuals and media. The technologies of the current media environment are embedded into the basic structure of society, including the classic institutions producing, preserving, and disseminating information – schools, libraries, museums, and more. I referred previously to context flows < in the case of mobile media; in and through mobile communication, entire social contexts move about. Also other practices of communication transport and translate information into diverse contexts of application and interaction. Schools (Peterson, Tierney, Baker, & McGaw, 2010), while offering skills for individual empowerment, have held an ambiguous potential in this regard. Typically organized around religious or vocational interests, education has helped to keep the faith and get the job done. (Luckily, what schools bring out in the open are generic competences that may be turned to contestable issues and against vested interests.) Libraries (Lerner,

flows between individuals and between institutions

> context flows – p. 178

education

2009; Wiegand & Davis, 1994), further, have evolved from being closed treasures for scholars and clergy to being public resources. In a modern worldview, people must be able to see and read for themselves, if they are to dare to know. Museums and other archives (Bennett, 1995), finally, have been opened up to the general public on the assumption that a good life in the present is informed by an awareness of the lives, good and bad, of others in the past. All these institutions – schools, libraries, museums – house factual and fictional, possible as well as actual worlds to consider with a view to the future.

libraries

museums

Many-to-one communication

digitalization

> rights of privacy – Chapter 7, p. 212

Digitalization is currently reshaping media, libraries, museums, schools, and other social institutions; digitalization is, once again, calling the very idea of communication into question. In digital systems, the right to privacy < has recently emerged alongside rights of information and communication as a key conceptual as well as practical issue. Who has access to which data, with what implications for the people who said something to each other?

If humans have always been speaking into the air (Peters, 1999), and increasingly interact through technological media channels, in recent decades we have also been communicating into the system (Jensen & Helles, 2017). It is now common knowledge that, in and of their reliance on digital systems, users leave behind bit trails that are accumulated, and which serve to structure future communications, with or without the users' knowledge and consent, within and beyond the medium in question. In digital media, we communicate not only one-to-one, one-to-many, and many-to-many, but also many-to-one.

Many-to-one communication has implications far beyond media as dedicated institutions of communication. One example is real-time bidding for advertising space, in which the information that is available about users and their earlier trajectories serves to personalize the push of commercial messages. Another example is the documentation of general user preferences over time that drives the recommendation of media titles, but also the marketing of other goods and services in systems such as Amazon, Netflix, and Spotify. In each case, what occurs is not so much an intentional communication *by* users, but an instrumental registration *of* users. What people do with digital media (Katz, 1959) is to orient their attention toward them, in sequences and networks that later come to inform what the same media, or third parties, do with and to users. The audience is the message.

the audience is the message

Performing justice

Positive and negative freedoms

institutions of governance

> the fourth branch of governance – p. 186

> rights of participation – Chapter 7, p. 207

Communication mediates human agency and social structure, enabling doubt, delay, and deliberation before collective decisions with, frequently, unpredictable and irreversible consequences pass through institutions of governance – the legislative, executive, and judicial branches of government, as monitored by what has come to be thought of as a fourth branch: media. < Rights of participation < pertain to the process of focusing and translating information and communication into beliefs that communities will be willing to act on: constitutions, legislative principles, policy formulations, administrative procedures, mechanisms of redress. In the process, justice is performed, and the participating citizens perform themselves as agents and constituents of (a more or less just) society.

democracy

Athenian democracy

direct democracy

> positive and negative freedom – Chapter 2, p. 36

Democracy is the term generally summarizing this complex process, even if "a general commitment to democracy is a very recent phenomenon," and although, today, "political regimes of all kinds describe themselves as democracies" (Held, 2006: 1). In an overview of different models of democracy, David Held highlighted two considerations cutting across the two traditions of republicanism and liberalism (which, beyond classical Athenian democracy and modern notions of direct democracy, can be considered key to contemporary research and debate). In doing so, he reiterated the distinction between positive and negative conceptions of freedom (Berlin, 1969), which have been key figures of thought and discourse in scholarly and public discussion of the ends and means of justice, up to and including Rawls' two principles of justice: < What should be the balance between the right of individuals to pursue their version of the good without interference from the collective (negative freedom), compared to the responsibility of the collective for addressing resulting inequalities and securing "compensating benefits for everyone, and in particular for the least advantaged members of society" (Rawls, 1999b/1971: 13) (positive freedom)? As important, how could and should different individuals and interests in society participate in striking such a balance?

republicanism

From the early Renaissance, Italian city-states had witnessed a form of republicanism in which (male, taxable) citizens would participate in self-governance through ruling councils with executive heads. The model of Renaissance republicanism, however, was given two distinctive formulations. *Developmental* republican theory, on the one hand, drew inspiration from classical Greek philosophy regarding "the inherent value of political participation and of the *polis* as a means to self-fulfilment [...] the development of citizens as human beings" (Held, 2006: 35). Political participation may be said to produce good citizens, who consequently will be in a better position to lead good lives; citizens and democracies are co-constructed through communication. On the other hand, *protective* republican theory was influenced from "republican Rome and its historians," stressing political participation for "its instrumental importance for the protection of citizens' aims and objectives," and noting "the highly fragile nature of civic virtue and its vulnerability to corruption if dependent solely upon the political involvement of any one major grouping, whether it be the people, the aristocracy or the monarchy" (p. 35). In this second version of republican theory, political participation is undertaken by already full-fledged citizens, who join forces to rein in the necessary collective arrangements; communication coordinates individual self-defense. Both formulations of republicanism could be heard to echo virtue ethics: < The political principles and procedures in question give priority either to the intrinsic process of individuals learning to be virtuous or to the instrumental enforcement of boundaries within which individuals may pursue virtue.

> virtue ethics – Chapter 2, p. 31

liberalism

The other main tradition – liberalism – emerged as a political articulation of modernity < vis-à-vis the *ancien regime* of feudal powers. In fact, political liberalism was paradoxically indebted to the absolutist monarchies dominating European states from the fifteenth to the eighteenth centuries:

> modernity – p. 170

> As the [absolutist] state's sovereign authority expanded and its administrative centres became more powerful, there was not simply [...] a concentration of power at the apex. For the increase in administrative power increased the state's dependence on cooperative forms of social relations; it was no longer possible for the state to manage its affairs and sustain its offices and activities by coercion alone. [...] Absolutism, in short, created within itself a momentum towards the development of new forms of and limits on state power – constitutionalism and (eventually) participation by powerful groups in the process of government itself.
>
> *Held, 2006: 57*

This momentum "paved the way for a national and secular system of power," accelerated by the Protestant Reformation, which entailed "bitter struggles between religious factions [...] across Europe during the last half of the sixteenth century [that] reached their most intensive expression during the Thirty Years' War in Germany" (p. 57), followed by the Westphalian Peace. < At issue were both the ends and the means of political participation. In a liberal optic, the end was one of "freeing the polity from religious control and freeing civil society (personal, family and business life) from political interference"; the means "a constitutional state, private property and the competitive market economy" (p. 59). The key issue became how 'free' individuals should relate to 'state' institutions, both as a matter of principle and through procedures balancing what is good for the individual against what is right for the collective.

> the Westphalian Peace – p. 168

Like republicanism, liberalism developed and practiced protective and developmental variants. Advanced by John Locke (2018/1690) in his *Two Treatises of Government*, and refined by utilitarian philosophers, protective democracy emphasized an instrumental approach to political participation and governance as such. The state is for the sake of the individual; a burdensome, but necessary invention circumscribing citizens' coexistence:

protective democracy

> The creation of a political community or government is the burden individuals have to bear to secure their ends. Thus, membership of a political community, i.e. citizenship, bestows on the individual both responsibilities and rights, duties and powers, constraints and liberties.
>
> *Held, 2006: 64*

In this vein, Jeremy Bentham and James Mill went on to extend the utilitarian principle of 'the greatest happiness for the greatest number' to politics. As a proposed scientific criterion replacing individual and collective virtue, this principle was advanced as the standard by which also political institutions and their deliveries to the public would be measured. <

> utilitarianism – Chapter 2, p. 38

James Mill's son, John Stuart Mill (2011/1859), in *On Liberty*, advocated a developmental variant of liberal democracy, which brought the distinction between positive and negative freedoms into focus. Compared to developmental republicanism, which retained the teleological flavor of virtue ethics, developmental liberalism reemphasized the process in which modern individuals define themselves. But, as recognized by (John Stuart) Mill, self-development within a complex social structure could only be

developmental democracy

accomplished through various devices of representation, < literally the re-presentation of interests and viewpoints, in parliamentary proceedings and political presses. "Liberal democratic or representative government was important for [John Stuart Mill], not just because it established boundaries for the pursuit of individual satisfaction, but because it was an important aspect of the free development of individuality" (Held, 2006: 79). Self-development depends on the opportunity to exercise reason, as represented in deontological principles rather than by utilitarian consequences or Aristotelian *phronesis*: "Active involvement in determining the conditions of one's existence is the prime mechanism for the cultivation of human reason and moral development" (p. 82). Justice requires not just a measure of positive and material "compensating benefits" (Rawls, 1999b/1971: 13), but participation in any definition of such benefits.

> re-presentation – p. 187

The distinction between positive and negative freedoms has remained a backdrop to political and policy debates on justice; I return to Amartya Sen's capability approach < as an important recent engagement with the issue. Aspects of John Stuart Mill's position, further, foregrounded positive freedom and advocated "a fully fledged 'social democratic' conception of politics," even though "it was left by and large to the extensive and often violently suppressed struggles of working-class and feminist activists in the nineteenth and twentieth centuries to accomplish a genuinely universal suffrage in some countries" (Held, 2006: 93f.). And it would take multiple economic crises and two world wars for an "expanding, Keynesian, interventionist state" to emerge (p. 186), followed by still continuing debates about the right measure of 'state' regulation of 'free' individuals. This was also the historical background to John Rawls' works and the critiques from both right and left of the political spectrum: libertarianism < as a fundamentalist liberalism and communitarianism < as a contemporary restatement of republicanism. Like other political philosophers, however, Rawls remained largely silent on the institutions and practices of communication that are necessary for citizens to participate in self-governance. Alongside the three classic branches of modern governance – legislative, executive, and judicial – a heterogeneous fourth branch of governance operates through communication.

> Sen's capability approach – Chapter 7, p. 193

the Keynesian welfare state

> libertarianism – Chapter 4, p. 120

> communitarianism – Chapter 4, p. 121

Branches of governance

The idea that a division of political powers is both practically necessary and normatively desirable, had been noted in classical

Athens, and was restated by John Locke, but it was Charles Louis de Secondat, Baron de Montesquieu (2008/1748) who consolidated the distinction between three branches of government: legislative, executive, and judicial. Legislators will reflect and deliberate on principles of coexistence and coordination at increasingly granular levels of implementation and operation; executives will enact these principles through procedures deriving from legislatures and civil service agencies; and judges will assess and evaluate the relationship between principles and procedures, enactments and outcomes, theory and practice, deferring also to legal precedent. While all three branches can be studied as communicative practices, it is a fourth branch that has come to be associated with institutions of communication, the political press in particular. Since the emergence of a modern public sphere, < the press has served a dual role of monitoring the powers that be – the other three branches of government – while at the same time carrying news and opinion back and forth between the general public and its elected and appointed representatives.

legislative, executive, and judicial branches of government

> the public sphere – Chapter 3, p. 52

Two different terminologies – the fourth estate and the fourth branch of government – both suggest the intermediate position of the media at the intersection of institutionalized politics, economic entrepreneurship, and the cultures of everyday life. First, the notion of a fourth estate is normally attributed to the eighteenth-century Irish statesman, political theorist, and member of parliament, Edmund Burke (Schultz, 1998: 49). Following the opening up of the House of Commons of Great Britain to press reporting, Burke commented that the press had entered into politics as a fourth force to be reckoned with alongside the social classes of nobility, clergy, and commoners; his use of the term was "a derogatory reference to the self-importance of parliamentary reporters in 1787" (p. 49). As such, his terminology pointed to a social formation that, like other classes, could be expected to represent particular interests – their readers, but also the newspaper entrepreneurs feeding the watchdog. Second, the reference to a fourth branch of government has been dominant in the United States (Cater, 1959). Supposedly, the US populace has not been characterized by estates or classes. More important, with a First Amendment emphasizing freedom of speech as an institutional as well as ideological construct, the press has come to be perceived as a quasi-official political agent, an understanding that has been reasserted at regular intervals by the media themselves, from the muckrakers of the Progressive Era to the revelations of Watergate to Edward Snowden documenting US government surveillance of its own citizens. What the two perspectives share,

the fourth estate

the fourth branch of government

nevertheless, is an assumption that the press and, more generally, institutions and practices of communication play a special role in the basic structure of modern society. *There's no business like show business* (Irving Berlin, 1946), no branch of governance like the media, feeding public communications into political institutions.

With modernization, as amplified by analog and digital technologies, has come an open-ended vision of how civil society, as a residual entity, could and should relate to the established institutions of state and market, being a source of imagined realities and a resource for emergent collective agency. The double secularization of culture < has entailed a culturalization of politics and economy: a continuous questioning of the boundaries between established institutions, in and through communications that extend across the entire basic structure of society. The feminist insight that the private is political, is one major example of how definitions of which issues may legitimately be deliberated on in public are subject to contestation and change. Other examples of issues crossing institutional boundaries include consumer rights and corporate social responsibility. Even the number of branches of government or governance has been subject to debate with reference to a fifth branch that has been equated, variously, with state administrations as political forces in their own right, with national and international special-interest lobbies, and with the scientific institutions that inform both material production and its social uses. The examples suggest why a terminology of 'governance' may be preferred over 'government,' which, in much public communication, has come to be associated with excessive bureaucracy and interventionism.

civil society

> the double secularization of culture – p. 169

the culturalization of politics and economy

a fifth branch of government

The question of how the different branches of governance re-present the interests of citizens, cuts across political philosophy and communication theory. Facts, issues, arguments, and inferences are all re-presented in discourse for each branch to work; the branches themselves are instantiated by human beings – delegates – re-presenting various powers, positions, and interests in their internal as well as external communications. A classic issue in political philosophy has been the status of such representatives or delegates, specifically in parliamentary assemblies, whether they are to be understood as autonomous agents engaging in communication and deliberation with other agents or, rather, as relays presenting the predefined positions of their constituencies (Pitkin, 1967). In the perspective of communication theory, the question is how citizens' interests and stakes in primary social goods < are represented in discourses, practices, and institutions of communication and subsequently translated – legislated on, executed,

re-presentation

> primary social goods – Chapter 4, p. 101

> justice as representativity – Chapter 7, p. 201

and judged – in established branches of governance. In Chapter 7, I elaborate on representativity < as a principle of communication and justice.

The mediation of agency and structure

To sum up the historical trajectory of media as conditions and constituents of justice, information and communication technologies have been developed and transformed over time as mediators of human agency and social structure, articulating the potentials for justice and anticipating their actualization. Media have made information *available*, depending on different and distinctive technologies and on the institutions embedding these into the basic structure of society. Media have made communication about public issues *accessible* to a greatly increased proportion of national citizenries and of the world's population. And, media have facilitated the enactment or *performance* of justice through the three branches of modern governance. In each respect, human communication has been and remains integral to the structuration of society (Giddens, 1984); communication prefigures and configures society through signs and symbols (Jensen, 1995).

the communicative structuration of society

In Chapter 5, I recovered the philosophical substream of pragmatism, and characterized individual cognition and communal communication as orientations toward the future. Having communicated in communities – expert as well as lay – we hold beliefs that we choose to act on, or must act on, by natural and social deadlines. Peirce's model of the sign < suggested that all knowledge *of* and interaction *about* the world is mediated by signs, which feed into extensive processes of interpretation and interaction – communication across time and space. Figure 6.1 reiterates the basic model, and relates its elements to the key concepts of information, communication, and action: Information constitutes a relation in which something stands for something else; in and through communication, people gain confirmatory, complementary, as well as alternative understandings of this and that something else; and from the vantage point of interpretants, people are in a position to engage in action, individually and in concerted efforts.

> Peirce's model of the sign – Chapter 5, p. 138

Figure 6.2 scales up the mechanism of semiosis or communication to the level of the social structure: Social agents continuously produce, maintain, repair, and transform the structure they inhabit, always with reference to meaningful signs or media. Whereas the social sciences, like political philosophy, have traditionally focused attention to the dialectic of agency and structure,

agency, structure, medium

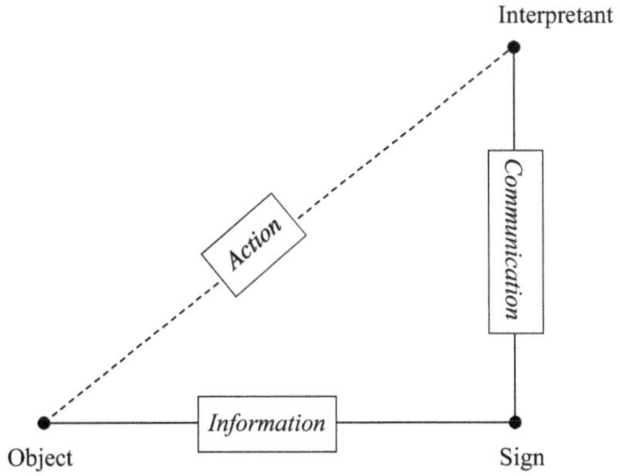

FIGURE 6.1 Peirce's model of the sign

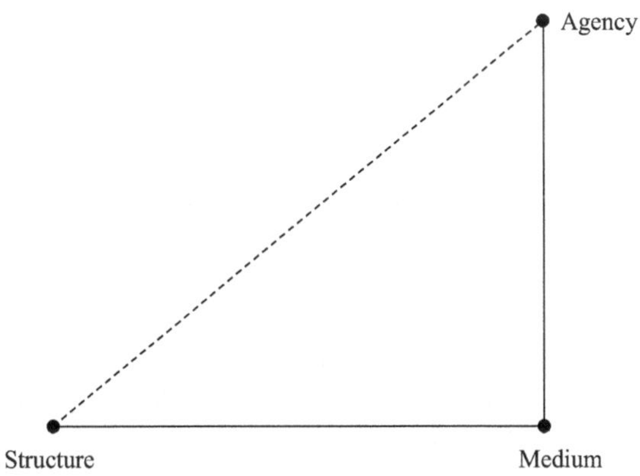

FIGURE 6.2 The communicative structuration of society

in this volume I have reemphasized the constitutive role of communication in all social life. As part of the description and pursuit of justice, communication must be conceived and studied on a par with agency and structure. Whether face-to-face or technologically mediated, communication is the fundamental process by which individuals and collectives relate to sources of information in considering, contesting, and coordinating what should be done.

In and through communication, citizens perform societies and themselves – and approximations of justice. Communication flows through many media, but ends in ways that make a practical, performative difference < for the good life and the common good. It is for this reason that a theory of communication and justice is both called for and overdue; Chapters 7 and 8 present the constituents of such a theory.

> performative difference – Chapter 5, p. 157

7

THE COMMUNICATIVE POSITION

The right to communicate

> modernization – Chapter 6, p. 168

human rights

The idea that all human beings have certain fundamental, inalienable rights was articulated over the span of 150 years (Moyn, 2018). Modernization < had presented an open political, economic, and cultural question of which basic rights humans ought to assign to themselves. Statements from the 1789 French Declaration of the Rights of Man and of the Citizen to the 1948 United Nations Universal Declaration of Human Rights, along with scholarly interventions from Bentham and Kant to Rawls and Sen, have all sought to advance such rights in different definitions and through different vocabularies. But while the universal human practice of communication has figured prominently in reference to freedom of expression and political governance (for overview, see Tumber & Waisbord, 2017), communication has not normally been treated as a general condition or constituent of justice. In this chapter, I develop the idea of a communicative position in which humans exercise the right to reflect and deliberate on their plans in life and the terms of their coexistence. Compared to Rawls' quasi-natural original position < and Habermas' primordial ideal speech situation, < in the communicative position universal rights, primary social goods, and human capabilities are all actualized, contested, and defended with the benefit of historical hindsight and communicative foresight, but within natural and social deadlines, and without guarantees.

> the original position – Chapter 4, p. 99

> the ideal speech situation – Chapter 3, p. 77

> the capabilities approach – p. 193

The first section introduces the capabilities approach, < pioneered by Amartya Sen (1999) and Martha C. Nussbaum

(2011), as a complement and corrective to John Rawls' account of those principles of coexistence that people *would* choose in the original position. Foregrounding historical contingencies and empirical variations, the capabilities approach has refocused attention on the distinction between the potential capabilities and the actual functionings of humans – what we can (and cannot) do and be in practice. Recognizing the many enabling conditions of a good life, capabilities scholars have reinvigorated a positive understanding of freedom as a collective, social accomplishment, if only with occasional or implicit reference to communication (for applications to communication studies, see, e.g., Birdsall, 2011; Britz, Hoffmann, Ponelis, Zimmer, & Lor, 2013; Coleman, Moss, & Martinez-Perez, 2018; Couldry, 2012; Garnham, 1997; Hesmondhalgh, 2017; Jacobson, 2016; Kleine, 2013; Mansell, 2002; Moss, 2018). It is not so much that people *can* choose to re-enter the original position to reflect and deliberate at any time, as suggested by Rawls; humans *must* communicate to arrive at sustainable beliefs and an overlapping consensus on the configurations of capabilities and functionings that they have reason to value as individuals and communities.

The second section lays out two principles of communication and justice, reworking Rawls' two principles of justice as fairness. < Whereas the first principle asserts basic liberties and opportunities for communication, the second principle addresses the enabling and compensatory arrangements that are needed, both for communicative resources to accumulate in society and for the available resources to be distributed fairly among its members. Highlighting the practical limitations of human cognition and communication, I refer to bounded rationality < (Simon, 1957) – the notion that the exercise of reason is constrained by cognitive and communicative capacities in the face of complex problems and contexts of solution, in addition to unavoidable time limits. Communication ends; the window of opportunity closes. <

> two principles of communication and justice – p. 196

> bounded rationality – p. 199

> the window of opportunity for communication – Chapter 2, p. 23

To specify how the two principles of communication and justice may be met, the third section develops an understanding of justice as representativity. < The availability of information, the accessibility of communicative resources, public participation in governance, and privacy – all four aspects of communication and justice lend themselves to analysis and assessment through the concept of representation. Ideas and issues, social agents and their interests, are all represented in discourse within institutions of knowledge, communication, and governance. At issue is the performativity of communication – the difference that specific communicative practices make for the engagement of problematic

> justice as representativity – p. 201

situations (Dewey, 1903), the negotiation of ends and means, and the long-term structuration and transformation of society. Joining the Rawlsian and capabilities perspectives and terminologies, the section refers to information, communication, participation, and privacy as primary social goods that instantiate citizens' rights and opportunities, and which facilitate the actualization of their general, potential capabilities as actual functionings in real-life settings.

> communication as condition and constituent of justice – p. 214

The fourth section elaborates on human communication as, at once, a condition and a constituent of justice. < Whereas public debate and political activism have traditionally been foregrounded as enabling conditions of justice, communication is also a constituent of justice, a source of self-respect and self-realization. Communication prefigures and configures the enjoyment of other entitlements. In the capabilities terminology, it is not only that communication conditions *doing* particular things; communication also constitutes *being* a particular individual or community. It is in and through communication that a life lived according to a plan and to the full can be imagined, represented, and shared. It is the task of a theory of communication and justice to qualify and systematize – broaden and deepen – an understanding of the communicative position as a local and global window of opportunity.

Human rights have been given a variety of philosophical and practical definitions; I use the term as a familiar common denominator for what different thinkers and practitioners of justice have found to be at stake, and which are currently being reconsidered with reference to the internet and worldwide digitalization (Jørgensen, 2019). John Rawls did not integrate human rights into either his 1971 or 1993 frameworks, but made passing reference to human rights in the 1999 *Law of Peoples* (Wilkins, 2008). Both Amartya Sen (2005) and Martha C. Nussbaum (1997) have devoted explicit attention to human rights as preparatory conditions of human flourishing, "an especially urgent and morally justified" set of claims that are constitutive of being human (Nussbaum, 1997: 292). In Chapter 6, I traced the emergence of rights of information, communication, participation, and privacy as practical concepts relating to the historical development of modern media – what justice has been. < In the following sections, I present systematic conceptions of information, communication, participation, and privacy, and of representativity and multi-step communications – what communication ought to be. These systematic conceptions also point forward to the empirical conceptualization and operationalization, in Chapter 8, of concrete choices and dilemmas – what justice could be. <

> practical concepts – Chapter 6, p. 163

systematic conceptions

> empirical conceptualizations – Chapter 8

The capability of communication

The capabilities approach has revitalized a positive conception of freedom: < Freedom is not the original state of an individual in any natural or social circumstance, but a collective and historical accomplishment that must be maintained and reenacted, day by day and generation to generation. Restating Aristotle's figure of potentiality and actuality, capabilities scholars have taken steps toward resolving the ambiguity inherent in Rawls' original position. Humans have the capability of transcending themselves, less by reverting to an imagined zero of civilization than through diverse cognitive and communicative practices actualizing the future. The human condition is historical, the preliminary outcome of choices and struggles that have been consolidated in the institutions of the basic structure of contemporary society. <

> positive and negative freedom – Chapter 2, p. 36

> the basic structure of society – Chapter 4, p. 103

Focusing attention on "enhancing justice and removing injustice" in specific social contexts and through empirical reasoning, Sen (2009: ix) has distinguished between freedom as an intrinsic value of human lives and as a set of instrumental rights designed to realize this basic value. On the one hand, freedom covers a set of means, of which he lists five: "(1) political freedoms, (2) economic facilities, (3) social opportunities, (4) transparency guarantees and (5) protective security" (Sen, 1999: n.p.). On the other hand, the capabilities approach treats freedom as an end in itself, "the freedoms of individuals as the basic building blocks. Attention is thus paid particularly to the expansion of the 'capabilities' of persons to lead the kind of lives they value – and have reason to value." In this way, capabilities are said to manifest as "functionings" or "the various things a person may value doing or being." A capability can be defined as what people *could* do or be:

capabilities and functionings

doing and being

> A person's "capability" refers to the alternative combinations of functionings that are feasible for her to achieve. Capability is thus a kind of freedom: the substantive freedom to achieve alternative functioning combinations (or, less formally put, the freedom to achieve various lifestyles).
>
> *Sen, 1999: n.p.*

As one illustration, Sen (1999: n.p.) has referred to the difference between an affluent person fasting and a destitute person starving. While both have the same functioning and are, in a sense, doing the same thing, each evidently has a different "capability set." There is an existential difference between what the first and the second person *could* do. Like the affordances of media, <

capability sets

> the affordances of media – Chapter 6, p. 165

the capabilities of humans must be assessed in relational terms, including the historical time and cultural space in which they are exercised. Also in more affluent countries, it is essential to ask what money can buy: "Being relatively poor in a rich country can be a great capability handicap, even when one's absolute income is high in terms of world standards."

> measuring capabilities – Chapter 8, p. 226

One implication of the capabilities approach is that the evaluation of potential and actual human flourishing around the world calls for more complex or sophisticated measures < than standard ones such as income – personal or national. "For example, family income levels may be adjusted downward by illiteracy and upward by high levels of education, and so on, to make them equivalent in terms of capability achievement" (Sen, 1999: n.p.). Capability sets amount to life packages, beyond physical survival and material sufficiency. Most generally, capabilities "exceed the domain of *potential*, as opposed to *actual*, legal rights." Capabilities can be reinterpreted with reference both to ethically motivated human rights and to what was once inconceivable even as a human right, for example, personalized medicine or digital privacy. In sum, Sen's account of capabilities allows for a diverse and processual understanding of what freedom and justice are, have been, and could become.

how many capabilities are there?

a minimal standard of capabilities?

Among the contested issues in the capabilities literature have been how many capabilities there are, and whether a minimal standard applies to any given capability. Whereas Sen has refrained from judgment in both respects, emphasizing the general minimization of injustice through concrete social choices, Martha C. Nussbaum (2011) has proposed a list of ten central capabilities, ranging from life and bodily integrity to senses, imagination, and thought. For each of these, she has advocated a threshold or "ample social minimum" (p. 40) as a necessary requirement for justice. Her summary question is, "among the many things that human beings might develop the capacity to do, which ones are the really valuable ones, which are the ones that a minimally just society will endeavor to nurture and support?" (p. 28).

mutually reinforcing capabilities

Of special interest here is Nussbaum's treatment of what Sen (1999: n.p.) had referred to as a "capability set," which she has reformulated in terms of an interplay of capabilities that may be mutually reinforcing. Nussbaum (2011) has pointed to two capabilities that "play a distinctive *architectonic* role: they organize and pervade the others" (p. 39). First, *affiliation* refers to the ability to live with others and "to be able to imagine the situation of another," but also affiliation to oneself: "having the social bases of self-respect and nonhumiliation." Second, *practical reason* means "being able to form a conception of the good and to engage in critical reflection about the planning of one's life" (p. 34), which, in turn, entails the "opportunity to choose and order the functionings corresponding to the various other capabilities" (p. 39). Nussbaum's argument aligns with Rawls' (1999b/1971: 358) suggestion that self-respect follows from "a human life lived according to a plan," actualizing one's self-defined potentials.

communication as architectonic capability

Each of these architectonic capabilities, further, depends on the capability of communication, not listed by Nussbaum (2011) and only briefly gestured at by Sen (2009). Communication is a necessary condition and constituent of any affiliation with others as well as of the exercise of practical reason. Whereas, quantitatively, most communications by far belong to the micro-interactions that inform the ongoing structuration of society, < some interactions address essentially contestable choices regarding decisive actions that have long-term and sometimes unforeseeable consequences. Individuals and communities discursively produce – hypothesize < and anticipate – solutions to problematic situations by devising procedures, < some of which are consolidated as institutions and practices of governance. In mundane as well as momentous interchanges, people find themselves in a communicative position, circumscribed by horizons of past experience and confronted by agendas for future action, questions of what could and ought to be done.

> the communicative structuration of society – Chapter 6, p. 189

> beliefs as hypotheses – Chapter 5, p. 145

> communication as public procedure – p. 198

justice is made, not found

While neither the capabilities approach nor the Rawlsian framework has integrated a communicative position, the two traditions share an Aristotelian common ground, the understanding that the potential of justice is actualized in practice and over time. Justice is made, not found. To one side, Rawls assumed that, in the original position, citizens *would* choose the two fundamental principles of justice, and would could go on to establish the institutions of the basic structure of society in a multi-step process. Equal rights and duties would obtain from the outset, while the inequalities resulting from historical and social contingencies would be compensated for through the difference principle. In Rawls' system, at least implicitly, equal rights and subsequent compensations are articulated and implemented through multi-step procedures supported by information and carried by communication. To the other side, Sen and Nussbaum have treated capabilities as potentials, and functionings as actualizations, which are manifested in discursive as well as material and institutional forms – beings and doings. Thus, the capabilities approach helps to specify the sense in which Rawls' framework of justice as fairness represents a practical theory, < whereas the communicative

> justice as fairness as practical theory Chapter 4, p. 110

position explicates some of the necessary premises and procedures of both traditions.

The communicative position historicizes Rawls' original position, simultaneously pointing to the substantial discursive labor that goes into the practical translation of capabilities into functionings. Both Sen and Nussbaum, like Rawls and Habermas, have noted the role of public reasoning as the royal road toward an actionable, overlapping consensus. Communication produces possible worlds, which may or may not be actualized in material and institutional forms. As part of the long communicative turn in the history of ideas, the American pragmatists and, later, Wittgenstein had realized that language and other sign use is, at once, hypothetical and performative, < an orientation toward the future through beliefs that communities are willing to act on. In the communicative position, people depart from a state of knowledge – the available information – and from a state of communication – the accessible media – as they reflect, deliberate, and enact the future. Rawls' two principles of justice translate into rights of information, communication, participation, and privacy.

public reasoning

> communication is performative – Chapter 5, p. 140

Principles of communication and justice

Rawls' dual aim – of ensuring equality of basic rights and duties while limiting economic and other social inequalities to the extent practically possible – was expressed in his two principles of justice. < In a final statement, Rawls (2001: 42f.) summed up the principles as follows:

> Rawls' two principles of justice – Chapter 4, p. 100

(a) Each person has the same indefeasible claim to a fully adequate scheme of equal basic liberties, which scheme is compatible with the same scheme of liberties for all; and
(b) Social and economic inequalities are to satisfy two conditions: first, they are to be attached to offices and positions open to all under conditions of fair equality of opportunity; and second, they are to be to the greatest benefit of the least advantaged members of society (the difference principle). <

equal basic liberties

> the difference principle – Chapter 4, p. 100

As in earlier formulations, *Justice as Fairness: A Restatement* (Rawls, 2001) indicated both that the first principle is prior to the second, and that, within the second principle, fair equality of opportunity is prior to the difference principle – a set of priorities that has fueled much of the debate on the Rawlsian agenda. < The 2001 restatement, further, specified the basic liberties in a list, which, in part, addressed rights of communication:

> the Rawlsian agenda – Chapter 4, p. 120

> freedom of thought and liberty of conscience; political liberties (for example, the right to vote and to participate in politics) and freedom of association, as well as the rights and liberties specified by the liberty and integrity (physical and psychological) of the person; and finally, the rights and liberties covered by the rule of law.
>
> *p. 44*

The two corresponding principles of communication and justice can be stated as follows:

(1) Each person has the same indefeasible claim to a fully adequate scheme of equal rights of information, communication, participation, and privacy, which scheme is compatible with the same scheme of rights for all; and

(2) Communicative inequalities are to satisfy two conditions: first, they are to relate to institutions, practices, and discourses open to all under conditions of fair equality of opportunity; and second, they are to be to the greatest benefit of the least advantaged participants in communication (the difference principle).

equal rights of information, communication, participation, and privacy

The first principle of communication and justice refers to four types of rights – regarding information, communication, participation, and privacy – that have been discovered and asserted over time, as reviewed in Chapter 6. All the information in the world can be considered a common resource, to become available on the widest possible basis for individuals and communities to reflect and deliberate on, as they plan their existence and coexistence. As elaborated below, this necessitates an understanding of communication as a multi-step process across the institutions within the basic structure of society. < Next, everybody should be in a position to both send and receive information, fact as well as fiction, as nodes in the widest possible network of social interaction, including contacts between persons who had no previous knowledge of or interest in each other. Everybody, further, should be able to participate in all deliberations and decisions affecting the distribution of primary social goods and, thus, the actualization of their capabilities. Finally, nobody should be treated as a means of information and communication without informed consent and public regulation. The idea of *habeas data* < extends the Kantian notion that humans should never be treated as means, only as ends, < in this case as subjects that have, hold, and *are* unique information.

> multi-step communications – Chapter 6, p. 178

> *habeas data* – p. 209

> humans as ends in themselves – Chapter 2, p. 37

The second principle of communication and justice addresses the enabling and compensating arrangements that institutions of knowledge, communication, and governance must be designed to procure – compensations for the contingent outcomes of highly distributed interactions, but also for the constitutive, practical limitations of the communicative position: No one can know everything; everybody cannot be heard on each matter of public interest; no collective decision can be overseen or assented to by everybody. Rawls' deontological scheme had admitted consequentialism through a conceptual backdoor in the form of the difference principle; as he recognized, a theory of justice that does not take consequences into account "would simply be irrational, crazy" (Rawls, 1999b/1971: 26). Equally, any principle of communication and justice must weigh rights and consequences on a practical scale in order to assess the difference they each make for the good life over time. In addition, the principles imply a consideration of virtue, not as any metaphysical command, but as a capability that is actualized through both formal training and the life-long exercise of communication, enabled through institutions of education and socialization. The first principle asserts the human potential for communication; the second principle addresses the historical actualization of this capability, as a set of valued functionings and as a further enabler of other capabilities.

rights and consequences

communicative virtue

Among human capabilities, communication is distinguished by being a generic and public procedure for articulating, reflecting, and deliberating on other capabilities – a vehicle of information and a resource for social participation and self-governance. Communication is a way of knowing things, speaking of things, and changing things. Communication is also limited in scope and duration; only certain things will be known by so many, only a certain number and variety of people will be in contact by natural and social deadlines, and only certain representatives will be in a position to affect collective decisions and actions, following input from so many other people. The question is how to represent the different interests of unique individuals and shifting constituencies in society, in such a way that the process of representation may respect both different versions of the good and necessary boundaries to the right, the "boundaries that men's systems of ends must respect" (Rawls, 1999b/1971: 27f.).

communication as public procedure

Additional boundaries to communication follow, on the one hand, from the affordances of the prevailing technologies of communication and, on the other hand, from the capabilities of humans as biological and historical beings. The affordances of print media are relative to the capability of literacy; the affordances

the interrelation of affordances and capabilities

of digital systems are relative to humans as more or less capable users (and sources) of data. But because people pursue their rights and interests over time, enabling and compensatory arrangements can be introduced to make up for deficits and excesses. This is the role of the institutions within the basic structure of society, which make up public systems of rules (Rawls, 1999b/1971: 47) – and which are themselves subject to deliberation and debate in distinctive institutions-to-think-with encompassing knowledge and communication. <

> institutions-to-think-with – Chapter 2, p. 27

availability of information

The availability of information is promoted by institutions of knowledge, which have yielded greatly increased quantities and qualities of information since the marriage of modern natural and social sciences to the printing press. Specialized sciences and scholarly fields have explored what is and what could be, with ancillary functions assessing what ought to be. To become accessible to publics beyond communities of specialists, all this information must, further, be reformulated in familiar repertoires of ordinary language and images, whether as part of dedicated science communication or as integral elements of mass communication, feeding into multi-step flows of communication one-to-one and many-to-many. As emphasized in Chapter 6, such dissemination involves institutions beyond media as mostly understood, including libraries and museums; here, public-service media occupy an intermediate position, being charged with covering diverse social domains and genres of presentation for the widest possible public. The performativity of information and communication, finally, depends on public participation in the institutions of governance, incorporating long lines of communication that involve voices from civil society organizations as well as established media organizations within the fourth branch of governance.

accessibility of communication

performativity of information and communication

Communication is potentially unending, notably in contestable matters; < in a sense, there is never enough time to think and talk about either international conflicts or national budgets. But communications end – to avoid continued atrocities or the shutting down of entire state administrations. As suggested by the pragmatists, the truth of the matter is what communities would arrive at if they had unlimited time and resources available for their inquiries – which they don't. That line of argument has been extended to economic and social theory by Herbert A. Simon (1957), who developed the idea of bounded rationality. In situations of planning and choice, people will "construct a simplified model of the real situation in order to deal with it" (p. 199), because they have limited access to information, have limited

> communication as contestation – Chapter 1, p. 13

bounded rationality

cognitive capacities, and are limited by the nature of the task itself and of the environment in which it must be accomplished. Accordingly, they 'satisfice' (satisfy and suffice) in "finding a course of action that is 'good enough'" (p. 205). Simon also noted how the process of satisficing unfolds in organizations or communities of inquiry and action:

satisficing

> It is only because individual human beings are limited in knowledge, foresight, skill, and time that organizations are useful instruments for the achievement of human purpose; and it is only because organized groups of human beings are limited in ability to agree on goals, to communicate, and to cooperate that organizing for them becomes a "problem."
>
> *p. 199*

Simon (1957) added that the social roles people take up, or are given, amount to "decision premises" (p. 201) – practical orientations toward the future that are informed by past experiences and interactions. In criticizing the idea that optimal rational choices are feasible, even typical, in economic and other social matters, Simon's position aligned with other theories of practice, including Amartya Sen's social choice theory. < Anthony Giddens' (1984) category of practical consciousness and Pierre Bourdieu's (1984/1979) concept of an embodied habitus both suggest that human cognition and communication – beliefs and orientations toward action – typically are not explicated in any full, discursive form of consciousness. Nor is communication about problematic situations and critical decisions necessarily carried through to any full, explicit consensus. (Also Rawls had noted that reason commonly serves as a practical resource for knowing-how to do things, rather than any explicit or representational knowing-that particular procedures are being mobilized.) < Nevertheless, processes of communication and participation must and do end. The open question, subject to human and social intervention in a historical window of opportunity, is whether and how the available media and the accessible communicative practices serve to represent both the ideas and issues at stake, and the individuals and stakeholders affected, as good-enough arrangements (Simon, 1957: 205) are worked out, resolving problematic situations for now.

> social choice theory – Chapter 2, p. 48

practical consciousness

habitus

> Rawls on practical reason – Chapter 4, p. 111

Whereas justice as fairness summed up Rawls' distinctive configuration of absolute, modern rights and contingent, historical compensations, I introduce the idea of justice as representativity to capture the constitutive role of communication in explicating and enacting justice. In the next section, I specify the two principles of communication and justice with reference to rights and goods – the general *rights* that people have and the specific *goods* that facilitate their social participation and self-determination and, thus, their functionings. Information, communication, participation, and privacy are primary social goods: something that people will want "whatever else they want" in life (Rawls, 1999b/1971: 230). Information must be representative, including the available ideas and insights – what is currently known by someone – for application to the matter at hand. Communication must be representative, including anyone as someone (Scannell, 2000), as party to the definition and resolution of problematic situations, when social orders, large and small, come into question or break down. And participation must be representative, as multi-step communications feed into institutions of political representation and social governance.

anyone as someone

Justice as representativity

Rights of information

The currently available information, accumulated through centuries and millennia of human inquiry and enterprise, can be understood as a "communicative commons" (Murdock, 2013: 160), enabling the cultivation of ever more information for humans to do, be, and coexist across time and space. Information constitutes a non-rival, non-depletable good that lends itself to recycling and reformulation in the face of material and social contingencies – and inevitable errors. More than items of factual description or reporting, information includes stories and arguments, fictions and fabulations, about the human condition in the widest possible sense. Externalized in matter and experienced by minds, information amounts to a coin of exchange between the personally subjective and the socially objective, what Popper had referred to as a World 3 mediating between a World 1 of physical objects and states and a World 2 of states of consciousness. < Humans want to know about the natural (and human-made) circumstances of their lives; they equally seek to know about other subjects with whom they must coordinate their plans and projects, and with whom they may identify (or not) as 'like me' and 'one of us.' The available information can be considered representative to the extent that what is known by someone could potentially be known by anyone, through institutions of knowledge and communication performing translation and dissemination.

the communicative commons

information as non-rival good

> Worlds 1, 2, and 3 – Chapter 1, p. 17

information goods

objects of interest

Rights of information entail the availability of three kinds of information goods. First, objects of interest range from the elements and processes of the natural environment to the human-made habitats and social formations within which lives unfold. As such, the objects of interest include all of the things that condition the present and future distribution of primary social goods: "rights, liberties, and opportunities, and income and wealth" (Rawls, 1999b/1971: 79). From primary education, to public libraries, to Wikipedia, the institutions of knowledge and communication that make information accessible, make up resources through which plans in life are informed and revised over time in response to contingencies and errors.

subjects of interest

Second, subjects of interest equally include persons, representatives, and collective or corporate agents. The question is *what*, but also *who* should be represented and how, so as to be reflected and deliberated on, and to be engaged in coordination as well as contestation. Most generally, representation in public is a minimal condition for anyone to become someone, to gain a presence, and to maintain an identity across time. We become ourselves in interactions with others, from para-social relations with mass media figures (Horton & Wohl, 1956) to the strong (and weak) social ties (Granovetter, 1973) that are maintained through social media and other one-to-one and many-to-many communications. To illustrate, one particularly divisive issue in international debates on cultural globalization has been what constitutes balanced and relevant representations of distant others, in news coverage as in fictional depictions (MacBride, 1980; Tunstall, 1977). <

> cultural globalization – Chapter 2, p. 42

> the world as frame of reference – Chapter 2, p. 47

Third, in an increasingly globalized and multicultural world, media serve to represent the world as a constantly available frame of reference, < which informs local beliefs and the readiness to act. One essential information good is a diverse set of representations of what this frame might look like, what the world could be: World 3 is a site of self-reflective interpretation and recursive negotiation. In contemporary communications, we encounter not one, but multiple worlds of interest.

worlds of interest

Like other primary social goods, information goods must be resourced, produced, and maintained; they are made, not found. The right to information about objects in the world, and about other subjects and worldviews, is conditioned by the availability and distribution of other goods: information infrastructures, literacy, background knowledge, etc. Questions of availability blend into questions of accessibility: How may ordinary citizens or typical constituencies access, comprehend, and benefit from what was once thought, said, and done by a comparatively few people with specialist knowledge and intellectual or aesthetic visions or, in rarer cases, by average citizens with the resources to record their planned and actualized lives? The prototype of eighteenth-century encyclopedia < had been intended and designed to make all the world's knowledge universally available and practically applicable. What was required then, and is required now, far beyond a simple reformulation of linguistic and mathematical notations, is a remediation (Bolter & Grusin, 1999) of actionable insights. The remediation of information for economic entrepreneurship, political activism, and cultural engagement involves the dissemination and reappropriation of information across media, other social institutions, and contexts of action. Information moves in multistep flows, without any centralized, institutionalized logic, across the basic structure of society. The central question for justice is how flows of information become available and accessible for users to orient their distributed contexts of action. < Information is a necessary condition for the citizen-users of media to dare to know, actualize their capabilities, and pursue their plans in life.

> modern encyclopedias – Chapter 6, p. 169

remediation

> flows of information, users, and contexts – Chapter 6, p. 177

A final aspect of information goods has to do with their continued availability: the preservation and potential recovery of information over time. The vast majority of communicative events and artifacts are gone forever, spoken into the air (Peters, 1999), decayed, or perhaps intentionally destructed. It is even in the nature of information to go missing: Whether in public or in private, for instrumental or reflective purposes, information will be selected and synthesized to make a difference in a particular context, for a concrete purpose, and with uncertain transfer value. Beyond local museums, national archives, and UNESCO lists of tangible and intangible cultural heritage, the communicative commons needs tending and curation, not to deselect, but to enable the reselection of information as goods and resources for the future. In this regard, high and low cultural forms represent different, but equal sources of past and present worldviews. < Despite the self-documenting functions of current digital systems, relatively few aspects also of contemporary information production and use are being recorded. What *is* being recorded for now, and digitized from the past, is subject to a new variant of decay and destruction: Rapidly changing versions of hardware and software mean that historians of the future likely will miss not just artifacts, but algorithmic points of entry to their past, our present. What is sometimes described, in the early twenty-first century, as a historical case of information overload may translate into future information deficits (Borgman, 2015).

information archives

> high and low cultures – Chapter 6, p. 169

information overloads and deficits

> natural and social capacities as collective assets – Chapter 4, p. 101

communication goods

What is known, and who knows what, are historically contingent facts. Rawls considered the natural and social capacities of historical individuals as collective assets, an outcome of chance and luck that calls for social regulation. < Also the current state and distribution of information can be understood as collective assets. "What is just or unjust is the way that institutions deal with [...] facts" (Rawls, 1999b/1971: 87) such as information and communication inequalities. In the case of information goods, equal rights and inequalities are associated with concrete *discourses* carrying information. When it comes to communication goods, equal rights and inequalities relate to the wider *practices* of communication that serve to socialize individuals and structure societies.

Rights of communication

representations as resources

centrifugal and centripetal communication

> many-to-one communication and privacy goods – p. 212

In my communications, I represent events in and states of the world – objects and subjects and worlds of interest – to others, sharing hypotheses and proposals for what could and should be done. Through communication, representations become resources. In communication, I also represent myself to others for what I am, or would like to become, simultaneously asserting my individuality and my sociality. Communication is, at once, a centrifugal and a centripetal process: We disseminate our ideas and interests far and wide to others; we also seek a common ground in which a shared understanding and an overlapping consensus may become possible. Humans cannot *not* communicate (Watzlawick et al., 1967: 49): Communication presents an inescapable circumstance for Aristotle's *zoon politicon*, but also a source of rights that have been asserted, reasserted, and reformulated in view of historically changing technologies and institutions of communication. Rights of communication entail the accessibility of a variety of communication goods that are afforded by one-to-one, one-to-many, as well as many-to-many interactions (I return to the case of many-to-one communication in a separate section below). <

one-to-one communication as socialization

At a biographical, existential level, individual human beings have a right of access to goods of socialization through one-to-one (and few-to-few) communications, from familial upbringing and basic education to secondary socialization throughout work settings, leisure activities, and community involvement. Extended through technologies of writing, telephony, and computing, one-to-one communication is both an evolutionary archetype and an essential element of participation in current everyday social interactions. Seemingly banal, but constitutive of becoming and remaining a person, such interactions are symbolic processes whereby not just shared social structures and realities, but social agents themselves are "produced, maintained, repaired, and transformed" (Carey, 1989a: 23). < Current social media are but one illustration of the communicative practices through which socialization and individualization proceed in tandem. Challenging a common critique, that the presentation of self to others (Goffman, 1959) via social media is a viciously narcissistic activity, Lee Humphreys (2018) has shown how social media rather reinvigorate past traditions of staying in close touch with personal relations across space and time, for example, by circulating diaries to family members and friends. Even me-to-me communication, making personal notes or images and surrounding oneself with heirlooms, children's drawings, and media clippings, contributes simultaneously to one's individuality and sociality.

> the ritual view of communication – Chapter 2, p. 41

one-to-one communication as individualization

me-to-me communication

Mass communication represented a major civilizational advance, introducing a historically unique communication good through which public reflection and deliberation and the governance of societies through communication became conceivable. This is in spite of still widespread concerns, that one-to-many communication may be alienating and disempowering, so that one-to-one and, recently, many-to-many formats might be preferred and planned for in information infrastructures. But no social system of some complexity and diversity could exist over time without the sort of coordinating mechanism that first writing and later print, broadcast, and digital media have afforded. Compared to the two-step flow of scribal communication, centered in authorities with emissaries, < modern mass media have allowed individuals and local constituencies to access an unprecedented range of mediated objects, subjects, and worlds, and to receive daily or, at least, periodical updates on events with public ramifications. In contrast to one more concern, that one-to-many communications make identical information accessible to large numbers of people, it is precisely this feature of the goods of mass communication that enables publics to remain updated on initiatives and interventions by institutional centers, without which modern societies would disintegrate – economically, politically, and culturally. Mass communication enables a measure of bottom-up surveillance or sousveillance (Rainie & Wellman, 2012) of the powers that be.

one-to-many communication as social structuration

> two-step scribal communication – Chapter 6, p. 166

sousveillance

Digital technologies have introduced additional communication goods for individuals and communities to employ and benefit from through many-to-many interactions. Whereas the social implications may equal or supersede those of mass communication, the juries of public and scholarly debate are still out in this

many-to-many communication goods

crowdsourcing

connective action

virtual and augmented aesthetics

regard (e.g., Benkler, 2006; Curran, Fenton, & Freedman, 2012). For now, research on digital technologies and the institutions emerging to regulate them, must defer to historical hindsight and communicative foresight. Rawls (1999b/1971: 43) recognized the practical limitations to what can be known about justice: "The most we can do is to study the conceptions of justice known to us through the tradition of moral philosophy and any further ones that occur to us, and then to consider these," in conjunction with the accumulated historical and empirical evidence. There is little question that networked forms of social coordination hold significant transformative potentials in economic, political, as well as cultural domains; the historical predecessors laid out in Chapter 6 suggest as much. Current examples of many-to-many communication goods include crowdsourcing (Brabham, 2013) in economic production, the organization of collective political action as networked or connective action (Bennett & Segerberg, 2012), and collaborative aesthetic expressions at the intersection of the material and the virtual (Paul, 2008).

> flows of information, users, and contexts – Chapter 6, p. 177

> meta-media – Chapter 6, p. 176

press, broadcast, and common-carrier models of regulation

> the communicative commons – p. 201

Because communication moves in multiple steps, communication goods can be more difficult to delimit, study, and assess than information goods. Despite its so-called News Feed, Facebook is not a news medium, but one step in multi-step flows of communication in diverse genres. Media users flow across sources of information and contexts of action. < With digitalization, moreover, several classic media are accessible in the same meta-medium < or platform, and asynchronous formats such as serial fiction lend themselves to synchronous commentary and viewer interaction. In institutional terms, and for historical reasons, the public regulation of media has varied considerably for press, broadcasting, and common carrier systems such as telecommunications and the internet (McQuail, 2010: 235–238); regulatory structures are in transition around the world. Farther afield, multi-step flows of communication include libraries, museums, and educational institutions, which traditionally have been financed and overseen through separate regulatory regimes. From the citizen-users' perspective, however, and in terms of their rights, communication goods derive from all these social institutions and sectors, and proceed in flows, sequences, and networks. Once again, "What is just or unjust is the way that institutions deal with" (Rawls, 1999b/1971: 87) the full range and configuration of communication goods from the media that be. Communication rights must be asserted, and inequalities assessed and remedied, with reference to the entire media environment of the present and the communicative commons inherited from the past. <

Rights of participation

Whereas information and communication goods are general, lending themselves to public and private, instrumental as well as reflective applications, participation goods relate to specific *institutions* – the three branches of governance that have been given priority by political philosophy and social sciences examining justice. Just as we cannot all speak at the same time, so we cannot all participate directly in the institutional speech acts – legislative decisions, executive enactments, and judicial reviews – that focus widely shared beliefs and translate them into material and discursive realities. As reflected in diverse models of representative democracy, devices of re-presentation < are key to the actualization of rights of participation, and to the recognition of inequalities. Such devices include lines of contact and communication, between electorates and representatives, but also among citizens and among the multiple media of the fourth branch of governance, which represent, build, and maintain policy agendas and frames of interpretation. In each case, formal or informal representatives of the public communicate on behalf of different constituencies. Representative democracy articulates the modern idea that communities and societies know best how to govern themselves, and must dare to communicate in order to explicate their plans and make their own history.

participation goods

> democratic re-presentation – Chapter 6, p. 187

Participation goods are of three kinds. First, rights of participation entail continuous access to other citizens and constituencies in and through communication, including records of what was thought, said, and done in the past. Such mediated records bear witness to other subjects of interest and to the multiple worlds that are the cumulative product of past interactions. < To engage in individual reflection and collective deliberation, it is essential that people enjoy the conditions to be reasonable, < being able to take the position of their others and to appreciate the background of extant positions. Crosscultural understanding, like dialogue between sociodemographic groups, takes practice and learning, on biographical and historical time scales.

citizens and constituencies

> subjects and worlds of interest – p. 202

> the reasonable vs. the rational – Chapter 4, p. 108

Second, public participation in politics depends on socially structured forms of access to representatives in the legislative, executive, and judicial branches of governance. Here, communications range from those of classic party organizations to channels of consultation involving non-party-affiliated citizens and more or less ad hoc, more or less issue-focused social movements. Much consultation necessarily occurs in multi-step and distributed fashion through established media

citizen–representative interaction

party communications

social movements

organizations: the reporting and debating of institutional politics, coupled with traditional letters-to-the-editor and, recently, social media commentary, all of which feeds back, through journalism, into one-to-many political communication. Mass communication remains an indispensable good for participation in a representative democracy. And while legislative and executive politics may have the most obvious, immediate relevance for citizens, participation goods importantly include coverage and analysis of legal decisions and precedents; some rulings become the last word trumping other political speech acts.

mass-mediated participation

Third, participation goods include the agendas and frames of interpretation that define and delimit what participation is *about*. Whereas policy agendas will morph and merge more frequently than historical and cultural frames of interpretation, access to both current agendas and predominant frames is a *sine qua non* of informed political participation. This is in spite of the fact that the political process itself commonly revolves around the definition and promotion of some agendas and frames above others. As a public service and in the aggregate, journalistic media are to make broadly accessible the available agendas and frames that apply to elections, referenda, and other contested procedures. The question is what media afford, not just potentially, but actually, as people exercise the capability of communication and their right to political self-governance.

agendas and frames

> culturalization of politics and economy – Chapter 6, p. 187

> from government to governance – Chapter 6, p. 164

The culturalization of politics and economy < through communications that pervade the entire social structure has challenged traditional institutional boundaries. In addition to the terminological shift from government to governance, < this ongoing development raises questions concerning the very category of participation: Who is in a position to participate in which institutions and practices of representation – internally and externally, privately and publicly, locally and globally? Humans cannot *not* communicate and, thus, participate in society; the terms of participation are conditioned by the availability and accessibility of particular information and communication goods.

But participation may be neither consensual nor explicated in communication. In the next section, I treat privacy goods as different from, yet related to participation goods. Here, the rights at stake have to do with a specific "right 'to be let alone'" (Warren & Brandeis, 1890: n.p.) < – *not* being rendered as information, *not* being communicated about, and *not* in effect participating in certain ways of socializing individuals and structuring societies (for overview, see Westin, 1967).

> the right to be let alone – p. 210

ANALYSIS BOX 7.1 *HABEAS DATA*

As noted by Philip E. Agre (1994) 25 years ago, digital systems have entailed a shift in the understanding of privacy. What used to require dedicated activities can now be accomplished through "automatic real-time data collection and analysis" (p. 103) of user actions and related events within digital systems. The final word of the quotation – analysis – is important because it suggests the extent to which the configuration of digital systems prefigures the analysis of who did what. The relationship between data collection and data analysis is not what it used to be: A notion of 'collect now, analyze later' has been emerging, as advocated in a growing literature on big data. The suggestion is that instead of sampling data in order to support inferences to a wider population, research should be gathering "as much [data] as possible, and if feasible, getting everything: *N=all*" (Mayer-Schönberger & Cukier, 2013: 26).

automatic real-time data collection and analysis

big data

N = all data

One response to such notions has been presented by Helen Nissenbaum (2011) in a theory of contextual integrity, which develops a communicative understanding of the principles and procedures at stake. Nissenbaum argues that the normative implications particularly of personal information cannot be decided once and for all, at the moment of capture or according to general terms of service. Information travels through unpredictable contexts; it may be accessed and acted upon by third or fourth parties in an uncertain future. Users cannot – should not – waive their right to decide whether or not to be associated with information that they originated or co-created through human–machine interactions. It is in both the personal and public interest to regulate the social uses of information according to certain "context-specific substantive norms" (p. 32). To specify these norms, Nissenbaum introduces three parameters – actors, attributes, and transmission principles: Who are the subjects, senders, and recipients in question; which types of information are part of their transactions; and, most important perhaps, "what are the constraints under which information flows" (p. 33) – who else might become end users of the information in question? The problem, Nissenbaum suggests, is that, for now, "the dominant approach to [...] achieving privacy online is a combination of *transparency*

contextual integrity

and choice." The unrealistic, impracticable assumption is that complicated terms of service regulating the potential future uses of information will be transparent to ordinary users as they choose to accept them by default. Like information in other markets, information in digital media is imperfect, and the users' rationality in making choices is bounded. < With a view to future unknown and unknowable contexts, so-called "notice-and-consent, or informed consent" (p. 34) cannot be considered informed. (For a critical discussion of Nissenbaum's position, see Rule, 2019.)

> bounded rationality – p. 199

un-informed consent

In a longer historical perspective, bit trails recall classic legal questions concerning measures "for the protection of the person, and for securing to the individual what Judge Cooley calls the right 'to be let alone'" (Warren & Brandeis, 1890: n.p.). In the late nineteenth century, Samuel D. Warren and Louis D. Brandeis had worried about the impact of "instantaneous photographs and newspaper enterprise" on "the sacred precincts of private and domestic life." Private information and individual identity have remained two sides of the same coin. The phenomenological philosopher, Maurice Merleau-Ponty (1962/1945), made the point that whereas people typically say that they *have* a body, they also *are* a body (p. 174). Humans *have* information, about themselves and others; they also *are* information that they themselves and others may access and act upon, depending on the practices and institutions regulating appropriate representations and interactions.

the right to be let alone

having and being information

Habeas data has been advanced, by analogy to *habeas corpus*, as a legal principle addressing such concerns (for overview, see Guadamuz, 2001). *Habeas corpus*, deriving from the English Magna Carta of 1215 and integral to modern jurisprudence around the world, literally means 'you may have the body.' The principle has been intended to protect individuals from unlawful imprisonment through the possibility of appeal, and courts are thus required to establish the whereabouts of a prisoner – his/her corporeal existence. *Habeas data* – 'you may have the data' – has been designed, in turn, to give individuals access to registers in which information is held about them and, if needed, to have the information corrected or removed. The principle has been given different interpretations, and was first implemented in the constitution of Brazil in 1988 (Doneda & Mendes, 2014). The European General Data Protection Regulation, which

habeas corpus

took effect in 2018, addresses such issues, with implications for other regions of the world.

The idea of *habeas data* refocuses attention on the fact that people exist and coexist in and by information and communication. Communities are imagined (Anderson, 1991), in part, with reference to the data that the users of media both access and leave behind. Online and offline, individuals and collectives will be social in distinctive ways, depending on how information about them is documented, processed, and applied. Like *habeas corpus, habeas data* is no absolute principle; societies assign certain rights for individuals to have, hold, and use their information as well as their bodies. Rights of data protection and privacy, < then, need to be considered on a par with rights of information and communication. Media users increasingly speak into systems that not only structure their communications, but which condition their agency far beyond the media as traditionally understood.

> rights of privacy – p. 212

For some time, an emerging generation of digital technologies have been referred to in terms of their ubiquity and pervasiveness (for overview, see Greenfield, 2006). Information technologies everywhere, in everything, and for everybody have been the commercial and policy buzzwords. The originator of the idea of ubiquitous computing, Mark Weiser (1991), contrasted ubiquity with virtuality. Early versions of virtual media environments during the 1980s–90s were based on a model of 'the world *in* a medium' – one local, stationary, and multimodal interface, including goggles, gloves, and a treadmill that enabled the user to enter a separate, virtual reality (for overview, see Levy, 1993). In contrast, ubiquitous media embed interfaces into diverse social settings, artifacts, and natural objects – 'the world *as* a medium.' The development has also been referred to as the coming of an Internet of Things (IoT) (ITU, 2005), including public transportation systems and home appliances. At the intersection of hardware and humans, life support systems and implants are examples of media as body parts. At the very least, digital technologies are enabling significantly more location-dependent and personalized communication; ubiquitous access to other people in image, text, as well as sound; and more actions at a distance, in ways that are still waiting to be imagined and realized.

ubiquity

pervasiveness

virtual reality

the world as a medium

the Internet of Things

In a future perspective, mobile, ubiquitous, and pervasive interactions challenge received ideas of 'media' and 'communication' and, hence, received agendas regarding communication and justice. Cognitive science has described the bandwidth of human cognition and communication with reference to so-called basic-level categories (Lakoff & Johnson, 1999), whose yardstick is the human body. We have, and are, a particular neurophysiological structure that taps into certain levels and aspects of reality, and not others. We have access to things that are about our size and within the reach of our senses: luminous surfaces and loud music, but not infrared radiation or the echoes of the Big Bang (at least not without technological extensions). Basic-level categories enable humans to think and speak about what is up and down, in and out, before and after, both literally and metaphorically in terms of who is up or down in a society, in or out as far as a culture is concerned. The "metaphors we live by" (Lakoff & Johnson, 1980), while determined in the first instance by the human body, have been extended into information and communication technologies, with unforeseen consequences for the human condition.

basic-level categories

metaphors we live by

> Peirce's pragmatism – Chapter 5, p. 136

The originator of pragmatism, Charles Sanders Peirce, < had speculated on the trails that historical individuals might have left behind: "Give science only a hundred more centuries of increase in geometrical progression, and she may be expected to find that the sound waves of Aristotle's voice have somehow recorded themselves" (Peirce, 1931–58: 5.542). In fact, communication is already recording itself in ways whose potentials and implications for justice await more scholarly inquiry and social interventions.

Rights of privacy

> many-to-one communication – Chapter 6, p. 175

The category of many-to-one communication < presents special challenges, for defining the right to communicate and, thus, for communication theory. At stake is a right *not* to be communicated about in further steps and networks, which might harm or disadvantage individuals as well as groups. Historical examples of many-to-one communication have been tax registers, military drafting, and the census; the centers of registration typically have been public, (more or less) regulated authorities. With digitalization, the nature of such registration is changing (Agre, 1994), quantitatively, but also qualitatively. For one thing, what is being amassed is big data (Mayer-Schönberger & Cukier, 2013). For another thing, the uses of big (and small) data amount to big business, including a new type of centralized infrastructure in which a few nodes in the network have the technology, capital, and legal resources at their disposal to accumulate and monopolize information from and about other nodes. We cannot *not* communicate into an unknown future recycling and remediating both public and private information. It is on this point that a principle of *habeas data* < – a right of informational and communicative self-determination – becomes essential. Beyond technical and legal issues, the ongoing global process of digitalization recalls Kant's categorical imperative < in its two aspects: "Universalize your maxim" and "Treat persons as ends" (Sandel, 2009: n.p.): Treat all persons – who *are* their data – as ends, who will define which uses of their data are good for them.

> *habeas data* – p. 209

> the categorical imperative – Chapter 2, p. 37

privacy goods

individuality

Privacy goods are of two kinds. First, the individuality of persons, as manifested both physically and discursively, can be considered uniquely private, to be shared through an explicit, positive choice. However, as representations – verbal statements, photographs, videos, and more – discourses travel in communication across contexts whose nature and consequences will be unforeseeable for any individual. In the digital media environment, it is this feature of communication that has led Helen Nissenbaum (2011) to focus attention not on the moment of information capture, as covered by market-based terms of service, but on its contexts of use, to be regulated according to public norms. < People cannot – should not – waive, across the board, the right to decide whether or not to be associated with specific items of information that they have originated (or co-created through human–machine interactions). Compared to long-established practices of copyright, which promote innovation and creativity in public, individuality may be protected through reverse copyright (Jensen, 2012f: 367): the right *not* be associated with any and all information generated and recorded for other purposes. Once again, information is performative, in the future as in the present, affecting the life choices and chances of individuals, from job prospects to insurance terms.

> contextual integrity – p. 209

reverse copyright

Second, from the census through traditional market surveys to digital metadata, individuals have been categorized and profiled; individuality is social. Profiling focuses the availability of information about others and the accessibility of communications with others, for better or worse. While enabling contact with likely objects, subjects, and worlds of interest, profiling also constrains

> serendipity – Chapter 8, p. 238

sociality

the choices through which individuals and communities make contact with new topics and issues: what they did not know they had an interest in. Communication is a source of serendipitous insights. < Because humans cannot *not* be socialized in and through communication, it is essential that the affordances of media and the capabilities of their human users leave significant scope for the unexpected, from moments of *Eureka!* to surprisingly relevant or enjoyable trivia. Sociality – being the individual that one is, or would like to become – is a privacy good: becoming and being part of society through a process of choice, error, and insight. As noted by Rawls (2005/1993: 313), with "the liberty of conscience" comes "the liberty to fall into error and to make mistakes," which are informed and corrected by communications.

> the communicative structuration of society – Chapter 6, p. 189

the audience commodity

Socialization and structuration can be considered two sides of the same social coin. In and through communication, society is structured in contestable and negotiable ways. < During the age of television, Dallas W. Smythe (1977) introduced the idea of an audience commodity: Though the viewers of television might think of themselves as consumers relaxing after a long and hard working day, they could also be characterized as laborers in front of their television sets, their eyeballs producing surplus value for broadcasters and advertisers. The perspective has continued and renewed salience in a digital media environment where data flow both to and from users within interlinked services and into opaque networks of monetization, with the business model of Google as a case in point (Lee, 2011). More or less private and personal data are the goods that such companies produce and distribute. The distributed communications that are summed up as data, condition the course of society; they also constitute the lived realities by which justice is measured.

Communication as condition and constituent of justice

> transmission and ritual models of communication – Chapter 2, p. 41

Communication is a way of doing; it is equally a way of being. This pragmatist point was summed up by John Dewey in a formulation that has fed into contemporary communication theory through James W. Carey's (1989a: 13f.) contrasting of transmission and ritual models of communication: < "Society exists not only by transmission, by communication, but it may fairly be said to exist in transmission, in communication." While being final products of communication, social relations are established in continuous processes, being "produced, maintained, repaired, and transformed" (Carey, 1989a: 23) over time and, increasingly, space.

By communication, humans act on realities and each other; *in* communication, they inhabit realities that may be explored and contested in ever more interactions.

by communication, in communication

Communication is both a condition and a constituent of justice, a means and an end. *By* communication, people rework the conditions in which they find themselves; *in* communication, they experience and share the current terms of their coexistence as well as future alternatives. As means, communication is a source of power, not as "a *common will* formed in noncoercive communication" or as the "'violence' (*Gewalt*)" of a system world (Habermas, 1996/1992: 147f.), but as a transformative capacity < (Giddens, 1984): the capability of humans to change their social and material circumstances by hypothesizing and anticipating alternatives. The goods of information, communication, participation, and privacy all enable and constrain how the capability of communication may be actualized as an instrument of justice. As ends, communications serve to manifest and maintain states of self-respect and mutual respect – being and knowing who I am and who we are. The same goods enable and constrain the possible, historical worlds < that humans articulate in fact and fiction, as they, potentially, "enjoy one another's excellences and individuality" (Rawls, 1999b/1971: 459).

> power as transformative capacity – Chapter 3, p. 75

> possible worlds – Chapter 3, p. 81

The capabilities literature has devoted specific attention to the distinction between doing and being as two aspects of human functionings: what it is feasible for individuals and groups to enact and experience in the context of their life circumstances. To Sen (1999: n.p.), functionings are actualizations of a person's capabilities, and taken together, they constitute "the substantive freedom to achieve alternative" ways of living – freedom in the positive and plural sense of the collective accomplishments of people pursuing different versions of the good within the limits of the right. < Nussbaum (2011), importantly, added that capability sets are dynamic constructs in which some capabilities are more architectonically central than others, because they mediate and catalyze the actualization of other capabilities: Affiliation and practical reason facilitate the recognition of others as subjects of interest and sources of additional worlds of interest. < As argued, communication constitutes a further architectonic, generic capability for reflecting and deliberating on justice. As such, communicative functionings serve ends of doing as well as being: designing institutions and practices of communication, and articulating the good life in discourse. Communication constitutes an iterative, self-reflective procedure, exploring and assessing what justice could be.

> positive freedom – p. 193

> subjects and worlds of interest – p. 202

> the prehistory of communication – Chapter 2, p. 28

Universal Declaration of Human Rights

> practical concepts – Chapter 6, p. 163

> theoretical conceptions – p. 192

The communicative position is, at once, an evolutionary condition and a historical accomplishment of institutions and infrastructures. Communication brings things out in the open, publicizing projects and promises, so that others cannot *not* know about them. < With the 1948 United Nations Universal Declaration of Human Rights (United Nations, 1948) (UDHR) as a benchmark, universal rights and duties of information, communication, participation, and privacy have been widely asserted, adopted, and communicated about. Most commonly cited regarding rights of communication is Article 19: "Everyone has the right to freedom of opinion and expression; this right includes freedom to hold opinions without interference and to seek, receive and impart information and ideas through any media and regardless of frontiers." In addition, rights of participation are recognized: "Everyone has the right to take part in the government of his country, directly or through freely chosen representatives" (Article 21), as are rights of privacy: "No one shall be subjected to arbitrary interference with his privacy, family, home or correspondence" (Article 12). Such statements incorporate practical concepts < that have articulated historically emergent rights of information, communication, participation, and privacy, as traced in Chapter 6; this chapter has presented systematic, theoretical conceptions < of the goods that substantiate these rights.

> the overlapping consensus – Chapter 4, p. 108

> publicity and translatability – Chapter 4, p. 113

> conflict and error – Chapter 4, p. 105

> the reasonable vs. the rational – Chapter 4, p. 108

The overlapping consensus < was Rawls' conception of how, at the end of communication, communities, large and small, may be able to go on together even when they cannot agree on many of the premises and arguments motivating their conclusions and actions. The theory of communication that remained unarticulated in Rawls' *oeuvre* held up the twin principles of publicity and translatability < between different comprehensive doctrines as necessary moments of arriving at an actionable consensus; he also recognized conflict as conducive to the clarification of premises and arguments, and error as a natural ingredient of reflection and deliberation on the good life. < In *Political Liberalism*, Rawls (2005/1993) elaborated how reasonable communication, as distinct from rational communication, "take[s] into account the consequences of [...] actions on others' well-being," bearing witness to a "moral sensibility" (pp. 49, 51). < In this way, "reasonable people [...] can reason in common," so that "the reasonable is public in a way the rational is not" (pp. 49, 53). Rawls remained silent, however, on the ways in which rights and principles of communication are to be translated into concrete goods and procedures.

The communicative position presents a window of opportunity for justice; the human capability of communication is actualized through goods of information, communication, participation, and privacy, and is put to work through institutions, practices, and discourses that make such goods available, accessible, and performative. Human communication serves to re-present – to make worlds present to subjects, and subjects to each other. First, the representativity of the available information – about objects, subjects, and worlds of interest – must be assessed in the aggregate, with reference to the sets of institutions and the sequences of communicative steps by which it is disseminated to the widest possible public. Second, the representativity of communicative flows will depend on their general accessibility – one-to-one, one-to-many, and many-to-many. *In* communication, both socialization and social structuration are continuous and contestable processes; communication is constitutive of society. Third, communication conditions society, specifically its institutions of collective agency; representative participation in self-governance is conditioned by communication among citizens and elected representatives and by the widest possible dissemination of extant agendas and frames of interpretation. *By* communication, the institutions of governance are in-formed and per-formed. Fourth, privacy entails a right *not* to be represented – identified and profiled – without informed consent and public regulation of the uses of personal information over time.

The present chapter has outlined an ideal theory < of communication and justice. Living with and communicating about injustice, however, is part of the human condition; the articulation of injustice anticipates justice. In Chapter 8, I turn to empirical and methodological questions of how justice *could* be served in and through communication.

> ideal theory – Chapter 4, p. 107

8

JUSTICE – MEASURE FOR MEASURE

Measures and meanings

> practical concepts – Chapter 6

> theoretical conceptions – Chapter 7

empirical conceptualizations

> possible worlds – Chapter 3, p. 81

Practical concepts < of communication and justice bear witness to continuing struggles for the good life; theoretical conceptions < have been the contribution of philosophers and other thinkers to specifying what might constitute the common good. In this chapter, I turn to empirical conceptualizations (Jensen, 2013a): operationalizations and methodologies for measuring whether and how communication can and does serve justice. Methodologies, to one side, involve epistemologies: procedures relating empirical evidence to further inferences and conclusions about what could be done. To the other side, epistemologies imply ontologies: premises regarding the possible worlds < in which justice might finally be realized. Beyond the institution of science and scholarship, empirical studies provide input to political deliberation and public debate about proposed solutions to problematic situations (Dewey, 1903). In a pragmatist lineage, I approach measures of justice, and the meanings that publics ascribe to them, as orientations toward the future – beliefs that communities and societies will be willing to act on, to stake their lives and coexistence on, at the end of communication.

> critical realism – p. 220

The first section presents critical realism < as a framework for empirical studies of communication and justice. Following the science wars of the twentieth century (Ashman & Baringer, 2001; Labinger & Collins, 2001), critical realism has charted a third way and a middle road between the two conflicting paradigms that had prioritized *either* the objects of inquiry as elementary and manifest (positivism) *or* the inquiring subject as their origin and source (constructivism). Recognizing *both* a reality independent of human inquirers *and* their active role in comprehending and communicating about reality, critical realists emphasize the discovery of what they take to be underlying or generative mechanisms: natural forces and social factors that explain why humans have particular experiences of reality and witness a certain range of events. < Some forms of justice are impossible, given the capabilities of humans (Sen, 1999) and the affordances of their environments (J.J. Gibson, 1979); other forms are possible, but depend for their realization on the development and maintenance of the right mechanisms: institutions and infrastructures. Critical realism is realist in that it seeks to identify material and institutional boundaries to the good life; it is critical insofar as it enables the questioning and shifting of such boundaries. Empirical studies explore the real degrees of freedom for individual and collective agency – the window of opportunity between chance and necessity. <

> mechanisms, events, and experiences – p. 222

> the window of opportunity between chance and necessity – Chapter 2, p. 23

Second, I elaborate on the goods of information, communication, participation, and privacy, identified in Chapter 7, as elements of an empirical research agenda. John Rawls (1999b/1971: 349) had shifted attention from *the good* in the abstract to the concrete *goods* that all humans will want in practice, "whatever else they want" (p. 230). While associated with a wide variety of human experiences and social events, the goods of information, communication, participation, and privacy depend for their realization on a small number of fundamental mechanisms – institutional, technological, and discursive – that span decades and centuries. Throughout the chapter, I illustrate the empirical agenda with reference to the internet as the centerpiece of an ongoing transformation of the global media environment (for overview, see Neuman, 2016). Digitalization – of the available information, the accessible media of communication, the institutions for participating in political governance, and the means of managing privacy – has reopened classic discussions concerning the legitimate principles and procedures, for example, for curating the world's information and protecting the individual's data. Parts of the research agenda present challenges on the order of big science: < the post-1945 development of national and international scientific collaborations relying on large-scale machineries and infrastructures. Justice, as enabled by digital information and communication technologies, is a worthy candidate for another historical round of big science.

digitalization

> big science – p. 228

The third section, finally, considers ways and means of monitoring the state of communication about and for justice, with reference to the three classic forms of inference: induction, deduction, and abduction. < Abduction articulates the rules or standards that deduction serves to specify, and which induction applies to identify particular instances of (in)justice. Far from being the prerogative of scientists and scholars, such inferences pervade human cognition and everyday interaction, lending themselves to operationalization in indexes that focus and facilitate public debate. With reference to the two principles of communication and justice, < which address equal rights and persisting inequalities, respectively, I note the dual role of empirical research in documenting inequalities and evaluating the compensating benefits which, in accordance with the difference principle, must be allocated to the least advantaged participants in communication. Public and private, national and international agents and stakeholders all refer to empirical baselines regarding problematic situations and proposed solutions, as they engage the different kinds and degrees of injustice that are part of the human condition. <

> deduction, induction, and abduction – p. 237

> the two principles of communication and justice – Chapter 7, p. 197

> living with injustice – p. 235

Normative questions lend themselves to empirical examination. Whereas David Hume's (2010/1739) objection stands – one cannot infer an 'ought' from an 'is' – I follow Ludwig Wittgenstein and, before him, the American pragmatists in noting that representations of what is, derive their meaning and relevance from their orientation toward the future – as hypotheses concerning what will be or could be. < As instances of the human capability to consider how things might be different, < empirical studies anticipate possible futures in which particular aspects of justice will be realized.

> representations as hypotheses on the future – Chapter 5, p. 145

> the human capability to consider how things might be different – Chapter 1, p. 3

The reality of justice

The empirical, the actual, and the real

Realism has witnessed a revival in recent decades, in a number of disciplines and fields, including communication theory (Pavitt, 1999). In the human and social sciences, an influential tradition has been the critical realism originally formulated by Roy Bhaskar (1979) (for overview, see Archer, Bhaskar, Collier, Lawson, & Norrie, 1998; Danermark, Ekström, & Karlsson, 2019). The tradition joins three premises:

critical realism

- *Ontological realism.* Critical realism approaches reality as a limit condition – a presupposition or premise of further inquiry into the specifics of what is, and what could be. Ontological realism reverses the burden of proof that modern science and scholarship have sought to lift since Descartes: Doubts arise in concrete instances, in practice, not as any theory-driven or abstract skepticism. The proof of reality is the interactions we have with it, and its resistance to some kinds of interventions < (Hacking, 1983). As a field of human enterprise, reality has material as well as immaterial boundaries.

> *erro, ergo sum* – Chapter 5, p. 127

- *Epistemological relativism*. Critical realism, further, assumes that human understanding of nature, culture, and other minds depends on a range and sequence of perceptions, cognitions, and inferences, all of which may be questioned, rejected, or revised – communicated about. Relativism does not imply that "anything goes" (Feyerabend, 1975), but rather that different aspects of reality call for different types of inquiry. Critical realism, thus, allows for normative research questions concerning just and sustainable forms of human existence and social coexistence.
- *Judgmental rationality*. Finally, all research – empirical and theoretical, quantitative or qualitative – involves an exercise of rationality which, at some point, must end in (fallible) judgments about what is the case, and what to do next. Like reality, rationality is bounded by evolutionary circumstances and historical contingencies. <

> bounded rationality – Chapter 7, p. 199

anthropocentrism

logical positivism

Roy Bhaskar ascribed the continued attraction of anti-realist positions to a persistent anthropocentrism in philosophy and theory of science: "Copernicus argued that the universe does not revolve around man. And yet in philosophy we still represent things as if it did" (cited in Archer et al., 1998: 45). Logical positivism, for one, had proposed to reduce reality to what is immediately accessible to the senses of the individual human being. Instead, the question must be what levels of reality humans are able to tap into, alone or in concert, through all manner of technological and institutional extensions. Following Aristotle, < critical realism allows for a diversified and distributed reality of entities, events, and emergents – which, over time, may prove accessible to humans through representation or inference, immediately or by media of registration and dissemination < still to be imagined or invented.

> Aristotelian realism – Chapter 2, p. 33

> media of registration and dissemination – Chapter 6, p. 170

With one of Bhaskar's key concepts, reality is, in grammatical terms, intransitive. As an object, it does not take – does not need – a human subject. It is humans who make material reality, such as optical fibers, transitive for purposes of enterprise and inquiry. Reality is, moreover, transfactual. Facts of several kinds exist: fiber intransitive, transfactual, and stratified reality

optics, local email exchanges, and the internet as a global institution. And, reality is stratified: Fibers, emails, and the internet are not reducible to each other, nor are they *incommunicado*, but constitute intertwined aspects of the real. Most important for empirical studies, a differentiated reality calls for a differentiated repertoire of research designs and analytical approaches: Measures and methods cannot be transferred directly from natural and physical sciences to human and social sciences, or vice versa. As suggested by Charles Sanders Peirce (1992: 29), "reasoning should not form a chain which is no stronger than its weakest link, but a cable whose fibers may be ever so slender, provided they are sufficiently numerous and intimately connected."

To specify the several levels and stages of empirical research, critical realism distinguishes three aspects or domains of reality (Bhaskar, 1979) (Table 8.1). First, the *empirical* domain is the concrete source of evidence – *experience* of the world. By documenting and describing, for instance, the images and verbal formulations by which people present themselves on social media to family, friends, acquaintances, as well as anonymous visitors, communication studies take a first step towards understanding how social networks are established, developed, and maintained over time, from the local to the global level.

experiences, events, and mechanisms

Second, further analysis and interpretation of the resulting quantitative or qualitative evidence serve to establish the *actual* status of social media use as particular kinds of *events* relating to specific practices and institutions. Representations of personal life transitions or participation in public-political manifestations serve as expressions, simultaneously, of individuality and sociality: < speech acts asserting personal identities and maintaining meaningful networks of affiliation.

> the goods of individuality and sociality – Chapter 7, p. 213

Third, critical realism places special emphasis on uncovering *mechanisms* of a general nature that may explain why certain events and experiences do (not) occur in particular contexts. Personal and political posts on social media are enabled and constrained by the material availability and institutional accessibility of digital networks and devices, the political regulation of

TABLE 8.1 Three domains of reality

	The real	*The actual*	*The empirical*
Experiences	x	x	x
Events	x	x	
Mechanisms	x		

communication services, and cultural conventions of expression and interaction.

Experiences, events, and mechanisms are all equally *real*. This is in spite of the fact that experiences seem to 'push' themselves on scholar and layperson alike as primary manifestations of reality. A central task of research is to mount countervailing interpretive and explanatory 'pulls' in order to identify a middle range of significant events, and to infer the structuring mechanisms underlying both the experiences and the events. The goods of information, communication, participation, and privacy that the internet delivers (or not) are structured – realized – by institutional, technological, as well as discursive mechanisms.

reality as push and pull

Institutional, technological, and discursive mechanisms

Originating as an initiative of the US military in the shape of the ARPANET from 1969, the internet was shifted as an institution, first, into a research network (NSFNET) from 1985 and, from 1995, consolidated as a commercially operated common carrier (for overviews, see Abbate, 1999; Radu, 2019). As a network relating social entities and agents, then, the internet has lent itself to implementation as a closed command-and-control system, a specialized sectoral infrastructure, or a general-purpose public medium. The 1990s witnessed both its popular breakthrough in the form of the World Wide Web as an audiovisual, user-friendly medium and its political and economic deregulation, which made it accessible to corporate, state, as well as civil society interests and stakeholders. In each of its three institutional incarnations – military, scientific, and commercial – the internet has made certain forms of communication likely or unlikely, possible and impossible.

institutional mechanisms

Compared to previous media, the internet has blurred institutional boundaries. For one thing, the internet integrates the press and other media of the fourth branch of governance; < the internet is a meta-medium < hosting all previous media. For another thing, it has developed into a more general means of production and distribution, collaboration and conflict, crisscrossing private and public sectors, spheres of work and leisure, and different national jurisdictions. The field of communication studies (Park & Pooley, 2008; Simonson, Peck, Craig, & Jackson, 2013) emerged in response to the newly recognized centrality of information and communication for social coordination – the control revolution < – with (mass) media systems as the dedicated carriers of public

> the fourth branch of governance – Chapter 6, p. 186

> meta-media – Chapter 6, p. 176

> the control revolution – Chapter 6, p. 171

> communication systems – p. 230

information and communication that would sustain representative democracy. With the internet, a new breed of communication systems < presents new empirical research questions along with many old (and some new) normative issues.

technological mechanisms

> determination in the first instance – Chapter 6, p. 163

> Aristotle on causation – Chapter 5, p. 130

technological momentum

Chapter 6 recounted how certain forms of communication were materially impossible before the invention of writing, or printing, or computing: Technologies determine communication, if only in the first instance. < Like Aristotle's bronze figure, < technologies are shaped as material means to social ends in long lines of causation – and coincidences. Instant messaging over the internet, for one, was predated by texting via telephony (sms). In fact, telephone companies had only thought of such messages as a way to contact their customers, or to offer specialized services, not as communications between subscribers (Gow & Smith, 2006: 55). But especially young users happened on the potential, making texting the first killer application of mobile communication and a central factor in its diffusion around the world (Castells, Fernández-Ardèvol, Qiu, & Sey, 2007). In stepwise fashion, practices of instant one-to-one and many-to-many communication thus acquired a momentum of their own (Hughes, 1994), and came to be taken for granted (Ling, 2012) by users as a standard component of diverse internet services.

suppression of radical potential

> communicative utopias and dystopias – Chapter 1, p. 7

> many-to-many and many-to-one communications – Chapter 6, p. 172

Rather than being discovered or recovered, technological potentials may be suppressed. In a history of communication technologies since the telegraph, Brian Winston (1998) presented and substantiated the argument that each of these has been subject to a suppression of radical potential. Telephony, broadcasting, and the internet could all be described as sources of individual empowerment and institutional democratization which have, however, been curtailed through an unhappy alliance of aggressive market forces and passive regulatory agencies. History, of course, has witnessed repeated narratives of such communicative utopias and dystopias. < Early utopias of the internet as a participatory medium (Rheingold, 1994) were questioned, during the 2010s, by the revelation of pervasive state surveillance of citizens and by the common recognition that citizens are subject to commercial surveillance, as well, as part of what Shoshana Zuboff (2019) has termed surveillance capitalism. The point is that both many-to-many participation and many-to-one surveillance < are historically new forms of communication, determined in the first instance by digital technologies. The two prototypes, and the momentum of each, hang in the balance, presenting both empirical questions and normative issues with global implications.

discursive mechanisms

> the evolutionary basis of communication – Chapter 2, p. 28

literacy

digital divides

Lastly, discursive mechanisms condition communication at the level of individual cognition and social interaction. Also on the internet, the question is who is able to do what with which words. Bounded by evolution, < the human capability of communication is cultivated through socialization and education, and extended through the historically available technologies. Against a background of media history, the idea of literacy has been redefined, beyond reading, writing, and counting, to refer to a range of generic competences of understanding and applying information for personal and social ends (Hobbs & Mihailidis, 2019). A critical component of literacy is the ability to evaluate the origins and often implicit interests of the information on offer, as one condition of self-determination. Internet studies have identified three levels of digital divides between the haves and the have-nots: a first level concerning basic access (or not) to networks and devices; a second level addressing users' (unequal) opportunities in terms of necessary skills for comprehending and utilizing information; and a third-level divide that refocuses attention on the (lack of) outcomes of internet use in terms of enhanced political, economic, or cultural participation (for overview, see Scheerder, van Deursen, & van Dijk, 2017). Digital divides serve as one reminder that institutional, technological, as well as discursive factors must be included in assessments of the diffusion and distribution of the goods of information, communication, participation, and privacy, globally and locally.

overdetermination

Empirical studies explore how the different determinants of an event or action intersect and interact in a process that Sigmund Freud (1911/1900) had referred to as overdetermination. Just as the happenings of an ordinary day will mix and merge with long gone and perhaps repressed experiences in the contents and forms of a person's dreams, institutional, technological, and discursive mechanisms jointly produce certain predominant forms of communication: particular events in and experiences of the world. Political philosophy and ethics traditionally have bracketed empirical inquiry altogether; communication studies have detailed the constituents, processes, and consequences of human communication, but with limited explicit reference to normative research questions. In the following section, I outline an agenda for empirical studies of communication and justice. The summary question is how the goods of information, communication, participation, and privacy are produced and distributed, to whom, with what implications for their place in society and the world, as well as for their self-respect and self-realization.

The empirical goods of justice

Information goods

> objects, subjects, and worlds of interest – Chapter 7, p. 202

Chapter 7 identified three kinds of information goods: objects, subjects, and worlds of interest; < Table 8.2 lays out these goods in the terminology of critical realism. Information goods present themselves, most concretely, as human *experiences* of representations of reality in text, image, and sound, which lend themselves to diverse instrumental and reflective uses. Such uses are configured as specific kinds of social *events*, as embedded in wider political, economic, and cultural practices, and expressed in the conventions of factual and fictional genres. Both the representations and their uses depend for their efficacy and durability on structuring *mechanisms*, centered in the institutions that produce, disseminate, and curate information as a social resource.

> the public-sphere model – Chapter 3, p. 54

content analysis

science communication

> climate change and justice – Chapter 1, p. 4

> intercultural communication – Chapter 2, p. 41

Empirical communication research has given priority to information as it relates to the political and cultural public spheres, < that is, to human subjects as social agents and to the communities and societies in which they organize their lives and coexistence. A mainstay of empirical studies has been content analyses (Krippendorff, 2018) of the quantity and, to a degree, the quality of the information available about different sociodemographic groups and different regions of the world. In comparison, objects of interest, specifically the natural and increasingly human-made environment, have been addressed in smaller, separate, and specialized areas such as science communication (National Academies of Sciences, Engineering, and Medicine, 2017). Climate change, for one, has only recently entered the mainstream study of mainstream media. < Similarly, worlds of interest – the comprehensive doctrines or worldviews within which different societies and cultures approach information – have commonly been delegated to intercultural studies < (Kim, 2018), rather than

TABLE 8.2 Information goods as objects of empirical inquiry

Experiences *Information about:*	*Events* *Information as:*	*Mechanisms* *Information actualized by:*
• Objects of interest • Subjects of interest • Worlds of interest	• Factual accounts • Imaginary constructions • Instrumental and reflective resources	• Institutions of knowledge • Institutions of dissemination • Institutions of curation

being recognized as part and parcel of any information about any reality. Inventories of the information available on subjects, objects, as well as worlds of interest – organized as a public resource or communicative commons < – can be considered one of the key deliverables of communication research as a practical discipline.

> the communicative commons – Chapter 7, p. 201

It is the conceptualization of information as a resource for acting in and on reality that most directly addresses information as a condition and constituent of justice. < This is in contrast to the more common notion of information as a representation of reality as one finds it – more or less true or beautiful – which also has been the premise of the social-scientific and humanistic mainstreams of communication research (see further Jensen, 1988, 1991). Factual accounts of politics and economy in news and other journalistic genres (Mazzoleni, 2016) constitute resources for public debate, opinion-formation, decision-making, and concerted action. But also fiction – imaginary constructions of possible worlds – serves to orient citizens' actions in the real world (Richardson, in press), as suggested by science fictions that have fed the idea of cyberspace (W. Gibson, 1984) and of certain basic laws of robotics (Asimov, 1974/1950) into scholarly, policy, and public debates on digitalization and artificial intelligence. For the individual, information resources enable a life lived according to a plan and to the full. < For the collective, information resources provide a necessary condition for arriving at an overlapping consensus of conflicting comprehensive doctrines. <

> information as resource and/or representation – Chapter 1, p. 9

> justice as self-realization – Chapter 4, p. 102

> the overlapping consensus – Chapter 4, p. 113

The production and distribution of information resources depends on three mechanisms as implemented in institutions of knowledge, curation, and dissemination. It is the institutions of public dissemination – the press and other media – that most communication researchers (and many fewer philosophers) have focused on (and to which I return in the next section). But the antecedent question is which information is available in the first place, for anyone to consider and act on. Information is made, not found. Science and scholarship make information available (or not), depending on their organization, funding, and prevailing knowledge interests. < As sources of evidence and insight enabling planning and forecasting, the institutions of knowledge belong on the research agenda for communication and justice on a par with the institutions of public dissemination. <

> knowledge interests – Chapter 3, p. 60

> institutions of knowledge and communication – Chapter 2, p. 26

Both within and beyond science and scholarship, digital technologies are producing exponentially increasing amounts of information, raising questions of how to preserve and prepare extant information for later use. In print culture, the task had been entrusted to libraries, museums, and other archives, with

> libraries, museums, and archives – Chapter 6, p. 181

big science

gradually increased public access; < sustainable institutions of digital curation have yet to emerge from diverse public and private initiatives, from national digital archives (e.g., https://dp.la) to Google Books (https://books.google.com). The present challenge calls for initiatives on the scale of big science (Weinberg, 1961), as exemplified by CERN, the European Organization for Nuclear Research (which spawned the World Wide Web (Berners-Lee, 1999)): grand, collaborative, basic research that prepares the ground for more specialized and applied projects, many still to be thought of. Importantly, both technical, humanistic, and social-scientific perspectives are needed to develop the principles and procedures which, for different areas of human activity, will select some qualities and quantities of information while, inevitably, discarding or making others unretrievable. Whether by design or default, institutions of curation circumscribe not just what can be known about the past, but also which futures may be envisioned and made.

Communication goods

Compared to information goods as carried by specific discourses, communication goods are relational and processual, emerging from meaningful human interactions over time and across social and cultural space. We have communicative *experiences* in face-to-face encounters as well as in interactions with distant or imagined others through technological media (Table 8.3). In both instances, we partake of communicative *events*, accessing information, being socialized as individuals, and contributing to the structuration of society in the long run. The *mechanisms* enabling socialization and social structuration include the media as institutions of public dissemination, but also the unique biographical individual; the two are, increasingly, intertwined in institutional, material, and discursive networks of communication.

interpersonal and mass communication

> two-step and three-step flows of communication – Chapter 6, p. 178

It is a sad and surprising fact that communication research has studied both embodied individuals and technological media as sites and sources of communication, but largely in separate traditions of interpersonal and mass communication research (Rogers, 1999). This is in spite of the founding of the field on the insight that communication flows in multiple steps and across the interpersonal–mass divide. < With digital technologies integrating these prototypes, it has become imperative to bridge the long and deep divide within the discipline – theoretically, methodologically, as well as empirically. In theory development, a growing body of work has begun to relate the classic literature on multi-step

TABLE 8.3 Communication goods as objects of empirical inquiry

Experiences *Communication among:*	*Events* *Communication as:*	*Mechanisms* *Communication actualized by:*
• Embodied others • Imagined others	• Information access • Socialization • Social structuration	• Biographical individuals • Media systems • Communication systems

flows of communication to the digital media environment (e.g., Brosius & Weimann, 1996; Campus, 2012; Himelboim, Gleave, & Smith, 2009; Karlsen, 2015; Vu & Gehrau, 2010; Zhang, Zhao, & Xu, 2016). In methodological terms, automated data collection via mobile and other digital devices (Salganik, 2018) provides increasingly fine-grained quantitative measurements of information and user flows across physical contexts, < complementing qualitative, naturalistic evidence from the social contexts of interaction (Jensen, 2012a).

> information flows, user flows, and context flows – Chapter 6, p. 177

As empirical social events – speech acts – communication is the vehicle, at once, of individual socialization and social structuration. Given the constitutive role of communication – access to and sharing of information – in all social life, its specific contribution to either the maintenance of the individual social subject or the long-term structuration of society has been notoriously difficult to operationalize in empirical studies (Jensen, 2012c: 167–170). Several research traditions, however, have documented the systematic and systemic interdependence of different kinds of inequality – the unequal distribution of both symbolic and material resources. Key references have been the work of sociologist Pierre Bourdieu (1984/1979) on economic and cultural capital and of political scientist Ronald Inglehart (1990) on value systems; the latter framework underlies the comparative World Values Survey (www.worldvaluessurvey.org/wvs.jsp, accessed August 15, 2020). A literature specifically on knowledge gaps anticipated current work on digital divides, suggesting how gaps and divides may be accumulated over time and, indeed, may be reinforced rather than closed through media use (Gaziano, 1997; Hwang & Jeong, 2009; Tichenor, Olien, & Donohue, 1970; Viswanath & Finnegan, 1996). The social-structural patterning of communicative practices is testified, further, by qualitative case studies, historical analyses, and culturally comparative research <

socialization

social structuration

knowledge gaps

> culturally comparative studies – Chapter 2, p. 41

(Esser & Hanitzsch, 2012), including the World Internet Project (www.worldinternetproject.com/index.html, accessed August 15, 2020).

media systems

In the early twenty-first century, technological mechanisms can be seen to trump institutional mechanisms in what appears to be an epochal transformation of the institutions of communication through digitalization. Concretely, the traditional model of the press that used to deliver "public service for private money" (Lund, 2001: 41) – publicistic content funded through commercial markets – is being eroded by multi-step communications and interlinked services in a new marketplace of attention (Webster, 2014). European-style public-service broadcasting, equally, is struggling to legitimate its model of public communication (Goldsmiths, 2016). As noted in Chapter 1, media systems are one of the few topics that have been subject to sustained normative analysis in communication research. More than a research opportunity, the current transition presents a threat to received models for the political economy of media from the last two centuries. At stake is the continued economic and institutional viability of the fourth branch of governance. <

> the fourth branch of governance – Chapter 6, p. 186

communication systems

> the control revolution – Chapter 6, p. 171

> big science – p. 228

> the printing press – Chapter 6, p. 167

As media systems are being reconfigured, a different category of communication systems is emerging (Flensburg & Lai, 2019). Compared to media systems (Hallin & Mancini, 2004), communication systems incorporate the full range of communicative prototypes – one-to-one, one-to-many, many-to-many, and many-to-one – as they are practiced across public, private, and intimate spheres of social activity. Communication systems, further, interface – intersect and interact — with other institutions in the basic structure of society: the institutions of knowledge and curation, along with markets, states, families, educational institutions, and civil society. Digital communication systems recall those of the control revolution, < which, from the late nineteenth century, helped to manage a greatly increased material production and a rebuilt natural environment. Like the curation of the world's information, communication systems present research questions on the order of big science. < Compared to the late 1800s, institutions are now in place to undertake empirical research to support normative evaluation of different potential lines of development for communication systems in a future perspective. "What is just or unjust is the way that institutions deal with" (Rawls, 1999b/1971: 87) facts such as technologies transforming the production and distribution of material as well as immaterial goods on a scale and with a scope that may overshadow the consequences of the printing press. <

Amid technological and institutional change, the unique biographical individual remains a key mechanism of human communication – as an embodied communicator, a giver and taker of socialization, and an agent of social structuration. This is true even as the latest generation of artificial intelligence is adding another layer of agency to communication systems (Gunkel, 2020). As an idea, *mass* communication came first; < in research, mass and interpersonal communication studies have remained alienated from each other. Digital technologies present a historical opportunity for more empirical studies of embodied human beings as central nodes in institutional, technological, and discursive networks – necessary conditions and constituents of communication about and for justice.

artificial intelligence

> mass communication came first – Chapter 1, p. 7

Participation goods

In communication, humans become both unique individuals and constituents of communities and societies; *by* communication, they participate in the governance of their communities and societies. Contacts with other citizens and constituencies, elected and appointed representatives, as well as mass-mediated representations of people and policies furnish the *experiences* that may qualify deliberation and dialogue (Table 8.4). As *events*, these myriad interactions aggregate and amount to self-governance through communication, which is the distinctive feature of modern political democracy. < Above and beyond any specific content, the acts of communication maintain the institution of representative governance, which is also the key *mechanism* lending meaning, focus, and relevance to the distributed interactions, translating them into procedures and decisions with practical consequences. Alongside the formal institutions of political democracy,

> self-governance through communication – Chapter 6, p. 186

TABLE 8.4 Participation goods as objects of empirical inquiry

Experiences *Participation with:*	*Events* *Participation as:*	*Mechanisms* *Participation actualized by:*
• Other citizens and constituencies • Elected and appointed representatives • Agendas and frames of interpretation	• Self-governance • Institutional maintenance	• Representative governance • Publicity • Translatability

additional mechanisms of publicity and translatability may ensure the informed consent of the governed.

Empirical studies of political communication (Mazzoleni, 2016) have emphasized the exchanges back and forth between public opinion as expressed by citizens, and policies as enacted by parliaments, executives, and judiciaries. The political system could be seen as a mediating entity receiving an input of demands and preferences, and returning an output of goods and entitlements (Easton, 1953). That emphasis is suggested by a standard

agenda-setting

operationalization of political agenda-setting (McCombs & Shaw, 1972) as an interplay between the different agendas of the public, the media, and the political system, which lend themselves to comparative measurements (Dearing & Rogers, 1996). Less attention has been given to the processes in which different

> practical concepts – Chapter 6, p. 163

practical concepts < of 'politics' and its constituent 'agendas' are articulated and negotiated as 'public opinion' takes shape, including extended agenda-building (Lang & Lang, 1981). Such

interpretive frames

processes bear witness to more basic and more permanent frames of interpretation (Borah, 2011) that imply worldviews with nor-

> critical literacy – p. 225

mative ramifications. Critical literacy < – including citizens' ability to relate the agendas of seasonal politics to long-term interests (their own as well as those of others, including future generations) – represents an essential participation good and an empirical research question bearing directly on communication and justice.

As noted in Chapter 6, participation can – must – take place through different devices of re-presentation: elections, hearings,

> justice as representativity – Chapter 7, p. 201

and other communications that delegate authority and agency. < There are constitutive, practical limitations to political communication: No one can hold all the relevant information; everybody cannot be heard on each public matter; and no collective decision can involve everybody. Whereas, for instance, the idea of 'clicktivism' tends to denigrate the online expression of commitment to a cause, it is important to recognize different kinds and degrees of participation in self-governance. The current age may be characterized as one of monitorial citizens and monitory democracy (Keane, 2009; Schudson, 1998), in which people will monitor society and the world for when (political) action may (not) be needed, rather being formally and continuously involved in the practice of politics. For empirical purposes, the salient political events or actions include party membership and participation in popular movements, but also material and symbolic contributions to causes and campaigns, as well as more or less regular attention to and interaction about the news. It is all of these actions that, together, produce, maintain, repair, and transform the institution of representative governance (Carey, 1989), including preparation for times of contestation and crisis. Institutional maintenance must be considered not only a byproduct, but a primary outcome of political communication.

The institution of representative governance embodies the mechanism that lends meaning and relevance to particular items of information and instances of communication as goods of participation; Chapter 6 reviewed the multi-step flows of communication at work, and I return in the last section of this chapter to empirical indexes of the quality of governance in local and global perspectives. Representative governance is enabled, further, by two complementary mechanisms that operate across the institutions of the basic structure of society. To one side, participation goods are produced and circulated through publicity, as traditionally associated with political and economic issues in the public sphere. As part of the culturalization of politics and economy, < however, an expanded right to know (Schudson, 2015) has come to include domains such as corporate social responsibility, consumer safety, personal health, and cultural identity. Increasingly, the burden of proof lies with those who might argue that the general public should *not* be in a position to know certain things. To the other side, translatability < had been referred to by John Rawls as a necessary condition for arriving at an overlapping consensus between incompatible comprehensive doctrines: the multiple worlds of interest in globalized and multicultural circumstances. But, also translatability between specialized (scientific) knowledge and politically actionable information, for example, about the objects of interest for material production and environmental sustainability, is key to public participation in self-governance. In both respects – publicity and translatability – comprehensive empirical studies are needed to trace the long and tortuous lines of supply that feed information resources (or not) into public communication and the institution of representative governance.

publicity

> culturalization of politics and economy – Chapter 6, p. 187

the right to know

> translatability – Chapter 4, p. 109

Privacy goods

Privacy covers *experiences* of individuality as well as sociality: being a unique individual and, simultaneously, being an equal part of and partner in a greater whole (Table 8.5). Compared to the goods of information, communication, and participation, privacy goods can be defined negatively as the products of *non-events*: the safeguarding of personal enclosures and the protection of individuals from social discrimination. Like other goods, however,

TABLE 8.5 Privacy goods as objects of empirical inquiry

Experiences *Privacy regarding:*	*Events* *Privacy as:*	*Mechanisms* *Privacy actualized by:*
• Individuality	• Personal enclosure	• Contextual integrity
• Sociality	• Non-discrimination	• Ombudsman

> contextual integrity – Chapter 7, p. 209

privacy depends on positively defined *mechanisms* to regulate the boundaries between the personal, the private, and the public: a principle of contextual integrity < and its enforcement through public institutions with democratic oversight – which do not yet exist.

> moderns define their own ends – Chapter 2, p. 35

> justice as self-respect and self-realization – Chapter 4, p. 102

search engines

The value commonly attached to the experience of being the individual that one is, follows from the modern idea and ideal of humans as autonomous agents with the right to define their own ends: < Self-definition is a constituent of self-respect and a condition of self-realization. < At the same time, individuality is social: The experience of being who one is, or would like to become, is an outcome of socialization and acculturation. Whereas personal and social identities are, in general, nourished by information and communication, justice is served by making some kinds of information about individuals unavailable or inaccessible, and by limiting certain forms of analysis of and communication about them. Sustained profiling brackets and filters the information that people get access to, for example, via internet search engines (Halavais, 2018); systematic comparisons may inform decisions – in unrelated, unforeseen, and unforeseeable contexts – on who gains which entitlements and benefits. In both respects, digital technologies hold potentials that are still being discovered in commercial research and development, and through empirical studies (on internet research ethics, see Franzke, Bechmann, Zimmer, Ess, & Association of Internet Researchers, 2020). The likely conclusion, in many cases, is that what could be, ought not to be.

personal enclosures

information *becomes* personal

Privacy goods are produced and maintained, first, through personal enclosures, material as well as immaterial: a home, a diary, an image archive. Such enclosures constitute privileged domains – sites of individuality – to which the person in question is the legitimate gatekeeper, but whose boundaries are being blurred by digital technologies: Given a sufficient number of data points, it is increasingly possible to establish the identities and activities of people without traditional identifying or 'personal' information (Rocher, Hendrickx, & de Montjoye, 2019). Information is not, but *becomes* personal in the context of other information. A second type of privacy goods relate to sociality, and are associated specifically with the data and metadata that users communicate into digital systems, and which may lead to social discrimination. As accumulated, analyzed, and applied in other contexts of decision and action, such data may determine which information people will (not) encounter as they try to cope with crises or life choices; data on past behaviors may also prejudice, for example, the terms of insurance that people are offered for the rest of their lives. At stake is, in the first case, a right to be *included* in communication and, in the second case, a right to have certain information *excluded* from communications with personal, existential implications.

non-discrimination

Whereas privacy has recently attracted significant public as well as scholarly attention (Monahan & Murakami Wood, 2018), including a subspecialty of data justice (Taylor, 2017), the institutional and discursive mechanisms that may regulate digitalization in the common interest remain underdefined, and call for much further theoretical and empirical inquiry. The idea of contextual integrity < offers a preliminary principle by which to evaluate the recommunication and enactment of information across contexts; relevant models of comparison include patient–doctor and client–attorney privileges, but also so-called state secrets: Some aspects of individuality and sociality could be considered top secret. The task will be to specify the status of individuals *as* data or information and the implications of this perspective for diverse social institutions and practices, as articulated in policies and procedures, and enforced by democratically accountable agencies. Such agencies have not yet been formalized at either national or international levels, but could be modeled on the institution of an ombudsman (Cheng, 1968). The institution would operate through double insight – into the workings of the communication system in question (for instance, proprietary algorithms) and into their implications for the rights, opportunities, and compensations < of citizens. Exercising transparency by proxy, while ensuring the confidentiality of systems as well as citizens, the ombudsman would perform the role of an arbiter, with executive powers and procedures of appeal still to be defined by national legislation and international treaty.

> contextual integrity – Chapter 7, p. 209

ombudsman

double insight

> rights, opportunities, and compensations – p. 241

transparency by proxy

ANALYSIS BOX 8.1 LIVING WITH INJUSTICE

"Poverty [...] needs no explanation. In a world governed by entropy and evolution, it is the default state of humankind" (Pinker, 2018: 24). Injustice, too, can be considered

> natural and social lotteries – Chapter 4, p. 101

part of the human condition. Because of the natural and social lotteries < that endow individuals with unequal starting points in life, societies must develop and maintain institutions to approximate justice over time. The historical, empirical record shows that such institutions will deliver imperfect outcomes. Globally and locally, humans live with different kinds and degrees of injustice.

> representations as hypotheses – Chapter 5, p. 145

> the ritual model of communication – Chapter 2, p. 41

Communication is a resource for justice: a source of hypotheses < about as well as hopes for the future, articulating and anticipating how reality could be changed for the better. As suggested by the ritual model of communication, < communication produces, maintains, repairs, and transforms reality (Carey, 1989a: 23). Communication *produces* the representations of reality that enable publics, large and small, to identify injustice. Communication *maintains* the worldviews that recognize and react to injustice. Communication *repairs* both worldviews and representations in response to the crises or contingencies associated with specific injustices. And, over time, communication *transforms* the beliefs that individuals and collectives will be willing to act on, so as to reduce and remedy injustice. Communication constitutes the generic human capability to compare and contrast what is, what ought to be, and what could be, thus informing conclusions on what should be done.

Communication itself, however, is also a source of injustice; communication frequently fails as either a condition or a constituent of justice. *Information* is a non-rival, non-depletable good, but depends for its availability and practical relevance on continuous renewal. Information goes missing within and around systems of curation; information proves inaccessible to people without the necessary economic means and educational competences. As social acts, *communications* reflect and reinforce the social structure generating them: Society speaks to itself, about itself. Information and communication both enable and constrain equal *participation* in the institutions and practices of democratic governance. And, in systems of many-to-one communication that recycle and repurpose information, *privacy* is at risk in unprecedented ways.

> the practical-productive turn of science – Chapter 5, p. 132

Communication unfolds in the window of opportunity between chance and necessity, which has been widened by the long practical-productive turn of science and scholarship:

< More material and immaterial goods are available than ever before in human history. Modern information and communication technologies are themselves unique products of the practical turn: self-reflective resources for exploring and shifting the limits to what could be, in research and public debate. And yet, communication remains limited by human capabilities, by the affordances of each new technology, and by the historical institutions that regulate the end of communication. We can't just talk about justice, < and must live with injustice under material, institutional, and discursive circumstances "transmitted from the past" (Karl Marx in Feuer, 1969: 360), but monitored and critiqued through empirical studies.

> we can't just talk about it – Chapter 1, p. 4

Monitoring injustice

Inferring justice

As a basis of collective decisions and actions, humans depend on inferences, as exchanged and examined in communication. We identify instances of the same kinds of experiences and events (induction), specify the categories that capture such instances (deduction), and articulate new categories to explain how and why certain experiences and events present themselves to us in particular contexts (abduction). Grounded in natural evolution, < induction, deduction, and abduction emerged as practical concepts; were formalized as logical conceptions; and shaped the modern conceptualizations and empirical research designs devised to inform the control of nature and the governance of societies.

three forms of inference

> the prehistory of communication and justice – Chapter 2, p. 28

While deduction and induction have enjoyed pride of place in histories and textbooks of science and scholarship, abduction had been identified by Aristotle (Florez, 2014), and was reintroduced to modern philosophy by Charles Sanders Peirce as part of a systematic relating the three types. His basic point was that there are three components to any inference: a rule which, when applied to a case, produces a conclusion or result. These components yield three possible combinations:

DEDUCTION

Rule. All the beans from this bag are white.
Case. These beans are from this bag.
Result. These beans are white.

INDUCTION

Case. These beans are from this bag.
Result. These beans are white.
Rule. All the beans from this bag are white.

[ABDUCTION

Result. These beans are white.
Rule. All the beans from this bag are white.]
Case. These beans are from this bag.

Peirce, 1986: 325–326

Formally, only the deduction is a valid inference. Here, given the meaning of the constituent terms, the rule can be applied without any uncertainty to the case; the result follows as a matter of course. In the induction, the implication is that, if one examines a sufficient number of beans (cases), one may be willing to conclude that they are all white. The point of the abduction, finally, is that it introduces a rule that might explain why one encounters particular (more or less surprising) facts, such as white beans, in a particular context. The bean example is, of course, trivial. In other cases, the newly devised rule represents an exceptionally bright idea, as in Sherlock Holmes solving crime mysteries, which are fictional feats of abduction (Sebeok & Umiker-Sebeok, 1983).

In practice, the three forms of inference are rarely found in any pure form in empirical studies; indeed, a combination of all three types is commonly required to produce relevant insights. Take the prototypical survey gauging public opinion and feeding into formal and informal deliberations about political agendas and plans of action. > political agendas – p. 232 < Such studies depart from hypotheses deriving from more general sociological or psychological theories (deduction), which can be tested empirically (against a null hypothesis) with reference to a sufficient number of concrete responses (induction). The findings likely provide, at best, partial support for the hypotheses in question, giving rise to the formulation of new or specified rules (abduction) to be investigated in further research. The original premise, equally, was the product of a (more or less) bright idea – abduction. Empirical studies *of* empirical research activities themselves support such a combinatorial understanding of how inferences are, in fact, produced, received, accepted, and translated into further scientific and other social practices (e.g., Hacking, 1983; Latour, 1987). Many important and influential insights from science and scholarship have been the outcome of serendipity (Merton & Barber, 2004): contingencies

serendipity

and confluences of the right questions being asked and answered at the right time and place.

Also studies of normative research questions involve deduction, induction, as well as abduction; here, the rules constitute rules of action, as applied to actual cases with contestable results. The modern understanding of human rights, including the right to communicate, is a product of abduction. As noted by the philosopher Michael J. Sandel (2009: 9) in his history of justice, "modern theories start with freedom" and balance individual liberty against the collective welfare or equality. Following a Renaissance that had placed humans at the center of the universe, and encouraged by scientific discoveries supporting humans' control of nature, the moderns faced the question of which rights they ought to assign to themselves for guiding social interaction and coexistence. The Enlightenment response was the rule that, in the words of the 1776 US Declaration of Independence, "all Men are created equal," endowed with "certain unalienable Rights" including "Liberty," as they pursue their diverse plans in life (https://guides.loc.gov/declaration-of-independence, accessed August 15, 2020). The rule notoriously left open questions of how it would be applied, beyond "Men," to cases across gender, class, and ethnicity, and how the unequal results or outcomes of its application would be addressed. As first premises of local and global coexistence, however, equality and liberty were reaffirmed and codified in the 1948 Universal Declaration of Human Rights. <

abduction

> communicative and other human rights – Chapter 7, p. 190

While sometimes manifesting themselves as flashes of creative insight (Eco, 1984: 42) or gestalt switches (Grinnell, 2019: 219), abductions are best thought of as rules of cognition and conduct that typically have been prepared and take effect over time, in and by communication. Enlightenment conceptions of human rights had grown out of a process of double hermeneutics < as philosophers took on board practical concepts of equality and liberty from contemporary politics, economy, and culture; the concepts have remained subject to centuries-long struggles. In the process, societies have been hard pressed to come to terms, at once, with secular rights and religious maxims and other comprehensive doctrines. < The US Declaration of Independence, for one, had assumed that it was "their Creator" that endowed humans with "certain unalienable Rights." In another creative abduction about a century later, Charles Darwin (2013/1859) introduced the rule that not just humans, but all animals are created equal under conditions of natural chance and environmental necessity.

> double hermeneutics – Chapter 2, p. 25

> comprehensive doctrines – Chapter 4, p. 108

Abductions may reinterpret thoroughly familiar entities, as in Darwin's reinterpretation of human beings, but have a special role to play when people try to fit unfamiliar experiences and events into a wider scheme of things for the first time. Chapter 6 recounted the history of how 'new' media have been cast in the image of the 'old': television as radio with pictures; the digital computer as a sophisticated calculator. As a technological potential, moreover, each new medium has raised questions of what it could and ought to become. The internet, as noted, has enabled forms of many-to-one communication which lend themselves to commercial and state uses that are still being discovered, and for which institutions of public regulation and democratic oversight are not yet in place. In response, *habeas data* < constitutes an abduction that introduces a rule by way of an analogy between the physical and informational existence of individuals.

> *habeas data* – Chapter 7, p. 209

deduction

The process of specifying the rules that abductions articulate relies on deduction. The modern rule that all humans are equal complicated another classic of logic textbooks: All human beings are mortal / Socrates is a human being // Therefore, Socrates is mortal. For one thing, if all human beings are equal, that arguably raised questions concerning what philosophers denote the *extension* (reference) of the term 'human being.' A solution, for a long time, was delivered by the dictum that some humans (animals) are more equal than others (Orwell, 2001/1945), excluding one (or some) gender(s), classes, and ethnicities from the category for all practical purposes. For another thing, the *intension* (meaning) of 'equal' is contestable in a way that 'mortal' is not. As an aspect of the 1776 formulation of equality, liberty or freedom could be defined either negatively or positively: < the freedom *from* collective agencies intervening into the individual's affairs, or the freedom *to* be the individual one would like to become precisely through the intervention of collective agencies. What might appear as philosophical hair-splitting entails very real, very different consequences for the institutions of the basic structure of society and for the individual lives they circumscribe.

> positive and negative freedom – Chapter 2, p. 36

The extension and intension of 'personal data' currently present questions of definition and delimitation, with practical ramifications for issues of transparency and trust in society at large. In digital systems, as noted, data *become* personal, depending on the contexts of other data in which they are analyzed and applied. Deductions help to specify the ways in which data may become personal. Deductions also serve to develop the hypotheses through which different kinds and degrees of privacy can be examined empirically. Like abductions, deductions contribute to preparing the principles and procedures by which injustice can be assessed, addressed, and acted on.

induction

Inductions, finally, identify instances of (in)injustice according to rules which, while contestable, < serve as common denominators, for the time being, for a given community or society. As such, inductions yield indexes – measures with meanings – that facilitate a continuous and public monitoring of the general state of justice: the production and distribution of the rights and goods of information, communication, participation, and privacy.

> essentially contestable concepts – Chapter 1, p. 13

Identifying injustice

The two principles of communication and justice < noted three standards for assessing whether and how justice is served: rights, opportunities, and compensations. As a first priority, each person has an equal right to information, communication, participation, and privacy. The information that has been accumulated throughout history should be made available and accessible as part of a communicative commons; < in and by communication, each person should be able to participate in deliberations and decisions affecting the actualization of their capabilities; and no one should be treated as a means of information and communication without informed consent and public regulation. Such rights are articulated (or not) in national legislation and international conventions and treaties, and can be ascertained through historical, textual, and other qualitative studies of principles, procedures, and precedents. Compared to statements of what is the case (knowing-that) and what could be done to either maintain or transform the status quo (knowing-how) (Ryle, 1949), rights constitute imperative speech acts: socially sanctioned stipulations of what *must* be the case.

> the two principles of communication and justice – Chapter 7, p. 197

rights

> the communicative commons – Chapter 7, p. 201

opportunities

Opportunities, second, refocus attention on the difference or disjuncture between rights and goods, principle and practice. Who is in a position to say and do what, and not to be said certain things about and done certain things to? Equality of opportunity depends on the availability, accessibility, and performativity of the relevant goods of information, communication, participation, and privacy. Whereas quantitative surveys and observational studies are essential for monitoring who does what with which media and communications, qualitative case studies can help to uncover some of the mechanisms < underlying, for instance, structural discrimination (Altman, 2015). Because the principle of fair equality of opportunity does not allow for exceptions, single cases of inequality call both for an explanation and for an account of how they might be avoided or reduced in the future.

> mechanisms, events, experiences – p. 222

compensations

Third, the need for compensations follows from the difference principle: the idea that continued inequalities must be to the greatest benefit of the least advantaged participants in communication. Communities and societies are obliged to develop institutions that make information more available, communication more accessible, participation more performative, and privacy less at risk: targeted subsidies, programs of research and development, educational interventions, and more. Both quantitative and qualitative methodologies lend themselves to evaluating compensatory arrangements, their consequences, and relative success. This is in addition to action research (Bradbury, 2015; Greenwood & Levin, 2007), which collaborates with stakeholders in an area of practice and inquiry to discover what are, in fact, the problems on the ground and what could be (the road to) a solution. The field of (new) media and communication studies has been among the contributors to the interdisciplinary domain of action research (Hearn, Tacchi, Foth, & Lennie, 2009).

action research

indexes of communication and justice

Indexes addressing rights, opportunities, and compensations are produced and presented on a continuous basis, if to varying degrees, for information, communication, participation, and privacy. The rights and goods of public communication and political participation, in particular, have been centers of attention as part of the classic understanding of communication as the medium or vehicle of the fourth branch of governance. Yearly national indices seek to capture the quality of the freedom of the press, and range from the World Press Freedom Index of the NGO, Reporters without Borders (https://rsf.org/en/world-press-freedom-index), to the Freedom of the Press report from the US-government-funded Freedom House (https://freedomhouse.org/report/freedom-press/freedom-press-2017). Wider freedoms of expression, including academic and artistic freedom, are addressed by the Index of Censorship organization (www.indexoncensorship.org). The Economist Intelligence Unit publishes a general Democracy Index (www.eiu.com/topic/democracy-index); the World Justice Project provides a further Rule of Law Index (https://worldjusticeproject.org/our-work/wjp-rule-law-index). Privacy has recently attracted renewed attention as part of public debate on surveillance, and is included, for example, in the Corporate Accountability Index for key internet, mobile, and telecommunications companies that is produced by the Ranking Digital Rights organization (https://rankingdigitalrights.org).

While these various indexes integrate multiple measures, it has not been common to consolidate indicators of the rights and goods of information, communication, participation, and privacy in summary indices of communication and justice. One model has been outlined as part of the comparative study of media systems (Brüggemann, Engesser, Büchel, Humprecht, & Castro, 2014); a factor analysis of structural indicators with normative implications served to identify a typology of media systems with different kinds and degrees of representation and participation (see further Ahmed, Cho, Jaidka, Eichstaedt, & Ungar, 2020). To capture the communication systems < that are replacing traditional media systems, a next step would be to develop models that include more than mass communication as well as information beyond classic news and current affairs. On the one hand, a transnational or global index of communication and justice would complement the United Nations' Human Development Index (http://hdr.undp.org/en/content/human-development-index-hdi), which is grounded in research on human capabilities; in Chapter 7, I noted the architectonic role of communication in articulating and anticipating the actualization of other capabilities. < On the other hand, a standard measure of inequality is the Gini coefficient, which indicates the degree of economic inequality within a (national) population (Haughton & Khandker, 2009). A comparable measure would capture the degree to which different members of a community or society are in a position to be informed about, communicate about, and make their own future – call it GiniComm.

> communication systems – p. 230

the Human Development Index

> the architectonic role of the capability to communicate – Chapter 7, p. 195

the Gini coefficient

Practicing justice

In the words of the anthropologist Clifford Geertz (1974: 29), empirical research on humans, their cultures and communications, tries to figure out "what the devil they think they are up to," seeking explanations and suggesting alternatives. The resulting evidence and insights can make a practical difference through the double hermeneutics of research. < Institutions of communication monitor society; empirical communication studies monitor the monitors. Whereas indexes of (in)justice have a special role to play in public debate as coins of exchange regarding the practical value of information, communication, participation, and privacy, empirical research also informs the policies by which public agencies regulate institutions of communication on time scales of years, decades, and centuries. In the words of John Rawls (1999b/1971: 47), institutions are public systems of rules; it is the common practice of communication – in multiple steps involving citizens, representatives, as well as researchers – that writes and rewrites the rules.

> the double hermeneutics of research – Chapter 2, p. 25

In a classic article introducing the basic communication model, Harold D. Lasswell (1948) noted surveillance, broadly speaking, as one of the key functions of human communication. Looking out, societies will monitor their surroundings for events requiring attention and action; the article was written at the intersection of the hot World War II and the Cold War. Looking in, societies monitor themselves through professional and public institutions-to-think-with. < A good reason for maintaining such institutions is that they constitute a collective readiness to think, speak, and act when problematic situations (Dewey, 1903) present themselves. An equally good motivation is that they may avoid or, at least, anticipate problems by imagining and rehearsing them. Like injustice, contestation and conflict are part of the human condition. Sooner or later, it is time to think, speak, and act again.

> institutions-to-think-with – Chapter 2, p. 27

In the early twenty-first century, the institutions of knowledge and communication that are legacies of modernity still serve as essential institutions-to-think-with, even while digitalization is challenging received notions of knowledge and communication. In and through communication, justice is practiced in both senses of the word: Communication performs justice by expressing and enacting it; communication also trains the capability of individuals and collectives to recognize and appreciate justice. Aristotle had suggested that people *become* just by practicing what is just: "by doing acts of temperance and courage we become temperate and courageous […] by doing just acts we become just" (Aristotle, 1886: 35). The final chapter considers the future of justice.

9

THE FUTURE OF JUSTICE

What is, what has been, and what will be

In Chapter 1, I departed from three questions that humans ask about the reality in which they find themselves, together: what is, what ought to be, and what could be. < The practical relevance of answers to the question of justice – what ought to be – depends on detailed comparison with what is, and additional analysis of what could be. The intervening chapters have outlined a conceptual and methodological architecture for a theory of communication and justice. In this final chapter, I return to the place of communication in the future of justice. Communication articulates lessons of what has been, addresses what is not yet, and anticipates what will be. Communication for justice entails beliefs, value judgments, as well as plans of action < – hypotheses to be represented in the present and reconfirmed for the future. <

> what is, what ought to be, and what could be – Chapter 1, p. 2

> beliefs as plans of action – Chapter 5, p. 140

> representations as hypotheses on the future – Chapter 5, p. 145

The first section considers the state of justice in the world, as observed from two distinctive positions in international intellectual and public debate. From one perspective highlighting global progress in general living conditions and quality of life, the glass of justice could be seen as at least half full. From another perspective, the glass is almost empty: Not only is global (and local) inequality still massive in the twenty-first century, but the international institutions designed to define and defend the welfare of world citizens, as stipulated in the 1948 Universal Declaration of Human Rights, < may have nourished symbolic rather than substantial forms of justice. The two book-length interventions, between them, delineate a spectrum within which current research and debate on the present and future of justice can be seen to oscillate.

> human rights and communication – Chapter 7, p. 190

> the interdependence hypothesis – Chapter 2, p. 28

> the window of opportunity between chance and necessity – Chapter 2, p. 23

In Chapter 2, I noted the evolutionary background to the very idea of justice: the interdependence of human beings from prehistorical time into an Anthropocene future (Lewis & Maslin, 2015). < The second section of this final chapter takes another long and wide perspective on justice, drawing on recent studies of the human condition across the *longues durées* of history (Braudel, 1980). Amid continuing sub-sub-specialization of academic disciplines, interdisciplinary research has been on the rise since the 1980s (Van Noorden, 2015), delivering, among other things, a ground of grand narratives on which publics and policy-makers may make sense of the many detailed disciplinary figures on offer. I consider synthetic reviews of the agricultural, industrial, and informational ages of human civilization; a proposal for rewriting five millennia of recorded world history from a non-Western perspective; and an analysis of how, in recent centuries, shifting political and economic regimes have perpetuated and legitimated local and global inequalities. Such macro-histories offer reminders of some of the tectonic forces of nature and culture that frame the window of opportunity for communication about justice. <

> peoples and/vs. states – Chapter 4, p. 116

> *erro, ergo sum* – Chapter 5, p. 127

The third section sums up the potentials and limitations of human communication for collective reasoning about the common good. The historical record suggests that no community or society, no people or society of peoples, < could hope to sustain principles and procedures of justice centuries and millennia into the future. But contemporary societies have accumulated the necessary and sufficient resources – unprecedented material and immaterial goods – to build robust institutions for being right (and wrong) < about the many problematic situations (Dewey, 1903) of their coexistence in a future perspective. While subject to competing demands and conflicting priorities, it is the goods of information, communication, participation, and privacy that put people and peoples in a position to live their lives according to (fallible) plans and to make their own (contestable) histories.

> the overlapping consensus – Chapter 4, p. 113

I conclude by revisiting communication as both a condition and a constituent of justice. Communication is a condition and a means of arriving at a conclusion and a consensus, if only of the overlapping kind, < so that communities may get by and go on with their many other doings. Communication is also an end in itself – a mode of being and becoming: In communication, individuals and collectives produce, maintain, repair, and transform themselves. In a footnote addressing how, in the end, people might feel justified and secure in the beliefs guiding their actions, John Rawls (2005/1993), like Immanuel Kant and countless other philosophers, had centered on the reasoning individual, holding that "reason is the final court of appeal," and its "concepts of judgment and inference, and the rest, are irreducible. With these concepts explanations come to an end; one of philosophy's tasks is to quiet our distress at this thought" (p. 120f.). Communication introduces one more court of appeal; one of the tasks of the study of communication is to quiet our distress at the thought that also communication comes to an end.

Not enough

In a book entitled, *Enlightenment Now: The Case for Reason, Science, Humanism, and Progress*, the cognitive scientist Steven Pinker (2018) advanced a two-step argument, that enlightenment has delivered progress for the human species on a scale that is "heroic," "glorious," and "uplifting" (p. 452), but that political, religious, and other intellectual trends are currently undermining 250 years of clarity and insight. Approaching the human predicament on the million-year time scale of planet Earth and the universe as such, Pinker departed from three concepts: entropy, evolution, and information. In a pitiless material universe, the law of *entropy* dictates that dangerous disorder is constantly growing, even if humans can "deploy energy and knowledge to fight back the tide of entropy and carve out refuges of beneficial order" (p. 17). In an intermediate step of *evolution*, "self-organizing processes of physics and chemistry gave rise to a configuration of matter that could replicate itself" (p. 18): life and, with time, human life, which, in a third step, ended up commanding a big brain that "can transform the *information* about the world that it receives from the sense organs in a way that mirrors the laws governing that world, which in turn allows it to make useful inferences and predictions" (p. 21, emphasis added). Refined as knowledge, < information has been the vehicle both of productive sciences < improving the human lot and of institutions embodying "a social contract that puts us in a positive-sum game" (p. 28). In short, "the world is better than it was and can get better still" (p. 39).

entropy, evolution, and information

> data, information, knowledge, wisdom – Chapter 6, p.164

> theoretical, practical, and productive sciences – Chapter 5, p. 129

Pinker (2018) offered detailed documentation of progress by enlightenment, responding to such fundamental questions as:

> How many people are victims of violence as a proportion of the number of people alive? How many are sick, how many starving, how many poor, how many oppressed, how many illiterate, how many unhappy? And are those numbers going up or down?
>
> *p. 43*

Statistics from international institutions such as the United Nations and the World Bank provide the answer that, in each case, those numbers are going down, in some instances by orders of magnitude. Based on international adaptations of the Gini coefficient < (which measures the relative distribution of income or wealth, originally in a national population), Pinker concluded that "despite the anxiety about rising inequality within Western countries, *inequality in the world is declining*. That's a circuitous way to state the progress, though: what's significant about the decline in inequality is that it's a decline in poverty" (p. 105).

> the Gini coefficient – Chapter 8, p. 243

> the World Values Survey – Chapter 8, p. 229

Referring to the World Values Survey, < Pinker (2018) added that enlightenment has further manifested itself in "emancipative values," which reorient outlooks on the future: "People begin to prioritize freedom over security, diversity over uniformity, autonomy over authority, creativity over discipline, and individuality over conformity" (p. 224). While recognizing regional and socioeconomic variations in this regard, as well, he pointed to what might be an accelerating global process of emancipation by enlightenment:

> What is surprising [...] is that *in every part of the world, people have become more liberal*. A lot more liberal: young Muslims in the Middle East, the world's most conservative culture, have values today that are comparable to those of young people in Western Europe, the world's most liberal culture, in the early 1960s.
>
> *p. 227*

> institutions of knowledge and communication – Chapter 2, p. 26

And, as a final step of his argument, Pinker credited modern institutions of knowledge and communication < as agents of moral progress, too:

the World Bank's Knowledge Index

> [T]he single best predictor of emancipative values is the World Bank's Knowledge Index, which combines per capita measures of education (adult literacy and enrollment in high schools and colleges), information access (telephones, computers, and Internet users), scientific and technological productivity (researchers, patents, and journal articles), and institutional integrity (rule of law, regulatory quality, and open economies) [...] the Knowledge Index accounts for *seventy percent* of the variation in emancipative values across countries, making it a far better predictor than GDP. The statistical result vindicates a key insight of the

> Enlightenment: knowledge and sound institutions lead to moral progress.
>
> *p. 228*

Against this background, Pinker (2018) devoted a full chapter to "progressophobia" (Chapter 4) among the Enlightenment's detractors. While taking on both political populists and religious authoritarians, he especially targeted well-educated commentators who, perhaps, should know better: "public intellectuals, especially cultural pessimists perennially hungry for signs that Western civilization is (as always) on the verge of collapse" (p. 191). Counting political correctness (Levy, 1992) as one of the key obstacles to further progress, he discounted the "common criticism" that the Enlightenment is "a Western invention, unsuited to the world in all its diversity":

progressophobia

political correctness

> [A]ll ideas have to come from somewhere, and their birthplace has no bearing on their merit. Though many Enlightenment ideas were articulated in their clearest and most influential form in 18th-century Europe and America, they are rooted in reason and human nature, so any reasoning human can engage with them. That's why Enlightenment ideals have been articulated in non-Western civilizations at many times in history.
>
> *p. 29*

But perhaps the Enlightenment, after all, has been *Not Enough*, the title of law and history professor Samuel Moyn's (2018) volume on *Human Rights in an Unequal World*, its subtitle. Where Pinker had fast-forwarded from entropy and evolution to information and ideas as forces of history, Moyn reemphasized an intermediate range of institutions through which different societies and civilizations might work out the conditions of their coexistence.

Referencing the same Enlightenment as Pinker as his point of departure, specifically the 1789 French Declaration of the Rights of Man and of the Citizen, Moyn (2018) focused attention on the global setting in which the Universal Declaration of Human Rights (UDHR) was finally adopted in 1948. UDHR spelled out the vision of a welfare world, an idea developed by the economist, Gunnar Myrdal: "The concept of the welfare state, to which we are now giving reality in all the advanced nations, would have to be widened and changed into a concept of a 'welfare world'" (cited

the welfare world

in Moyn, 2018: 107). Extrapolating from the welfare states then emerging in "the advanced nations," the 30 articles of UDHR could be read as a "modular reproduction of the welfare state" in political, economic, and cultural spheres of life and scaling these up to the global level (p. 44). For Moyn (citing Myrdal), UDHR constituted the long overdue, logical, or, rather, historical conclusion to what had been asserted locally in 1776 and 1789: "the very idea of human rights and fundamental freedoms carr[ies] with it the concept of universality" (p. 106).

welfare states

Welfare states had been a long time coming, emerging from recurring economic crises and two world wars during the first half of the twentieth century. From the outset, both the welfare states and the welfare world were confronted by entrenched national and international interests. After the 1945 caesura, the world had been split into Eastern and Western blocs, and remained divided until 1989, exactly two centuries after the modern declaration of human rights. For individuals and movements seeking alternatives or correctives to Western-style capitalism, while remaining frustrated with Eastern-style socialism, a commitment to human rights offered "a morally pure form of activism" (Moyn, 2018: 122) that allowed the committed to sidestep the need for concrete political or economic reform in either camp. In a militarily as well as politically and economically divided world, people could organize selectively and safely around the idea of the right to express ideas. For four decades following World War II, Moyn argued, UDHR was mobilized as "a charter meant to save the individual from the state's depredations of civil liberties rather than to empower the state to make individual flourishing and equality a reality" (p. 122).

the Cold War

During the same Cold War decades, the more consequential idea of a welfare world came under attack in the context of national politics, too. The backdrop was the long legacy of the idea of freedom, either negative freedom (*less* government equals *more* freedom for the individual) or positive freedom (*more* government of the right kind equals *more* freedom for all). < A relative shift from negative toward positive freedoms in the public regulation of private enterprises and social services had been one of the main achievements of organized labor, feminism, and other left-leaning movements and political parties. Particularly from the 1970s, Keynesian welfare states were challenged by economic neoliberalism (Boas & Gans-Morse, 2009), symbolized by the Reagan and Thatcher administrations in the US and the UK, respectively. In the international arena, neoliberal principles were

> positive and negative freedom – Chapter 2, p. 36

neoliberalism

extended from donor countries in the Global North to recipient countries in the Global South as conditions of aid packages. In retrospect, "by 1980, human rights were far along in their transit from principles of an egalitarian *welfare* package for fellow citizens to aspirations of global *sufficiency* for fellow humans" (Moyn, 2018: 145, emphases added). Forty years on, Pinker (2018), in equating a decline in poverty with declining inequality, could be heard advocating such a principle of sufficiency.

In Moyn's (2018) summary, 1989 "set up a global moment in which freedom increasingly implied civil liberties on the basis of market freedom alone" (p. 180). The defense of classic freedoms of thought and opinion, information and communication, were supplemented by a "concern for the most indigent on a global scale, notably on the African continent." Amounting to a form of moral cosmopolitanism, < such concerns echoed "the much more longstanding call for humanitarian philanthropy that the global rich might give to the global poor" (p. 196). Moyn recognized that, by the beginning of the twenty-first century, the world had witnessed "a world-historic breakthrough of increasing recognition" of people across gender, "race, sexuality, indigeneity, or disability." Unfortunately, "everyone was treated more equally than ever before, except materially" (p. 202f.).

> moral cosmopolitanism – Chapter 2, p. 45

For Pinker (2018), in a universe of entropy, evolution, and information, not only is "poverty [...] the default state of humankind," but "misfortune may be no one's fault" (p. 24). *Sufficiency* might be an acceptable end, improved incrementally by *ideas* as the first movers of human emancipation. For Moyn (2018), misfortune is typically the fault of *institutions* to which individuals and communities delegate authority and agency, and on which they depend as local as well as global means of *welfare*.

sufficiency through ideas

welfare through institutions

The different time scales that the two authors invoked – from decades and centuries to millions of years – help to explain their diverging narratives about the human condition and the preconditions of justice. Philosophical theories of justice have traditionally focused on what Rawls (1999b/1971: 230) termed primary *social* goods < – "rights, liberties, and opportunities, and income and wealth" (p. 79). In this book, I have highlighted and detailed the place of information, communication, participation, and privacy among the primary social goods. But social goods depend for their actualization on the production and distribution of many other qualities and quantities of goods. Justice is determined in the first instance < by natural as well as historical contingencies.

> primary social goods – Chapter 4, p. 101

> determination in the first instance – Chapter 6, p. 163

Justice in time

Agricultural, industrial, and informational goods

the Black Death

Spanish conquests

Covid-19 pandemic

In the introduction to the second volume of one of the most widely diffused and debated recent grand narratives of the human condition, the historian Yuval Noah Harari (2017) noted that plagues – one of the three scourges of all time – no longer define the human condition (the other two being famines and wars, which also have declined). "For the first time in history, [...] more people die from old age than from infectious diseases" (p. 2). And yet, the natural environment has remained a source of threats as well as goods for *Sapiens* or *Homo Deus*, the titles of Harari's (2014, 2017) two volumes. In the mid-1300s, the Black Death traveled with traders and other unwitting hosts along the Silk Road and its byways, ultimately killing an estimated between 75 and 200 million, "more than a quarter of the population of Eurasia" (p. 8). In 1520, Spanish explorers (conquerors) landed in Mexico, carrying smallpox, flu, measles, and other ailments to its 22 million people, and "in 1580 its population was down to less than 2 million" (p. 10). And, at the time of writing, the Covid-19 pandemic has led to the death of more than one million people (WHO, 2020a), and was met with the first ever global lockdown of economic and other social interaction to avoid many more as well as impossible (by contemporary standards) choices in national healthcare systems.

> natural and social lotteries – Chapter 4, p. 101

environmental lotteries

the agricultural age

Guns, Germs, and Steel

Like the natural and social lotteries shaping an individual's life chances, < environmental lotteries have presented unequal conditions for human communities to develop durable societies and flourishing civilizations. In a volume subtitled, *A Short History of Everybody for the Last 13,000 Years*, Jared Diamond (1998) drove home the point that environmental differences, rather than genomic differences *within* the human species, gave Eurasian communities a head start into the agricultural age, following millennia upon millennia of nomadic hunting-and-gathering. Plants and animals that lent themselves to domestication, coupled with a climate sufficiently dry for storage, helped generate food surpluses, which, in turn, fed population growth and facilitated an early division of labor, prefiguring social and technological innovations that were consolidated in the institutions and infrastructures of cities and states, and extended into empires. As summarized in the title of Diamond's (1998) book, Eurasian states ended up dominating much of the rest of the world through *Guns, Germs, and Steel*: Guns ensured superiority in military encounters with other peoples; steel built the systems for transporting the exploits of empires and colonies back and forth; and, as noted, germs – to which the invaders, having lived for generations in close proximity to domestic animals in densely populated areas, had grown immune – killed off large proportions, even majorities, of indigenous peoples. Natural chance conspired with culturally, religiously legitimated conquest to produce a first round of globalization, 1500–1800 CE, with the West as hegemon.

Humans *found* plants and animals; they *made* crops and livestock. Humans also made and re-made – thought of and refined – distinctive varieties of immaterial goods that allowed them to imagine ways and means of modifying both the goods they found and those that they or others before them had made – call it knowledge, as shared in communication, embodied in writing and subsequent technologies, and embedded in social institutions. Chapters 5 and 6 recounted how, over the last five centuries, institutions and technologies of knowledge and communication supported a practical-productive turn of science and scholarship < that made possible the production of many more goods for much better (and much longer) human lives. As material and immaterial goods carried over from the agricultural age, northwest Europe spearheaded an industrial age that culminated in a Great Divergence of the West from the rest: a period of unprecedented economic growth yielding ever more goods for (very gradually and very locally) more people. While the author of *The Great Divergence* (Pomeranz, 2000) highlighted the period 1800–1900, it stands to reason that this small corner of Eurasia, coupled to its former North American colony and standing on the backs of other colonies until the mid-twentieth century, owed its eventual wealth and welfare to the accumulation and inheritance of goods, material as well as immaterial, across centuries and millennia.

goods – found and made

goods – material and immaterial

> practical-productive turn of science – Chapter 5, p. 132

the industrial age

the Great Divergence

The agricultural and industrial ages represented the first and second waves preceding what the futurist Alvin Toffler (1980) termed the third wave of human history: the information society (Porat, 1977). (Speaking of an information *age* (Castells, 1996–98) may be premature.) Prefigured by the control revolution of the nineteenth century, < when societies devised new modes of controlling growing masses of industrial goods and a rebuilt natural environment, the information society denotes an era in which, quantitatively, a majority of the workforce is employed in information and other service occupations, while, qualitatively, information has become a key means of production (and consumption) in its own right and a strategic component of both private business and public governance. Whereas a competing terminology spoke of the coming of a postindustrial society (Bell,

the information society

> the control revolution – Chapter 6, p. 171

1973), as if the industrial age were over, it was the vested national and corporate interests of the industrial age that, again, inherited the material and immaterial Earth. An essential feature of the information society has been a new global division of labor. In *The Great Convergence*, Richard Baldwin (2016) mapped how, since the 1990s, information and communication technologies have transported ideas – immaterial goods – to low-wage countries to expand the high-tech production there of material goods, as well: "up to 1990, globalization was mostly about [material] goods crossing borders; now it is also about know-how crossing borders" (p. 8). And, like the divergence picking up steam two centuries ago, convergence has been an unequal process so far: "Just six developing nations – [...] (China, Korea, India, Poland, Indonesia, and Thailand) – accounted for almost all of the G7's decline" (the G7 being the United States, Germany, Japan, France, Britain, Canada, and Italy) (p. 3).

the Great Convergence

The information society has been associated with a new era of enlightenment and emancipation – information everywhere, in everything, and for everyone. But the goods of information were not, and are not, found, but made – through long lines of production and dissemination, curation and education. Information may "want to be free," but it also "wants to be expensive because it can be immeasurably valuable to the recipient" (Brand, 1987: 202) – individuals, societies, and civilizations.

information wants to be free – and expensive

The silk roads

Complementing and, in important respects, challenging the story of global divergence and convergence driven by Western explorers and entrepreneurs, a second grand narrative has unfolded along the east–west axis of Eurasia: the Silk Road(s). Favored by environmental lotteries, Eurasia was the literal cradle of 'civilization' – the site of the first towns and cities (in Mesopotamia) – of systematized agriculture throughout the wider 'fertile crescent' stretching from the Persian Gulf to the Mediterranean, and of the writing systems (Powell, 2009) that came to record human doings and beings over the last five millennia: the 'historical' period. Across the full expanse between China and the Mediterranean, Eurasia was, and increasingly became, rich in resources – goods, found and made – that successive regional and world powers have sought to either conquer or control. And, as suggested by the plural titles of historian Peter Frankopan's (2017, 2019) two volumes – *The Silk Roads* and *The New Silk Roads* – multiple forms of interchange linked east and west for millennia before any divergence

civilization

the fertile crescent

the historical period

or convergence. The conquest of land and the trade in (other) goods trumped both physical distance and cultural difference. As important as the transmission of material goods (and of diseases such as the Black Death) was the incidental communication of immaterial goods that no trader or conqueror had bargained for – information and ideas, including recombinant elements of world religions – which might reinterpret the meaning of trade, conquest, and other human endeavors, for religious leaders and for their followers.

Frankopan's (2017) first volume included careful examination of the place of the silk roads in historical trajectories leading far beyond Eurasia toward different kinds and degrees of globalization. At its far western end, Europe is commonly depicted, in a Western Whig interpretation (Butterfield, 1931) of human history, as the site in which

Whig interpretation of history

> the Enlightenment and the Age of Reason saw a coming of age where ideas of absolutism were replaced by notions of freedom, rights and liberty. But it was Europe's entrenched relationship with violence and militarism that allowed it to place itself at the centre of the world after the great expeditions of the 1490s.
>
> *Frankopan, 2017: 250*

Centuries-long "fierce rivalry between states that frequently erupted into open hostility and war" had stimulated the development of "military technology" (material goods) and associated "tactics" (immaterial goods), underwritten by another immaterial, but forceful ideology of violence:

an ideology of violence

> European art and literature had long celebrated the life of the chivalrous knight and his capacity to use force judiciously – as an act of love and of faith, but also as an expression of justice. [...] In fact, Europe's distinctive character as more aggressive, more unstable and less peace-minded than other parts of the world now paid off.
>
> *p. 251*

After the travels of Christopher Columbus and Vasco da Gama had connected Europe to the Americas and to Asia by sea, the Eurasian connection remained strategically important throughout Spanish and British bids for world hegemony, and into the twentieth century. In the context of World War II, "Germany's alliance with the Soviet Union did pose a threat to

explorations of Columbus and da Gama

World War II alliances

British interests in the east" (p. 353) – India – even as centuries of European colonialism were coming to an end. At the end of an American century, when global terrorism hit the US at home on September 11, 2001, "attention in Washington quickly turned to the bigger picture: controlling the centre of Asia decisively and properly": Afghanistan and, next, "Iran and Iraq." "The 9/11 attacks transformed the way the United States engaged with the world as a whole. America's future depended on securing the spine of Asia, running from Iraq's western frontier with Syria and Turkey to the Hindu Kush" mountain range across Afghanistan (p. 483f.).

9/11

Frankopan's (2019) second intervention looked into both *The Present and Future of the World*, its subtitle. *The New Silk Roads* have been given concrete shape by the recent Belt and Road Initiative (BRI) of the People's Republic of China. "Since the project was announced in 2013, nearly $1 trillion has been promised to infrastructure investments, mainly in the form of loans, to around 1,000 projects" (p. 15). BRI covers more than 80 countries, including "the Central Asian republics, the countries of South and South East Asia, those of the Middle East, Turkey and Eastern Europe – as well as states in Africa and the Caribbean," with a combined population of 4.4 billion accounting for "more than 63 percent of the world's population" and "29 percent of total global output" (p. 91). Having lifted "more than 800 million [...] above the poverty line since the 1980s" at home (p. 25), the Party-state could be seen to pursue a global capitalism with Chinese characteristics, re-making the silk roads and remediating them (Bolter & Grusin, 1999) through a Digital Belt and Road, as well (www.dbeltroad.org, accessed August 15, 2020).

the Belt and Road Initiative (BRI)

the Digital Belt and Road

The information society is counted in decades so far. At a local and regional level, the West has pursued a "monetization of data," as compared to a "weaponization of data" (Frankopan, 2019: 41) designed to sustain a "networked authoritarianism" (MacKinnon, 2011) in China. In the medium term, a strategic plan, Made in China 2025, has been designed to shift Chinese industries from low-end toward high-value products and services, and a Chinese Dream recalling the American Dream has been promoted, originally by President Xi Jinping, as a common denominator for individual and national aspirations. In a long-term and global perspective, the new silk roads of belts and bits symbolize, and might eventually enact, a new world order in which a civilization dating back four millennia adopts and adapts a political economy dating back less than four centuries.

the Chinese Dream

Capital and ideology

A third grand narrative has been told by the economist, Thomas Piketty (2014, 2020), placing human flourishing and its other – inequality – in historical perspective. Relying on innovative time series of indicators particularly for key Western economies since the eighteenth century, Piketty's (2014) first book – *Capital in the Twenty-first Century* – distilled its argument into a formula: $r > g$. $r > g$
In a capitalist economy, the rate of return on capital (r) will be greater than the rate of growth of the economy as such (g), thus reproducing and exacerbating inequality, particularly when economic growth in a society is low (below 1 percent). In close to 700 pages of facts and figures, the volume recognized that the production and distribution of immaterial goods – knowledge, skills, and competences – contribute to the reduction of inequality at an individual as well as a societal level:

> Knowledge and skill diffusion is the key to overall productivity growth as well as the reduction of inequality both within and between countries. We see this at present in the advances made by a number of previously poor countries, led by China.
>
> *p. 21*

With the twentieth century as a case in point, however, Piketty concluded that it was a conjuncture of (world) wars and (consequent) institutional reforms that introduced (imperfect and intermittent) limits on inequality:

> [T]he reduction of inequality that took place in most developed countries between 1910 and 1950 was above all a consequence of war and of policies adopted to cope with the shocks of war. Similarly, the resurgence of inequality after 1980 is due largely to the political shifts of the past several decades, especially in regard to taxation and finance.
>
> *p. 20*

Even in the welfare states that were in place 1950–80 in a good number of Western countries, the reductions in inequality were modest and indirect:

> [M]odern redistribution does not consist in transferring income from the rich to the poor, at least not in so explicit a way. It consists rather in financing public services

> and replacement incomes that are more or less equal for everyone, especially in the areas of health, education, and pensions.
>
> *p. 479*

In summary, "the inequality $r > g$ has clearly been true throughout most of human history, right up to the eve of World War I, and it will probably be true again in the twenty-first century" (p. 358).

Piketty's (2020) second book broadened the scope of the analysis even further (in upward of a thousand pages), not just geographically and historically, but most significantly by shifting the focus from (economic) description toward (political) explanation: How might the persistence of "inequality regimes" (p. 2) across diverse historical and cultural settings be explained? The premise of an answer was given by its title – *Capital and Ideology* – which proposed "taking ideology seriously" (p. 7), as seriously as capital, in contradistinction to a classic Marxist position treating ideology as a secondary reflection of the basic relations of production. The premise was spelled out with reference to the combination of material and immaterial conditions that nurture human existence and social coexistence: "All societies have two essential needs – meaning and security" (p. 59). Taking premodern societies as a reference point, Piketty suggested that these needs are felt most urgently, and their dynamic particularly manifest, in "less developed societies, where the territory is fragmented, communication difficult, instability chronic, and existence precarious. Pillage, mayhem, and disease are constant threats." Referring to such societies as 'ternary' or 'trifunctional' (having three main classes: the clergy [voices of meaning], the nobility [sources of security], and "the common people [who] did the work," p. 51f.), he concluded:

inequality regimes

meaning and security

trifunctional societies

> If religious and military groups can provide credible responses to these needs by supplying institutions and ideologies adapted to their time and place, it should come as no surprise that trifunctional order emerges and is accepted as legitimate by the people.
>
> *p. 59*

The bulk of Piketty's (2020) second volume was devoted to tracing historical struggles over meaning and security, resulting in changing configurations of institutions that have assigned rights and delivered goods (or not) to individuals and groups. With 'ownership' (capitalist) societies as the inequality regime of

ownership (capitalist) societies

central interest, his analyses and interpretations included, on the one hand, slave and colonial societies and their intersections with ownership societies, and, on the other hand, the communist and social-democratic societies which, in distinctive ways, challenged the ideology of ownership as the meaningful core of social organization. Considering these and other key developments of the twentieth century, however, Piketty (2020) revised his explanation of how historical change comes about in fundamental ways:

> In both Europe and the United States, the compression [reduction] of inequality in the period 1914–1970 can be explained by legal, social, and fiscal changes hastened by two world wars, the Bolshevik revolution of 1917, and the Great Depression of 1929. In an intellectual and political sense, however, those changes were already under way by the end of the nineteenth century, and it is reasonable to think that they would have occurred in one form or another even if those crises had not occurred. Historical change takes place when evolving ideas confront the logic of events: neither has much effect without the other.
>
> *p. 30f.*

Piketty (2014), as already cited, had spoken of the two world wars as the more or less direct causes of the policies that, for a time, limited inequality; having rediscovered ideology, Piketty (2020) now referred to broader and deeper political-economic and social-structural trajectories: Even without the world wars, welfare societies, of some kind and degree, likely would have emerged. In the last quotation, history is said to be articulated and anticipated in "evolving ideas," which catalyzed the "events" that constitute change. Capital and matter, and ideology and mind, are all necessary, but insufficient conditions of equality and justice.

In a charitable interpretation, Piketty's (2020) second volume did not contradict his first, but added nuance and depth regarding the several mechanisms – material, institutional, and discursive – that account for (in)justice. < Meaning – shared, communicated concepts and conceptions of reality < – lends orientation to the actions that deliver security and a good life (or not). Toward the end of the second volume, he returned to a key formulation concerning a power of ideology that is "not surprising" when it takes effect, whether in trifunctional societies or information societies. Consider the final sentence of Piketty's (2020) diagnosis of the twenty-first century, which is worth quoting in full:

> material, institutional, and discursive mechanisms – Chapter 8, p. 223

> concepts, conceptions, and conceptualizations – Chapter 7, p. 192

> The conservative revolution of the 1980s, the collapse of Soviet communism, and the development of neo-proprietarian ideology vastly increased the concentration of income and wealth in the first two decades of the twenty-first century. Inequality has in turn heightened social tensions almost everywhere. For want of a constructive egalitarian and universal political outlet, these tensions have fostered the kinds of nationalist identity cleavages that we see today in practically every part of the world: in the United States and Europe, India and Brazil, China and the Middle East. When people are told that there is no credible alternative to the socioeconomic organization and class inequality that exist today, it is not surprising that they invest their hopes in defending their borders and identities instead.
>
> *p. 966*

ideology as a good thing

Communities express hopes for the future in ideologies. Ideology is a good thing: a good or resource in struggles transforming reality for the better. Clarifying his own ideological position, Piketty (2020) contrasted current local and global ownership societies, which were said to represent an emphatic variant of "hypercapitalism" (p. 648), with alternatives of "participatory socialism" (p. 967) and "social federalism on a global scale" (p. 1022) that would include shared ownership and decision-making powers in the means of production, and public regulation through wealth taxes alongside "progressive income taxes, universal basic incomes, and educational justice" (p. 967). Such institutions, he suggested, could be considered operationalizations of John Rawls' principles of justice (which also had figured in the first volume, alongside Amartya Sen's capability approach, as two lines in an extended family of egalitarian ideologies (Piketty, 2014: 480)). Responding to persistent inequalities before and after the 2008 financial crisis (and in the aftermath of the Covid-19 pandemic), and received with enthusiasm by activists around the world, Piketty's *oeuvre* so far has served as an intervention into the double hermeneutics of justice. < Recognizing that "history is the product of crises," of problematic situations writ large rather than of economic writings, Piketty (2020: 967) nevertheless concluded, on an (implicit) pragmatist note, that these are "the positions I would be inclined to defend if I had all the time in the world to deliberate." <

> the double hermeneutics of justice – Chapter 2, p. 25

> pragmatism on the long run of inquiry – Chapter 5, p. 141

Timing communications

> communication as an architectonic capability – Chapter 7, p. 195

Communication is a distinctive, architectonic capability < that enables humans to find and make innumerable material as well as immaterial goods, including the institutions to regulate the production and distribution of any good. The institutions of knowledge and communication that emerged as part of political, economic, and cultural modernization < support deliberation and debate while there is still time, before natural and social deadlines necessitate binding decisions and concerted actions with practical and, frequently, unforeseeable consequences. In this section, I sum up the potentials and limitations of communication about and for justice, with reference to the ongoing society-wide and world-wide process of digitalization. Now is a good time to take stock of what communication could be.

> modernization – Chapter 6, p. 168

rights and goods of information

Information has been accumulated throughout centuries and millennia of human inquiry and enterprise, institutionalized as knowledge, and applied by individuals and collectives as resources for diverse instrumental and reflective purposes. The sum total of available information constitutes a communicative commons, < which can be considered representative to the extent that what is currently known by someone could potentially be known by anyone. But because it is in the nature of information to go missing, it must continuously be made and re-made through institutions and technologies that are themselves subject to repair and transformation. The task of preserving and preparing extant information for later use has historically been entrusted to libraries, museums, and other archives, with gradually increased public access. Digitalization presents practical, conceptual, and normative issues on the order of big science: < large-scale basic research feeding into applied projects and policy debates to guide the selection and curation of information for the future. For the first time in human history, there are (admittedly imperfect and inherently fallible) local and global institutions of research and governance in place that may anticipate, motivate, and legitimate the design and regulation of the infrastructures carrying information across generations.

> the communicative commons – Chapter 7, p. 201

> big science – Chapter 8, p. 228

rights and goods of privacy

With digitalization, the information that is accumulated over time increasingly includes the diverse data and metadata that users communicate many-to-one into the system, and which are circulated and repurposed in weakly defined and delimited networks. Summarized in legislation and public debate as rights and goods of privacy, it is the individuality and sociality of natural persons that is at stake: being a unique end in oneself and, simultaneously, an equal part of and partner in larger communities. To protect personal enclosures and to counteract social discrimination, some types of information must be unavailable, inaccessible, or, minimally, subject to informed consent and public regulation. In a future perspective, such information includes not just socially, biologically identifying data

> *habeas data* – Chapter 7, p. 209

> contextual integrity – Chapter 7, p. 209

but biologically identifying data – personal genomes – which only raises the urgency of conceiving data as something that one *is*, and which others might *do* something with. < As discussed in Chapter 7, the principle of contextual integrity < – asserting that the legitimacy of subsequent uses especially of personal information must be judged not by any overriding terms of service, but by the concrete contexts of use – only offers a preliminary standard in this regard.

rights and goods of communication

> communication systems – Chapter 8, p. 230

If institutions and infrastructures still need to be *invented* to safeguard the world's information and the individual's privacy, the institutions and infrastructures of (public) communication and (political) participation call for varying degrees of *reinvention*. Communication constitutes a generic capability that has been extended across human history from one-to-one and few-to-few interactions, first to one-to-many mass communication and, recently, to many-to-many communication as typified, so far, by social media. Each prototype has come to be associated with distinctive rights and goods of communication enabling humans to *do* and *be* in a great variety of ways that they have reason to value, including the maintenance of media as institutions to collectively express and evaluate their plans in life. Media systems of the last three centuries, for all their imperfections and errors, have afforded societies a fourth branch of governance involving, in principle, anyone as someone (Scannell, 2000) in self-governance through communication. The first decades of the twenty-first century have witnessed the early stages of a transition from media systems to communication systems, < which intersect and interact with other political, economic, and cultural institutions in the basic structure of society. A reinvention of the fourth branch of governance awaits the development of new models of financing and regulating communication systems in the public interest, for either private or public money (Lund, 2001).

> justice as re-presentation – Chapter 7, p. 201

rights and goods of participation

> the culturalization of politics and economy – Chapter 6, p. 187

Public participation in the institutions of political governance, finally, occurs through long lines of communication, between electorates and representatives, among citizens, and across the multiple media of the fourth branch of governance. All these communications constitute re-presentation in action, < delivering the goods which enable the exercise of the core right of participation. But the culturalization of politics and economy < has been shifting the boundaries of formal institutions, and has stretched the idea of participation, raising questions of who is, in fact and in practice, in a position to effectively participate in which forms of representation – internally and externally to parliamentary institutions, publicly and privately, locally as well as globally. This last question – of global forms of representation and participation – has remained the most difficult of all. Theoreticians from Rawls and Habermas to multiculturalist, cosmopolitan, and intercultural communication scholars < have provided, at best, broad outlines of global governance; elected representatives, activists, and other practitioners still struggle to deliver an approximation of global justice.

> multiculturalism, cosmopolitanism, and intercultural communication – Chapter 2, p. 41

Communication takes time – hours, days, and years – if it is to translate information into actionable knowledge, distributed interactions into meaningful communities, public opinion into informed consent by the governed, and personal data into valued experiences of individuality and sociality. Much more time – decades and centuries – is needed to produce the institutions through which communication may *condition* justice. < If the short (as well as nasty and brutish) twentieth century, 1914–91 (Hobsbawm, 1995), produced a global framework of international institutions and conventions, capped by the United Nations and the Universal Declaration of Human Rights, the twenty-first century confronts further challenges of how to maintain, repair, and transform these institutions and conventions in the face of additional existential risks < to human civilization and the species.

> communication as condition and constituent of justice – Chapter 7, p. 214

> existential risks – p. 268

Communication also produces, maintains, repairs, and transforms the people communicating: Communication is a mode of becoming, of realizing things that were previously unknown, by individuals and collectives, for the longest or shortest time. It is this quality that makes communication a *constituent* of justice, as well – an end in itself:

> No one knows everything the others know, or can make all the same inferences that they can draw in concert. Discussion is a way of combining information and enlarging the range of arguments. At least in the course of time, the effects of common deliberation seem bound to improve matters.
>
> *Rawls, 1999b/1971: 315*

Unknown knowns

At a press conference addressing the lack of evidence for weapons of mass destruction in Iraq before the 2003 invasion by the United States and its allies (which was being justified by the existence of such weapons), then US Secretary of Defense, Donald Rumsfeld, commented:

Donald Rumsfeld

> [A]s we know, there are known knowns; there are things we know we know. We also know there are known unknowns; that is to say we know there are some things we do not know. But there are also unknown unknowns – the ones we don't know we don't know. And [. . .] it is the latter category that tend to be the difficult ones.
>
> *Department of Defense, 2002*

This figure of thought and discourse was a legacy of psychological research, begun during the 1950s by Joseph Luft and Harry Ingham (Luft, 1969: 6), on the different levels of awareness that people have of the motivations underlying what they do. In Luft's terminology, "behavior, feelings, and motivation" may be either known or not known, by oneself or by others. In a standard two-by-two matrix, this produces four possible states: Something can be "open" to both self and others (known knowns); it can be "unknown" to all (unknown unknowns); it may be known to oneself, but "hidden" from others (known unknowns); or one may be "blind" to what others know (p. 13). The terminology had traveled via private and public research administration, including the NASA space agency (NASA, 1981), from where it reached Rumsfeld and public discourse. Rumsfeld, notably, did not consider the fourth possibility: being blind to what others know (neither before nor after the invasion could evidence of weapons of mass destruction in Iraq be presented). Embracing the ridicule that had greeted his remarks, Rumsfeld (2011) later titled his memoirs, *Known and Unknown: A Memoir.*

Slavoj Žižek

Abu Ghraib

The missing fourth position was later called out by the philosopher, Slavoj Žižek (2004), in an article on the torture and humiliation of Iraqi prisoners by US soldiers, caught on camera in Baghdad's Abu Ghraib prison, entitled, "What Rumsfeld Doesn't Know That He Knows about Abu Ghraib." In Žižek's psychoanalytic perspective, the Abu Ghraib images represented the return of the repressed, with Rumsfeld as the symptom and mouthpiece of a political regime and a wider public culture deriving energy and enjoyment from dehumanizing others. Whereas President George W. Bush framed the scenes as "isolated incidents," to Žižek (2004: n.p.) they constituted a moment of truth: "Thus, Bush was wrong. What we get when we see the photos of humiliated Iraqi prisoners is precisely a direct insight into 'American values,' into the core of an obscene enjoyment that sustains the American way of life."

Žižek (and Bush) missed the larger point, whereas Rumsfeld got it at least partly right. Žižek's (2004) psychoanalytic perspective invited grandiose extrapolation from individual to social psychology, and hyperbole in the resulting indictment of the entire way of life of a people; Bush, in his turn, failed to appreciate the animal in humans < that wars tend to arouse. Rumsfeld's wording, in comparison, recognized both that knowledge is something that "we" have (or not) as a collective or public, and that knowledge is coupled to "difficult" decisions about what "we" as a community, small or large, ought (not) to do. In and through media and communication, publics make unknown knowns more widely known; they debate which known unknowns should be examined further in either journalistic or scientific research; they contest < whether known knowns are *really* known; and publics regularly encounter unknown unknowns, when problematic, and sometimes unprecedented, situations present themselves for attention and action.

> the animal in humans – Chapter 2, p. 24

> communication as contestation – Chapter 1, p. 13

Communication enables doing, being, as well as becoming. Humans become themselves in communication, with individualities, socialities, and plans in life that they have reason to value, and equally good reasons to revise in response to unavoidable errors and constant contingencies. *Erro, ergo sum.* <

> *erro, ergo sum* – Chapter 5, p. 127

ANALYSIS BOX 9.1 FINAL JUSTICE

Death marks the end of natural existence, but not of cultural presence, given the right technologies and institutions of communication. Aristotle, Kant, Rawls, and other extraordinary figures of the past are still in print and on loan from libraries; the present cohort of ordinary individuals can expect to live on in curated social media entries and other digital legacies. Communication, further, mediates and affirms the individual's entry to and exit from life – in birth and death certificates, suicide notes, and last wills and testaments. And, for civilizations and the human species as such, the right communication at the right time may mean the difference between extinction and continued existence.

An individual constitutes a chance event that is recognized by the collective as a necessity. Article 3 of the Universal Declaration of Human Rights (UDHR) stipulates that, "Everyone has the right to life" (United Nations, 1948). UDHR, in comparison, does not include a right to die, whether motivated by terminal illness, unbearable suffering, an experienced loss of meaning, or a completed life plan. Voluntary euthanasia or (physician-)assisted suicide

the right to life

the right to die

(Young, 2020) has only been legalized in a small number of jurisdictions around the world. Though traditionally condemned by major world religions, suicide could be considered one of the rights that modern humans assign themselves as part of their self-governance. It is communication through legislation and codes of conduct that enables and constrains such a right; it is a speech act – informed consent – that transfers agency to a medical professional or lay relative. But because this final act is fraught with personal and professional dilemmas – a physician may oppose voluntary euthanasia on religious grounds – an overlapping consensus of agent and patient is of the essence: Also a society permitting voluntary euthanasia must leave it up to the individual on the line to decide whether or not to end a life.

organ donation

As bodies, humans lend themselves to recycling – cells, tissues, and organs for others to live by. Whereas people will give one of their kidneys to a close relative while alive, body parts are typically donated and transplanted upon death. Procedures in the area bring back classic philosophical as well as physiological questions concerning the nature and delimitation of death (DeGrazia, 2016; Luper, 2019); organ donation puts vulnerable individuals and populations at risk, and has been addressed in guidelines by the World Health Organization (WHO, 2020c). Even with self-governance as a premise, societies confront the issue of whether organ donation ought to be the default option. In England, as of 2020, the National Health Service (NHS) has introduced an "opt-out system," and informs citizens that if you

> have not confirmed whether you want to be an organ donor – either by recording a decision on the NHS Organ Donor Register, or by speaking to friends and family – it will be considered that you agree to donate your organs when you die.
>
> *NHS, 2020: n.p.*

postmortem communications

As minds, as well, human beings leave their mark. With the rise of social media over the past two decades, anyone can have not only a public presence, but an afterlife that previously was reserved for tiny elites (for overview, see, e.g., Christensen & Sandvik, 2015). Facebook (2020), for one, has in place detailed procedures for preserving and memorializing accounts when their owners pass. Beyond online memorials, the general issue is that of *habeas data*: < Who should be in a position to access and process information and communications by and about individuals, with what kinds and degrees of informed consent and public regulation? In the European Union, what had been referred to as a 'right to be forgotten' – to have information removed from digital archives – was included in its 2018 General Data Protection Regulation as a 'right of erasure' (European Union, 2020). As discussed in Chapter 8, as growing quantities and qualities of information are stored and interlinked, information *becomes* personal. At stake is a human right not to be forgotten, but to be remembered, in particular forms, contents, and contexts still waiting to be addressed in national and international legislation and codes of conduct.

> *habeas data* – Chapter 7, p. 209

the right to be remembered

Humans can expect to live increasingly longer (if not always better) lives. Since 1800, life expectancy at birth (LEB) has risen dramatically (Riley, 2001), from around 30 years as a global average to 72 years in 2016 (WHO, 2020b), even while Europeans still live longer (77.5 years) than Africans (61.2 years) (and women outlive men at 74.2 compared to 69.8 years). In *Homo Deus*, Yuval Noah Harari (2017) even suggested that, having limited the frequency and intensity of disease, famine, and war, humankind may turn its energies toward the lifespan: "In the twenty-first century humans are likely to make a serious bid for immortality [even if] so far modern medicine hasn't extended our natural life span by a single year. Its great achievement has been to save us from *premature* death" (p. 24, 31).

life expectancy

immortality

The future of the human species hangs in balance like never before. The practical-productive turn of science and scholarship of the last half millennium has empowered Aristotle's *zoon politicon* to give itself laws and to exercise capabilities that can either make or break it. The most clear and present danger – nuclear war – has been kept in check, for half a century so far, by the principle of Mutual Assured Destruction (MAD); climate change holds the prospect of mutual probable destruction. < To avoid further degradation of the environment for other species, pessimists have joined in The Voluntary Human Extinction Movement (http://vhemt.org, accessed August 15, 2020) to end this particular life form as part of a cosmic kind of justice.

> climate change and justice – Chapter 1, p. 4

Returning to the potentials as well as the responsibilities of the human species into an indefinite future, the philosopher,

existential risks

Toby Ord (2020), has categorized and weighed what he terms existential risks: "risks that threaten the destruction of humanity's longterm potential" (p. 6), covering extinction but also various forms of civilizational collapse. The specific risks include, in addition to nuclear war and climate change, asteroids and stellar explosions along with the potentially disastrous consequences of emerging and still unimagined technologies, from genetic engineering to artificial intelligence. Human-made risks outweigh natural chance events: Asteroids like the one that hit planet Earth around 66 million years ago, resulting in mass extinction and famously ending the dinosaurs, present the least of our problematic situations. Ord's reference to humanity's "longterm" potential should be taken literally and emphatically: On current evidence that he cites in meticulous detail, Earth will remain habitable for at least a billion years; if humanity were to settle elsewhere, life might be extended to trillions of years (p. 21); so that we ought to communicate, as well, about "successors to *Homo sapiens*, or creatures elsewhere in the cosmos." In the end, it is not that

> only humans count. Instead, it is that humans are the only beings we know of that are responsive to moral reasons and moral argument – the beings who can examine the world and decide to do what is best. If we fail, that upwards force, that capacity to push towards what is best or what is just, will vanish from the world.
>
> *p. 38*

REFERENCES

Abbate, J. (1999). *Inventing the Internet*. Cambridge, MA: MIT Press.

Aboulafia, M., Bookman, M., & Kemp, C. (Eds.). (2002). *Habermas and Pragmatism*. London and New York: Routledge.

Adorno, T. (Ed.). (1976). *The Positivist Dispute in German Sociology*. London: Heinemann.

Agre, P. E. (1994). Surveillance and Capture: Two Models of Privacy. *The Information Society, 10*(2), 101–127.

Ahmed, S., Cho, J., Jaidka, K., Eichstaedt, J. C., & Ungar, L. H. (2020). The Internet and Participation Inequality: A Multilevel Examination of 108 Countries. *International Journal of Communication, 14*, 1542–1563.

Alexander, J. (1991). Habermas and Critical Theory: Beyond the Marxian Dilemma. In A. Honneth & H. Joas (Eds.), *Communicative Action: Essays on Jürgen Habermas's The Theory of Communicative Action* (pp. 49–73). Cambridge, MA: MIT Press.

Alexander, L. (2016). Deontological Ethics. Retrieved from https://plato.stanford.edu/entries/ethics-deontological/.

Alexander, S. S. (2003). Social Evaluation through Notional Choice. In C. Kukathas (Ed.), *John Rawls* (Vol. 1, pp. 305–328). London, New York: Routledge. (Original work published 1974.)

Altman, A. (2015). Discrimination. Retrieved from https://plato.stanford.edu/entries/discrimination/.

Anderson, B. (1991). *Imagined Communities: Reflections on the Origin and Spread of Nationalism* (2nd ed.). London: Verso.

Anscombe, G. E. M. (1958). Modern Moral Philosophy. *Philosophy, 33*(124), 1–19.

Apel, K.-O. (1981). *Charles S. Peirce: From Pragmatism to Pragmaticism*. Amherst, MA: University of Massachusetts Press.

Archer, M., Bhaskar, R., Collier, A., Lawson, T., & Norrie, A. (Eds.). (1998). *Critical Realism: Essential Readings*. London: Routledge.

Aristotle. (1886). *Nicomachean Ethics* (F. H. Peters, Trans. 3rd ed.). London: Kegan Paul.

Aristotle. (2007a). *Metaphysics*. Retrieved from http://etext.library.adelaide.edu.au/a/aristotle/metaphysics/complete.html.

Aristotle. (2007b). *On Interpretation*. Retrieved from http://etext.library.adelaide.edu.au/a/aristotle/interpretation/complete.html.

Aristotle. (2015). *Politics*. Retrieved from https://ebooks.adelaide.edu.au/a/aristotle/a8po/.

Ashcroft, B., Griffiths, G., & Tiffin, H. (Eds.). (2006). *The Post-Colonial Studies Reader* (2nd ed.). London: Routledge.

Ashman, K. M., & Baringer, P. S. (Eds.). (2001). *After the Science Wars*. London: Routledge.

Asimov, I. (1974). *I, Robot*. London: Dobson Books. (Original work published 1950.)

Augustine. (2009). The City of God. Retrieved from www.newadvent.org/fathers/1201.htm.

Austin, J. L. (1962). *How to Do Things with Words*. Oxford: Oxford University Press.

Bacon, F. (2014). *Novum Organum*. Retrieved from www.gutenberg.org/ebooks/45988 (Original work published 1620.)

Baehr, A. R. (1999). Toward a New Feminist Liberalism: Okin, Rawls, and Habermas. In H. S. Richardson & P. J. Weithman (Eds.), *The Philosophy of Rawls: A Collection of Essays* (Vol. 3, pp. 295–312). New York, London: Garland Publishing. (Original work published 1996.)

Baldwin, R. (2016). *The Great Convergence: Information Technology and the New Globalization*. Cambridge, MA: The Belknap Press.

Barlow, J. P. (1996). A Declaration of the Independence of Cyberspace. Retrieved from www.eff.org/cyberspace-independence.

Barthes, R. (1973). *Mythologies*. London: Paladin. (Original work published 1957.)

Bateson, G. (1972). *Steps to an Ecology of Mind*. London: Granada.

Baudrillard, J. (2007). *Forget Foucault* (New ed.). Cambridge, MA: MIT Press. (Original work published 1977.)

Baumard, N., Hyafil, A., Morris, I., & Boyer, P. (2015). Increased Affluence Explains the Emergence of Ascetic Wisdoms and Moralizing Religions. *Current Biology, 25*, 10–15.

Bay, M. (2017). The Ethics of Unbreakable Encryption: Rawlsian Privacy and the San Bernardino iPhone. *First Monday, 22*(2).

Baynes, K. (2014). Critical Theory and Habermas. In J. Mandle & D. A. Reidy (Eds.), *A Companion to Rawls* (pp. 487–503). Malden, MA: Wiley-Blackwell.

Bell, D. (1973). *The Coming of Post-Industrial Society*. New York: Basic Books.

Bellah, R. N., Madsen, R., Sullivan, W. M., Swidler, A., & Tipton, S. M. (1985). *Habits of the Heart: Individualism and Commitment in American Life*. Berkeley, CA: University of California Press.

Bellinger, G., Castro, D., & Mills, A. (2004). Data, Information, Knowledge, and Wisdom. Retrieved from www.systems-thinking.org/dikw/dikw.htm.

Beniger, J. (1986). *The Control Revolution: Technological and Economic Origins of the Information Society*. Cambridge, MA: Harvard University Press.

Benkler, Y. (2006). *The Wealth of Networks: How Social Production Transforms Markets and Freedom*. New Haven, CT: Yale University Press.

Bennett, L. W., & Segerberg, A. (2012). The Logic of Connective Action: Digital Media and the Personalization of Contentious Politics. *Information, Communication & Society, 15*(5), 739–768.

Bennett, T. (1995). *The Birth of the Museum*. London: Routledge.

Bentham, J. (1823). *An Introduction to the Principles of Morals and Legislation*. Oxford: Clarendon Press.

Benveniste, É. (1985). The Semiology of Language. In R. E. Innis (Ed.), *Semiotics: An Introductory Anthology* (pp. 228–246). Bloomington, IN: Indiana University Press. (Original work published 1969.)

Berger, C. R., Roloff, M. E., & Roskos-Ewoldsen, D. E. (Eds.). (2009). *The Handbook of Communication Science* (2nd ed.). Los Angeles, CA: Sage.

Bergman, M. (2004). *Fields of Signification: Explorations in Charles S. Peirce's Theory of Signs*. Helsinki: University of Helsinki.

Bergman, M. (2008). The New Wave of Pragmatism in Communication Studies. *Nordicom Review, 29*(2), 135–153.

Berlin, I. (1969). Two Concepts of Liberty. In I. Berlin (Ed.), *Four Essays on Liberty* (pp. 118–172). Oxford: Oxford University Press. (Original work published 1958.)

Berman, M. (1982). *All That Is Solid Melts into Air: The Experience of Modernity*. London: Verso.

Berners-Lee, T. (1999). *Weaving the Web: The Original Design and Ultimate Destiny of the World Wide Web by Its Inventor*. San Francisco, CA: Harper.

Bernstein, R. J. (1983). *Beyond Objectivism and Relativism: Science, Hermeneutics, and Praxis*. Philadelphia, PA: University of Pennsylvania Press.

Bernstein, R. J. (1987). One Step Forward, Two Steps Backward: Richard Rorty and Liberal Democracy and Philosophy. *Political Theory, 15*(4), 538–563.

Bernstein, R. J. (1998). The Retrieval of the Democratic Ethos. In M. Rosenfeld & A. Arato (Eds.), *Habermas on Law and Democracy: Critical Exchanges* (pp. 287–305). Berkeley, CA: University of California Press.

Bernstein, R. J. (2010). *The Pragmatic Turn*. Cambridge: Polity.

Bernstein, R. J. (2012). Foreword. In J. Hannan (Ed.), *Philosophical Profiles in the Theory of Communication* (pp. ix–x). New York: Peter Lang.

Bevir, M. (2017). John Rawls in Light of the Archive: Introduction to the Symposium on the Rawls Papers. *Journal of the History of Ideas, 78*, 255–263.

Bhaskar, R. (1979). *The Possibility of Naturalism*. Brighton, UK: Harvester Press.

Birdsall, W. F. (2011). Human Capabilities and Information and Communication Technology: The Communicative Connection. *Ethics and Information Technology, 13*(2), 93–106.

Bloor, D. (1983). *Wittgenstein: A Social Theory of Knowledge*. New York: Columbia University Press.

Blumer, H. (1954). What Is Wrong with Social Theory? *American Sociological Review, 19*, 3–10.

Boas, T. C., & Gans-Morse, J. (2009). Neoliberalism: From New Liberal Philosophy to Anti-Liberal Slogan. *Studies in Comparative International Development, 44*(2), 137–161.

Bobzien, S. (2015). Ancient Logic. Retrieved from https://plato.stanford.edu/entries/logic-ancient/.

Bod, R. (2013). *A New History of the Humanities: The Search for Principles and Patterns from Antiquity to the Present*. Oxford: Oxford University Press.

Boettcher, J. W. (2009). Habermas, Religion, and the Ethics of Citizenship. *Philosophy & Social Criticism, 35*(1–2), 215–238.

Bohman, J., & Rehg, W. (2014). Jürgen Habermas. Retrieved from http://plato.stanford.edu/archives/fall2014/entries/habermas/.

Bolter, J. D., & Grusin, R. (1999). *Remediation: Understanding New Media*. Cambridge, MA: MIT Press.

Borah, P. (2011). Conceptual Issues in Framing Theory: A Systematic Examination of a Decade's Literature. *Journal of Communication, 61*(2), 246–263.

Borgman, C. L. (2015). *Big Data, Little Data, No Data: Scholarship in the Networked World*. Cambridge, MA: MIT Press.

Botti, D. (2019). *John Rawls and American Pragmatism: Between Engagement and Avoidance*. Lanham, MD: Lexington.

Bou-Habib, P. (2019). Climate Justice and Historical Responsibility. *The Journal of Politics, 81*(4), 1298–1310.

Bourdieu, P. (1984). *Distinction*. Cambridge, MA: Harvard University Press. (Original work published 1979.)

Brabham, D. C. (2013). *Crowdsourcing*. Cambridge, MA: MIT Press.

Bradbury, H. (Ed.). (2015). *The SAGE Handbook of Action Research*. London: Sage.

Brand, S. (1987). *The Media Lab: Inventing the Future at MIT*. New York:Viking.

Braudel, F. (1980). *On History*. Chicago, IL: Chicago University Press.

Bray, D. (2011). *Pragmatic Cosmopolitanism: Representation and Leadership in Transnational Democracy*. London: Palgrave Macmillan.

Brecht, B. (1993). The Radio as an Apparatus of Communication. In N. Strauss & D. Mandl (Eds.), *Radiotext(e)*. New York: Columbia University Press. (Original work published 1932.)

Briggs, A., Burke, P., & Ytreberg, E. (2020). *A Social History of the Media* (4th ed.). Cambridge: Polity.

Britz, J., Hoffmann, A., Ponelis, S., Zimmer, M., & Lor, P. (2013). On Considering the Application of Amartya Sen's Capability Approach to an Information-based Rights Framework. *Information Development, 29*(2), 106–113.

Brosius, H.-B., & Weimann, G. (1996). Who Sets the Agenda? Agenda-Setting as a Two-Step Flow. *Communication Research, 23*(5), 561–580.

Brüggemann, M., Engesser, S., Büchel, F., Humprecht, E., & Castro, L. (2014). Hallin and Mancini Revisited: Four Empirical Types of Western Media Systems. *Journal of Communication, 64*(6), 1037–1065.

Butterfield, H. (1931). *The Whig Interpretation of History*. Retrieved from www.eliohs.unifi.it/testi/900/butterfield/index.html.

Calhoun, C. (Ed.). (1992). *Habermas and the Public Sphere*. Cambridge, MA: MIT Press.

Calhoun, C., Florence, L., & Mirchandani, R. (1992). Concluding Remarks. In C. Calhoun (Ed.), *Habermas and the Public Sphere* (pp. 462–479). Cambridge, MA: MIT Press.

Camargo, M. (1996). Where's the Brief? The Ars Dictaminis and Reading/Writing between the Lines. *Disputatio: An International Transdisciplinary Journal of the Late Middle Ages, 1*, 1–18.

Campus, D. (2012). Political Discussion, Opinion Leadership, and Trust. *European Journal of Communication, 27*(1), 46–55.

Carey, J. W. (1989a). A Cultural Approach to Communication. In J. W. Carey (Ed.), *Communication as Culture* (pp. 13–36). Boston, MA: Unwin Hyman. (Original work published 1975.)

Carey, J. W. (1989b). *Communication as Culture*. Boston, MA: Unwin Hyman.

Carroll, N. (1988). *Mystifying Movies: Fads and Fallacies in Contemporary Film Theory*. New York: Columbia University Press.

Castells, M. (1996). *The Rise of the Network Society*. Oxford: Blackwell.

Castells, M. (1996–98). *The Information Age: Economy, Society, and Culture*. Oxford: Blackwell.

Castells, M., Fernández-Ardèvol, M., Qiu, J. L., & Sey, A. (2007). *Mobile Communication and Society*. Cambridge, MA: MIT Press.

Cater, D. (1959). *The Fourth Branch of Government*. Boston, MA: Houghton-Mifflin.

Charmaz, K. (2006). *Constructing Grounded Theory: A Practical Guide through Qualitative Analysis*. London: Sage.

Cheney, G., May, S., & Munshi, D. (Eds.). (2011). *The Handbook of Communication Ethics*. New York: Routledge.

Cheng, H.Y. (1968). The Emergence and Spread of the Ombudsman Institution. *The Annals of the American Academy of Political and Social Science, 377*(1), 20–30.

Christensen, D. R., & Sandvik, K. (Eds.). (2015). *Mediating and Remediating Death*. London: Routledge.

Christians, C., & Nordenstreng, K. (Eds.). (2014). *Communication Theories in a Multicultural World*. New York: Peter Lang.

Christians, C., & Traber, M. (Eds.). (1997). *Communication Ethics and Universal Values*. Thousand Oaks, CA: Sage.

Christians, C. G., Glasser, T. L., McQuail, D., Nordenstreng, K., & White, R. A. (2009). *Normative Theories of the Media: Journalism in Democratic Societies*. Urbana, IL: University of Illinois Press.

Clarke, B. (1979). Eccentrically Contested Concepts. *British Journal of Political Science, 9*(1), 122–126.

Coleman, S., Moss, G., & Martinez-Perez, A. (2018). Studying Real-Time Audience Responses to Political Messages: A New Research Agenda. *International Journal of Communication, 12*, 1696–1714.

Collier, D., Hidalgo, F. H., & Maciuceanu, A. O. (2006). Essentially Contested Concepts: Debates and Applications. *Journal of Political Ideologies, 11*(3), 211–246.

Corchia, L. (2020). *Jürgen Habermas: A Bibliography*. Pisa, Italy: Arnus University Press.

Corlett, J. A., Norzagary, M., & Sharpless, J. (2010). Rawls and Habermas on the Cosmopolitan Condition. *The Philosophical Forum, 41*, 459–477.

Couldry, N. (2012). *Media, Society, World: Social Theory and Digital Media Practice*. Cambridge: Polity.

Couldry, N., Madianou, M., & Pinchevski, A. (Eds.). (2013). *Ethics of Media*. Houndmills, UK: Palgrave Macmillan.

Coulthard, G. S. (2014). *Red Skin, White Masks: Rejecting the Colonial Politics of Recognition*. Minneapolis, MN: Minnesota University Press.

Cox, R. (2013). *Environmental Communication and the Public Sphere* (3rd ed.). Los Angeles, CA: Sage.

Craig, R. T. (1989). Communication as a Practical Discipline. In B. Dervin, L. Grossberg, B. J. O'Keefe, & E. Wartella (Eds.), *Rethinking Communication* (Vol. 1: Paradigm Issues, pp. 97–122). Newbury Park, CA: Sage.

Craig, R. T. (1999). Communication Theory as a Field. *Communication Theory, 9*(2), 119–161.

Craig, R. T. (2007). Pragmatism in the Field of Communication Theory. *Communication Theory, 17*(2), 125–145.

Craig, R. T. (2014). Selected Bibliography on Grounded Practical Theory. Retrieved from https://sites.google.com/a/colorado.edu/robert_craig/projects.

Craig, R. T. (2018). For a Practical Discipline. *Journal of Communication, 68*(2), 289–297.

Craig, R. T., & Muller, H. L. (Eds.). (2007). *Theorizing Communication: Readings across Traditions*. Los Angeles, CA: Sage.

Craig, R. T., & Tracy, K. (1995). Grounded Practical Theory: The Case of Intellectual Discussion. *Communication Theory, 5*(3), 248–272.

Craig, R. T., & Tracy, K. (2014). Building Grounded Practical Theory in Applied Communication Research: Introduction to the Special Issue. *Journal of Applied Communication Research, 42*(3), 229–243.

Craig, R. T., & Tracy, K. (2021). *Grounded Practical Theory: Investigating Communication Problems*. San Diego, CA: Cognella.

Crenshaw, K. (1989). Demarginalizing the Intersection of Race and Sex: A Black Feminist Critique of Antidiscrimination Doctrine, Feminist Theory and Antiracist Politics. *University of Chicago Legal Forum* (1), 139–167.

Curran, J., Fenton, N., & Freedman, D. (2012). *Misunderstanding the Internet*. London, New York: Routledge.

D'Agostino, F. (2004). The Legacies of John Rawls. *Journal of Moral Philosophy, 1*(4), 349–365.

Danermark, B., Ekström, M., Jakobsen, L., & Karlsson, J. C. (2019). *Explaining Society: Critical Realism in the Social Sciences* (2nd ed.). London, New York: Routledge.

Darwin, C. (2013). *On the Origin of Species*. Retrieved from www.gutenberg.org/files/1228/1228-h/1228-h.htm. (Original work published 1859.)

Davies, P. J. E., Hofrichter, F. F., Jacobs, J. F., Simon, D. L., Roberts, A. S., & Janson, F. T. (2015). *Janson's History of Art* (8th ed.). New York: Pearson.

de Sola Pool, I. (Ed.). (1977). *The Social Impact of the Telephone*. Cambridge, MA: MIT Press.

Dearing, J., & Rogers, E. M. (1996). *Agenda-Setting*. Thousand Oaks, CA: Sage.

DeGrazia, D. (2016). The Definition of Death. Retrieved from https://plato.stanford.edu/entries/death-definition/.

Dennett, D. (1982). Comments on Rorty. *Synthèse, 53*, 349–356.

Denning, M. (1987). *Mechanic Accents: Dime Novels and Working-Class Culture in America*. London: Verso.

Department of Defense. (2002). DoD News Briefing – Secretary Rumsfeld and Gen. Myers. Retrieved from https://archive.defense.gov/Transcripts/Transcript.aspx?TranscriptID=2636.

Derrida, J. (1973). *Speech and Phenomena: And Other Essays on Husserl's Theory of Signs*. Evanston, IL: Northwestern University Press. (Original work published 1967.)

Derrida, J. (1976). *Of Grammatology*. Baltimore, MD: Johns Hopkins University Press. (Original work published 1967.)

Dewey, J. (1903). *Studies in Logical Theory*. Retrieved from www.gutenberg.org/files/40665/40665-h/40665-h.htm.

Dewey, J. (1927). *The Public and Its Problems*. New York: Holt.

Diamond, J. (1998). *Guns, Germs, and Steel: A Short History of Everybody for the Last 13,000 Years*. London: Vintage.

Dickstein, M. (Ed.). (1998). *The Revival of Pragmatism*. Durham, NC: Duke University Press.

Dieleman, S., Rondel, D., & Voparil, C. (Eds.). (2017). *Pragmatism and Justice*. Oxford: Oxford University Press.

Dissanayake, W. (Ed.). (1988). *Communication Theory: The Asian Perspective*. Singapore: Asian Mass Communication Research and Information Center.

Divers, J. (2002). *Possible Worlds*. London: Routledge.

Doneda, D., & Mendes, L. S. (2014). Data Protection in Brazil: New Developments and Current Challenges. In S. Gutwirth, R. Leenes, & P. de Hert (Eds.), *Reloading Data Protection: Multidisciplinary Insights and Contemporary Challenges* (pp. 3–20). New York: Springer.

Drake, S. (1978). *Galileo at Work: His Scientific Biography*. Mineola, NY: Dover.

Duff, A. S. (2012). *A Normative Theory of the Information Society*. New York, London: Routledge.

Easton, D. (1953). *The Political System: An Inquiry into the State of Political Science*. New York: Alfred A. Knopf.

Eco, U. (1976). *A Theory of Semiotics*. Bloomington, IN: Indiana University Press.

Eco, U. (1984). *Semiotics and the Philosophy of Language*. London: Macmillan.

Eisenberg, A., & Spinner-Halev, J. (Eds.). (2005). *Minorities within Minorities: Equality, Rights, and Diversity*. Cambridge: Cambridge University Press.

Eisenstein, E. L. (1979). *The Printing Press as an Agent of Change: Communication and Cultural Transformation in Early-Modern Europe*. Cambridge: Cambridge University Press.

Elstub, S. (2010). The Third Generation of Deliberative Democracy. *Political Studies Review, 8*(3), 291–307.

Enzensberger, H. M. (1972). Constituents of a Theory of the Media. In D. McQuail (Ed.), *Sociology of Mass Communications*. Harmondsworth: Penguin. (Original work published 1970.)

Ess, C. (2020). *Digital Media Ethics* (3rd ed.). Cambridge: Polity.

Esser, F., & Hanitzsch, T. (Eds.). (2012). *The Handbook of Comparative Communication Research*. London, New York: Routledge.

European Union. (2020). Everything You Need to Know about the "Right to be Forgotten." Retrieved from https://gdpr.eu/right-to-be-forgotten/.

Eysenck, M. W., & Keane, M. T. (2020). *Cognitive Psychology: A Student's Handbook* (8th ed.). New York: Psychology Press.

Facebook. (2020). Memorialized Accounts. Retrieved from www.facebook.com/help/1506822589577997.

Fagan, B. (2000). *The Little Ice Age: How Climate Made History 1300–1850*. New York: Basic Books.

Fallon, D. (1980). *The German University: A Heroic Ideal in Conflict with the Modern World*. Boulder, CO: Colorado Associated University Press.

Feuer, L. S. (Ed.). (1969). *Marx and Engels: Basic Writings on Politics and Philosophy*. London: Fontana.

Feyerabend, P. (1975). *Against Method: Outline of an Anarchistic Theory of Knowledge*. London: New Left Books.

Fink, E. J., & Gantz, W. (1996). A Content Analysis of Three Mass Communication Research Traditions: Social Science, Interpretive Studies, and Critical Analysis. *Journalism and Mass Communication Quarterly, 73*(1), 114–134.

Finlayson, J. G. (2019). *The Habermas-Rawls Debate*. New York: Columbia University Press.

Finlayson, J. G., & Freyenhagen, F. (2011a). The Habermas-Rawls Dispute: Analysis and Reevaluation. In J. G. Finlayson & F. Freyenhagen (Eds.), *Habermas and Rawls: Disputing the Political* (pp. 1–21). New York, London: Routledge.

Finlayson, J. G., & Freyenhagen, F. (Eds.). (2011b). *Habermas and Rawls: Disputing the Political*. London, New York: Routledge.

Fisch, M. H. (1954). Alexander Bain and the Genealogy of Pragmatism. *Journal of the History of Ideas, 15*(3), 413–444.

Fischer, C. S. (1992). *America Calling: A Social History of the Telephone to 1940*. Berkeley, CA: University of California Press.

Flensburg, S., & Lai, S. S. (2019). Mapping Digital Communication Systems: Infrastructures, Markets, and Policies as Regulatory Forces. *Media, Culture & Society*, 1–19.

Florez, J. A. (2014). Peirce's Theory of the Origin of Abduction in Aristotle. *Transactions of the Charles S. Peirce Society, 50*(2), 265–280.

Flyvbjerg, B. (2006). Five Misunderstandings about Case-Study Research. *Qualitative Inquiry, 12*(2), 219–245.

Fowler, W. W. (1911). Book Review by W. Warde Fowler (Oxford) of "De Nuditate Sacra Sacrisque Vinculis" by Josephus Heckenbach. *Review of Theology & Philosophy, 6*(12), 730–731.

Frankopan, P. (2017). *The Silk Roads: A New History of the World*. New York: Vintage.

Frankopan, P. (2019). *The New Silk Roads: The Present and Future of the World*. London: Bloomsbury.

Franzke, A. S., Bechmann, A., Zimmer, M., Ess, C., & the Association of Internet Researchers. (2020). Internet Research: Ethical Guidelines 3.0. Retrieved from https://aoir.org/reports/ethics3.pdf.

Freud, S. (1911). *The Interpretation of Dreams*. Retrieved from www.psywww.com/books/interp/toc.htm. (Original work published 1900.)

Friedman, M. (1962). *Capitalism and Freedom*. Chicago, IL: University of Chicago Press.

Furnham, A. F. (1988). *Lay Theories: Everyday Understanding of Problems in the Social Sciences*. Oxford: Pergamon Press.

Galisanka, A. (2019). *John Rawls: The Path to a Theory of Justice*. Cambridge, MA: Harvard University Press.

Gallie, W. B. (1956). Essentially Contested Concepts. *Proceedings of the Aristotelian Society, 56*, 167–198.

Gamson, W. A. (1992). *Talking Politics*. New York: Cambridge University Press.

Garnham, N. (1997). Amartya Sen's "Capabilities" Approach to the Evaluation of Welfare: Its Application to Communications. *Javnost – The Public, 4*(4), 25–34.

Gaziano, C. (1997). Forecast 2000: Widening Knowledge Gaps. *Journalism and Mass Communication Quarterly, 74*(2), 237–264.

Geertz, C. (1973). *The Interpretation of Cultures*. New York: Basic Books.

Geertz, C. (1974). "From the Native's Point of View": On the Nature of Anthropological Understanding. *Bulletin of the American Academy of Arts and Sciences, 28*(1), 26–45.

Gelder, K. (Ed.). (2005). *The Subcultures Reader* (2nd ed.). London: Routledge.

Gibson, J. J. (1979). *The Ecological Approach to Visual Perception*. Boston, MA: Houghton-Mifflin.

Gibson, W. (1984). *Neuromancer*. New York: Ace.

Giddens, A. (1979). *Central Problems in Social Theory*. London: Macmillan.

Giddens, A. (1984). *The Constitution of Society*. Berkeley, CA: University of California Press.

Giddens, A. (1991). *Modernity and Self-Identity*. Cambridge: Polity Press.

Giles, H., Reid, S., & Harwood, J. (Eds.). (2010). *The Dynamics of Intergroup Communication*. New York: Peter Lang.

Gitlin, T. (1978). Media Sociology: The Dominant Paradigm. *Theory and Society, 6*(2), 205–253.

Goffman, E. (1959). *The Presentation of Self in Everyday Life*. New York: Anchor Books.

Goldsmiths. (2016). A Future for Public Service Television: Content and Platforms in a Digital World. Retrieved from http://futureoftv.org.uk/wp-content/uploads/2016/06/FOTV-Report-Online-SP.pdf.

Goody, J., & Watt, I. (1963). The Consequences of Literacy. *Comparative Studies in Society and History, 5*, 304–345.

Gow, G. A., & Smith, R. K. (2006). *Mobile and Wireless Communications: An Introduction*. Maidenhead, UK: Open University Press.

Granovetter, M. S. (1973). The Strength of Weak Ties. *The American Journal of Sociology, 78*(6), 1360–1380.

Greenfield, A. (2006). *Everyware: The Dawning Age of Ubiquitous Computing*. Indianapolis, IN: New Riders.

Greenwood, D. J., & Levin, M. (2007). *Introduction to Action Research: Social Research for Social Change* (2nd ed.). Thousand Oaks, CA: Sage.

Grinnell, F. (2019). Abduction in the Everyday Practice of Science: The Logic of Unintended Experiments. *Transactions of the Charles S. Peirce Society, 55*(3), 215–227.

Guadamuz, A. (2001). Habeas Data vs the European Data Protection Directive. *Journal of Information, Law & Technology* (3). Retrieved from https://warwick.ac.uk/fac/soc/law/elj/jilt/.

Gudykunst, W. B., & Kim, Y. Y. (1992). *Communicating with Strangers: An Approach to Intercultural Communication* (2nd ed.). New York: McGraw-Hill.

Gudykunst, W. B., & Mody, B. (Eds.). (2002). *Handbook of International and Intercultural Communication*. Thousand Oaks, CA: Sage.

Gunkel, D. J. (2020). *An Introduction to Communication and Artificial Intelligence*. Cambridge: Polity.

Habermas, J. (1971). *Knowledge and Human Interests*. Boston, MA: Beacon Press. (Original work published 1968.)

Habermas, J. (1973). A Postscript to Knowledge and Human Interests. *Philosophy of the Social Sciences, 3*(1), 157–189.

Habermas, J. (1977). Martin Heidegger: On the Publication of Lectures from the Year 1935. *Graduate Faculty Philosophy Journal, 6*(2), 155–180. (Original work published 1953.)

Habermas, J. (1979). *Communication and the Evolution of Society*. London: Heinemann. (Original work published 1976.)

Habermas, J. (1984). *The Theory of Communicative Action* (Vol. 1). Boston, MA: Beacon Press. (Original work published 1981.)

Habermas, J. (1987a). *The Philosophical Discourse of Modernity*. Cambridge: Polity. (Original work published 1985.)

Habermas, J. (1987b). *The Theory of Communicative Action* (Vol. 2). Cambridge: Polity Press. (Original work published 1981.)

Habermas, J. (1989). *The Structural Transformation of the Public Sphere*. Cambridge, MA: MIT Press. (Original work published 1962.)

Habermas, J. (1991). A Reply. In A. Honneth & H. Joas (Eds.), *Communicative Action: Essays on Jürgen Habermas's* The Theory of Communicative Action (pp. 214–264). Cambridge, MA: MIT Press.

Habermas, J. (1992a). *Faktizität und Geltung: Beiträge zur Diskurstheorie des Rechts und des demokratischen Rechtsstaats*. Frankfurt am Main: Suhrkamp.

Habermas, J. (1992b). Further Reflections on the Public Sphere. In C. Calhoun (Ed.), *Habermas and the Public Sphere* (pp. 421–461). Cambridge, MA: MIT Press.

Habermas, J. (1992c). Peirce and Communication. In J. Habermas (Ed.), *Postmetaphysical Thinking* (pp. 88–112). Cambridge, MA: MIT Press.

Habermas, J. (1992d). *Postmetaphysical Thinking*. Cambridge, MA: MIT Press.

Habermas, J. (1996). *Between Facts and Norms: Contributions to a Discourse Theory of Law and Democracy*. Cambridge: Polity Press. (Original work published 1992.)

Habermas, J. (1998). Reply to Symposium Participants, Benjamin N. Cardozo School of Law. In M. Rosenfeld & A. Arato (Eds.), *Habermas on Law and Democracy: Critical Exchanges* (pp. 381–452). Berkeley, CA: University of California Press.

Habermas, J. (2001). *The Postnational Constellation*. Cambridge, MA: MIT Press. (Original work published 1998.)

Habermas, J. (2003). *Truth and Justification*. Cambridge, MA: MIT Press.

Habermas, J. (2006). Political Communication in Media Society: Does Democracy Still Enjoy an Epistemic Dimension? The Impact of Normative Theory on Empirical Research. *Communication Theory, 16*(4), 411–426.

Habermas, J. (2008). *Between Naturalism and Religion*. Cambridge: Polity. (Original work published 2005.)

Habermas, J. (2009). *Europe: The Faltering Project*. Cambridge: Polity. (Original work published 2008.)

Habermas, J. (2011a). "Reasonable" versus "True," or the Morality of Worldviews. In J. G. Finlayson & F. Freyenhagen (Eds.), *Habermas and Rawls: Disputing the Political* (pp. 92–113). New York, London: Routledge. (Original work published 1996.)

Habermas, J. (2011b). Reconciliation through the Public Use of Reason: Remarks on John Rawls' Political Liberalism. In J. G. Finlayson & F. Freyenhagen (Eds.), *Habermas and Rawls: Disputing the Political* (pp. 25–45). New York, London: Routledge. (Original work published 1995.)

Habermas, J. (2019a). *Auch eine Geschichte der Philosophie* [This too a history of philosophy]. Berlin: Suhrkamp.

Habermas, J. (2019b). *Auch eine Geschichte der Philosophie. Band 2: Vernünftige Freiheit. Spuren des Diskurses über Glauben und Wissen* [This too a history of philosophy. Volume 2: Rational freedom: tracing the discourse on faith and knowledge]. Berlin: Suhrkamp.

Hacking, I. (1983). *Representing and Intervening: Introductory Topics in the Philosophy of Natural Science*. Cambridge: Cambridge University Press.

Halavais, A. (2018). *Search Engine Society* (2nd ed.). Cambridge: Polity.

Hall, S. (1983). The Problem of Ideology: Marxism without Guarantees. In B. Matthews (Ed.), *Marx: A Hundred Years On* (pp. 57–85). London: Lawrence & Wishart.

Hallin, D. C., & Mancini, P. (2004). *Comparing Media Systems: Three Models of Media and Politics*. Cambridge: Cambridge University Press.

Hannan, J. (2015). Justice Implicit: The Pragmatism of Amartya Sen. *Contemporary Pragmatism, 12*(2), 317–339.

Hansen, K., & Gregersen, T. (2020). The Habermas Forum. Retrieved from www.habermasforum.dk.

Harari, Y. N. (2014). *Sapiens: A Brief History of Humankind*. London: Vintage.

Harari, Y. N. (2017). *Homo Deus: A Brief History of Tomorrow*. London: Vintage.

Haughton, J., & Khandker, S. R. (2009). *Handbook on Poverty and Inequality*. Washington, DC: The World Bank.

Havelock, E. A. (1963). *Preface to Plato*. Oxford: Blackwell.

Hawthorn, G. (1991). *Plausible Worlds: Possibility and Understanding in History and the Social Sciences*. Cambridge: Cambridge University Press.

Hay, C. (2012). Consonances between Liberalism and Pragmatism. *Transactions of the Charles S. Peirce Society, 48*(2), 141–168.

Hearn, G., Tacchi, J., Foth, M., & Lennie, J. (2009). *Action Research and New Media: Concepts, Methods, and Cases*. Creskill, NJ: Hampton Press.

Hedrick, T. (2010). *Rawls and Habermas: Reason, Pluralism, and the Claims of Political Philosophy*. Stanford, CA: Stanford University Press.

Held, D. (2006). *Models of Democracy* (3rd ed.). Cambridge: Polity.

Herman, D., Jahn, M., & Ryan, M.-L. (Eds.). (2005). *Routledge Encyclopedia of Narrative Theory*. New York, London: Routledge.

Hesmondhalgh, D. (2017). Capitalism and the Media: Moral Economy, Well-being and Capabilities. *Media, Culture & Society, 39*(2), 202–218.

Heyes, C. (2016). Identity Politics. Retrieved from https://plato.stanford.edu/entries/identity-politics/#Aca.

Himelboim, I. (2010). The International Network Structure of News Media: An Analysis of Hyperlinks Usage in News Web Sites. *Journal of Broadcasting and Electronic Media, 54*(3), 373–390.

Himelboim, I., Gleave, E., & Smith, M. (2009). Discussion Catalysts in Online Political Discussions: Content Importers and Conversation Starters. *Journal of Computer-Mediated Communication, 14*, 771–789.

Hobbes, T. (2009). *Leviathan*. Retrieved from www.gutenberg.org/etext/3207. (Original work published 1651.)

Hobbs, R., & Mihailidis, P. (Eds.). (2019). *The International Encyclopedia of Media Literacy*. Hoboken, NJ: Wiley-Blackwell.

Hobsbawm, E. (1995). *The Age of Extremes: A History of the World, 1914–1991*. New York: Random House.

Hoffmann, A. L. (2014). *Google Books as Infrastructure of In/justice: Towards a Sociotechnical Account of Rawlsian Justice, Information, and Technology*. (PhD). University of Wisconsin Milwaukee.

Honneth, A., & Joas, H. (Eds.). (1991). *Communicative Action: Essays on Jürgen Habermas's The Theory of Communicative Action*. Cambridge, MA: MIT Press.

Horton, D., & Wohl, R. (1956). Mass Communication and Parasocial Interaction: Observations on Intimacy at a Distance. *Psychiatry, 19*(3), 215–229.

Hsieh, Y. P. (2012). Online Social Networking Skills: The Social Affordances Approach to Digital Inequality. *First Monday, 17*(4).

Hughes, R. (1991). *The Shock of the New: Art and the Century of Change* (Updated and enlarged ed.). London: Thames & Hudson.

Hughes, T. P. (1994). Technological Momentum. In M. R. Smith & L. Marx (Eds.), *Does Technology Drive History? The Dilemma of Technological Determinism* (pp. 101–113). Cambridge, MA: MIT Press.

Hume, D. (2010). *A Treatise of Human Nature*. Retrieved from www.gutenberg.org/ebooks/4705. (Original work published 1739.)

Humphreys, L. (2018). *The Qualified Self: Social Media and the Accounting of Everyday Life*. Cambridge, MA: MIT Press.

Huntington, S. (1993, June 6). The Coming Clash of Civilizations, Or, the West against the Rest. *The New York Times*, p. E19.

Hursthouse, R. (2016). Virtue Ethics. Retrieved from https://plato.stanford.edu/entries/ethics-virtue/.

Hutchby, I. (2001). *Conversation and Technology: From the Telephone to the Internet*. Cambridge: Polity.

Huyssen, A. (1986). *After the Great Divide: Modernism, Mass Culture, and Postmodernism*. London: Macmillan.

Hwang, Y., & Jeong, S.-H. (2009). Revisiting the Knowledge Gap Hypothesis: A Meta-Analysis of Thirty-Five Years of Research. *Journalism and Mass Communication Quarterly, 86*(3), 513–532.

Inglehart, R. (1990). *Culture Shift in Advanced Industrial Society*. Princeton, NJ: Princeton University Press.

Innis, H. A. (1951). *The Bias of Communication*. Toronto: University of Toronto Press.

Innis, H. A. (1972). *Empire and Communications*. Toronto: University of Toronto Press. (Original work published 1950.)

Internetlivestats. (2020). Internet Users. Retrieved from www.internetlivestats.com/internet-users/.

ITU. (2005). The Internet of Things: Executive Summary. Retrieved from www.itu.int/dms_pub/itu-s/opb/pol/S-POL-IR.IT-2005-SUM-PDF-E.pdf.

Jacobson, T. L. (2016). Amartya Sen's Capabilities Approach and Communication for Development and Social Change. *Journal of Communication, 66*(5), 789–810.

Jakobson, R. (1960). Closing Statement: Linguistics and Poetics. In T. A. Sebeok (Ed.), *Style in Language* (pp. 350–377). Cambridge, MA: MIT Press.

James, W. (1919). *The Will to Believe and Other Essays in Popular Philosophy*. New York: Longmans, Green, & Co. (Original work published 1897.)

James, W. (2013). *Pragmatism: A New Name for Some Old Ways of Thinking.* Retrieved from www.gutenberg.org/ebooks/5116. (Original work published 1907.)

Jaspers, K. (2010). *The Origin and Goal of History.* London, New York: Routledge. (Original work published 1949.)

Jauss, H. R. (1982). *Toward an Aesthetic of Reception.* Brighton, UK: Harvester Press.

Jay, M. (1996). *The Dialectical Imagination: A History of the Frankfurt School and the Institute of Social Research, 1923–1950* (2nd ed.). Berkeley, CA: University of California Press.

Jenkins, H. (1992). *Textual Poachers: Television Fans and Participatory Culture.* New York: Routledge.

Jensen, K. B. (1988). News as Social Resource. *European Journal of Communication, 3*(3), 275–301.

Jensen, K. B. (1991). When Is Meaning? Communication Theory, Pragmatism, and Mass Media Reception. In J. Anderson (Ed.), *Communication Yearbook* (Vol. 14, pp. 3–32). Newbury Park, CA: Sage.

Jensen, K. B. (1994). Reception as Flow: The "New Television Viewer" Revisited. *Cultural Studies, 8*(2), 293–305.

Jensen, K. B. (1995). *The Social Semiotics of Mass Communication.* London: Sage.

Jensen, K. B. (2009). Three-Step Flow. *Journalism – Theory, Practice, and Criticism, 10*(3), 335–337.

Jensen, K. B. (2010). *Media Convergence: The Three Degrees of Network, Mass, and Interpersonal Communication.* London, New York: Routledge.

Jensen, K. B. (2012a). The Complementarity of Qualitative and Quantitative Methodologies in Media and Communication Research. In K. B. Jensen (Ed.), *A Handbook of Media and Communication Research: Qualitative and Quantitative Methodologies* (2nd ed., pp. 283–301). London, New York: Routledge.

Jensen, K. B. (2012b). Introduction: The state of convergence in media and communication research. In K. B. Jensen (Ed.), *A Handbook of Media and Communication Research: Qualitative and Quantitative Methodologies* (2nd ed., pp. 1–19). New York, London: Routledge.

Jensen, K. B. (2012c). Media Effects: Quantitative Traditions. In K. B. Jensen (Ed.), *A Handbook of Media and Communication Research: Qualitative and Quantitative Methodologies* (pp. 153–170). London, New York: Routledge.

Jensen, K. B. (2012d). Media Reception: Qualitative Traditions. In K. B. Jensen (Ed.), *A Handbook of Media and Communication Research: Qualitative and Quantitative Methodologies* (pp. 171–185). London, New York: Routledge.

Jensen, K. B. (Ed.). (2012e). *A Handbook of Media and Communication Research: Qualitative and Quantitative Methodologies* (2nd ed.). London, New York: Routledge.

Jensen, K. B. (2012f). The Social Origins and Uses of Media and Communication Research. In K. B. Jensen (Ed.), *A Handbook of Media and Communication Research: Qualitative and Quantitative Methodologies* (2nd ed., pp. 351–370). London, New York: Routledge.

Jensen, K. B. (2013a). Definitive and Sensitizing Conceptualizations of Mediatization. *Communication Theory, 23*(3), 203–222.

Jensen, K. B. (2013b). What's Mobile in Mobile Communication? *Mobile Media and Communication, 1*(1), 26–31.

Jensen, K. B., & Helles, R. (2011). The Internet as a Cultural Forum: Implications for Research. *New Media & Society, 13*(4), 517–533.

Jensen, K. B., & Helles, R. (2017). Speaking into the System: Social Media and Many-to-One Communication. *European Journal of Communication, 32*(1), 16–25.

Johansen, J. D. (1985). Prolegomena to a Semiotic Theory of Text Interpretation. *Semiotica, 57*(3–4), 225–288.

Johansen, J. D. (1993). *Dialogic Semiosis*. Bloomington, IN: Indiana University Press.

Johnson, J. H. (1995). *Listening in Paris: A Cultural History*. Berkeley, CA: University of California Press.

Jørgensen, R. F. (Ed.). (2019). *Human Rights in the Age of Platforms*. Cambridge, MA: MIT Press.

Kakihara, M., & Sørensen, C. (2002, January 7–10). *Mobility: An Extended Perspective*. Paper presented at the Hawai'i International Conference on System Sciences, Big Island, Hawai'i.

Kant, I. (1970). An Answer to the Question: 'What Is Enlightenment?'. In H. Reiss (Ed.), *Kant's Political Writings*. Cambridge: Cambridge University Press. (Original work published 1784.)

Kant, I. (1992). *The Conflict of the Faculties* (M. J. Gregor, Trans.). Lincoln, NE: University of Nebraska Press. (Original work published 1798.)

Kant, I. (1998). *The Critique of Pure Reason* (2nd ed.). Retrieved from http://etext.library.adelaide.edu.au/k/kant/immanuel/k16p/. (Original work published 1787.)

Kant, I. (2004a). *The Critique of Judgment*. Retrieved from http://etext.library.adelaide.edu.au/k/kant/immanuel/k16j/. (Original work published 1790.)

Kant, I. (2004b). *Fundamental Principles of the Metaphysic of Morals*. Retrieved from www.gutenberg.org/etext/5682. (Original work published 1785.)

Kant, I. (2016). *Perpetual Peace: A Philosophical Essay*. Retrieved from www.gutenberg.org/ebooks/50922. (Original work published 1795.)

Karlsen, R. (2015). Followers Are Opinion Leaders: The Role of People in the Flow of Political Communication on and beyond Social Networking Sites. *European Journal of Communication, 30*(3), 301–318.

Katz, E. (1959). Mass Communication Research and the Study of Popular Culture: An Editorial Note on a Possible Future for this Journal. *Studies in Public Communication, 2*, 1–6.

Katz, E., & Lazarsfeld, P. F. (1955). *Personal Influence*. Glencoe, IL: The Free Press.

Kay, A., & Goldberg, A. (1999). Personal Dynamic Media. In P. A. Mayer (Ed.), *Computer Media and Communication: A Reader* (pp. 111–119). Oxford: Oxford University Press. (Original work published 1977.)

Keane, J. (2009). *The Life and Death of Democracy*. London: Simon & Schuster.

Kenix, L. J. (2009). Blogs as Alternative. *Journal of Computer-Mediated Communication, 14*, 790–822.

Kim, H. (2019). An Extension of Rawls's Theory of Justice for Climate Change. *International Theory, 11*(2), 160–181.

Kim, Y.Y. (Ed.). (2018). *The International Encyclopedia of Intercultural Communication*. Hoboken, NJ: Wiley-Blackwell.

Kincaid, D. L. (Ed.). (1987). *Communication Theory: Eastern and Western Perspectives*. San Diego, CA: Academic Press.

Kjørup, S. (2001). *Humanities, Geisteswissenschaften, Sciences humaines: Eine Einführung* [The human sciences: an introduction]. Stuttgart: J.B. Metzler.

Kleine, D. (2013). *Technologies of Choice: ICTs, Development, and the Capabilities Approach*. Cambridge, MA: MIT Press.

Kleingeld, P., & Brown, E. (2013). Cosmopolitanism. Retrieved from https://plato.stanford.edu/entries/cosmopolitanism/.

Knapp, M. L., & Daly, J.A. (Eds.). (2011). *The SAGE Handbook of Interpersonal Communication*. Los Angeles, CA: Sage.

Knight, J., & Johnson, J. (2011). *The Priority of Democracy: Political Consequences of Pragmatism*. Princeton, NJ: Princeton University Press.

Krippendorff, K. (2018). *Content Analysis: An Introduction to Its Methodology* (4th ed.). Thousand Oaks, CA: Sage.

Kristeva, J. (1984). *Revolution in Poetic Language*. New York: Columbia University Press. (Original work published 1974.)

Kukathas, C. (Ed.). (2003). *John Rawls*. London, New York: Routledge.

Kymlicka, W. (1996). *Multicultural Citizenship: A Liberal Theory of Minority Rights*. Oxford: Oxford University Press.

Labinger, J. A., & Collins, H. (Eds.). (2001). *The One Culture? A Conversation about Science*. Chicago, IL: University of Chicago Press.

Ladurie, E. L. R. (1972). *Times of Feast, Times of Famine: A History of Climate since the Year 1000*. London: Allen & Unwin. (Original work published 1967.)

Lafont, C. (2009). Religion and the Public Sphere: What Are the Deliberative Obligations of Democratic Citizenship? *Philosophy & Social Criticism, 35*(1–2), 127–150.

Lakoff, G., & Johnson, M. (1980). *Metaphors We Live By*. Chicago, IL: University of Chicago Press.

Lakoff, G., & Johnson, M. (1999). *Philosophy in the Flesh: The Embodied Mind and Its Challenge to Western Thought*. New York: Basic Books.

Lamb, H. H. (1995). *Climate, History, and the Modern World* (2nd ed.). London: Routledge.

Lang, G. E., & Lang, K. (1981). Watergate: An Exploration of the Agenda-Building Process. In G. C. Wilhoit & H. d. Bock (Eds.), *Mass Communication Review Yearbook* (Vol. 2, pp. 447–468). Beverly Hills, CA: Sage.

Lasswell, H. D. (1948). The Structure and Function of Communication in Society. In L. Bryson (Ed.), *The Communication of Ideas* (pp. 32–51). New York: Harper.

Latour, B. (1987). *Science in Action*. Milton Keynes, UK: Open University Press.

Lazarsfeld, P. F. (1941). Remarks on Administrative and Critical Communications Research. *Studies in Philosophy and Social Science, 9*(1), 2–16.

Lazarsfeld, P. F., Berelson, B., & Gaudet, H. (1944). *The People's Choice*. New York: Duell, Sloan, and Pearce.

Lee, M. (2011). Google Ads and the Blindspot Debate. *Media, Culture & Society, 33*(3), 433–447.

Lerner, F. (2009). *The Story of Libraries: From the Invention of Writing to the Computer Age* (2nd ed.). New York: Continuum.

Lessig, L. (1999). *Code and Other Laws of Cyberspace*. New York: Basic Books.

Levine, D. N. (1995). *Visions of the Sociological Tradition*. Chicago, IL: University of Chicago Press.

Levy, M. (Ed.). (1992). Symposium: Communication Scholarship and Political Correctness. *Journal of Communication, 42*(2).

Levy, M. (Ed.). (1993). Symposium: Virtual Reality: A Communication Perspective. *Journal of Communication, 43*(4).

Lewis, L. (Ed.). (1991). *The Adoring Audience*. London: Routledge.

Lewis, S. L., & Maslin, M. A. (2015). Defining the Anthropocene. *Nature, 519*, 171–180.

Ling, R. (2012). *Taken for Grantedness: The Embedding of Mobile Communication into Society*. Cambridge, MA: MIT Press.

Liszka, J. J. (1998). Reading Peirce Postmodernly. *Semiotica, 121*(1/2), 113–132.

Lobkowicz, N. (1967). *Theory and Practice: History of a Concept from Aristotle to Marx*. Notre Dame, IN: University of Notre Dame Press.

Locke, J. (2018). *Two Treatises of Government*. Retrieved from http://oll.libertyfund.org/titles/locke-the-two-treatises-of-civil-government-hollis-ed. (Original work published 1690.)

Lord, A. B. (2000). *The Singer of Tales* (2nd ed.). Cambridge, MA: Harvard University Press.

Luft, J. (1969). *Of Human Interaction*. Palo Alto, CA: National Press.

Lull, J. (2020). *Evolutionary Communication: An Introduction.* New York, London: Routledge.

Lund, A. B. (2001). The Genealogy of News: Researching Journalistic Food-Chains. *Nordicom Review, 22*(1), 37–42.

Luper, S. (2019). Death. Retrieved from https://plato.stanford.edu/entries/death/.

MacBride, S. (Ed.). (1980). *Many Voices, One World.* Paris: UNESCO.

MacGilvray, E. (2014). Democratic Doubts: Pragmatism and the Epistemic Defense of Democracy. *The Journal of Political Philosophy, 22*(1), 105–123.

MacIntyre, A. (2007). *After Virtue: A Study in Moral Theory* (3rd ed.). Notre Dame, IN: University of Notre Dame Press. (Original work published 1981.)

MacKinnon, R. (2011). Liberation Technology: China's "Networked Authoritarianism." *Journal of Democracy, 2*, 32–46.

Macleod, C. M. (2014). Applying Justice as Fairness to Institutions. In J. Mandle & D. A. Reidy (Eds.), *A Companion to Rawls* (pp. 164–184). Chichester, UK: Wiley-Blackwell.

Malcolm, N. (1958). *Ludwig Wittgenstein: A Memoir.* London: Oxford University Press.

Mandle, J., & Reidy, D. A. (Eds.). (2014). *A Companion to Rawls.* Chichester, UK: Wiley-Blackwell.

Mannheim, K. (1976). *Ideology and Utopia.* London: Routledge & Kegan Paul. (Original work published 1922.)

Mansell, R. (2002). From Digital Divides to Digital Entitlements in Knowledge Societies. *Current Sociology, 50*(3), 407–426.

Mayer-Schönberger, V., & Cukier, K. (2013). *Big Data: A Revolution That Will Transform How We Live, Work, and Think.* Boston, MA: Houghton Mifflin Harcourt.

Mazzoleni, G. (Ed.). (2016). *The International Encyclopedia of Political Communication.* Hoboken, NJ: Wiley-Blackwell.

McCombs, M. E., & Shaw, D. L. (1972). The Agenda-Setting Function of Mass Media. *Public Opinion Quarterly, 36*, 176–187.

McLuhan, M. (1964). *Understanding Media: The Extensions of Man.* New York: McGraw-Hill.

McMahon, C. (2002). Why There Is No Issue between Habermas and Rawls. *The Journal of Philosophy, 99*(3), 111–129.

McQuail, D. (2010). *McQuail's Mass Communication Theory* (6th ed.). London: Sage.

Menand, L. (2001). *The Metaphysical Club.* New York: Farrar, Strauss, and Giroux.

Meraz, S. (2009). Is There an Elite Hold? Traditional Media to Social Media Agenda Setting Influence in Blog Networks. *Journal of Computer-Mediated Communication, 14*, 682–707.

Merleau-Ponty, M. (1962). *Phenomenology of Perception.* London: Routledge & Kegan Paul. (Original work published 1945.)

Merton, R. K., & Barber, E. (2004). *The Travels and Adventures of Serendipity: A Study in Sociological Semantics and the Sociology of Science.* Princeton, NJ: Princeton University Press.

Meyrowitz, J. (1994). Medium Theory. In D. Crowley & D. Mitchell (Eds.), *Communication Theory Today* (pp. 50–77). Cambridge: Polity Press.

Mill, J. S. (2004). *Utilitarianism.* Retrieved from www.gutenberg.org/cache/epub/11224/pg11224.txt. (Original work published 1861.)

Mill, J. S. (2009). *A System of Logic.* Retrieved from www.gutenberg.org/files/27942/27942-0.txt. (Original work published 1843.)

Mill, J. S. (2011). *On Liberty.* Retrieved from www.gutenberg.org/files/34901/34901-h/34901-h.htm. (Original work published 1859.)

Millard, A. (1995). *America on Record: A History of Recorded Sound.* Cambridge: Cambridge University Press.

Miller, R. (2003). Rawls and Marxism. In C. Kukathas (Ed.), *John Rawls* (Vol. 3, pp. 69–87). London, New York: Routledge. (Original work published 1974.)

Misak, C. (2000). *Truth, Politics, Morality: Pragmatism and Deliberation*. London, New York: Routledge.

Misak, C. (2013). *The American Pragmatists*. New York: Oxford University Press.

Misak, C. (2016). *Cambridge Pragmatism: From Peirce and James to Ramsey and Wittgenstein*. Oxford: Oxford University Press.

Misak, C. (2019). Habermas's Place in the History of Pragmatism. *International Journal of Constitutional Law, 17*(4), 1064–1067.

Monahan, T., & Murakami Wood, D. (Eds.). (2018). *Surveillance Studies: A Reader*. Oxford: Oxford University Press.

Monod, J. (1997). *Chance and Necessity: An Essay on the Natural Philosophy of Modern Biology*. London: Penguin. (Original work published 1970.)

Montesquieu. (2008). *The Spirit of Laws*. Retrieved from https://archive.org/details/spiritoflaws01montuoft. (Original work published 1748.)

Moon, J. D. (2003). Rawls and Habermas on Public Reason: Human Rights and Global Justice. *Annual Review of Political Science, 6*, 257–274.

Morris, M. (2001). *Rethinking the Communicative Turn: Adorno, Habermas, and the Problem of Communicative Freedom*. Albany, NY: State University of New York Press.

Mortensen, F. (1977). The Bourgeois Public Sphere: A Danish Mass Communications Research Project. In M. Berg, P. Hemanus, & J. Ekecrantz (Eds.), *Current Theories in Scandinavian Mass Communication* (pp. 293–354). Grenaa, Denmark: GMT.

Moss, G. (2018). Media, Capabilities, and Justification. *Media, Culture & Society, 40*(1), 94–109.

Moyn, S. (2018). *Not Enough: Human Rights in an Unequal World*. Cambridge, MA: The Belknap Press.

Müller-Doohm, S. (2016). *Habermas: A Biography*. Cambridge: Polity Press.

Murdock, G. (2013). Communication in Common. *International Journal of Communication, 7*, 154–172.

Murphy, J. P. (1990). *Pragmatism: From Peirce to Davidson*. Boulder, CO: Westview Press.

Nagel, T. (1986). *The View from Nowhere*. Oxford: Oxford University Press.

Nagel, T. (1997). *The Last Word*. New York: Oxford University Press.

Nagel, T. (2003). Rawls on Justice. In C. Kukathas (Ed.), *John Rawls* (Vol. 1, pp. 25–37). London, New York: Routledge. (Original work published 1973.)

NASA. (1981). NASA Program Management and Procurement Procedures and Practices: Hearings Before the Subcommittee on Space Science and Applications of the Committee on Science and Technology, U.S. House of Representatives, Ninety-seventh Congress, First Session, June 24, 25, 1981. Retrieved from https://books.google.dk/books?id=dRMrAAAAMAAJ&pg=PA73&dq=%22unknown+unknowns%22&redir_esc=y&hl=da#v=onepage&q=%22unknown%20unknowns%22&f=false.

National Academies of Sciences, Engineering, and Medicine. (2017). *Communicating Science Effectively: A Research Agenda*. Washington, DC: The National Academies Press.

Nerone, J. C. (Ed.). (1995). *Last Rights: Revisiting Four Theories of the Press*. Urbana, IL: University of Illinois Press.

Neuberger, H. (1970). Climate in Art. *Weather, 25*(2), 46–56.

Neuman, W. R. (2016). *The Digital Difference: Media Technology and the Theory of Media Effects*. Cambridge, MA: Harvard University Press.

NHS. (2020). Organ Donation Law in England Has Changed. Retrieved from www.organdonation.nhs.uk/uk-laws/organ-donation-law-in-england/.

Nielsen, J. (2006). The 90-9-1 Rule for Participation Inequality in Social Media and Online Communities. Retrieved from www.nngroup.com/articles/participation-inequality/.

Nietzsche, F. (2001). *The Gay Science*. Retrieved from www.holybooks.com/wp-content/uploads/The-Gay-Science-by-Friedrich-Nietzsche.pdf. (Original work published 1882.)

Nissenbaum, H. (2011). A Contextual Approach to Privacy Online. *Dædalus* (Fall), 32–48.

Nott, J. J. (2002). *Music for the People: Popular Music and Dance in Interwar Britain*. Oxford: Oxford University Press.

Nozick, R. (2013). *Anarchy, State, and Utopia*. New York: Basic Books. (Original work published 1974.)

Nussbaum, M. C. (1997). Capabilities and Human Rights. *Fordham Law Review, 66*(2), 273–300.

Nussbaum, M. C. (2011). *Creating Capabilities: The Human Development Approach*. Cambridge, MA: The Belknap Press.

O'Mahoney, P. (2013). *The Contemporary Theory of the Public Sphere*. Bern: Peter Lang.

Okin, S. M. (1999). Reason and Feeling in Thinking about Justice. In H. S. Richardson & P. J. Weithman (Eds.), *The Philosophy of Rawls: A Collection of Essays* (Vol. 3, pp. 273–293). New York, London: Garland Publishing. (Original work published 1989.)

Ong, W. (1982). *Orality and Literacy*. London: Methuen.

Ord, T. (2020). *The Precipice: Existential Risk and the Future of Humanity*. London: Bloomsbury.

Orwell, G. (2001). *Animal Farm*. Retrieved from http://gutenberg.net.au/ebooks01/0100011.txt. (Original work published 1945.)

Park, D.W., & Pooley, J. (Eds.). (2008). *The History of Media and Communication Research: Contested Memories*. New York: Peter Lang.

Paul, C. (2008). *Digital Art* (Revised and expanded ed.). London: Thames & Hudson.

Pavitt, C. (1999). The Third Way: Scientific Realism and Communication Theory. *Communication Theory, 9*(2), 162–188.

Pedersen, J. (2008). Habermas' Method: Rational Reconstruction. *Philosophy of the Social Sciences, 38*(4), 457–485.

Pedersen, J. (2012). Justification and Application: The Revival of the Rawls-Habermas Debate. *Philosophy of the Social Sciences, 42*(3), 399–432.

Peirce, C. S. (1931–58). *Collected Papers*. Cambridge, MA: Harvard University Press.

Peirce, C. S. (1955). *Philosophical Writings of Peirce*. New York: Dover.

Peirce, C. S. (1958). *Selected Writings*. New York: Dover.

Peirce, C. S. (1982). *Writings of Charles S. Peirce: A Chronological Edition* (Vol. 1). Bloomington, IN: Indiana University Press.

Peirce, C. S. (1986). *Writings of Charles S. Peirce: A Chronological Edition* (Vol. 3). Bloomington, IN: Indiana University Press.

Peirce, C. S. (1992). *The Essential Peirce* (Vol. 1). Bloomington, IN: Indiana University Press.

Peirce, C. S. (1992–98). *The Essential Peirce*. Bloomington, IN: Indiana University Press.

Peirce, C. S. (1998). A Neglected Argument for the Reality of God. In C. S. Peirce (Ed.), *The Essential Peirce* (Vol. 2, pp. 434–450). Bloomington, IN: Indiana University Press. (Original work published 1908.)

Perry, D. K. (Ed.). (2001). *American Pragmatism and Communication Research*. Mahwah, NJ: Lawrence Erlbaum.

Peters, J. D. (1986). Institutional Sources of Intellectual Poverty in Communication Research. *Communication Research, 13*, 527–559.

Peters, J. D. (1999). *Speaking into the Air: A History of the Idea of Communication*. Chicago, IL: University of Chicago Press.

Peters, J. D. (2015). *The Marvelous Clouds: Toward a Philosophy of Elemental Media*. Chicago, IL: University of Chicago Press.

Peterson, P., Tierney, R., Baker, E., & McGaw, B. (2010). *International Encyclopedia of Education* (3rd ed.). Oxford: Academic Press.

Pike, K. L. (1967). *Language in Relation to a Unified Theory of the Structure of Human Behavior* (2nd ed.). The Hague: Mouton.

Piketty, T. (2014). *Capital in the Twenty-First Century*. Cambridge, MA: The Belknap Press.

Piketty, T. (2020). *Capital and Ideology*. Cambridge, MA: The Belknap Press.

Pinker, S. (2018). *Enlightenment Now: The Case for Reason, Science, Humanism, and Progress*. New York: Viking.

Pitkin, H. F. (1967). *The Concept of Representation*. Berkeley, CA: University of California Press.

Plaisance, P. L. (Ed.). (2018). *Communication and Media Ethics*. Berlin: De Gruyter.

Plato. (2016). *The Republic*. Retrieved from www.gutenberg.org/cache/epub/1497/pg1497.txt.

Pogge, T. (2007). *John Rawls: His Life and Theory of Justice*. New York: Oxford University Press.

Pomeranz, K. (2000). *The Great Divergence: China, Europe, and the Making of the Modern World Economy*. Princeton, NJ: Princeton University Press.

Popper, K. R. (1972a). *The Logic of Scientific Discovery*. London: Hutchinson. (Original work published 1934.)

Popper, K. R. (1972b). *Objective Knowledge: An Evolutionary Approach*. London: Oxford University Press.

Porat, M. (1977). *The Information Economy: Definition and Measurement*. Washington, DC: Government Printing Office.

Powell, B. B. (2009). *Writing: Theory and History of the Technology of Civilization*. Malden, MA: Wiley-Blackwell.

Prado, C. (1987). *The Limits of Pragmatism*. Atlantic Highlands, NJ: Humanities Press International.

Putnam, H. (1994). Pragmatism and Moral Objectivity. In J. Conant (Ed.), *Words and Life – Hilary Putnam* (pp. 151–181). Cambridge, MA: Harvard University Press.

Radu, R. (2019). *Negotiating Internet Governance*. Oxford: Oxford University Press.

Rainie, L., & Wellman, B. (2012). *Networked: The New Social Operating System*. Cambridge, MA: MIT Press.

Rao, S., & Wasserman, H. (Eds.). (2015). *Media Ethics and Justice in the Age of Globalization*. Houndmills, UK: Palgrave Macmillan.

Rasmussen, D. M. (2012). The Emerging Domain of the Political. *Philosophy & Social Criticism, 38*(4–5), 457–466.

Rawls, J. (1946). *A Brief Inquiry into the Nature and Function of Ethical Theory*. Student paper. Princeton University.

Rawls, J. (1958). Justice as Fairness. *The Philosophical Review, 67*(2), 164–194.

Rawls, J. (1971). *A Theory of Justice*. Cambridge, MA: Harvard University Press.

Rawls, J. (1999a). *The Law of Peoples*. Cambridge, MA: Harvard University Press.

Rawls, J. (1999b). *A Theory of Justice* (Revised ed.). Cambridge, MA: Harvard University Press. (Original work published 1971.)

Rawls, J. (2001). *Justice as Fairness: A Restatement*. Cambridge, MA: The Belknap Press.

Rawls, J. (2005). *Political Liberalism* (Expanded ed.). New York: Columbia University Press. (Original work published 1993.)

Rawls, J. (2011). Political Liberalism: Reply to Habermas. In J. G. Finlayson & F. Freyenhagen (Eds.), *Habermas and Rawls: Disputing the Political* (pp. 46–91). New York, London: Routledge. (Original work published 1995.)

Redding, P. (2015). Georg Wilhelm Friedrich Hegel. Retrieved from https://plato.stanford.edu/entries/hegel/#PheSpi.

Reichenbach, H. (1938). *Experience and Prediction: An Analysis of the Foundations and Structure of Knowledge*. Chicago, IL: University of Chicago Press.

Reidy, D. A. (2014). From Philosophical Theology to Democratic Theory: Early Postcards from an Intellectual Journey. In J. Mandle & D. A. Reidy (Eds.), *A Companion to Rawls* (pp. 9–30). Chichester, UK: Wiley-Blackwell.

Renfrew, C., & Bahn, P. (Eds.). (2014). *The Cambridge World Prehistory*. Cambridge: Cambridge University Press.

Rennie, E. (2006). *Community Media: A Global Introduction*. Lanham, MD: Rowman & Littlefield.

Rheingold, H. (1994). *The Virtual Community*. London: Minerva.

Richardson, H. S., & Weithman, P. J. (Eds.). (1999). *The Philosophy of Rawls: A Collection of Essays*. New York, London: Garland Publishing.

Richardson, K. (in press). Mediated Fiction. In K. B. Jensen (Ed.), *A Handbook of Media and Communication Research: Qualitative and Quantitative Methodologies* (3rd ed.). London, New York: Routledge.

Ricoeur, P. (1981). *Hermeneutics and the Human Sciences: Essays on Language, Action and Interpretation*. Cambridge: Cambridge University Press.

Riley, J. C. (2001). *Rising Life Expectancy: A Global History*. Cambridge: Cambridge University Press.

Robertson, R. (1992). *Globalization: Social Theory and Global Culture*. London: Sage.

Rocher, L., Hendrickx, J. M., & de Montjoye, Y.-A. (2019). Estimating the Success of Re-identifications in Incomplete Datasets Using Generative Models. *Nature Communications*, 1–9. Retrieved from https://doi.org/10.1038/s41467-019-10933-3.

Rogers, B. (2002, November 27). John Rawls. Retrieved from www.theguardian.com/news/2002/nov/27/guardianobituaries.obituaries.

Rogers, E. M. (1999). Anatomy of Two Subdisciplines of Communication Study. *Human Communication Research, 25*(4), 618–631.

Rorty, R. (Ed.). (1967). *The Linguistic Turn*. Chicago, IL: University of Chicago Press.

Rorty, R. (1979). *Philosophy and the Mirror of Nature*. Princeton, NJ: Princeton University Press.

Rorty, R. (1982). *Consequences of Pragmatism*. Minneapolis, MN: University of Minnesota Press.

Rorty, R. (1989). *Contingency, Irony, and Solidarity*. Cambridge: Cambridge University Press.

Rorty, R. (1991a). *Philosophical Papers: Essays on Heidegger and Others* (Vol. 2). Cambridge: Cambridge University Press.

Rorty, R. (1991b). *Philosophical Papers: Objectivity, Relativism, and Truth* (Vol. 1). Cambridge: Cambridge University Press.

Rorty, R. (1998). *Philosophical Papers: Truth and Progress* (Vol. 3). Cambridge: Cambridge University Press.

Rorty, R. (2003). The Priority of Democracy to Philosophy. In M. D. Peterson & R. C. Vaughan (Eds.), *The Virginia Statute for Religious Freedom: Its Evolution and Consequences in American History* (pp. 257–282). Cambridge: Cambridge University Press. (Original work published 1988.)

Rorty, R. (2007). *Philosophical Papers: Philosophy as Cultural Politics* (Vol. 4). Cambridge: Cambridge University Press.

Ross, D. (1923). *Aristotle*. London: Methuen.

Rousseau, J.-J. (1920). *The Social Contract and Discourses*. Retrieved from www.gutenberg.org/ebooks/46333. (Original work published 1762.)

Rudy, W. (1984). *The Universities of Europe 1100–1914: A History*. London: Associated University Presses.

Rule, J. B. (2019). Contextual Integrity and Its Discontents: A Critique of Helen Nissenbaum's Normative Arguments. *Policy & Internet, 11*(3), 260–279.

Rumsfeld, D. (2011). *Known and Unknown: A Memoir*. London: Penguin.

Russill, C. (2005). The Road Not Taken: William James' Radical Empiricism and Communication. *Communication Review, 8*, 277–305.

Ryan, M.-L. (1991). *Possible Worlds, Artificial Intelligence, and Narrative Theory*. Bloomington, IN: Indiana University Press.

Ryle, G. (1949). *The Concept of Mind*. New York: Hutchinson's University Library.

Sachs, J. D. (2020). *The Ages of Globalization: Geography, Technology, and Institutions*. New York: Columbia University Press.

Salganik, M. J. (2018). *Bit by Bit: Social Research in the Digital Age*. Princeton, NJ: Princeton University Press.

Sandel, M. J. (1998). *Liberalism and the Limits of Justice* (2nd ed.). Cambridge: Cambridge University Press. (Original work published 1982.)

Sandel, M. J. (2009). *Justice: What's the Right Thing to Do?* New York: Farrar, Straus, and Giroux.

Saussure, F. d. (1959). *Course in General Linguistics*. London: Peter Owen. (Original work published 1916.)

Scannell, P. (2000). For-Anyone-as-Someone Structures. *Media, Culture & Society, 22*(1), 5–24.

Scheerder, A., van Deursen, A., & van Dijk, J. (2017). Determinants of Internet Skills, Uses, and Outcomes: A Systematic Review of the Second- and Third-Level Digital Divide. *Telematics and Informatics, 34*, 1607–1624.

Schejter, A. M., & Tirosh, N. (2016). *A Justice-Based Approach for New Media Policy*. Cham, Switzerland: Palgrave Macmillan.

Scheufele, D. (1999). *Agenda-Setting, Priming, and Framing Revisited: Another Look at Cognitive Effects of Political Communication*. Paper presented at the International Communication Association, San Francisco, CA.

Schudson, M. (1998). *The Good Citizen: A History of American Civic Life*. Cambridge, MA: Harvard University Press.

Schudson, M. (2015). *The Rise of the Right to Know: Politics and the Culture of Transparency*. Cambridge, MA: The Belknap Press.

Schultz, J. (1998). *Reviving the Fourth Estate: Democracy, Accountability and the Media*. Cambridge: Cambridge University Press.

Schulz, K. (2010). *Being Wrong: Adventures in the Margin of Error*. New York: Ecco.

Schwarzenbach, S. A. (1999). Rawls, Hegel, and Communitarianism. In H. S. Richardson & P. J. Weithman (Eds.), *The Philosophy of Rawls: A Collection of Essays* (Vol. 4, pp. 261–293). New York, London: Garland Publishing. (Original work published 1991.)

Scribner, S., & Cole, M. (1981). *The Psychology of Literacy*. Cambridge, MA: Harvard University Press.

Searle, J. R. (1969). *Speech Acts*. London: Cambridge University Press.

Sebeok, T. A., & Umiker-Sebeok, J. (1983). "You Know My Method": A Juxtaposition of Charles S. Peirce and Sherlock Holmes. In U. Eco & T. A. Sebeok (Eds.), *The Sign of Three*. Bloomington, IN: Indiana University Press.

Sen, A. (1999). *Development as Freedom*. New York: Random House.

Sen, A. (2005). Human Rights and Capabilities. *Journal of Human Development, 6*(2), 151–166.

Sen, A. (2009). *The Idea of Justice*. Cambridge, MA: The Belknap Press.

Shields, C. (2014). Aristotle. Retrieved from http://plato.stanford.edu/archives/spr2014/entries/aristotle/.

Shirky, C. (2008). *Here Comes Everybody: The Power of Organizing without Organizations*. London: Penguin.

Shotter, J. (1996). "Now I Can Go On": Wittgenstein and Our Embodied Embeddedness in the "Hurly-Burly" of Life. *Human Studies, 19*(4), 385–407.

Siebert, F., Peterson, T., & Schramm, W. (1956). *Four Theories of the Press*. Urbana, IL: University of Illinois Press.

Simon, H. A. (1957). *Models of Man: Social and Rational. Mathematical Essays on Rational Human Behavior in a Social Setting*. New York: Garland Publishing.

Simonson, P., Peck, J., Craig, R. T., & Jackson, J. P. (Eds.). (2013). *The Handbook of Communication History*. New York: Routledge.

Sinnott-Armstrong, W. (2015). Consequentialism. Retrieved from https://plato.stanford.edu/entries/consequentialism/#ClaUti.

Smythe, D. W. (1977). Communications: Blindspot of Western Marxism. *Canadian Journal of Political and Social Theory, 1*(3), 1–27.

Song, S. (2016). Multiculturalism. Retrieved from https://plato.stanford.edu/entries/multiculturalism/#ClaMul.

Standage, T. (1998). *The Victorian Internet: The Remarkable Story of the Telegraph and the Nineteenth Century's On-line Pioneers*. London: Walker and Company.

Strate, L. (2016). Media Ecology. In K. B. Jensen & R. T. Craig (Eds.), *International Encyclopedia of Communication Theory and Philosophy* (Vol. 3, pp. 1159–1167). Hoboken, NJ: Wiley-Blackwell.

Talisse, R. B. (2011). Toward a New Pragmatist Politics. *Metaphilosophy, 42*(5), 552–571.

Taylor, C. (1985). *Philosophy and the Human Sciences: Philosophical Papers 2*. Cambridge: Cambridge University Press.

Taylor, L. (2017). What Is Data Justice? The Case for Connecting Digital Rights and Freedoms Globally. *Big Data & Society* (July–December), 1–14.

Thompson, J. B. (1995). *The Media and Modernity*. Cambridge: Polity Press.

Tichenor, P., Olien, C., & Donohue, G. (1970). Mass Media Flow and Differential Growth in Knowledge. *Public Opinion Quarterly, 34*(2), 159–170.

Toffler, A. (1980). *The Third Wave*. New York: Bantam.

Tomasello, M. (2016). *A Natural History of Human Morality*. Cambridge, MA: Harvard University Press.

Tomlinson, J. (1999). *Globalization and Culture*. Cambridge: Polity.

Tufte, E. (1983). *The Visual Display of Quantitative Information*. Cheshire, CT: Graphics Press.

Tufte, E. (1990). *Envisioning Information*. Cheshire, CT: Graphics Press.

Tumber, H., & Waisbord, S. (Eds.). (2017). *The Routledge Companion to Media and Human Rights*. New York, London: Routledge.

Tunstall, J. (1977). *The Media Are American*. London: Constable.

United Nations. (1948). The Universal Declaration of Human Rights. Retrieved from www.un.org/en/universal-declaration-human-rights/.

Van Noorden, R. (2015). Interdisciplinary Research by the Numbers. *Nature, 525*, 306–307.

Viswanath, K., & Finnegan, J. R. (1996). The Knowledge Gap Hypothesis 25 Years Later. *Communication Yearbook, 19*, 187–227.

Vu, H. N. N., & Gehrau, V. (2010). Agenda Diffusion: An Integrated Model of Agenda Setting and Interpersonal Communication. *Journalism and Mass Communication Quarterly, 87*(1), 100–116.

Walker, J. R. (2007). Letter Writing in the Late Age of Print: Electronic Mail and the Ars Dictaminis. In C. Poster & L. C. Mitchell (Eds.), *Letter-Writing Manuals and Instruction from Antiquity to the Present* (pp. 230–243). Columbia, SC: University of South Carolina Press.

Wallerstein, I. (1974). *The Modern World-System* (Vol. 1). New York: Academic Press.

Walzer, M. (1983). *Spheres of Justice: A Defense of Pluralism and Equality*. Oxford: Blackwell.

Wang, G. (Ed.). (2011). *De-Westernizing Communication Research: Altering Questions and Changing Frameworks*. London: Routledge.

Ward, L. (2019). Rekindling "Radical Democratic Embers": Rawls and Habermas on Public Reason. *The European Legacy, 24*(7–8), 819–839.

Warren, S. D., & Brandeis, L. D. (1890). The Right to Privacy. *Harvard Law Review, 4*(5). Retrieved from www.lawrence.edu/fast/BOARDMAW/Privacy_brand_warr2.html.

Watt, I. (1957). *The Rise of the Novel*. London: Chatto & Windus.

Watzlawick, P., Beavin, J. H., & Jackson, D. D. (1967). *Pragmatics of Human Communication: A Study of Interactional Patterns, Pathologies, and Paradoxes*. New York: Norton.

Weber, E. T. (2010). *Rawls, Dewey, and Constructivism*. London: Continuum.

Webster, J. G. (2014). *The Marketplace of Attention: How Audiences Take Shape in a Digital Age*. Cambridge, MA: MIT Press.

Webster, J. G., & Phalen, P. F. (1997). *The Mass Audience: Rediscovering the Dominant Model*. Mahwah, NJ: Lawrence Erlbaum.

Weinberg, A. M. (1961). The Impact of Large-Scale Science in the United States. *Science, 134*(3473), 161–164.

Weiser, M. (1991). The Computer for the Twenty-First Century. *Scientific American, 265*(3), 94–104.

West, C. (1989). *The American Evasion of Philosophy: A Genealogy of Pragmatism*. Madison, WI: University of Wisconsin Press.

Westin, A. F. (1967). *Privacy and Freedom*. New York: Atheneum.

White, S. (2014). Democratic Equality as a Work-in-Progress. In J. Mandle & D. A. Reidy (Eds.), *A Companion to Rawls* (pp. 185–199). Chichester, UK: Wiley-Blackwell.

Whitehead, A. N. (1978). *Process and Reality: An Essay in Cosmology* (Corrected ed.). New York: Free Press. (Original work published 1929.)

WHO. (2020a). Coronavirus Disease (COVID-19) Pandemic. Retrieved from www.who.int/emergencies/diseases/novel-coronavirus-2019.

WHO. (2020b). Life Expectancy. Retrieved from www.who.int/gho/mortality_burden_disease/life_tables/situation_trends_text/en/.

WHO. (2020c). WHO Task Force on Donation and Transplantation of Human Organs and Tissues. Retrieved from www.who.int/transplantation/donation/taskforce-transplantation/en/.

Wiegand, W. A., & Davis, D. G., Jr. (1994). *Encyclopedia of Library History*. London: Garland Publishing.

Wieland, W. (1962). *Die aristotelische Physik* [Aristotelian physics]. Göttingen, Germany: Van den Hoeck & Ruprecht.

Wilkins, B. (2008). Rawls on Human Rights: A Review Essay. *The Journal of Ethics, 12*, 105–122.

Williams, R. (1974). *Television: Technology and Cultural Form*. London: Fontana.

Williams, R. (1975). *Culture and Society 1780–1950*. Harmondsworth: Penguin. (Original work published 1958.)

Winston, B. (1998). *Media, Technology, and Society: A History: From the Telegraph to the Internet*. London: Routledge.

Wittgenstein, L. (1953). *Philosophical Investigations*. London: Macmillan.

Wittgenstein, L. (1972). *Tractatus Logico-Philosophicus*. London: Routledge & Kegan Paul. (Original work published 1921.)

Young, R. (2020). Voluntary Euthanasia. Retrieved from https://plato.stanford.edu/entries/euthanasia-voluntary/.

Zhang, L., Zhao, J., & Xu, K. (2016). Who Creates Trends in Online Social Media: The Crowd or Opinion Leaders? *Journal of Computer-Mediated Communication, 21*(1), 1–16.

Žižek, S. (2004). What Rumsfeld Doesn't Know That He Knows about Abu Ghraib. Retrieved from http://inthesetimes.com/article/747/what_rumsfeld_doesn_know_that_he_knows_about_abu_ghraib.

Zuboff, S. (2019). *The Age of Surveillance Capitalism: The Fight for a Human Future at the New Frontier of Power*. New York: Public Affairs.

INDEX

Note: Page numbers in *italic* denote figures and in **bold** denote tables.

Ingram Content Group UK Ltd.
Milton Keynes UK
UKHW050843230323
419024UK00017B/46

9 781138 807266